Steamboats and Ferries on the White River

Steamboats and Ferries on the White River

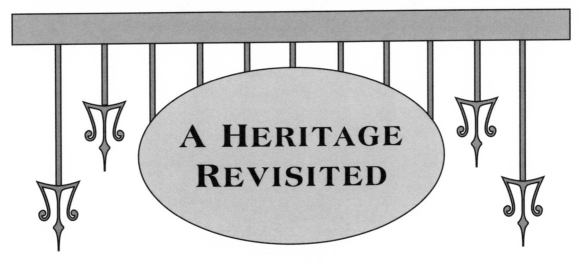

A Heritage Revisited

New Edition

Duane Huddleston, Sammie Cantrell Rose,
and Pat Taylor Wood

The University of Arkansas Press Fayetteville 1998

First edition, 1995, *Steamboats and Ferries on White River: A Heritage Revisited,* published by UCA Press, Conway, Arkansas

02 01 00 99 98 5 4 3 2 1

Designed by Alice Gail Carter

⊗ The paper used in this publication meets the minimum requirements of the American National Standard for Permanence of Paper for Printed Library Materials Z39.48-1984.

Library of Congress Cataloging-in-Publication Data

Huddleston, Duane.

Steamboats and ferries on the White River : a heritage revisited / by Duane Huddleston, Sammie Cantrell Rose, and Pat Wood.

p. c.

Includes bibliographical references (p.) and index.

ISBN 1-55728-538-1 (pbk. : alk. paper)

1. White River (Ark. and Mo.)—History. 2. River steamers—White River (Ark. and Mo.)—History. I. Rose, Sammie, 1941– . II. Wood. Pat, 1935– . III. Title.

F417.W5H83 1998

976.7'2—dc21 98-13808

CIP

Dedicated to Duane Huddleston, the consummate historian,

and to our husbands, Chuck Wood and Frank Rose, for their ever present support.

ACKNOWLEDGMENTS

No project of this nature can ever be accomplished without the assistance of many. This book is no exception. While there is inadequate space to list everyone, there are some individuals we feel compelled to recognize. The late Elmo Ingenthron is one of them. Two of a kind, Duane Huddleston and he corresponded for years about their historical pursuits. Mr. Ingenthron's love of history and his elation in sharing it with others made an early impression upon us.

Once our interest was whetted and we were on the trail of the steamboats and ferries, Wilson Powell, of the *Batesville Guard,* provided the encouragement needed to propel us forward at just the appropriate time. A good judge of character, he seemed to recognize that we were hooked by the subject. We owe him a huge debt.

The late Mrs. Lady Elizabeth Luker, former curator of the Jacksonport Courthouse Museum in Jacksonport, also rendered invaluable information on the Lower White River, as did Paul Yarber and his daughter, Cora Lee Looney.

We cannot exclude Linda Pine of the University of Arkansas, Little Rock, Archives and Special Collections, who was delightfully helpful and patient with our research. This book would not have been complete without the photographs from the Huddleston Collection housed at University of Arkansas, Little Rock. We are indebted for their use.

A special thanks goes to those individuals who graciously allowed us into their homes and gave so generously of their time to share with us their memories of the White River. Not only was their information unique, the opportunity to visit with them was a special treat for us.

Lastly, we must thank Mary Huddleston, who trusted us enough to share her husband's research with us. Duane died in 1982, but he left a lasting legacy of historical research, particularly in the field of steam travel in the White and Arkansas Rivers. It has been a joy to incorporate his writings with ours. We hope this book brings as much joy to the reader.

Sammie Rose and Pat Wood

Contents

ILLUSTRATIONS

Introduction

I christen thee Ozark Queen. Glide smoothly to thy home on the beautiful White. Float lightly, speed swiftly and safely! Long live the Queen.

These words of little June Glenn rang crystal as the water beneath the vessel she was christening, and with surprising strength the young girl shattered a bottle containing sparkling White River water against the bow of the steamboat. The air was filled with hearty cheers from the assembled crowd when the craft glided to the water's edge and was cradled by the river.

By Miss Glenn's side at the Batesville, Arkansas, landing stood a gray-haired gentleman with a broad smile upon his face. The date was September 12, 1896, a year that had been particularly disastrous for rivermen who traveled the upper reaches of the White River. The gentleman was Charles B. Woodbury, one of the most competent and well-liked steamboat captains in the region. Captain Woodbury was enchanted by the challenge and beauty of the Upper White as it wandered through the heart of the Ozark Mountains, hence the name for this his newest steamboat. He would continue to navigate the river until his death in 1903.

Local citizens came by wagon, bicycle, horseback, buggy, and on foot for this gala occasion, gathering well ahead of the designated launch time. Their excitement reflected the importance of steam travel along the White River. This mode of transportation began on the river in 1831 and became a major contributing factor in the settlement and economic development of the area. Steamboats remained a primary method of travel into the twentieth century when the arrival of rail transportation put them out of

Ozark Queen *shown at unknown landing on Upper White River in 1896. Built at Batesville by Capt. Charles B. Woodbury, the boat ran as far as Lead Hill from 1896 until railroad was built to Cotter in 1903. It then ran in Lower White from Newport to Rosedale, Mississippi, through 1904.*

Courtesy of the Missouri Historical Society and the University of Arkansas, Little Rock, Archives and Special Collections.

business. Ironically, they played a significant role in their own demise by carrying supplies for the construction of the railroad.

Prior to the arrival of the steamboats, ferries had been built along the course of the White. For pioneer travelers who found it necessary to cross the waterway, the sight of a ferry to "carry" them across, rather than having to ford the river, was like an answer to a prayer, particularly in times of heavy rains. A number of the ferries were originally built because of the need by farmers to reach a portion of their land that lay on the opposite shore. Many of these farmers shared their crafts with neighbors and travelers, becoming the first ferry operators. Members of their families assisted at times and often followed in their relatives' footsteps. Since they were established sites, ferry landings frequently became the regular steamboat stops as well.

There is something about river travel that captures our hearts. Perhaps it is the thought of gliding idly along reflecting on nature's beauty as we are gently carried by the current. It is a misleading image, for river travel can be far from gentle. Beguiling, yes; gentle, no. Ask any riverman and he will delight in plying you with stories of a river's challenge. It is a challenge that exists today and was even more demanding during the period we are about to discuss. Despite such peril, however, waterways in the 1800s offered a far better means of travel than the overland alternative along the animal trails that served as primary pathways through a vast woodland covered with a carpet of dense undergrowth.

With this book, we pay homage to the steamboats and ferries that operated on the White River and to the courageous men who built and navigated them. We wish to share with our readers the beauty and magnificence of these vessels and the pioneering spirit of their rivermen. They were major players in the development of a region. We will carry you to a time when life may have seemed slow-paced but was actually quite the opposite; a time when physical survival was a constant battle and the difficulties of a struggling, young society were ever present; the time of river traffic on the White. While our story is regional, it is representative of happenings that occurred in many portions of this country during the period discussed—events consequential in the building of our nation.

Within these pages, we pay homage, as well, to an enchanting, beguiling, beautiful, and occasionally terrifying part of our environment, the White River, a waterway that continues to contribute substantially to the welfare of its people.

Because we feel your rendezvous with the steamboats and ferries will be enhanced by a review of the water craft that were the forerunners of the steamboats, we have begun our book with a brief discussion of keelboats and flatboats, the vessels that served the wilderness White River basin and remained on the river for some time following the arrival of steam travel.

"Float lightly, speed swiftly and safely" through this adventure along the White.

PART I

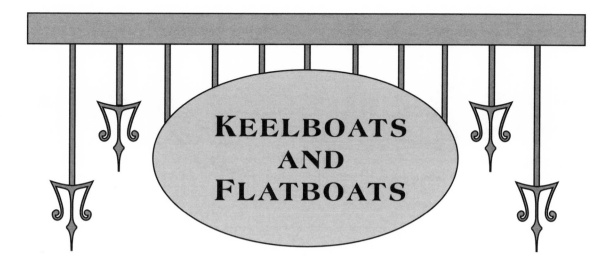

Keelboats and Flatboats

The White River originates in a quiet meadow surrounded by densely wooded hills near the hamlet of Boston, in the Boston Mountains of Arkansas. The rivulet grows from this spring branch into a major regional waterway that travels 720 miles before emptying into the Mississippi River. Like a child eager to roam but reluctant to leave home, the White meanders through much of the Ozarks before departing the rounded old hills to flow across the Arkansas delta region on its journey to the Mississippi.

Simply judging by direction of flow, one might have difficulty knowing the White River's final destination. If the waterway chose a "crow's route" to the Mississippi, the trip would be a much shorter one, a journey of only 225 miles. The White, however, prefers to follow the natural valleys rather than cut a course of its own as many rivers do, hence the 720 miles mentioned earlier. After departing the meadow near Boston, the river heads west on its roving trip, then saunters north to Fayetteville. Flowing northwest from Fayetteville, it crosses the Arkansas-Missouri border and turns east to wander through the Missouri counties of Barry, Stone, and Taney. As though on a playful romp, it then zigzags along the Missouri-Arkansas line before rambling through the hill country of northeast Arkansas on its way to Batesville. At Batesville the river bids farewell to the mountains and travels across the Arkansas delta until it empties into the Mississippi. Like a drover going to market, White River gathers water from a multitude of streams along the way. Brimming with such contributions, the enlarged river spills into the Mississippi below Helena, just above the mouth of the Arkansas River. Flowing near one another at this point, the two rivers are connected by a channel called the Arkansas Cut-Off. The channel forms a huge island around which a craft can circle, if desired, by traveling up the White River from its mouth, through the cut-off, down the Arkansas, and up the Mississippi to the White's mouth again. The cut-off was greatly utilized by early river travelers and by steamboat commerce.

Prior to the 1800s, the countryside through which the White River flowed was a rugged wilderness that contained an abundance of wildlife. Since there were no roads and limited trails, the river became the highway of commerce for early explorers and trappers. While the fur trade along the White had become well established with the building of a trading post by Francois d'Armand in 1766 at the river's mouth, few white people lived in the area until after the Louisiana Purchase and the War of 1812. The white men who arrived at this time were a new breed, seeking land to clear and cultivate. They brought with them their families, household goods, tools, and supplies and came to stay. Many traveled in keelboats down the Ohio, the Tennessee, and the Mississippi Rivers to traverse the White. They brought their dreams of a new life in a land full of promise and found the White River region to be a domain that offered bountiful rewards for those willing to work.

The keelboats bringing these early pioneers were large, heavy-timbered crafts with rounded bottoms. They ranged in size from forty to seventy-five feet long and from eight to twelve feet wide. They laid on a keel that was three or four inches thick, strong enough to withstand scraping over sandbars and bumping into snags along the trip. A cargo box for freight storage occupied a major portion of the boat, but space was left on either side for the crew to walk when poling the vessel. Cargo boxes were usually about four or five feet high and extended from ten to twelve feet from each end. Many of the larger boats also had an additional covered area to provide rooms for passengers.

Keelboats, though shallow draft, could carry heavy loads. The boats were built of heavy four-inch-square timbers that extended from bow to stern along the bottom of the boat. This timber, known as the keel, was placed so as to take the shock of a collision with underwater objects without wrecking the boat. They usually ranged from forty to seventy feet long and seven to nine feet wide.

Sketch by Sammie Rose.

The keelboats were propelled by oars, pushed by setting poles, and on occasion, equipped with sails. The usefulness of the sails on a tree-lined waterway such as the White River, however, was minimal. The setting poles for the boats ranged from ten to twelve feet in length, with their lower ends covered in iron to better handle the constant stress placed upon them. On the upper end was a knob to somewhat protect the shoulder of the user. The crew members manning the instruments placed the poles on the river bottom, then walked in single file, starting at the bow, along the gunwales on each side of the cargo box, and pushed the boat ahead. When the stern was reached, the crewmen walked rapidly forward again and the process was repeated. In times of calm currents, oars could be used to propel the boat. The pilot or captain guided the craft by a long, heavy, wide-bladed oar that was placed in a pivot on the stern and usually extended beyond the top of the cargo box.

All of the keelboats were also equipped with a cordelle, a rope fastened to the bow of the craft, with which the vessel could be pulled upstream, if necessary. The line was quite long to lessen the likelihood of the boat's being drawn toward the shore. A cordelle was particularly needed when the river was too deep for poling the vessel, in times of swift water, or in times of extremely low water. Due to the dense vegetation in many areas along the White, the crewmen would often have to first clear a path along which to walk before they could tow the boat. In such situations, crew members would disembark, chop a trail if necessary, then throw the cordelle over their shoulders, and walk in a stooped position along the riverbank or gravel bar, dragging the boat behind them until the difficult portion of the river was passed. If it was impossible for the boatmen to haul the keelboat, two or three of them would carry the end of the rope up the river and tie it to a tree. The crew remaining on the boat would then drag in the line, thereby pulling the craft forward. Such a process was called warping. A cordelle was also utilized by steamboats for the same navigational problems.

Although keelboats were useful and offered a degree of comfort when floating downstream, the vessels drew resounding curses from their helmsmen as they struggled to navigate the White. The river, with its many sharp bends and rapids, provided a major challenge to the keelboat pilots, especially when traveling up the river in the unwieldy craft. Long stretches of calm water were interspersed with impressive shoals along the river's path. Sometimes all three of the above means of propelling the vessel were used to traverse six or eight miles a day. While three men could usually navigate a keelboat downstream, six to ten men were required to propel one upstream. Despite such difficulties, it was the keelboat that brought many of the early settlers to the White River region, and the craft continued in use on the river for a number of years.

Though there were many keelboat operators on the White, John Lafferty was one of the first to establish a trading post on the upper river. Lafferty, who was from Sumner County, Tennessee, had explored the river as early as 1802 and was no stranger to keelboats. In 1808, Lafferty and his oldest son, John, were living at Arkansas Post, though the rest of their family remained in Tennessee. At the time, his keelboat was running between St. Charles, on the Missouri River, and points along the Cumberland River in Tennessee and was under the command of Charles Kelly, later commander of the steamboat *Volant* in the White River.

In the fall of 1809, Kelly took a hunting party on the keelboat from St. Charles to Arkansas Post, then up the White to above what is now Independence County. The party returned to the post in the spring of 1810, and John Lafferty accompanied Kelly back to Tennessee, where Kelly married Lafferty's oldest daughter. Kelly and his wife were back at Arkansas Post by September of 1810 in anticipation of the entire family's move to the Upper White.

By December of that year, the Lafferty property at Arkansas Post was sold and the family had settled on the south bank of White River opposite what was to become known as Lafferty Creek, about forty-five miles above the mouth of the Black River. The landing and trading post there served as the base for Lafferty's keelboat operations on the White River. The landing was almost destroyed by the New Madrid earthquake of 1811. A bottomless well was created on the property by the turbulence. There was a tremendous shaking, and muddy water rose from one side of the river to the other followed by a gigantic explosion near the south bank of the river where the well appeared. The basin was sounded for over two hundred feet with no sign of finding the bottom. Lafferty's enterprise proved unsuccessful and a financial suit brought against him in 1812 struck a fatal blow to the business. When he died, his administrator's bond was only four hundred dollars.

Robert Bean, who operated a trading hut at the mouth of Rocky Bayou near the present town of Guion, Arkansas, was one of Lafferty's primary competitors for the White River trade. The presence of his business was recorded as early as 1810 and was still in existence when Schoolcraft toured the region in 1819. Goodspeed, another early historian, states that John Reed and Bean operated trading posts at the mouth of Poke Bayou, now Batesville, in 1812 and 1814, respectively.

The largest trader and keelboat operator on the White River prior to 1819 was John C. Luttig. Luttig was an agent for Christian Wilt of St. Louis. Luttig had, at one time, been quite a prosperous Baltimore, Maryland, shipping merchant, but he moved to St. Louis in 1809 and became employed by the Missouri Fur Company. In 1813, Christian Wilt persuaded Luttig to work for him. His first assignment was a trading expedition along the White River. During 1814, convinced by Missouri's Governor Clark, one of the company's partners, Luttig briefly returned to the Missouri Fur Company, but he soon rejoined Wilt's endeavors on the White River at the trading post established near the mouth of Poke Bayou. The initial inventory for the post, valued at $2,388.37, was conveyed by keelboat.

Utilizing Poke Bayou as his base, Luttig ran his keelboat up and down the river, trading with Indians, hunters, and settlers. In September of 1814, he returned to St. Louis with one thousand dollars worth of pelts and hides and, due to lack of space, left behind at his post five thousand pounds of buffalo tallow and other unsold goods. Entries in his ledgers of that period included the following:[1]

1814	Sept 5	By cash for 317 Raccoon skins	$91.63
	Sept 7	By Ditto per J. C. Luttig	16.12
	Sept 17	245 lb. tallow at .12½	31.75
	Oct 8	260 bearskins at .87½	227.50
	Oct 8	127 lb. Beaver at $2	254.00
	Oct 8	17 Otter skins	20.00
	Oct 28	46 galls Bears Oil $1	46.00

Quickly transacting his business in St. Louis, Luttig left for the White River post with a large invoice of merchandise. The shipment included an ample supply of whiskey and several yards of Levant silk, which Wilt felt should bring four dollars a yard at the Poke Bayou post. Evidently, a taste for refinement was arriving in White River country. Luttig was also traveling on a new keelboat, the expenses of which were listed as follows:[2]

1814	Sept 7	Paid boat hands	$221.00
	Sept 7	Paid Patroon	15.00
	Sept 7	Provisions for boat	60.00
	Sept 7	Cash paid Patroon in full	19.05½
	Sept 7	Invoice #2 per J. C. Luttig	1723.57¼
	Sept 9	Store-Herculaneum- 45 gal. Whiskey @ .80	36.00
	Sept 24	Cash per 337 Galls Whiskey	294.87¼
	Oct 28	P. Lindell & Co. for a Boat	300.00

After his return to Poke Bayou, business boomed. In late December of 1914, Luttig was apparently so busy he was forced to hire another riverman, John Duncan, and his keelboat to transport a large shipment of freight down the White and up the Mississippi to the mouth of the Ohio River. The cargo carried by Duncan included one thousand pounds of shaved and unshaved deerskins, numerous other animal pelts, three barrels of tallow, buffalo tongues, beef, salted trout, turkey wings, hams, and venison. The decision to pay another keelboatman rather than use his own boat, thereby avoiding the loss of trading time up and down the White while the craft made the long journey, must have been a difficult one for Luttig. It also proved to be a wrong one.

Duncan's keelboat took thirty-five days to travel from the Poke Bayou trading post to the mouth of the White River and up the Mississippi to the Ohio. At the Ohio's mouth, Duncan was supposed to be met by an agent of Christian Wilt; however, the connection was not made, resulting in the boat being taken to Kentucky. By the time the hides and pelts were sold and the remaining cargo was shipped to Wilt in St. Louis, there was a considerable financial loss. Wilt was particularly disappointed with the small amount of tallow included in the shipment, but Luttig had been unable to purchase more because the Osage had "put on their war paint" and prevented other Indian tribes and the white men in the area from hunting buffalo.

On April 16, 1815, Luttig wrote Wilt about recent tradings with the Indians. In his correspondence, Luttig spoke of particular dealings with the Delaware. The first of the tribe had arrived that day, and, while he had only traded thirty-two dollars of merchandise, he expected the bulk of the Delaware Nation, under Chief Pompus, to arrive shortly with about one thousand beaver and five hundred raccoon pelts to barter. Due to warfare among the Indians and high waters along the White, the corn crop that year had been seriously affected, so Luttig knew the demand for corn was high. Wisely, he had purchased a large quantity of the crop on Spring River, providing him with a strong bargaining position at the time. He felt he could show profits of five thousand dollars from his dealings with the Delaware.[3]

The Shawnee were another of the Indian tribes with whom Luttig dealt. In 1815, there were three settlements of Shawnee living near the White River, one located near the mouth of Livingston's Creek, one at the mouth of Pine Bayou, and one near the mouth of the Big North Fork (Norfork) River. Colonel Lewis was the Shawnee chief at the North Fork settlement. Luttig was evidently working with Colonel Lewis on the possibility of mining lead in that area. In his April 15 letter to Wilt, Luttig requested that Wilt secure a claim for lead mines on the lower North Fork of White River and that the permit be placed in one of three names: Colonel Lewis, Luttig, or Wilt.

Luttig also mentioned that the settlers were calling the location at Poke Bayou "Luttigsville," but he said that if he recorded it, he would name the settlement "Christianstadt" in honor of his employer. Had Luttig lived, the present community of Batesville, Arkansas, might have been given one of the above German names, but two months following this communication, Luttig died. Operations at the store ceased, as did the trading with the keelboat. The craft remained moored at the mouth of Poke Bayou while Wilt and Luttig's widow became involved in litigation over the assets of the trading post. Settlement of the property proved to be a lengthy process, with numerous witnesses, including some White River keelboat operators, called to testify.

Most of the Indian tribes located along the White at the time lived peacefully with their white neighbors. Outbreaks of animosity did occur, however, sometimes initiated by young Indian braves and sometimes by white settlers. In the fall of 1823, some youthful Cherokee braves roamed the countryside, robbing and ravishing their white neighbors. Adding to the problem was the presence of large numbers of displaced Indians who had congregated in the upper reaches of the White. A multitude of rebel tribes, including the Delaware, Kickapoo, Shawnee, Weas, Peoria, and Piankashaw, were rendezvousing at the mouth of the North Fork. According to a message sent on September 28, 1823, to J. C. Calhoun, secretary of war, by Robert Crittenden, acting governor of Arkansas Territory, there were at least ten thousand dissident Indians gathered at North Fork, in addition to the dissatisfied Cherokees in the Batesville area. White settlers were, understandably, more than a little concerned and by December were pressuring officials to alleviate the situation. Because the region was still wilderness, the task was not an easy one. Fortunately, while administrators debated about how to deal with the Indians, nature provided a deterrent. In late January of 1824, the White River flooded the valley with levels ten to fifteen feet higher than any known before in some places. While the damage was major, the calamity did curb the actions of the dissatisfied Indians for a while, though the problem was far from resolved. It was not until May of that year, following lengthy negotiations, that tensions were relieved.

Generally, the relationships between the various Indian tribes and their white neighbors were not only peaceful, but quite amicable. In the 1820s, two Indian chiefs, Johnny Cake, a Delaware, and Peter Cornstalk, were particularly remembered for their kindness. While some references identify Cornstalk as Cherokee, others say he was Shawnee, and the strongest evidence supports the latter. Many white settlers often joined the Indians at the Green Corn Celebration of the Delaware. Frequently, the celebration was held at a large spring near the present Tucker Bottom on the Upper White. The location served as headquarters for Johnny Cake. Not only did the pioneers join in the festivities, they helped with the work such galas require. At one Corn Dance, John Tabor, who built the first cabin in the Flippin Barrens of Upper White River country, helped drag several slain buffalo down to the Indian village for the occasion. Some of the animals were roasted for the dance, and the rest were dried for future use.

Asa McFeltch, a riverman from Ohio, was another of the early keelboat businessmen on the upper reaches of the White River. He established a water-powered grist mill and trading post at Athens, near the mouth of Pine Bayou, in the early 1820s. McFeltch ran his keelboat as far up the river as the mouth of Swan Creek near the later location of Forsyth, Missouri. Purchasing products from white settlers and the Indians, McFeltch then floated the commodities to New Orleans where they were traded for pioneer staples, supplies, and dry goods. According to some records, McFeltch and his family lived for a while near the Swan Creek site prior to their move to Athens, so he probably had good marketing contacts there. Later, McFeltch moved to Marion County, Arkansas, near Talbert's Ferry, where he lived until his death in the 1840s. He was known to be a generous, gracious man and a shrewd businessman.

A contemporary of Asa McFeltch's was John E. Stallings. Stallings moved to the Sylamore, Arkansas, area about 1827; there he established a keelboat business and trading post. For a while, Stallings had owned a store in what is now Boone County in northern Arkansas near Dubuque, a spot that became a major landing when the steamboats arrived. His son, Thomas Benton Stallings, later became a noted steamboat captain on the White River.

The first recorded keelboat operator in Marion County, Arkansas, on the Upper White, was Jesse Goodman, who arrived there in 1837. Goodman and a number of his relatives and friends had lived in Tennessee and Indiana but decided to move west. In the fall of 1836, the group selected three men, Jesse Goodman and two teachers named Wright and John Rutherford, to scout out the wilderness that was to be their future home. The men returned with wondrous tales of the White River country and the beautiful spot they had selected for their colony. While on the scouting trip, Goodman even bought a farm and ferry situated on the river. The land was purchased from Walter Talbert and was an established trading site.

Since Goodman had experience with keelboats, he navigated a thirty-ton keelboat purchased in Louisville, Kentucky, to the chosen site at Talbert's Ferry. The women and children of the group made the long trip on the keelboat, while most of the men traveled overland with the stock belonging to the families. The keelboat was maneuvered along the Ohio River to the Mississippi, where the travelers journeyed to the mouth of the White and began the final leg of their arduous trip to their new home. The overland group herding the stock arrived first, about the end of March, after a trip of approximately six weeks. When days passed with no news of the keelboat, the concern for their families mounted.

Finally, a messenger arrived with word of the keelboat. The courier had been told to request that all the men of the colony who could be spared come down the river to assist in pushing the craft up the White. Goodman also asked the men to construct two dugouts and load them with supplies of meat and other necessities for the travelers. Relieved, the men worked quickly and met the keelboat a short distance above Batesville. Such a large vessel had never traveled that far up the White before, and when word spread of the appearance of Goodman's craft, settlers came from miles around to see the huge boat.

At the time Goodman purchased the keelboat in Louisville, he had also purchased staples he felt would be needed by the new settlers and their neighbors. In addition to basic supplies were included such specialties as old peach brandy, Spanish brandy, rye whiskey, and cherry and mint cordials, so the vessel was well supplied with rewards for the hard-working pioneers. The keelboat was successfully transported up the White to the settlers' new home site and Goodman operated it from Talbert's Ferry for about three years.

The challenges facing these early rivermen were varied, with each trip presenting new problems to be faced. During the latter part of May 1860, a keelboat carrying a load of bacon and corn left Talbert's Ferry enroute to Batesville. Also consigned to the vessel for delivery in Batesville was $800 from a branch of a financial establishment called the House of Burr. The craft ran aground at Buffalo City and could not be dislodged. Since they would have to spend at least one night there, perhaps more, delaying their arrival in Batesville, the keelboat captain decided to forward the money the following morning by yawl. For safekeeping, he hid the cash for the night. His caution, however, proved unsuccessful as, except for $120 in gold that was concealed among some mutilated bills, the money was gone the next morning. A young crewman suspected of the robbery was closely watched by the captain following the incident. At Batesville, the young man bought a razor, some perfumery, and a watch before he bought a skiff in which he fled. When apprehended at Jacksonport, the crewman denied guilt and so was tied with a rope and transported back to Batesville. Upon arrival at Batesville, he decided to confess to taking the money, saying he had delayed that confession because he would rather be whipped in Independence County than taken to the penitentiary in Little Rock, which he thought would happen had he confessed in Jacksonport.

The White River claimed its fair share of keelboats through the years. In the fall of 1866, a keelboat carrying goods for Batesville merchants sank at the head of Bluch Island between Jacksonport and Batesville. The sinking inflicted heavy losses on some of the merchants. Included in the craft's cargo were eleven barrels of sugar, a cask of bacon, two cotton gins, a lot of hardware and castings, and numerous other freight, much of which was never recovered.

Capt. Albert G. Cravens was another successful and well-known keelboat operator on the White, running several keelboats from 1866 until he began working with steamboats about 1871. His most popular keelboat was the *Eliza Jane* and, like all trips for rivermen, each junket held an element of surprise. In February of 1866, the surprise was a sad one. Cravens was en route from Batesville to Jacksonport with his muscle-powered craft when he found the lifeless body of a fourteen-year-old boy. A jaunt in March of 1868 afforded a happier note when Captain Cravens and the *Eliza Jane* provided transportation for a steamboat excursion party of fifty Jacksonport men and women who had experienced travel difficulties aboard a steamer and become stranded.

Capt. Albert G. Cravens, owner and operator of the keelboat Eliza Jane. *He was later a steamboat captain and owner of the* T. E. Morrison. *He was also a pilot of the* Lady Boone *and brought the steamer* Myrtle *to Batesville on its maiden voyage in 1894.*

Courtesy of the University of Arkansas, Little Rock, Archives and Special Collections.

On Saturday, March 21, the festive group had departed Jacksonport on the steamboat *John D. Perry* for an excursion upriver. The gala mood aboard the steamer was heightened by the music of a band called the Philharmonics of Jacksonport that had joined them for the outing. When the steamer landed at Batesville, word quickly spread about the Jacksonport party and the musicians. The *John D. Perry* was en route to Erwin's gin, some eighteen miles beyond Batesville, to take on a large load of cotton; and Capt. Pat Wheat, its master, issued an invitation to Batesville citizens to join the Jacksonport group for the remainder of the trip. Approximately two hundred Batesville citizens accepted the kind captain's offer and climbed aboard.

The trip to Erwin's gin was very enjoyable, with music and dancing that lasted until about midnight. Then disaster struck. Perhaps the party became a little too gay, at least for the pilot of the vessel. The *North Arkansas Times* described the incident: "Owing to the fact that the pilot on board was boosy (that is the mildest term we can apply) he didn't seem to know what he was about, and the boat ran into a sand bar and stuck hard and fast."[4]

Though the steamboat crew tried valiantly, the beautiful vessel refused to budge. Daylight found the crew and passengers in a quandary. They worked all of Sunday morning with no success and

Steamboat F. W. Brooks. *Built in 1863, the ninety-nine-ton boat was purchased by Captain Cable in September of 1867 and became a tri-weekly Little Red River packet. The boat then ran in Upper White River to Buffalo City; it sank above Jacksonport on October 18, 1868.*

Courtesy of the University of Arkansas, Little Rock, Archives and Special Collections.

were pondering what to do next when the whistle of another steamboat broke the silence downriver. Delighted, passengers and crew watched anxiously as the steamer *F. W. Brooks,* en route upriver to Buffalo City, came slowly into view and drew closer and closer.

When the *F. W. Brooks* stopped, Captain Wheat and the officers of the grounded side-wheeler boarded it and asked its captain to take the passengers back to Batesville. To their amazement, the request was denied. After a heated discussion, Captain Cable of the *F. W. Brooks,* with a sharp eye for business, finally agreed to change his course for the sum of $500. With tempers short, angry words followed before the officers of the *John D. Perry* returned to their steamboat where the sum of $450 was raised and offered to Captain Cable. Upon acceptance of the payment by the *F. W. Brooks*'s captain, the excursion passengers angrily boarded the vessel for the return trip downriver. It was a sullen group that debarked at the Batesville wharf. Knowing the mood of his reluctant passengers, Captain Cable hastily turned the *F. W. Brooks* upstream following the last guest's departure and fled the scene with all possible speed.

A night's rest in Batesville mellowed the travelers, and the following morning a rejuvenated Jacksonport party, including their brass band, gaily departed for home aboard Captain Cravens keelboat, the *Eliza Jane*. As the small crew of the *Eliza Jane* took their poles and pushed the tiny vessel into the current of the river, the band struck up a rousing tune, and the excursionists bade a happy farewell to the Batesville crowd that had assembled to see them depart. The band was still playing and the Jacksonport excursionists were still waving as the keelboat slowly vanished from sight. The group reached home at ten o'clock that night.

Captain Cravens was originally from the Yellville, Arkansas, area. His keelboat, *Eliza Jane,* was a regular semi-weekly packet between Batesville and Jacksonport, and he continued to run keelboats on the White long after other keelboatmen left the trade. In 1871, Captain Cravens was operating the keelboat *John F. Allen* in the upper river when it struck a snag a short distance above Jacksonport and sank. The craft was loaded with eighty bales of cotton belonging to Batesville merchants. The cotton floated off as the boat sank, but a number of men with flatboats were later hired to retrieve it, and most of the cargo was rescued from the river and taken to the Jacksonport wharf. The captain later plied steamboats between Newport and the Upper White River, serving in several positions on the vessels.

An avid riverman, Cravens was once traveling down the White

in a canoe with two other fellows. The river was quite high, almost out of its banks, and just above Buffalo City, navigation of their craft became increasingly difficult. To their delight, they spied the steamboat *Lady Boone,* churning up the river toward them. Quickly, they signaled its pilot that they wished to be taken aboard. With three short blasts of the boat's whistle, the pilot gave them a favorable reply and deckhands were hurriedly instructed by the steamboat's mate to stand by ready to grab the canoers when they came within reach. The *Lady Boone* was a square-bowed boat, similar to a ferry, and such construction made the rescue attempt particularly dangerous while still in midstream with the river so high. Carried by the swift current, the canoe, with Captain Cravens seated in its stern steering, was rapidly approaching the steamboat. His two companions were crouched in the bow, ready to leap to the steamer. When the canoe was within three feet of the *Lady Boone* deckhands grasped the hands of the two men forward and yanked them safely aboard. In the next instant, the bow of the canoe was sucked under that square bow of the steamboat, thrusting the canoe's stern into the air and catapulting Captain Cravens into the river near the center of the steamer's bow. Cravens was immediately sucked under the craft and could feel himself bumping against the boat's bottom as the current sped him along the 110 feet of the vessel's length. To add to his problems, he suddenly heard a terrifying noise that he recognized to be the paddles of the wheel at the boat's stern. Knowing he had to avoid that wheel if he wanted to live, the captain dove as deep as he could until he heard the wheel pass directly over him. When he knew he was safe, and with little breath left, Cravens swam for the surface, where he bobbed up in the middle of the large waves that followed in the wake of the steamboat. After spouting what seemed like gallons of water, he swam for the shore and seized an overhanging limb to which he clung until a yawl from the *Lady Boone* rescued him. His experience as a riverman served him well in this threatening situation.

In the early days along the White River, the arrival of a keelboat was an occasion for celebration. Sometimes the trading sessions inspired boisterous parties that ended in brawls. A favorite game of keelboat crews when they landed was "shooting the cup." The game consisted of two men taking turns shooting a tin cup filled with whiskey off each other's head. Needless to say, a great deal of the liquid was also guzzled by the participants before and during the contest. Surprisingly, few serious casualties occurred.

Schoolcraft, an Englishman who visited the area during the early 1800s, made less than positive remarks about the behavior displayed by some rivermen and traders. On one occasion, he and his group were unwilling witnesses to a trading festivity that occurred at the mouth of the Big North Fork of White River. Twelve or fourteen hunters and settlers gathered at the site to await the arrival of a keelboatman who would, hopefully, buy their items. An abundance of whiskey was freely passed around and as the consumption of the liquid refreshment increased, so did the activity level of the drinkers. Schoolcraft and his party, who were awaiting transportation, were merely observers, but shocked and frightened ones. Since there was only one small dwelling at the site, all the men, Schoolcraft and his party included, had to spend the night together. The frontiersmen drank, sang, danced, and brawled. As Schoolcraft said, every "mouth, hand, and foot [was] in motion." Occasionally, one man drunker than the rest would fall to the floor, where he would remain for the evening. Schoolcraft was appalled. He and his companions were afraid to sleep, even if they could have.[5] Needless to say, it was a long night for the Englishman and his party.

As mentioned, keelboats continued in use on the White River even after the appearance of steamboats on the waterway, though their popularity declined as that of the steamers increased. The keelboats were pressed into service in the upper river, however, when extreme low water prevented the steamboats from traveling there. In 1879, at least one keelboat, the *Sylamore,* made regular trips from Calico Rock to Batesville.

Some pioneers arrived in White River country by flatboat, a craft that became a favorite of the frontier families because it was more easily constructed than the keelboat. Flatboats varied in size from twenty to sixty feet long and from ten to twenty feet wide. The sides rose from three to six feet above the surface of the water and drew from one to two and one-half feet of water when loaded. Layers of earth could be placed on boards on the boats and fires built for cooking or for warmth when needed. Many were roofed over to protect their cargo, with only a few feet at each end left uncovered. Steered by a pole or long oar at the rear, they sometimes had one or two oars on either side and an oar in the bow for maneuvering if the water was swift. Because the side sweeps of the craft often projected outward, somewhat like horns, flatboats were sometimes called "broadhorns." They became the work horses of the river for a number of years. It was not unusual to see one of these broad-bottomed crafts piled high with grain or loaded with livestock drifting down the river to market or traveling along the waterway with supplies needed by the wilderness population. The vessel was frequently used by peddlers who wished to sell their wares to settlers along the river.

The shoals and currents of the Upper White provided a significant challenge for flatboats, particularly during the seasons of heavy rains. Because the White flows through mountainous country, its bottom consists of sand, heavy gravel, boulders, and, at several places, solid rock. Like all such winding rivers, the sand and gravel form bars on many points. These bars force the water into the bends where it is usually deep. At the foot of the bends, or the crossing from one bend to another, the sand and gravel drift across, eventually joining the bar in the next bend to form a sort of natural dam over which the water spreads wide and shallow. On the Upper White River, such shallow places were usually called shoals. In other locales, one might also hear them referred to as shallows, riffles, or simply bars. The numerous shoals and sharp bends on the White made the probability of an accident likely. Wrecks were common. A place near the Arkansas-Missouri border called Elbow Shoals was one of the trickiest to maneuver.

Flatboats used in the early 1800s were a forerunner of steamboats. Easily constructed, they varied in size from twenty to sixty feet long and from ten to twenty feet wide. Their sides rose from three to six feet above the surface of the water and drew from one to two and a quarter feet when loaded. Occasionally equipped with a sail, oars and long poles were the usual means of locomotion. Layers of earth could be placed on boards on the floor where fires were built for cooking and warmth.

Sketch by Sammie Rose.

S. C. Turnbo, an early historian of the area, recorded two flatboat disasters that occurred at Elbow Shoals. The first happened in 1835. The shoal was approached by a flatboat loaded with numerous iron vessels, including wash kettles, cooking pots, frying pans, and similar containers. The boat owner hoped to sell the merchandise to settlers along the White. The craft had been built near the mouth of the James River in Missouri and the iron utensils brought in freight wagons from St. Louis. Only a short distance into the rapids, the boat rammed against the right bank of the river and sank. Unfortunately, it was a rainy season when the sinking occurred and, before any of the merchandise could be rescued, fresh runoff emptying into the White buried both the flatboat and its contents under sand and gravel.

The second disaster recounted by Turnbo occurred in the spring of 1848, when Benjamin Majors was taking a load of corn and fattened cattle to market in New Orleans via flatboat on the White. At that same curvy shoal, the Elbow, the swift current forced the bow of the boat against the rocks along the bank and a bottom plank of the craft was torn away. The crew rushed to the bow of the boat as it was swinging around and jumped for the shore. All of them landed safely except Bob Rains, who fell backward into the water. Fellow crewmen noticed his plight and plucked him from the roiling rapids. The cattle, unfortunately, were securely tied to the boat and could not be extricated. Crewmen watched, helplessly, as the flatboat, cattle still aboard, was swept into deep water where it sank. Interestingly, during the following summer and fall, large numbers of fish gathered in and around the sunken boat. Word of this spread quickly, and pioneers living in the vicinity traveled to the spot in dugout canoes. With harpoons, they harvested the fish by the hundreds. Majors, the owner of the flatboat, had been a prosperous man, but he never fully recovered the loss he suffered in that accident.

By 1842, great interest in the expansion of river commerce on White River was shown. On the Upper White, a flotilla of more than fifty flatboats was planned to transport stock, produce, and other commodities from Missouri to markets downriver. However, Mother Nature didn't cooperate, providing little moisture for these enterprising businessmen. There was no measurable rain for two months, and by December 1842 the White was extremely low, making the trip by the flatboats impossible. While plans for this particular flotilla were thwarted, the number of such craft in the White increased substantially the following year and for years to come.

Flatboats were usually constructed for a single trip. Frequently a vessel was built, loaded with products, and floated down the White to markets along the river such as Batesville, or to New Orleans. Here, the cargo was sold and the craft was disassembled so that lumber from it could also be marketed. The owner would then return home by foot, wagon, horseback, or steamer.

J. J. Sams, an early Izard County, Arkansas, pioneer, not only helped build flatboats but learned to pilot them. In 1835, Sams worked for Asa McFeltch, the keelboat operator mentioned earlier. Sams's first trip to New Orleans was during that year when he piloted one of the flatboats included in a flotilla that McFeltch was sending to market. Some of the boats were carrying a variety of settler commodities. Others were loaded with beef cattle about two miles below the present site of Jacksonport. In

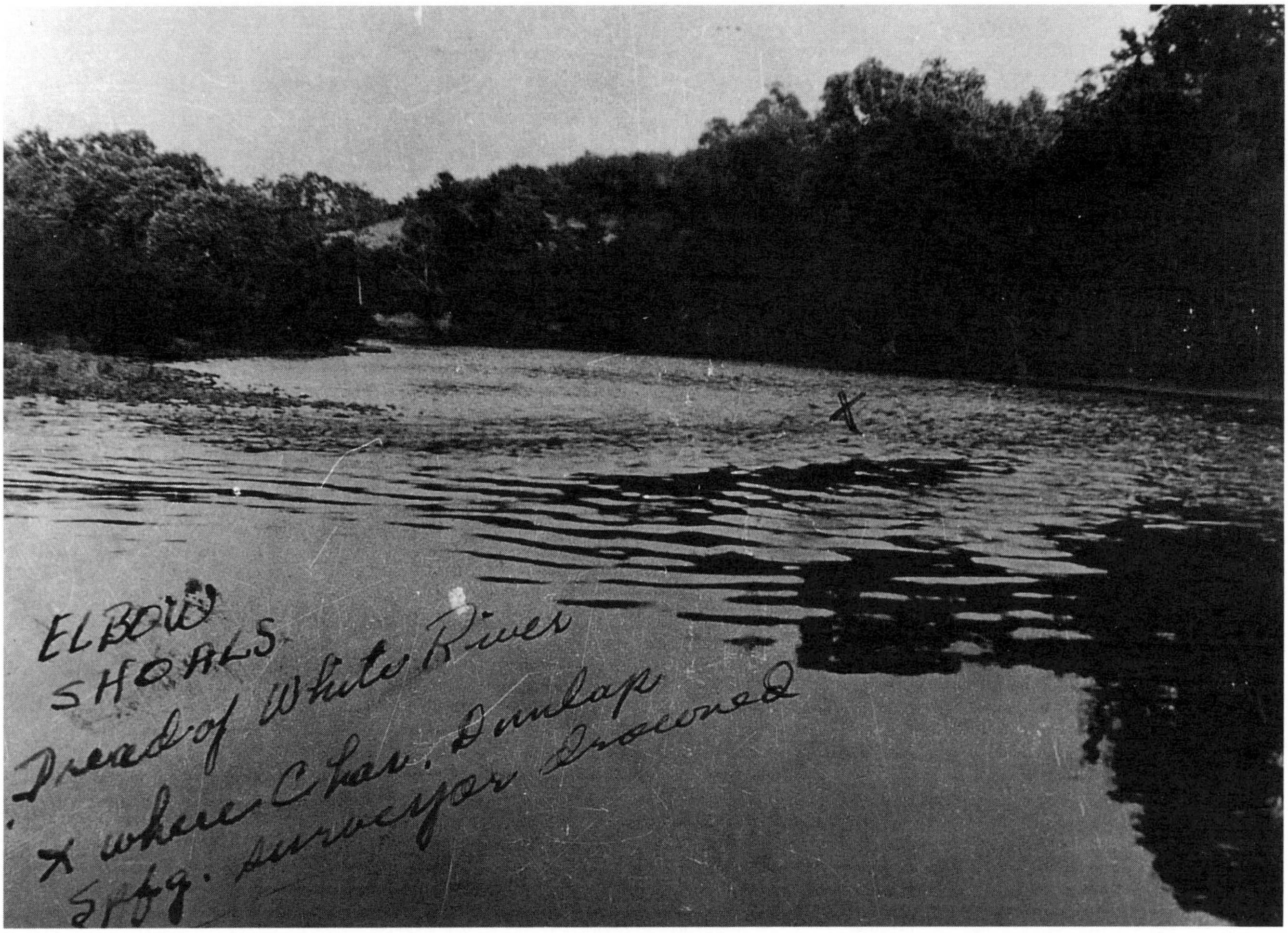

Elbow Shoals, known as the "Dread of the White River," was the site where two flatboat disasters occurred. A great deal of misery was dealt steamboat captains at this shoal also.

Photo by Gus Crumpler.

New Orleans, both freight and flatboats were sold. Sams had to spend six days in New Orleans while awaiting the arrival of an "old tub wheel steamboat" to return him to Jacksonport, a trip that took eight days and nine nights.[6]

The comments of John Dennis, another early operator of flatboats on the White, amply demonstrate the popularity and versatility of the craft. In the 1820s, Dennis and a friend, George Hatch, settled at the mouth of Taylor's Bay near where the town of Augusta, Arkansas, would one day exist. Dennis once told some acquaintances, while discussing his land, that in thirteen years of living at Taylor's Bay, the only time he ever broke the ground was to drive a stake to tie his "bar dog" to. (A dog well-trained to hunt bear was a valuable asset to these early pioneers.) When asked why he didn't farm, Dennis replied, why should he? Living in country like his, he commented, that was covered with fine cypress from which he could build himself a shanty where he could store his rifle and fiddle, where he could cut a raft that wouldn't cost him a cent and load it with venison hams, bear oil, and furs, and float it down the river to sell the goods, and then could travel on to New Orleans, where he could sell the craft for around a thousand or two dollars in gold—why in the world would he want to be a farmer? With money like that, he could buy plenty of traps and ammunition, a sack of coffee, a "bar'l" of sugar, a "bar'l of Dean's Liquor," and plenty of fiddle strings. Who could ask for more?[7]

The men who utilized the flatboats were sometimes looked down upon by keelboatmen, who thought themselves vastly superior to these "broadhorners." Not only did they feel they were better rivermen, but also far tougher and more fearless. Both groups did their fair share of "hell-raising," however. When either band arrived in a river town, local peaceable citizens tried to steer clear of them.

Due to the rugged nature of the wilderness, early settlers, particularly along the Upper White, were dependent upon these hardy boatmen to supply them with such basics as salt, flour, whiskey, coffee, and lead for bullets in exchange for pelts, bear's bacon and oil, venison, beeswax, honey, beef, pork, and other commodities produced by the pioneer. Coffee, which was regularly priced at two pounds for one dollar, dropped in price to three pounds for that same amount with delivery by flatboat or keelboat. Prices dropped even lower with the advent of steamboats on the river.

Bear oil was one of the more important commodities sold by

the pioneers. A major bear oil rendering plant operating in the early 1830s was located on Bear Creek, a tributary of the White, in northwestern Arkansas. The plant employed sixty men: twenty-five barrel makers, twenty-five bear skinners, five rendering-plant operators, and five or more boat operators. This particular endeavor lasted only four or five years due to the tremendous rate at which the bears were slain with the resultant decrease in abundance of the animals. The village of Oil Trough near Jacksonport was another well-known source of bear oil and received its name from the industry. In early days of settlement, bears were abundant in the canebrakes of the area. Cottonwood and poplar trees growing near the town were cut and hollowed out to make massive troughs, which were packed with bear grease and/or salted bear and buffalo meat and rafted together to float to New Orleans and other major ports. The oil was used not only for cooking and candle-making but also for grooming hair and dressing leather, and as axle grease for wagons.

Flatboats on the White were used at least once during the Civil War. In the spring of 1862, Gen. Samuel Curtis and his Union troops captured Batesville and Jacksonport, Arkansas, thereby controlling much of the traffic on the river. There was a great deal of bitterness in the area against the occupation, and atrocities were committed by both sides. Because of the skirmishes, the Union forces at Batesville had several wounded and sick men who needed evacuation to better medical facilities. Since it seemed the coolest and easiest mode of transportation, flatboats were constructed for the purpose of carrying the infirm soldiers down the river. Though a hospital flag flew over the vessels, the boats were fired upon by Rebels along the bank as the convoy floated along. Some of the men aboard pointed to the flag and begged for the shooting to stop, but to no avail. The passengers on the flatboats were at the mercy of the snipers until the shots attracted the attention of the rear guard, who returned the fire, dispersing the attackers along the shore.

While steamboats eventually brought an end to keelboating, in the early years of steam travel the two sometimes worked together. Occasionally, to increase carrying capacity, a steamer would arrive at a port with one or two keelboats in tow. As previously mentioned, keelboats were also utilized to transport cargo during the dry summer months when the upper reaches of the White could not be navigated by the steamers. Commercial flatboat traffic along the White continued into the twentieth century, though they shared the river with snake-barges as well as the steamboats and received competition from each.

PART II

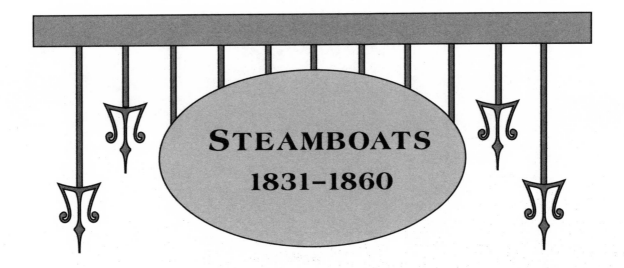

Steamboats 1831–1860

While popular history credits Robert Fulton with the invention of the steamboat in 1807, the idea for steam propulsion had been pondered by men in many countries long before. An American named John Fitch was one of those men. Fitch was a surveyor who in 1780, while watching the Ohio River, thought about river travel. He found it impossible to believe that God in His wisdom would create a river so long and with such irresistible current without providing man with some power to overcome that force of water in order to navigate it upstream as well as downstream. He set his mind to work and, in the summer of 1790, designed a vessel that traveled between Burlington, New Jersey, and Philadelphia, Pennsylvania, at the reported rate of eight miles per hour. The craft was shaped much like a dory and was equipped with large paddles that propelled the boat along in a turbulent fashion. The passengers aboard for this remarkable trip were seated quite near a steam engine that belched noise, sparks, and smoke. Interested observers lined the riverbank to watch, many of them shaking their heads in amusement.

From such humble beginnings came the gracious steamboats of the 1800s that captured the hearts of a nation smitten with their beauty. The sight of a steamer traveling serenely along a river, its ornate pilothouse perched atop several levels of decks, gangplanks suspended out over the bow, and paddle wheels churning the water as tall smokestacks belched smoke, was certainly a memorable sight. A steamboat's design, however, was not for beauty but for practicality. The shallow nature of many rivers required vessels with a wide, shallow hull or bottom. Decks stacked on top of one another provided needed space for both passengers and cargo, since there was little room in the hull of the boat for either. The position of the pilothouse afforded the pilot an excellent view of the waters ahead, and two smokestacks were used rather than one because a single stack in front of the pilothouse would have obstructed the pilot's view. The smokestacks were quite tall in order to increase their draft and enable the boilers to operate more efficiently. Gangplanks were necessary at most landings since few towns and none of the plantations and farms had docking facilities. While many of the steamboats displayed ornate trimmings, the fundamental design of the craft was very functional and related to the specific problems of river travel.

There were two basic types of steamboats, the stern-wheeler and the side-wheeler. As the names imply, their difference came from the placement of the paddle wheel. Stern-wheelers had the paddle wheel mounted on the back of the boat, while the side-wheelers had paddle wheels mounted on each side. The stern-wheelers could operate in shallower water, so that design was the more popular one used on the White River. Side-wheelers, however, were easier to maneuver and were faster. Speed was important to the steamboat captains because the faster boats, all else being equal, attracted more business. In order to increase speed, a boat's engineer would often increase boiler pressure to a dangerous level, with boiler explosions a frequent result. Injuries and loss of life were common.

Though there were only two basic types, steamboat design did reflect regional tastes and preferences. While there were numerous variations, most styles fit within one of four categories: East Coast, Mississippi, West Coast, and Coastal.

East Coast steamers were characterized by a long graceful hull and a straight vertical bow with an overhanging fantail stern. The pilothouse on these craft was usually situated forward on the top deck and had a round front. By the 1890s, boilers were located in

Replica of first steamboat built by Lt. John Fitch in 1786. Located on the common in Bardstown, Kentucky, where a monument to Fitch stands.

Photos by Pat Wood.

the hold on these vessels. One or more tall, vertical stacks could be seen on the steamer's center line. Propulsion of the East Coast type steamboat was usually by side wheel or propeller, rarely by stern wheel. The gingerbread decoration used in other regions was seldom seen on these boats. Their superstructure had the appearance of a "layer cake" since the plumb line of the stem was often carried up to the second or third deck.

The Mississippi or "Western Rivers" steamboat is probably the craft envisioned by most people when thinking of a steam vessel. The term Western Rivers came into being over one hundred years ago when the Mississippi was considered the western frontier. Though hardly "west" by today's standards, it still serves as a division line and the term remains in use. The White River is part of the Western Rivers system. Tall, twin smokestacks forward, with a square pilothouse located amidship, are classic on the Mississippi-style steamer. Many of the western rivers, including the White, have shallow, twisting routes and experience rapid rises and falls of water level. The Mississippi steamboat required minimal draft and had the ability to dock at a muddy bank or a sloping levee when necessary, so it was ideal for these rivers. The hull of this type craft was a low freeboard with the main deck only a foot or two above the waterline. The vessels were equipped with long gangplanks, called stages, that were suspended on booms over the foredeck, ready to be lowered when needed to facilitate loading and unloading along the riverbank. Usually, the boilers were located out in the open on the main deck. Exhaust steam on these boats escaped through a pair of "scape" pipes aft of the pilothouse. The deep "whoosh-whoosh" of the exhaust steam could often be heard on the shore. Initially, the superstructure of these steamers was constructed of the lightest possible materials. To conceal such fragile construction, gingerbread trim was utilized and became part of the basic style even after construction improved. Passenger boats were particularly ornate in their decorations.

While most of the steamers on the White River were two or three stories high, some truly magnificent four-story vessels from New Orleans and Memphis visited ports on the lower river. The cargo deck was at water level and comprised the engine room, boilers, and cargo space. Immediately above was the boiler deck where the cabins, bar, staterooms, pantry, and storage room were located. On the third or "texas deck" were the crew's quarters and, occasionally, additional staterooms for passengers. Poised atop the texas deck was the pilothouse. If there was no texas deck, the crew's quarters were usually on the main or cargo deck.

The West Coast classification covers a variety of boats. The San Francisco ferries were quite similar to the East Coast ones. In addition, many of the first steam-driven craft to appear on the West Coast were East Coast side-wheelers that had traveled around South America. As population of the area increased, a definite West Coast style emerged from California to Alaska. The boats seemed to be a mixture of the East Coast and Mississippi types. Their hulls rode high out of the water compared to the Mississippi steamers but were low when compared to East Coast craft. The pilothouse was placed forward, but the cabins, like on a Mississippi boat, stopped short of the bow, leaving a small open foredeck. Except at the bow, the main deck cabin was usually completely enclosed. Sometimes a paddle box was built to cover the stern wheel, so those stern wheels were often tall and narrow, unlike a Mississippi stern wheel. Occasionally, gingerbread could be seen on the pilothouse roof. Their machinery was similar to a Mississippi vessel except that due to a deeper hull, a single boiler could be installed in the hold.

The Coastal steamboats were, exactly as the name implies,

The Liberty *was an excellent example of a "Western Rivers" steamboat. This photo was taken at Grafton, Illinois.*
Photo courtesy of Ralph DuPae and the Murphy Library, University of Wisconsin, La Crosse.

vessels that plied the coast in generally unprotected waters. They were usually built with more enclosed space for protection from the sea and had a higher freeboard. Often their windows were round ports rather than the square ones found on the other types. Many were simply East Coast steamers that were constructed more sturdily. Some gave the appearance of a small steamship. One might ask, then, the distinction between a steamboat and a steamship. In simplified terms, the difference is the location of where the craft was designed to operate. A "boat," no matter its size, is built to run on inland waterways, while a "ship" is fashioned for ocean travel.

In descriptions of specific steamboats, their registered tonnage is often given. Many people err by thinking this number refers to the vessel's weight or displacement. It is, actually, a calculated measure of the volume of the hull, expressed as "gross" tonnage. "Net" tonnage is the gross minus certain allowable deductions, such as the space occupied by the engines. A "ton" equals one hundred cubic feet. The term comes from a time in Britain when sailing ships were rated by the number of standard-size wine casks, called "tuns," they could carry. In time, the spelling changed to "tons."

Prior to the appearance of the first steamboat on the White River, to think of travel as "pleasant" was to be considered deranged, so the arrival of a steam-propelled vessel traversing the White brought a revolutionary way of thinking as well as expanded commerce. Not only did it offer the possibility of elegant comfort while traveling, it also made more feasible the availability of many luxury items such as dressy shoes, fancy suits and dresses, and feathered hats. Even more important economically, the presence of steamboats meant planters would be far more inclined to emigrate to the area since their slaves could be shipped ahead to clear the land, and more adequate transportation for getting their crops to market would be available. Steam travel offered, too, a quicker and cheaper mode of transportation for pioneer staples. A single large steamboat from Memphis or New Orleans could carry one thousand barrels of salt to the White in eight or nine days, while it would take a wagon at least two weeks to make the round trip from Batesville to Little Rock, where the nearest railroad ran, for a load of only ten barrels.

The first steamboat to appear on the White River was the *Waverly*, commanded by Capt. Phillip Pennywit, with Thomas Todd Tunstall serving as the pilot. The *Waverly* arrived in Batesville, Arkansas, on January 4, 1831. Captain Pennywit had been operating steamboats on the Arkansas River since as early as 1828, with regular runs between Fort Gibson (near Muskogee, Oklahoma) and New Orleans, offering one of the first regular services on that river. His expansion to the White with the *Waverly* exhibited his strong belief in the importance of steam transportation in general

Steamboat engines and boiler from illustrated catalog of James Rees & Sons Company, Pittsburgh, Pennsylvania.

From the Duane Huddleston Collection.

CLOCKWISE FROM TOP: *Automatic Engine.*

Type of Boilers, used on Steamboats on Western and Southern Rivers.

Vertical Engine.

Propeller Engine.

and in the potential offered by the White. The *Waverly* had no difficulty ascending the river until it reached the mouth of the Black River, just twenty miles below Batesville. There, the vessel was detained because of the low stage of the White above that point. After two days, Mother Nature became more cooperative and the river rose ten feet, allowing the staunch little craft to steam on to Batesville. The steamboat was carrying merchandise for two businesses in Batesville as well as goods for the surrounding area, including some cargo destined for the Big North Fork, about one hundred miles farther up the White. The *Waverly*'s loud whistle announced its impending arrival, and the riverbank was lined with men, women, and children eager to witness this historic occasion. Batesville, just ten years old at the time, was second only to Little Rock in population, but few people in northern Arkansas had ever seen a steamboat prior to this event. On January 6, the *Waverly* departed Batesville loaded with over two hundred bales of cotton, various pelts, and other freight.

The success of the *Waverly* encouraged other steamboat owners to consider business on the White River, and on February 9, 1831, a small steamer named *Laurel* made a trip up the White to Batesville. The *Laurel* was a well-built vessel that drew only two feet of water when fully loaded, so it was superbly designed for navigation on the Arkansas and White Rivers, even at their lowest stages. The *Laurel* made a second trip to Batesville in February of 1831, towing two keelboats laden with cargo. In early March of that year, the steamer was purchased by Col. James Smith, who planned to run it in both the White and the Arkansas Rivers. The *Laurel* made another trip to Batesville on March 20 and continued to make regular trips to the city. The initial trip made by the *Waverly* was its only visit to Batesville, but that appearance proved to be the significant one that focused attention upon the market possibilities there.

The impact of steamboat travel on the White River is dramatically emphasized by the sharp price reductions that occurred in Batesville as a result of just those first three visits by the *Waverly* and the *Laurel*. Coffee and sugar, previously selling for fifty-five and twenty-five cents per pound, began to sell for twenty cents and ten cents per pound following the appearances of the steamboats. Other items were comparably lowered.

Prompted by the success of the *Waverly* and the *Laurel*, another steamboat, the *Bob Handy*, commanded by Captain Dooty, visited Batesville in May of 1831. After initial trips to Batesville, the vessel served primarily in the Black River, one of the White's tributaries.

Batesville may have been visited by at least one other steamboat during 1831. At that time, William Montgomery and his son-in-law, David Miller, operated a commission and forwarding firm at Montgomery Point, located at the mouth of White River. Settled initially by the French fur trader Francois d'Armand, who built a large house and several log warehouses there in 1776, the colony was a primary transfer point for river commerce. The Frenchman's house was utilized as a hotel by the Montgomery family, demonstrating the importance of the location. In 1831, Montgomery and Miller purchased a steamboat called the *Reindeer*. The craft was described as a fast-running vessel of some 130 tons with a passenger capacity of about seventy-five. While the steamer was acquired to run exclusively in the Arkansas River trade, there is some indication that the vessel made infrequent trips up the White and Black Rivers.

In 1832, two businessmen from Batesville joined Montgomery and Miller in their steamboat endeavor. Charles Kelly and John Ringgold purchased a steamboat called the *Volant* and formed a partnership with Montgomery and Miller. Unlike his keelboatman father-in-law, Lafferty, Kelly had prospered. This newest venture was named Montgomery, Kelly, and Company and was advertised in the *Arkansas Gazette*. Like the *Reindeer*, the *Volant* traveled primarily from New Orleans to locations on the Arkansas River, carrying both freight and hundreds of emigrants. Because, however, the Batesville firm of Kelly and Ringgold required a large supply of merchandise, the *Volant* made intermittent trips up the White River to serve area businessmen.

In June of 1833, disaster struck Montgomery, Kelly, and Ringgold. Cholera was raging in the river ports up and down the Mississippi River when Captain Miller and the steamer *Reindeer* left plague-ridden New Orleans, bound for the Arkansas River. Several passengers boarded the vessel at Vicksburg, one of whom spread cholera to the other passengers and crew. By the time the *Reindeer* reached the mouth of White River at Montgomery's Point, Captain Miller was sick and docked the boat. After only four or five hours, the captain succumbed to the disease. The boat proceeded upriver, taking the Arkansas Cut-Off to Little Rock. Upon its arrival there, six passengers and crew were dead, including the pilot and engineer. Another passenger died after reaching the city, but the vessel was scrubbed and continued on to Fort Smith. En route, an additional crew member died.

Bills of lading for White River steamboats are scarce, particularly those prior to 1850. However, Mrs. Betty L. Stroud of Desha, Arkansas, had an original, handwritten document from the *Volant*. Dated May 26, 1833, it is the oldest known bill of lading for a White River steamer. It reads:

	J. C. T. Wilson		
1833	in a/c with S. B. Volant		
May 26	For Freight as per first Book May 9	88.00	
	Passage of C. T. Wilson	12.00	
	7 Dozen Bottles	7.00	107.00

The death of Captain Miller caused the dissolution of Montgomery, Kelly, and Company on June 20, 1833, and the *Volant* and *Reindeer* were advertised for sale at New Albany, Indiana, in September. As the steamboats were being dismantled at New Albany, though, fire from the cook's room set the *Volant* ablaze. The flames spread quickly to the *Reindeer*, which was lying beside the *Volant*, and both boats were destroyed.

Another probable traveler to Batesville in the early 1830s was the small steamer *Ottawa*. The *Ottawa* sank in May of 1834 just below Little Rock on the Arkansas River. Its owners, however, were a group of gentlemen who lived on the White River and at least one historian mentioned the *Ottawa* as an early visitor to Batesville.

The next major breakthrough for steamboat travel on the White River occurred in 1833 when Capt. Thomas Todd Tunstall bought the steamboat *William Parsons* at New Orleans. Tunstall, as you may remember, served as the pilot on the famous *Waverly* trip to Batesville. When Tunstall purchased the *William Parsons* in 1833, he owned a section of land with an existing mill and had built a sawmill in the Magness, Arkansas, area. In 1839, Tunstall bought additional land and established the town of Jacksonport. The location of Jacksonport at the mouth of the Black River was ideal, and Jacksonport proved to be the head of steam navigation on the White for the larger steamers plying the Mississippi River. Because the channel of the White was wide and deep with a primarily sandy bed at this point and below, deep water vessels could usually travel to Jacksonport year round. The town became a major terminal for the steamboat industry. The part of the White River above Jacksonport became known as the Upper White and the portion below, the Lower White.

The *William Parsons,* a small craft of 116 tons, ran mostly in the Arkansas River and was the first steamer to travel up that waterway to the mouth of the Verdigris River. The vessel did, however, make occasional trips in the White. In fact, one of those trips was due to a second love of Tunstall's. The captain was a racing enthusiast and owned some thoroughbreds that were of the same fine quality as his steamboats. During the fall of 1834, Captain Tunstall loaded his prize race horses, Volcano and Greyhound, on the *William Parsons* and steamed down the White River to the cut-off to the Arkansas River where he traveled to Little Rock to enter the animals in the fall races sponsored by the newly formed Little Rock Jockey Club. Their arrival was announced in the *Arkansas Gazette* on October 31, 1834. On the opening day of the race, November 3, a large number of spectators came from as far away as Oklahoma to witness the event.

Capt. Thomas Todd Tunstall. In 1833 he bought the William Parsons *for White River use. He had served as the pilot on the famous* Waverly. *In 1839, Tunstall established the town of Jacksonport on the White. Tunstall was a racing enthusiast and owned some thoroughbred horses that were of the same quality as his steamboats. Other steamers owned by Tunstall were the* Tecumseh, *the* Neosho, *the* Harp, *the* De Kalb, *one-half interest in the* Steubenville, *and the* Batesville.
Courtesy of the University of Arkansas, Little Rock, Archives and Special Collections.

The ride on the *William Parsons* must have agreed with Volcano and Greyhound, for the two thoroughbred stallions dominated the meet. The first race, exhibiting horses other than Volcano and Greyhound, consisted of three one-mile heats, best two of three, with a thirty-five minute rest interval between heats. While the performance of the participating animals was described as "respectable," none of their owners were willing to pit them against Volcano, so Captain Tunstall's seven-year-old bay stallion won the four hundred dollar purse for the day's main event unchallenged. As was frequently the case, the match following the disappointing main race proved to be the most exciting. A favorite among those in attendance, it was the match when saddle horses and farm steeds belonging to the spectators were allowed to race. There was usually a lot of betting and joshing among both participants and onlookers during these races, as well as a lot of alcohol consumption. In some ways, it was the highlight of each day.

The featured meet of the second day was a race of two one-mile heats, best two of three. The purse was $250, and Captain Tunstall entered his five-year-old stallion, Greyhound. As happened the previous day, owners were reluctant to race against Tunstall's animals, but the race did draw one opponent, a gelding named Silverheels owned by a Mr. Leech. The gelding was apparently outclassed. Greyhound won the first heat handily. Excitement grew, momentarily, following the rest period, when Greyhound bolted at the start of the second heat and lost five hundred yards. The setback for Tunstall's stallion was minimal, however, and the beautiful animal came from behind to take the purse as he sped over the finish line fifty yards ahead of the gelding.

Captain Tunstall did not race either of his horses on the third day of the meet, saving their energies for the fourth and final day. Weather conditions were perfect on that day, as was the track. The main race consisted of one-mile heats, the best three in five. Tunstall entered Volcano and, to make the race more interesting, he allowed his competitors to enter a fresh horse against his stallion for each heat. Volcano's opponents were Leech's Silverheels, Steele's Blue Skin, and Col. Wharton Rector's Andrew Jackson. Volcano easily took the first heat but lost the second, bringing murmurs from the spectators. To the delight of the crowd, however, Captain Tunstall's valiant stallion went on to thunder across the finish line first in both the third and the fourth heats to take the purse.

In the early spring of 1835, disaster hit the *William Parsons* when, about forty miles above Arkansas Post on the Arkansas River, it struck a snag that knocked a huge hole in the hull. Hoping to save the sinking steamer, Captain Tunstall immediately ran the vessel toward a sandbar where he lodged it on a log. There he felt the boat was safe from submerging. Unfortunately, an unexpected drop of several feet in the river damaged the *William Parsons* beyond repair.

By May of 1836, Tunstall had bought another steamboat, the *Tecumseh*. The steamer was advertised in the *Arkansas Gazette* as "substantial and fast-running," with excellent accommodations for passengers. The *Tecumseh* was scheduled to run as a regular packet in both the White and the Arkansas Rivers, with occasional trips to New Orleans when business indicated. In his *Gazette* ad, Tunstall promised quick delivery of freight and competitive charges. Tunstall's business with the *Tucumseh* was so successful that he soon purchased an additional steamer, the *Neosho,* which was also to run in both the White and the Arkansas Rivers, making occasional trips to New Orleans. Young Stephenson served as master on the *Neosho,* while Captain Tunstall remained master on the *Tecumseh*. Misfortune struck the *Tecumseh* in the fall of 1836 while descending the Arkansas from Fort Gibson. There had been a significant rise in the river and, a few miles below Fort Smith, the steamer ran onto a sand island that was quite a distance from the regular channel but in an area where the water was fifteen to eighteen feet deep at the time. Unfortunately, the vessel was still stranded there, high and dry, at the end of February 1837. Needless to say, the inability to operate the *Tecumseh* created some business problems.

Captain Tunstall had entered into a partnership with his friend, Arkansas governor James S. Conway, and a small firm called Glasgow and Harrison. The men had contracted with the United States government to trade and transport provisions to the Creek and Seminole Indians on the Arkansas River for twelve months. It is thought both the *Neosho* and the *Tecumseh* were to be utilized for such delivery; however, an accident prevented the *Neosho* from making even one of the trips.

Just after midnight on an evening in February of 1837, the *Neosho* struck a snag about one mile above Judge Lucas's plantation on the Arkansas, near Arkansas Post. The vessel was a total loss, sinking in about five minutes. The death of one passenger, Barnard LaFarme, was reported. LaFarme was a goldsmith and silversmith from New Orleans who was planning to open a business in one of the towns on the Arkansas. He drowned just a few feet from the shore. Many of the passengers and crew lost all their belongings but were grateful to be alive. Fortunately, the boat and most of the cargo was insured. Most of the passengers had been on the boiler deck at the time of the mishap. As they were hurrying toward a lifeboat, the steamboat rolled wildly and, thinking the craft was going under, many of them plunged into the river. With the exception of LaFarme, all were rescued or swam to safety where they lay, exhausted, on the riverbank.

You can imagine their delight when, just a short time after reaching the shore, they saw another steamer, the *De Kalb,* in the river. Eagerly they yelled and waved to attract the attention of the vessel's crew but, to their dismay, the boat continued down the river. There was a great deal of anger and resentment over the incident, not directed toward Tunstall or Captain Stephenson, but toward the captain of the *De Kalb*. Versions of the misfortune differ. Passengers on the unfortunate *Neosho* stated that not only did the captain of the *De Kalb* pass them by, but he yelled, "What do you want?" They were so insulted by such a reaction, they "neither asked nor received favor" from the *De Kalb* captain when he did finally return. Captain Lemon, the master of the *De Kalb,* gave a different description of the mishap. Lemon stated that as soon as he saw the accident, he directed the pilot to turn around at the first place in the river that was wide enough. After returning to the scene of the accident, he then offered assistance to both passengers and crew and took some crew members and furniture, free of charge, to ports downriver.

Many of those on board the *Neosho* were cared for by a Mr. Thedford, who lived a short distance above the wreck. Thedford not only sent provisions to the disaster victims, but took some to his home for additional care. Tunstall "offered his purse" to any who were destitute.[1]

With the loss of the *Neosho,* and the *Tecumseh* still aground, Tunstall needed another craft. Following the *Neosho* disaster, Tunstall left immediately for New Orleans where he purchased a new steamboat, the *Harp,* to fulfill the contract for transporting provisions to the Indians on the Arkansas. While the *Harp* was primarily an Arkansas River craft, it is thought it made occasional trips on the White because of the business interests of its owners. The *Harp*'s history was short, however. In 1838, hardly two years after its purchase, the boat struck a snag in the Arkansas and sank in ten minutes. The *Tecumseh* was finally floated off the sandbar that had been its home for several months and resumed its service for Glasgow, Harrison, and Company, but it, too, was short lived. In August of 1838, the steamer struck a snag about eighteen miles below Little Rock and sank. With the loss of both steamboats, the partnership of Glasgow, Harrison, Tunstall, and Conway was dissolved.

Offering competition to Tunstall's steamboats in the White was the steamer *Mount Vernon*. In May of 1838, Capt. Samuel Taylor advertised in the *Batesville News* that the *Mount Vernon* would run as a packet from the mouths of the White and Arkansas Rivers to Batesville. Along with other cargo, the steamboat carried salt to the region.

Despite the steamboat mishaps mentioned, Captain Tunstall's financial interests continued to prosper during the late 1830s. The captain not only became a partner in the *De Kalb* but, in January of 1839, purchased one-half interest in the *Steubenville,* a beautiful steamer built in Liverpool, Ohio, and owned by William Marsh. The vessel was to be utilized in the trade of Little Rock and Batesville and became a favorite of the area. The forty-five ton vessel made frequent trips in the White and Arkansas Rivers, as well as occasional runs in the Black, the White's wonderfully navigable tributary. Among the many cargoes carried by the *Steubenville* was

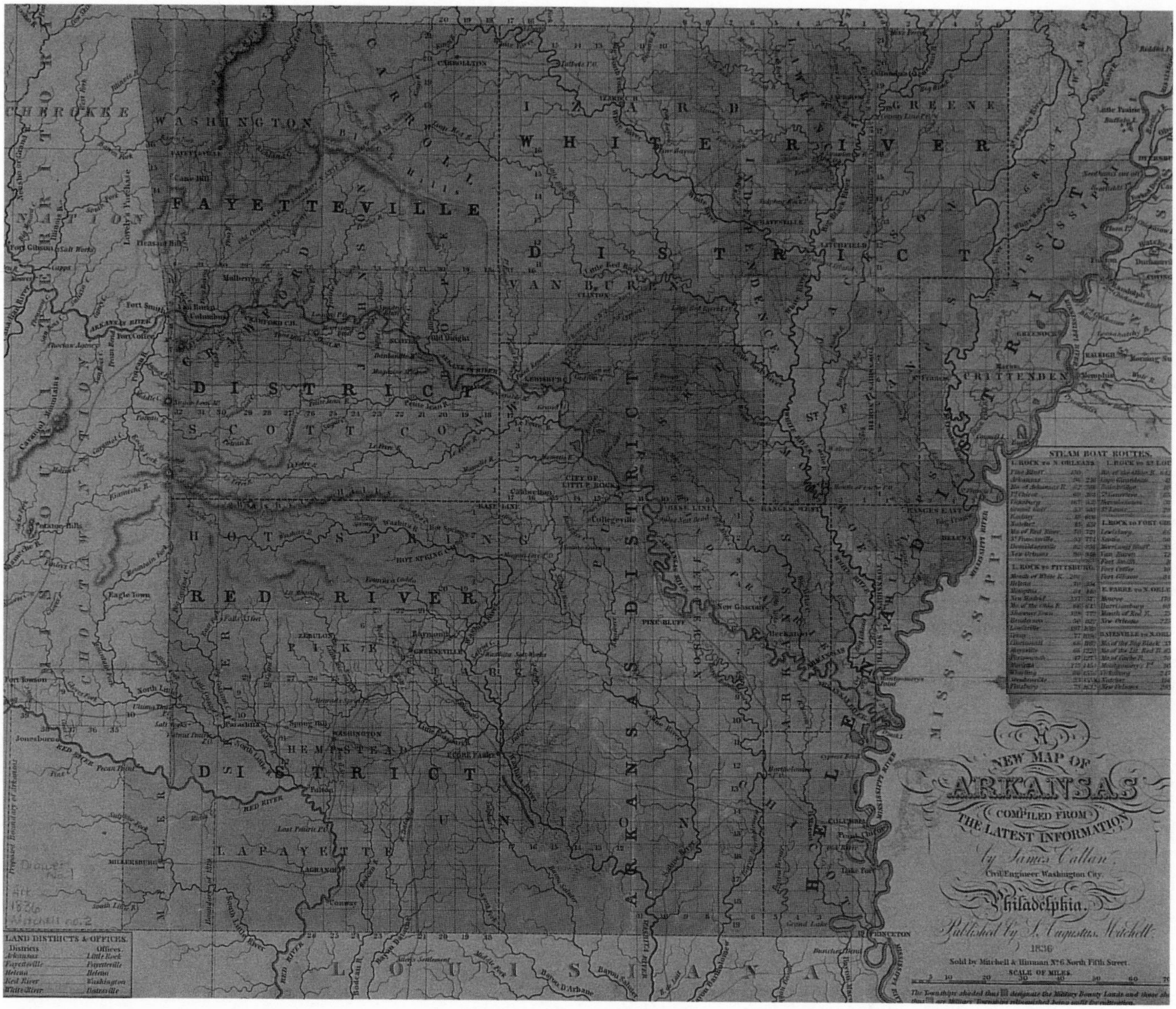

Steamboat routes: Batesville to New Orleans, 1836.

Courtesy of the Special Collections Division, University of Arkansas Libraries, Fayetteville.

pig copper from copper mines in the region. The *Steubenville* ran through most of 1840, when it was abandoned, a common practice for older or disabled craft. There was some indication that a part of its machinery was removed and installed in a new boat, the *Batesville,* which Tunstall began building in 1839.

Designed to carry 150 tons of freight, the *Batesville* (the first of three steamboats to be so named) was a light-draft boat that the captain hoped could "carry out sacked corn at all seasons."[2] While details about this *Batesville* are sketchy, the steamer made a number of trips to Batesville during 1840, supplying the merchants there with varied merchandise. On one trip it carried a fresh stock of paper for the *Batesville News,* and on another, seven hundred sacks of salt and one hundred barrels of "sup'r Rectified Whiskey, which . . . will sell lower than ever sold in this market."[3]

Like many of the steamers, the first *Batesville* was evidently short lived also. An article in the *Batesville News* in May of 1841 tells about the loss of the steamer *De Kalb* while towing the hull of the old steamer *Batesville.* Stripped of its boilers and machinery, the *Batesville* was loaded with lumber, cattle, and other freight when the disaster occurred. The *De Kalb* was traveling down the Mississippi toward New Orleans when it struck a snag near the mouth of the Big Red River. A part-owner of the steamer, Charles McArthur, was aboard the *Batesville* for the trip and was asleep when the accident happened. The noise of the mishap awakened McArthur and he arose, but, still half asleep, he wandered overboard. While gallant efforts were made to rescue him, the darkness, the swift, muddy waters, and the confusion caused by the misfortune made such efforts ineffective. The *Batesville* was cut loose from the sinking *De Kalb* so that its cargo might later be salvaged.

Another important development on the White River in the 1830s was the establishment of mail service by steamboat. In 1838, the *William Hurlbert* became the first known packet to run as a regular mail carrier on a portion of the White. The mail was dispatched from Memphis. The steamer traveled from Memphis down the Mississippi to the mouth of the White, then up the river to Rockroe, a site near the present town of Clarendon. From there, the mail was carried by stage to Little Rock and other points. Several years later, on October 3, 1850, river mail service from Memphis to Batesville was offered with the arrival of the forty-five-ton steamer *Dispatch,* commanded by Capt. W. L. McCullough. The first steamboat to provide mail service to Batesville, the aging vessel had just undergone a thorough overhauling in order to afford every facility needed for mail and passenger service. It was scheduled to leave Batesville each Saturday morning at ten o'clock, travel to Napoleon at the mouth of the Arkansas River, where it would connect with the Mississippi River mail boats, then return to Batesville within the week.

In late December of that year, misfortune befell the *Dispatch* when, on its upward trip, it struck a snag and sank thirty miles above the mouth of the White. Nothing could be salvaged from the wreck except the machinery and some of the furniture. The steamers *J. B. Gordon* and *Santa Fe* appeared as replacements for the *Dispatch.* White River patrons discovered, however, that river mail service could sometimes be erratic. One Batesville citizen complained, "We need a good mail boat—the *Santa Fe* is a terrible old concern."[4] The *Santa Fe* was later removed from the business and abandoned in 1851. The *J. B. Gordon* hit a snag and sank seven miles below Batesville in May of 1851.

In January of 1852, the Jacksonport newspaper contained these unfavorable comments about the mailboats: "The *General Ben* came up with the mail on Friday—she will be up again as soon as she can. The mailboats of late transport the mails with the speed of lightning—B-U-G-S!—in a walk."[5] In reporting the Jacksonport complaints, the *Memphis Weekly Appeal* said, "This speed reveals the velocity of a snail's gallop; and we in Memphis are, unfortunately, without any parallel to the expeditious transportation of our mails."[6]

Despite such criticism, river mail service expanded on the river and, through the years, improved. The steamers carried personal correspondence as well as newspapers from such cities as Little Rock, Memphis, and New Orleans, bringing closer contact with the rest of the country for the developing White River region. One of the favorite mail boats on the White in the mid-1850s was the *Sam Hale.* With Captain Adams as its master, the steamer plied between Napoleon and Jacksonport, with trips to Batesville when the water stage permitted.

The steamboats of the 1830s were rather crude when compared to those that appeared later. Still, every effort was made at providing comfort for their passengers, and, compared to travel overland, they were sheer delight. Most of the boats had a gentlemen's cabin that was lined on both sides with upper and lower bunks, which were draped with curtains for privacy. The ladies' cabin was smaller but offered individual staterooms.

The main cabin of a steamer was used as the dining area at mealtime, so it was equipped with drop-leaf tables. On most of the boats, these tables were set with fine china and silverware placed on beautiful linen cloths. Often, there was a piano in the room for the entertainment of the travelers. Occasionally they even danced here to the strains of a live band or orchestra.

There was also a bar and poker room on each vessel and the guests could rely upon the gambler aboard to be honest. If he wasn't, he didn't last long. The late Lady Elizabeth Luker of Newport, great-great-granddaughter of Thomas T. Tunstall and former curator of the Jacksonport Courthouse Museum, told how

The main cabin of Mary Woods II *would have been used for a dining area at mealtime, after which the drop-leaf tables were pushed against the walls and the cabin would serve as an entertainment center. A piano, band, or other musical diversion was usually provided. These beautiful chairs and sideboard date from about 1879.*

Photo by Sammie Rose.

Old stateroom in Mary Woods II *refurbished as it was in the 1890s. The beautiful old dress and suit are originals from that era. The wash basin and bunk beds complete the time frame.*

Photos by Sammie Rose.

dishonest gamblers were handled: they were simply placed on the next river island. Other craft, seeing a lone man on one of these islands, would never pick him up because everyone knew the reason for his being there, and there he remained.

The *Mary Woods II,* moored at Jacksonport State Park, is a lovely example of the grandeur of these steamers. The vessel was built in 1931 to haul log rafts on the White. Permanently docked at the park, the steamboat is the last triple-decked stern-wheeler on the river and one of only a few remaining on the Mississippi River system. In 1967, through the combined efforts of the Jackson County Historical Society, Arkansas State Parks, and the Potlatch Corporation, the *Mary Woods II* was donated to the park. Because the craft had always operated in the White River, those making the donation felt the steamboat belonged at Jacksonport. It was refurbished to represent an 1890s steamer and so is perhaps a bit more lavish than the earlier boats, but it is still a good representation of a White River steamboat.

In July 1997, the *Mary Woods II* suffered almost $300,000 worth of damage when a devastating tornado swept through the area and tossed the historic river boat approximately one hundred yards from its mooring. Fortunately, funds have been provided for repair of the steamboat, and the *Mary Woods II* will again be available to those who visit Jacksonport State Park.

Accommodations for deck passengers were quite different from the ones provided for cabin travelers. When night came, the deck sojourners slept wherever they could find a space amidst the cargo. Their meals were usually bought ashore or consisted of food they brought with them for the journey.

By 1841, at least three more steamboats, the *Victoria, Franklin,* and *Governor Yell,* entered the White and Black River trade. Formerly owned by Cherokee chief John Ross, the *Victoria* had been used to transport Cherokee Indians to their new home in the Oklahoma Territory. When offered for sale at Little Rock in 1840, it was purchased by John Brown of Batesville. Brown planned to run the *Victoria* regularly between Batesville and New Orleans. To firmly entrench the steamer in the White River business, Captain Brown, in 1841, signed a trade agreement with Noadiah Marsh of Elizabeth, Arkansas, in Jackson County. Marsh, a son-in-law of Capt. Charles Kelly, owned a large warehouse and was a keelboat operator who had been trading on the river since the early 1830s. In the possession of Betty L. Stroud of Desha, Arkansas, is an original copy of the agreement stating:

Bar and poker room on steamboat Mary Woods II. *The gambling table is set as if a game were in progress. Every steamboat had such a room.*

Photo by Sammie Rose.

> . . . Brown doeth agree to furnish the said Marsh . . . a good assortment of dry good of all discriptoon [*sic*] . . . also Nailes, iron steel Hardware & cutlery Sugar Coffe & avry other article found necessary to compose an assortment for a Country Store . . . Said Marsh is to allow the Said Brown on Articles of Merchandise (Except sugar coffe & Salt) fifty per cent over cost & charges. Sugar Coffe & Salt to be furnished at cost & charges of freight Insurance . . . Said Marsh is to pay the Said Brown in *Marketable* produce of the Country at the curent market price. Such as Beef Cattle, Stags & Bulls excepted, pork hogs, Horses, Tobacco, Cotton & free of any Extra Charge except the actual hire of Labour and hands to drive and asist in Loading . . . Should the Amount of goods purchased by said Brown exceed the amount of stock purchased by said Marsh and furnished to said Brown, he the Said Marsh agrees to pay the balance in good Current Money of the State of Arks. . . .

Apparently, Marsh had little competition for the keelboat trade in the region, so there were great expectations for the success of the arrangement between Brown and him.

During the early 1840s, the dream of regular steam traffic along a lengthy route of the White River seemed achievable. On May 10, 1841, the steamer *Victoria,* with Capt. John Brown, the owner, at the helm, became the first steamboat to travel to the mouth of the North Fork River, some one hundred miles above Batesville, setting the stage for a new era of steamboating on the White. By 1842, more and more steamers were traveling the river. In January of that year, the *Franklin,* with Captain Lee as its master, arrived at Batesville from the mouth of the White carrying 145 passengers, 95 of whom were emigrants to the area. New Orleans to Batesville packets were also more frequent. In the spring of 1842, the packet *Pawnee,* one of Tunstall's vessels, commanded by Captain Lott, who

The late Lady Elizabeth Luker, formerly curator of the Jacksonport Courthouse Museum, at Mary Woods II *in Jacksonport State Park on White River at Jacksonport.*

Photo courtesy of Sammie Rose.

later became a partner of Tunstall's, made the New Orleans–Batesville round trip fully loaded in about twenty days. The *Pawnee* was briefly replaced that summer by a large Mississippi River boat of 301 net tons called the *Bunker Hill.* Both the *Pawnee* and the mammoth *Bunker Hill* ran in the White until at least May of 1843 when the light-draft steamer *Carrier* displaced the *Pawnee.* By 1844, several other vessels, including the *Sarah,* the *Yucatan,* and the *Marietta,* competed with the Tunstall-Lott steamers.

As business increased during the 1840s and more and more emigrants migrated to the region, the steamboats began traveling greater distances above Batesville. The farther upstream they went, the more difficult the journey became, with navigational hazards increasing each mile advanced upriver. Demands for improvement of the Upper White channel escalated through most of the 1840s. The crude, cumbersome boats of the early 1830s were being replaced with the far superior vessels of the 1840s, and the steamboat industry was rapidly "coming of age" and wanting to expand.

Several important events occurred in the 1840s that advanced the steamboat business on the White River substantially. Packet lines were set up to run as frequently as possible from New Orleans, Memphis, Louisville, and other deep-water ports to Jacksonport and, when water would permit, above, providing regular service to White River communities. Jacksonport was thriving with the business. As previously mentioned, the river's channel to that point was quite good, allowing these large steamboats to travel there virtually year round. As at Montgomery Point, located at the White's mouth, cargo was then transferred at Jacksonport to smaller steamers which could navigate in shallower water. Such increased activity brought about even lower freight rates. One bill of lading in November of 1841 showed the costs of a shipment of livestock from Montgomery Point to Batesville on the steamboat *Franklin:*[7]

M. S. Denton Nov. 20, 1841

To Steamer *Franklin* Due

To Freighting from Montgomery Point to Batesville:

1 Durham Bull	$10.00
1 Do Heifer	10.00
Charges on same	7.50
Feeding cattle on passage	3.00
Passage for self from Mouth of Black River	3.00
	$33.50

When a steamer was carrying a cargo of cattle, a railing was placed a few feet inside the guardrail on the freight deck and the animals were tied to this railing as closely as possible to conserve space. At feeding time, a deckhand with a sack of corn would pass in the space between the guardrail and the temporary railing to give each animal an ear of corn. The procedure was repeated as often as necessary to complete the feeding. Watering of the cattle was accomplished in the same way.

With such an increase in vessels navigating the lower portions of the river, attention was drawn more and more to the potential of the upper reaches of the White. A number of the steamboat captains felt they were ready for the challenge offered on that portion of the waterway and recognized the fertile market that existed there. The *Victoria's* achievement in reaching the mouth of the North Fork contributed to that interest, and requests for improvement of the upper river to enable navigation to the mouth of Swan Creek in Missouri became stronger. While some of the more difficult portions had been improved for flatboat travel, additional work was needed to make regular steamboat navigation there more viable.

Buffalo Shoals in southeastern Marion County, Arkansas, like Elbow Shoals above it, was one of the more demanding shoals on the river. The arrival date of the first steamboat at Buffalo Shoals is uncertain, but on March 24, 1844, with the intensity of competition on the Lower White increasing, Capt. Thomas T. Tunstall announced that the steamboat *Carrier* would depart from Jacksonport, Arkansas, on April 20 en route to Forsyth, Missouri, a settlement at the mouth of Swan Creek that was 521 miles from the mouth of the White and was considered the head of navigation on the river. Forsyth offered great promise as a river town because of its strategic location as a connecting point for land routes to major commercial points in Missouri, such as Springfield. Successful navigation of the Upper White was considered vital to the growth of towns like Forsyth as well as to the commerce of the surrounding area. The expanded market was appealing to the steamboat owners as well.

The attempt by Captain Tunstall and the *Carrier* in 1844 was unsuccessful, but the captain was undaunted in his belief that the upper reaches of the river could be conquered. On May 12, 1844, Tunstall wrote from Jacksonport, Arkansas, to Maj. John P. Campbell of Springfield, Missouri, about the *Carrier* journey. Major Campbell was engaged in the boating business and was an interested promoter of commercial traffic along the White. Captain Tunstall stated that the *Carrier*, a steamer of 350 tons, could have made it to the mouth of Swan Creek had it not been for the significant rise in the White River, making it impossible to make any head against such a strong and rapid current without ample wood to make steam other than the water-soaked rails and the very green wood that was available along the way. Tunstall further stated that the White River, for its length and size, was one of the best in America for steam navigation as far up as the mouth of the Swan. With a small appropriation for minor improvements, he felt the navigation could become superior. Even under current conditions, Tunstall went on to say, if a boat could reach Batesville, it could go to Swan Creek.

As Tunstall mentioned, a good wood supply for the steamboats was always a concern. The primary fuel used by the steamers was pine cordwood. Ambitious farmers who lived near the White would cut and haul the wood to the riverbank where they would stack it in cords. The price paid by the boats was usually four dollars per cord. Pine was not only plentiful at the time but also preferred by the steamboatmen because it made a quick, hot fire that lasted a long time. Included in the cords of pine were plenty of pine knots to provide rapid ignition and a splendid light. The odor of the burning pine knots floating in the air was another delightful signal to those living along the river that one of the beautiful vessels was approaching.

When a fireman noticed that his fuel supply was low, he would warn the mate to keep a sharp eye for cordwood along the shore. The pilot would then make a stop at the first stack or wood yard he came to. Sometimes the fuel was supplied at a regular landing. Often, it was from one of the piles along the riverbank. It was never necessary for the workman who owned the wood to be present. If his wood was used, he would simply go to the most convenient landing near his place when the boat was again due and present his bill. The theft of cordwood stacked along the White was almost unknown.

Occasionally, the steamer's fuel supply would be depleted at a point where there was no cordwood available. In those instances, the boat would land near a farm, if possible, and proceed to remove as many boards of the farmer's rail fence as were needed. Understandably, such fuel always cost a stiff price. If even this source was not available, the crew disembarked and chopped some wood.

John Quincy Wolf, who lived by the White and worked on the steamboats, told about a trick, involving cordwood, that he once played on a friend. Wolf was working at Calico Rock at the time. His friend Sam Ivy hoped to earn some extra money by selling cordwood to the steamers. It was early autumn and, as rivermen knew, the river was too low for boating, but Ivy cut some pine anyway. With a yoke of oxen, he then hauled the wood about three miles to the river, where he neatly stacked it in cords on the bank. Each time he brought in a load, Ivy would sit by the stack of wood and longingly look down the river, hoping a steamer would come into view. Days passed, but still no steamboat because the White was so low. Ivy was persistent, however, and continued in his endeavor. One day, when Ivy was sitting expectantly by his stack of wood, Wolf spied him and saw the opportunity for some fun. Because of his early love of steamboats, Wolf had learned to perfectly imitate the whistle of one of the vessels. Staying out of sight, he gave the signal of a steamboat blowing for a landing—a moderately long blast, then a short one followed by a long, drawn-out one. To Wolf's delight, his friend Ivy jumped up, leaped in his wagon, and cracked his whip over the heads of the oxen as he yelled "git up" and raced away for another load of pine. One can imagine Ivy's disappointment when he returned later in the afternoon to find no steamboat and no wood missing from his stack.[8]

In 1845, Captain Tunstall again tried to ascend Buffalo Shoals with the steamer *Wasp* and again failed. The *Arkansas Gazette* of June 9, 1845, reported the attempt: "Capt. Tunstall has gone above with the *Wasp.* He left for the mouth of Swan, but I recon the Buffalo Shoals will be as high as he can make. The captain is working the fires now to make up for his default by old Stomper, who beat Eudora and Sally Carr for him. Stomper has Miss Bell, a consol mare that run well with Kirkman's Sartin at Nashville in a second heat, in 5:47."[9]

Captain Tunstall's racehorses had fared poorly in competition with those of "old Stomper," a gentleman from Georgia. Monetary side bets of rather large amounts often accompanied the running of the horses, and Captain Tunstall must have lost some of his extra cash, since he was "working the fires now to make up for his default by old Stomper." Both Batesville and Jacksonport had racetracks during this period.

Captain Tunstall continued to run his steamboats to Buffalo Shoals, making another fruitless attempt to conquer it with the steamboat *Kate Kirkwood* in May 1848.

Validating the importance that political leaders attributed to navigation along the White River, on December, 23, 1844, the fifth session of the General Assembly of Arkansas passed an act declaring the White River a navigable stream. Section one of that act stated that the White River was navigable from its junction with the Mississippi River to the mouth of Swan Creek near Forsyth, Missouri, for steamboats; and from there to Three Forks it was navigable for keelboats and flatboats. Section two of that act further stated that "if any person or persons should obstruct the navigation thereof, he or they so offending shall be deemed guilty of a misdemeanor and may be fined a penal sum of not less than five, nor more than fifty dollars, and costs of removing same." It is interesting the Arkansas legislature worded the act "navigable to mouth of the Swan" rather than to the Missouri state line since it would seem that body would have no authority past such a point.

The state of Missouri joined in the support of commerce on the White River, appropriating eight thousand dollars on March 3, 1851, for the improvement of the river along the Arkansas border. The Missouri legislature additionally appropriated, at that time and for the same purpose, all monies then or thereafter due the counties of Taney, Greene, and Barry from the internal improvement fund derived from the sale of government land given to the state by the U.S. Congress in 1841. Combining private capital with some of these state funds, men were hired to cut a new channel through the Elbow Shoals. Working under Hack Snapp, who allegedly paid the men in gold, the new channel was finished in late summer of 1851.

Reflecting the confidence placed in the promise offered by steamboat navigation, the official seal of the Missouri county of Taney bore a steamboat in its center, and steamboat traffic became one of the major topics of conversation among the inhabitants of southwestern Missouri and northwestern Arkansas.

The summer of 1845 was unusually hot and dry, and the drought lasted well into the early winter months, as shown by this item from Batesville, appearing in the *Arkansas Gazette* on December 19, 1845: "White River was never so low, by some five inches. If our river would only rise one foot, it would help; but if she would take up both, the *General Morgan* would be afloat, and she is the favorite craft of these parts. It is right that she should be so, for Captain Sept. Williams is some punkins anywhere."

Disaster struck one of Captain Tunstall's steamboats in 1846 when the ill-fated *Wabash Valley* had a collision and sank en route to New Orleans. The vessel struck an upriver boat about midnight near Memphis and submerged to its cabin floor. The other steamboat continued on its way, offering no help to the *Wabash Valley.* One of the hands was reported missing and several passengers were thought to have drowned. The steamer *Belle Creole* towed the wreck ashore opposite Jefferson College and took part of the crew and passengers to Memphis.

The steamboat that collided with the *Wabash Valley* may have been the *Bulletin*. These words of a Batesville citizen later appeared in the *Arkansas Gazette* of April 27, 1846: "The sinking of the *Wabash Valley* was a serious loss to Captain Tunstall and his son William. I never heard of so wanton a sporting with human life before. The pilot of the *Bulletin* should be gibbeted. She never even stopped, though the *Valley*'s distress bell was rang immediately. After the collision, but for the parting of the cabin from the hull, many would have drowned. I hope Mr. Tunstall will be able to score it on the *Bulletin* heavily." The Tunstalls were well respected along White River and remained active in the steamboat trade there throughout their lives.

The Mexican War was mentioned in White River steamboating news in 1847. In early December of that year, the *Governor Bent* arrived at Batesville with the body of Capt. Andrew R. Porter, one of Independence County's heroes, who died at Buena Vista, Mexico, on February 23, 1847. Through the kindness of Capt. Franklin W. Desha, the body had been placed in a secure coffin and transported to New Orleans, where it was then placed aboard the *Governor Bent.* When the steamer left Batesville for the return trip to New Orleans, it had aboard Lieutenant Magruder with about fifty new recruits for the Mexican War. They were accompanied by Dr. James E. Pelham, their surgeon.

During the spring of 1849, the dreaded disease cholera again appeared in the ports along the Mississippi River and induced justifiable uneasiness among the travelers on the White. While there were several cases of cholera on the steamer *Storm* when it arrived at Batesville on April 9 of that year, none of the local citizens who were passengers on the vessel were among the ill. Fortunately, of the other passengers and crew who were afflicted, none died from the ailment.

Those aboard the *Governor Bent* did not fare so well. Capt. Joseph Anthony of Randolph County, Arkansas, who had just been married in New Orleans, died of cholera shortly after his arrival at Pocahontas on the Black River. Crawford Walker, a passenger from White County, Arkansas, died on the boat, as did Joseph Spikes, sheriff of Randolph County. Another traveler aboard for that ill-fated trip of the *Governor Bent* left the steamer at Jacksonport but died before he could reach his home.

About a month later, death again visited the *Governor Bent,* taking one of the steamer's clerks. The vessel was steaming up the Mississippi River en route to Jacksonport when a boiler exploded and killed the crewman. Except for a chance happening, there would have been other fatalities in the accident. Just moments prior to the explosion, several crew members were gathered near the boilers when a rat was sighted and all but the victim left in pursuit of the rodent. The varmint chase saved their lives.

Perhaps its name influenced the career of the *Storm,* as another catastrophe in November of 1849 permanently removed the steamboat from the New Orleans to Batesville trade. The White River vessel was lying beside the big steamer *Louisiana* at New Orleans when the boilers on the *Louisiana* exploded. The blast hurled the *Storm* fifty feet out into the river, damaging it beyond repair. The *Storm*'s pilot fell to the deck of the wheelhouse when he heard the explosion. A dead man came flying through the window and landed on top of him. The cabin where the *Storm*'s clerk, Moody, sat at his desk was riddled with flying pieces of steel that completely tore away the walls. Miraculously, he was uninjured, but his wife, who was standing at the stern, was killed instantly, and it was not until the next morning that their child was found, unharmed.

By the late 1840s, a number of small steamboats were traveling regularly to the foot of Buffalo Shoals about nine months of the year and making year-round trips when river conditions permitted. As a result of its strategic location, the village there experienced considerable growth and was named Buffalo City with the establishment of a post office there. Among the early vessels running to Buffalo City were the *Lt. Maury,* the *Major Barbour,* and the *Eureka.* The *Eureka* was the craft that finally conquered Buffalo Shoals in June 1851 and traveled upstream to the next significant challenge, near the Missouri line, the infamous Elbow Shoals, which had been the pitfall for so many flatboats in the past. The steamer was loaded with cargo designated for Forsyth when it made its attempt to pass Elbow Shoals. S. C. Turnbo gave a vivid description of the occasion:

> In the month of June, 1851, when the earliest corn was nearly knee high, people along the river were surprised as well as delighted at seeing a steamboat shoving its way up the river. As the boat came in sight of each cabin it gave a loud whistle, and the people ran to the bank to see what made such a strange and fearful noise. The sight was wonderful to them, cattle were terrified and stampeded and horses snorted and ran away . . . The day was sultry, the air calm and charged with moisture. The atmosphere was almost suffocating, small cumulus clouds floated slowly along in the aerial regions . . . As the boat approached the shoal, the firemen were ordered to heave wood into the furnace that there might be plenty of steam to force the boat over the shoal. Great volumes of smoke ascended high in the air and slowly drifted away. Great jets of steam belched from the escape pipes and formed miniature white clouds that dissipated. The propelling wheel of the boat churned the water so rapidly and strongly as to dash water high on the bank; grown people, as well as we children, looked on with wonder and amazement. The steamer, as she plowed her way through the swift current of water, had attained good speed when she entered the old channel: her intended destination was Forsyth. The captain and passengers were anxious to pass the shoal; and as she was forced along against the strong current, the water leaped and foamed against the bow. The beautiful steamer succeeded in reaching the curve, where the speed was checked and she soon came to a standstill. The bow, in spite of efforts of the pilot to prevent it, turned toward the south

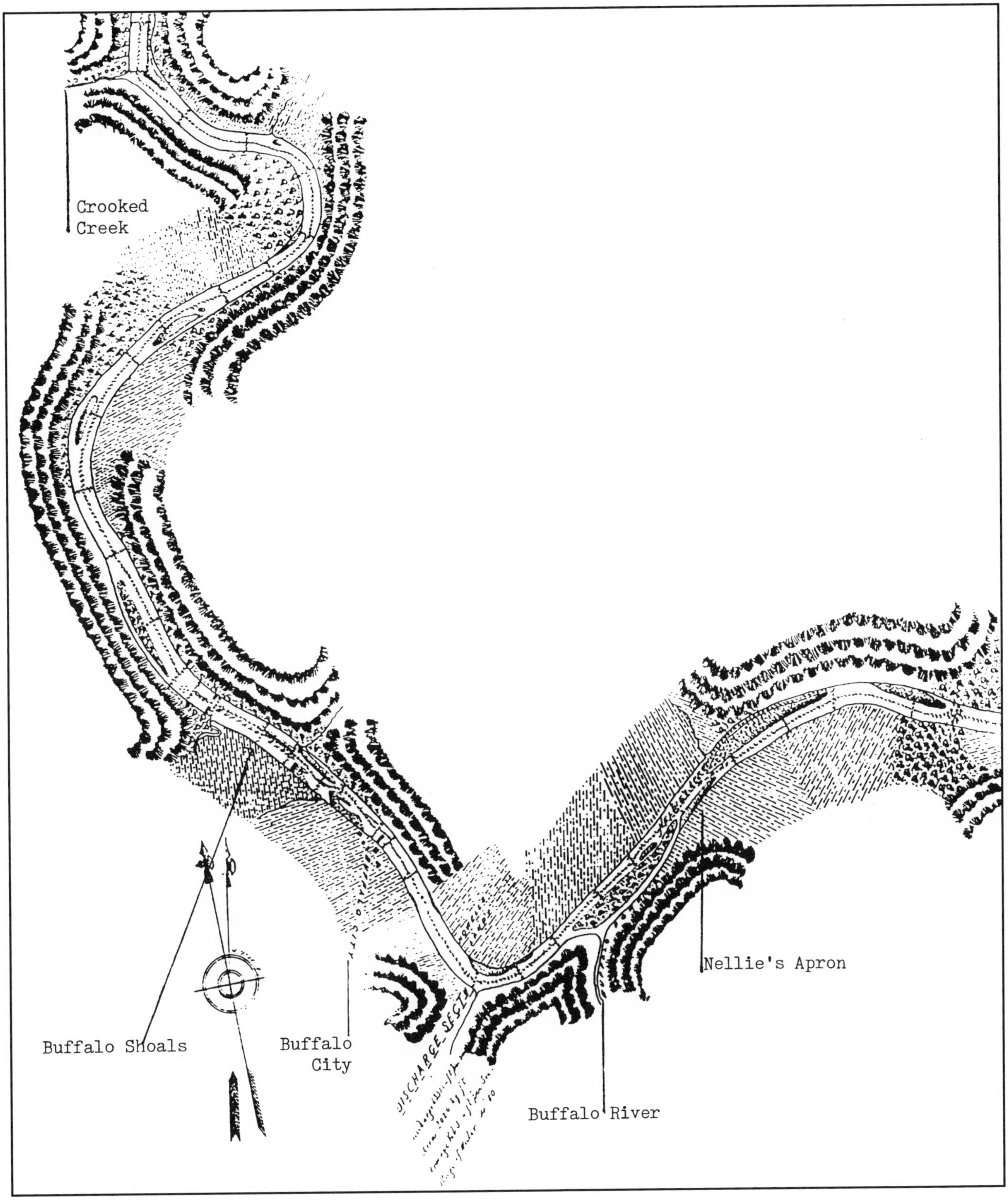

April 4, 1888, U.S. Army Corps of Engineers map, White River, Buffalo Shoals area. It was made under the direction of H. S. Taber, Captain, U.S. Army Corps of Engineers, by Jas. C. Long and Chas. E. Taft, Asst. Engineers.

Courtesy of the U.S. Army Corps of Engineers office, Little Rock, Arkansas.

> bank. For a moment the pilot had lost control of the boat, and there was imminent danger of a collision against the shore and the chimneys being swept off by the timber. The engines were instantly reversed, and the boat was righted again by its being backed downstream a short distance. Then another trial was made to stem the rolling tide of the swift-flowing water with no better success than in the first attempt. It was now evident that she could proceed no farther up the river; the efforts of the captain and crew were unavailing, and they had to drop back to the landing at Dubuque, 2 miles below the shoal.

The landing received its name from the *Eureka*'s captain when he was asked to name the town and he chose to name it after his home town of Dubuque, Iowa. Turnbo's narration about the *Eureka* continued:

> The boat remained there that night and early the following morning a crowd of men and women and children had collected at the landing to see the boat, and just before her departure from here back down the river, she gave a loud whistle which startled the entire assembly of people. Among the crowd was a young man with red hair and red complexion who when the steamer whistled thought the boat was rent asunder and started away on a fast run and was soon lost from view. Those of the crowd that quickly recovered from the fright created by the blast from the whistle yelled and laughed at the panic stricken fellow.[10]

Buffalo City's prosperity attracted numerous businessmen. In the fall of 1858, hoping to profit from the increased trade at the community, John H. Quisenberry decided to develop the settlement into a major port. The ambitious Quisenberry purchased land, platted it into lots and advertised such lots for sale. In his ad, he stated that river mail service would soon be extended to Buffalo City and that these packets would provide continuous transportation to the Mississippi. To fulfill his promises, Quisenberry worked with Capt. Pete Fleming and T. J. Wood to purchase a boat to run from Buffalo City to Augusta, where it would connect with the steamer *Admiral,* owned by Captain Fleming. Such a plan would establish a steamboat line from Buffalo City to the Mississippi, thence to Memphis and New Orleans. The steamboat *Oakland* was purchased by the three men, a craft they felt could run the entire year since it drew only fourteen inches of water.

Quisenberry's attempt to develop Buffalo City progressed nicely for a while. Sixty-seven back lots averaging $22 each and a few of the $150 riverfront lots sold. The developer was unable to make the *Oakland* a U.S. mail packet, however, and the steamer had difficulty withstanding the increased competition for trade on the Upper White, particularly with the entrance of the *Mary Patterson* upon the scene in April 1859.

The *Mary Patterson* passed Buffalo City that month en route to Forsyth with Capt. Morgan Bateman at its helm. The steamer, named after the daughter of a prominent Augusta businessman, proved to be a worthy competitor for the Upper White River trade. Although not completely finished at the time of the initial trip, the *Mary Patterson* was one of the lightest and staunchest vessels afloat and was well adapted to upper river navigation. Upon his return from Forsyth, Bateman stated he would make another trip to Taney County in about two weeks.

To keep up with such competition, Capt. Thomas J. Wood announced that he was taking the *Oakland* to Forsyth also, and as a further gesture of goodwill, he scheduled an excursion trip from Batesville to Buffalo City. The craft was to depart Batesville Thursday morning, April 21, and return Saturday evening. The local newspaper lauded the trip as an opportunity "for all lovers of the magnificent to visit the picturesque scenery of Upper White River."[11] In his estimation, the belles and beaux of the city and surrounding area would greet the news with delight since it would be one of the treats of the season. Fare for the round trip was four dollars. Due to unforeseen problems, however, the excursion trip was canceled; Wood had to move the *Oakland* to the lower river trade to replace the *Admiral* when that vessel became temporarily disabled. Once the pride of Buffalo City, the *Oakland* was finally sold at a U.S. marshall's sale on September 7, 1859, to meet unpaid debts acquired because of its inability to effectively compete with other steamers on the Upper White.

In a letter to the *Des Arc Citizen* expressing excitement about the expansion at Buffalo City, A. G. Cochran, the postmaster at Buffalo City, stated:

> The following boats are holding themselves in readiness to run the Upper White River trade the coming season, VIZ: the *Interchange,* Captain J. W. Gilchrist, to run from Buffalo City to New Orleans; *Mary Patterson,* Captain Morg Bateman, and *Nebraska,* Captain Cummins, to run from Buffalo City to Jacksonport; and I doubt not that several OTHER BOATS will be "in" in time to reap a share of the spoils. . . . The principal productions of the country are corn, wheat and tobacco, which has been raised this year in abundance. Cattle and hogs are also raised in almost INNUMERABLE QUANTITIES. Beef cattle could be bought at 3 cents per pound, good corn-fed pork, at not exceeding 4 cents, wheat is worth 50 cents per bushel, corn will be worth 25 per bushel. . . . The town was surveyed in October last, but very little improvement was done until the first of February. Since then there has been considerable. . . . To the tavern known as the "Shoal House," there has been added a room 20 feet square, with a passage 16 feet wide, and a porch 36 feet long, and a double stable and a smoke house. The warehouse at the steamboat landing has been thoroughly renovated and put in good order; which is of sufficient capacity to do an extensive receiving and forwarding business, and also to carry on an extensive mercantile business upstairs, which is now occupied by Messrs. Gilchrist and Co. A business 25 by 100 feet (new) is nearly completed; two residences have been built, and several others in contemplations. We suppose Messrs. G. and Co., Captain Morg Bateman, W. H. Fletcher, E. B. Tunstall, C. Duggins and Alex Moreland will build this fall, and probably others. I omitted to mention when speaking of new improvements, a STEAM GRIST MILL, built by the Messrs. Tunstalls, which makes a fine article of flour. There have been eleven families moved here since the town was surveyed.[12]

The August 24, 1859, issue of the *Des Arc Citizen* noted: "I find there are many citizens of our state, who do not know that the White River is navigable to Buffalo City, even during winter and spring. For the information of such persons, I will give the names of six different steamboats that went to Buffalo City during the past season: *City of Knoxville, Monongahela Belle, Oakland, Mary Patterson, Nebraska,* and the *Interchange*. Three of these boats will run to Buffalo City in the coming season."

The growing number of steamboats traversing the White increased the frequency of the unforgettable sound of a steamer's whistle resounding along the river. Each whistle had a distinctive tone that enabled the residents along the way to know which boat was approaching. It was a nostalgic sound that lived forever in the hearts of the people who experienced it. John Q. Wolf described the haunting signals:

> The famous steam whistles, forever linked in the memory of boats, were stationed above the roof on the pilothouse. They usually had three prongs, each prong keyed to a different tone, and were very musical, attracting almost as much attention as the rest of the boat. If atmospheric conditions were favorable, they could be heard for twenty-five miles. The *J. Harry (Josie Harry)* had a five pronged whistle that could be heard, it is said, for fifty miles. If a boat were going to land, it gave three blasts from the whistle, while yet a half or three-fourths mile away—one fairly long, one short one, and then a long drawn out blast. I think this custom was changed in later years to four blasts; one long, two short, then a very long one. When it was ready to depart, two or three taps of the bell out in front warned everybody who did not belong on the boat to get off. Likewise it was a warning to passengers loafing on shore to get on board.[13]

It was said one steamer, the *Ella No. 2,* had one thousand silver coins melted in its bell at the time of casting, creating a remarkable tone.

By the 1850s, steamboats were a common sight along the White. By no means do we imply the battle was easy. In arid times the river did not offer enough water and during the wet months, the rapids could be fierce and impossible to pass. The upper reaches of the White River, as briefly mentioned before, presented the severest challenge to the captains of the steamboats navigating the river because of the numerous sharp bends and difficult shoals. The business was fraught with difficulties. Sandbars, fires, snags, and boiler explosions were common. The average life of a boat was four years.

One of the worst disasters to occur on the White happened on December 4, 1851, when the *Clermont No. 2* sank on the lower river near Augusta, Arkansas. The steamboat struck a snag about midnight and quickly sank in eighteen feet of water. While the cabin passengers, officers, and crew members were all saved, twenty-two of the twenty-six deck passengers died.

Despite such difficulties however, the advantages of transportation by steam far outweighed the disadvantages and the promise of profit was there. Freight rates were quite reasonable, making the usage of steamboats very attractive. In 1848, such staples as whiskey were shipped from Cincinnati to local markets for $1.50 a barrel and the general going cargo rate was about $.40 per one hundred pounds. Travel by steamer was becoming increasingly popular as well.

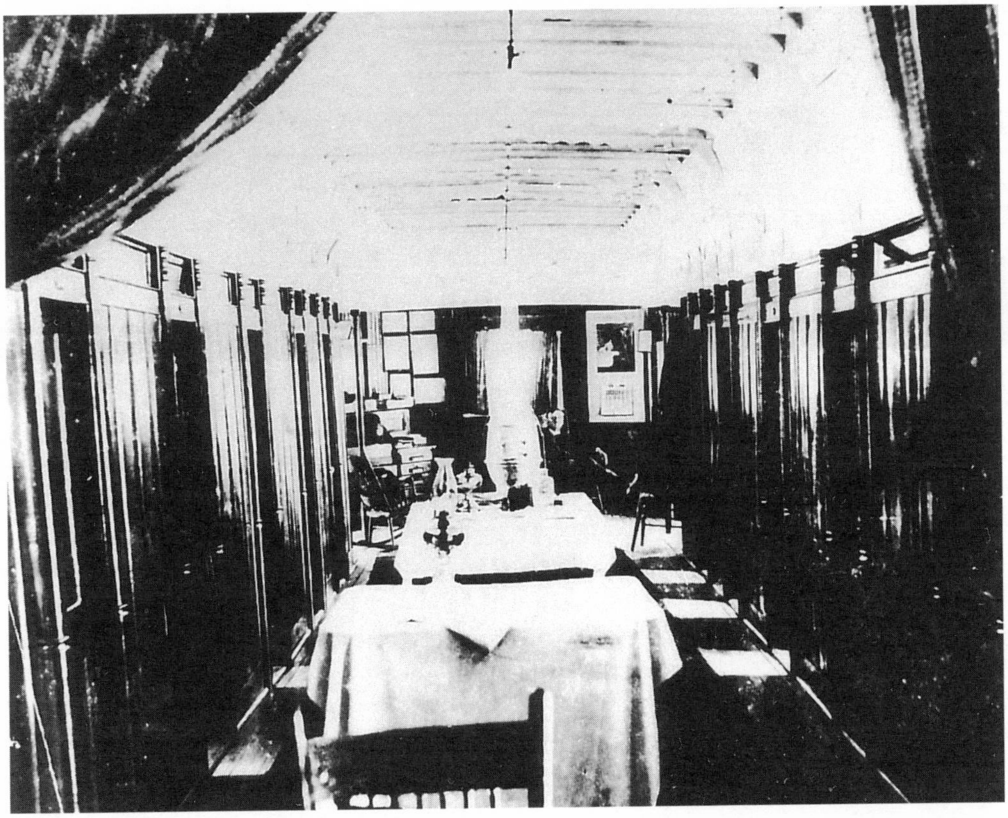

Inside the cabin of a small Upper White River steamer, believed to be the Home, *which was built at Calico Rock in 1885 by Capt. Thomas B. Stallings.*

Courtesy of the University of Arkansas, Little Rock, Archives and Special Collections.

With such incentives, believers in the steamboat industry were not only inspired but eager to take on the demands placed upon them by the White. The pilots and captains of the steamboats became remarkably ingenious in their methods of combating the obstacles presented by the river. When the White was low, these exceptional men could literally "jump" a boat drawing three feet of water over a shoal that was only two and a half feet deep. John Q. Wolf wrote of witnessing such a feat. Wolf was on the steamer *Home* when the vessel ran aground in a swift shoal near Wolf Bayou, sixteen miles below Batesville. The steamboat was heavily loaded. After sizing up the situation, Captain Stallings ordered the mate to lay a line to a tree about 350 feet up the river. The other end of this line was fastened around the capstan, which was then turned until the cable stretched so tautly that it appeared it could snap at any moment. Meanwhile, the pilot had signaled the engineer to turn the engine forward very slowly, keeping the water pulled from under the boat so that it was resting hard on the bottom. At the proper moment, the pilot rang the stopping bell, then immediately rang the backing bell. Upon receiving that signal, the engineer reversed his engine and quickly backed with all the power he could muster. These maneuvers resulted in the backing of the wheel forcing a great volume of water under the boat, which lifted it clear of the bottom so that the tautness of the cable literally "jerked" it forward several feet. The cable slack was then quickly tightened in order to maintain the gain accomplished and the process was repeated until the craft cleared the obstacle.[14]

The steamboat captains took great pride in their ability to navigate a craft in low water. One captain stated he could run a boat on just the "morning dew." Another declared all he needed was a "mere spit" in the channel and away he would go. There were times, however, when even the most talented masters had to tie up their boats and await a rise in the river, often a week or more. On one such occasion, a newspaperman commented that one of the boats became grounded so long the crew members were planting potatoes so they would have a cargo to fill the boat when the water rose in the fall.

Certainly, an adept crew contributed to a steamer's success in the trade. A knowledgeable crew was essential not only to economic success but also to the vessel's safety. The crewmen's responsibilities were very specific and of equal importance if the steamboat was to function at its highest capabilities—not so different from a properly run operation today.

The average crew of White River steamboats numbered from fifteen to thirty, and their "job descriptions," to use modern vernacular, adequately explained their responsibilities. Officers consisted of the master, the pilot, the engineer, the clerk, and the mate. In addition to these, there was usually a second pilot, second engineer, a "mud" clerk, a head fireman, his assistant, the steward, always a cook, a night watchman, cabin boys, and deckhands. Frequently, there were also chambermaids to care for the lady passengers.

The master was the executive officer. He was the one in command, the man who hired and fired, and usually, but not always, the owner of the boat. During the trip, he was not, necessarily, very visible; but when the steamboat was in trouble or at a landing, the master was always seen out in front directing the pilot and the mate. Landings were crucial. The boat must come in to the shore slowly, must not be jerked around, and must hit the bank gently.

Capt. Andy Pate, the last licensed pilot for the navigable length of White River from its mouth to Forsyth, Missouri.

Courtesy of Jimmie Jean Bowman, his daughter.

The pilot, who was at the wheel, was almost as important as the master. It was the pilot who decided if the night was too dark or the fog too thick or the wind too strong to navigate safely. The pilot was also the one who, if the boat was sinking, was required to stay at the wheel until there was no hope of saving the vessel. Most importantly, the pilot must know the river. He had to know where each shoal and reef was, where each submerged boulder or snag rested, where each sharp turn existed in the channel. When the water was high, he must be familiar with the currents so that he would know how close to the shore he could safely steer. When he was traveling upstream in high water, he must shun the middle of the river because that was where the current was the swiftest and strongest. Because of this, he must also know how to constantly shift the boat's position, from one side of the river to the other, to avoid the swift currents. The pilot had to know his

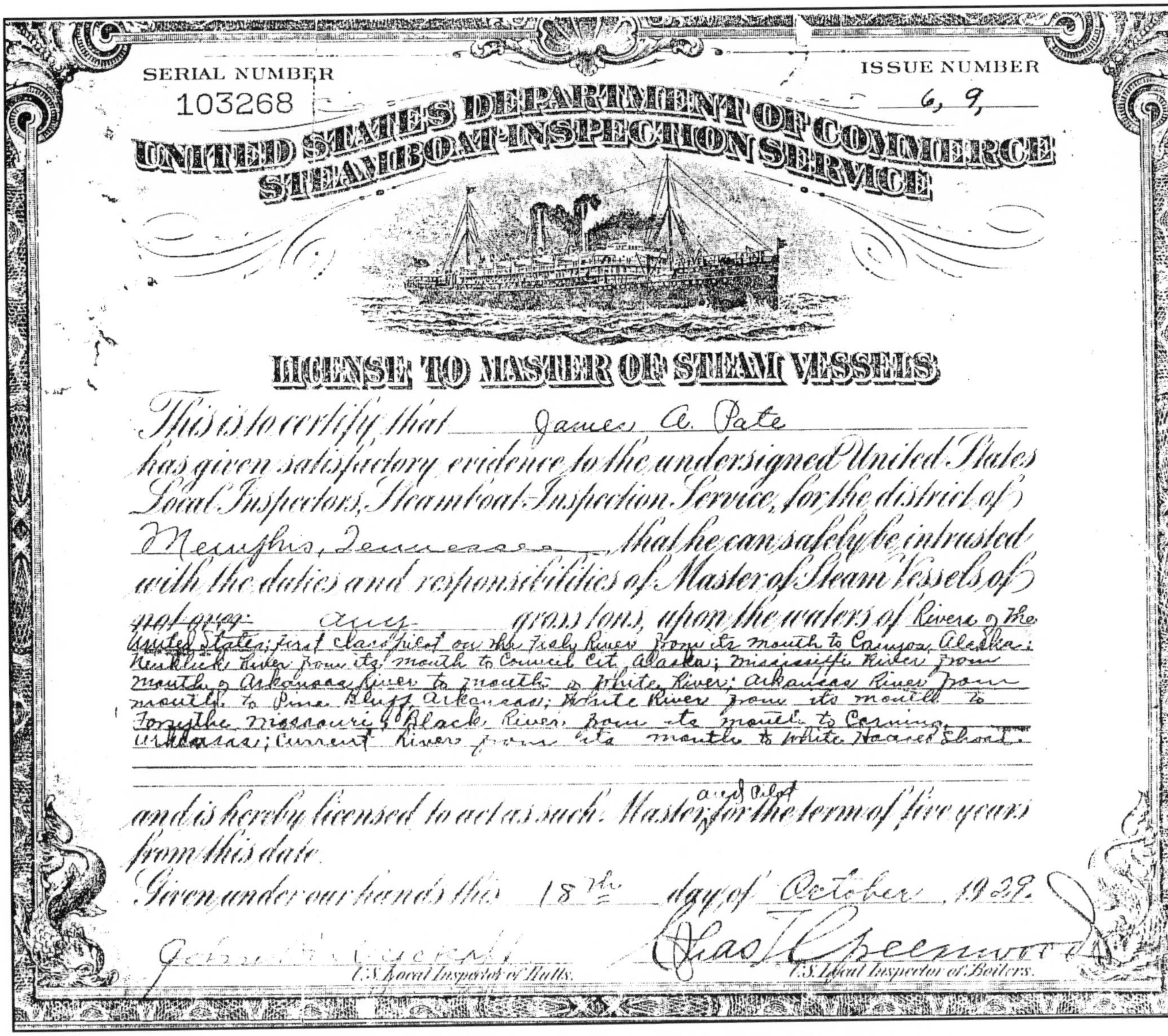

SERIAL NUMBER 103268

ISSUE NUMBER 6, 9,

UNITED STATES DEPARTMENT OF COMMERCE
STEAMBOAT-INSPECTION SERVICE

LICENSE TO MASTER OF STEAM VESSELS

This is to certify that James A. Pate
has given satisfactory evidence to the undersigned United States Local Inspectors, Steamboat-Inspection Service, for the district of Memphis, Tennessee that he can safely be intrusted with the duties and responsibilities of Master of Steam Vessels of not over any gross tons, upon the waters of Rivers of the United States; first class pilot on the Yukon River from its mouth to Canyon, Alaska; Knik River from its mouth to Council City, Alaska; Mississippi River from mouth of Arkansas River to mouth of White River; Arkansas River from mouth to Pine Bluff, Arkansas; White River from its mouth to Forsyth, Missouri; Black River from its mouth to Corning, Arkansas; Current River from its mouth to White Hare Shoal.

and is hereby licensed to act as such Master and Pilot for the term of five years from this date.

Given under our hands this 18th day of October 1929.

U.S. Local Inspector of Hulls.

U.S. Local Inspector of Boilers.

Pilot's license of Capt. Andy Pate.

Courtesy of Jimmie Jean Bowman, his daughter.

river extremely well so that he could take advantage of its currents at its different stages. He must also be very familiar with his boat, ever aware of its capabilities and limitations.

The engineer, as the title implies, ran the engine. It was vital that he and the pilot have quick and distinct communication since he was situated in the boat's belly with the engine, while the pilot was aloft in the pilothouse with the river in his full view. Their primary method of communicating was by usage of bells located just over the engineer's head and connected to the pilothouse by small wires. There were two bells, a deep one and a high one. The deep bell was known as the "come-ahead and stopping bell" while the high bell was the "slow and backing bell." They were used, for example, when it was time for the boat to depart. With all in readiness, the pilot would ring the "come-ahead" bell, and the engineer would turn on the steam, enabling the boat to move off. When the pilot rang this bell again, the engineer shut off the steam. If the pilot wished to back up when the boat was heading forward, he would first ring the deep bell to stop the engines, then he would ring the high bell, signaling for the boat to back up. It would keep on backing up until the pilot rang the deep bell again. If the boat was lying still and the pilot decided it should be backed up, he would ring only the high bell. Sometimes the pilot would ring the "come-ahead" bell and immediately ring the high bell. Such actions told the engineer to move ahead gently. In case of a problem with the bells functioning properly, there was also a speaking tube running from the engine room to the pilothouse. Both pilots and engineers had to be licensed in Memphis before working on the steamboats. A required portion of the test for pilots was to mark all obstacles (islands, boulders, overhangs, sandbars, etc.) on a map of the river they wished to navigate.

The last known person to hold a White River steamboat pilot's license that extended the navigable length of the White, from its mouth to Forsyth, Missouri, was Capt. Andy Pate. Born at Jamestown, Arkansas, in 1866, Captain Pate loved water and boats, even as a boy. He obtained his first riverboat job in 1892, as a clerk and helmsman, and worked on numerous riverboats in various capacities before receiving his pilot's license in 1896. In 1898, he received his master's ticket. He worked on several rivers across the country during that time. In 1898 he also traveled with some friends to Alaska, where he spent six winters and nine summers, working on the rivers and in the Bering Sea and Arctic Ocean. It was his only sea-going experience. In addition to his boat experiences, his stay in Alaska included a stint as a mail carrier, which required driving a dog sled from Golovin Bay to Council City, a distance of eighty miles. In 1907, Captain Pate returned to Arkansas where he married and, later, established a store in his hometown of Jamestown. He continued to work enough on the rivers to maintain his pilot's license, however. Four years later, following a fire that destroyed his store, he returned to his occupation on the rivers, serving on both the White and the Arkansas. In December of 1923, Pate and his family moved to Newport, Arkansas, where he was headquartered. Among the White River steamboats that Captain Pate served on were the *Dauntless* and the U.S. government boats *Quapaw* and *C. B. Reese*.

The clerk on a steamboat was also a busy person. It was his responsibility to check on every item of freight, make out the manifest that included where every item was to be delivered, then check the cargo taken off as the vessel arrived at the various landings. He also checked in all freight taken aboard for the downriver trip. John Q. Wolf served for a while as clerk on the steamboat *Home*. Wolf told of one trip he made when the *Home* left Batesville about nine o'clock at night headed for the Upper White. The

UNITED STATES Inspectors' License to MASTERS

Issue No. 25-25

This is to Certify that Charles M. Engles has given satisfactory evidence to the undersigned Local Inspectors of Steam Vessels for the District of Memphis, Tenn that he is a skillful MASTER of River Steam Vessels, and can be entrusted to perform such duties upon the Waters of Rivers whose waters flow into the Gulf of Mexico, also first class pilot on White river between its mouth and Forsyth, Mo; and on the tributaries of White river above Newport, Ark

and he is hereby Licensed to act as such Master and Pilot on Steam Vessels for the term of five years from this date.

Given under our hands this 14th day of May 1913

William J. Hodge, Inspector of Hulls.

46551

Chas [illegible], Inspector of Boilers.

Pilot's license of Charles Engles.

From the Duane Huddleston Collection.

Ozark Queen *at a landing in extreme Upper White River about 1897. The boat ran during boating season from Newport and Batesville to Buffalo City and McBee's Landing, near Cotter, Arkansas; but when water permitted, it ran to Lead Hill and above. It was owned by Capt. Charles B. Woodbury, with Capt. John T. Warner as one of its pilots. After completion of the railroad up White River, the* Ozark Queen *ran from Augusta, Arkansas, to Rosedale, Mississippi, during the 1903–04 boating season, making twenty-four trips and carrying 250 passengers. It was then sold for service in Louisiana.*

Courtesy of the University of Arkansas, Little Rock, Archives and Special Collections.

vessel was carrying a rather heavy load of freight and as they were leaving the dock, he began making out his manifest. He was seated on a high stool at an office desk, comparable to those used by early-day accounting clerks. About 2 A.M., his eyes ceased to function properly. Thinking just a brief nap would help, he rested his head on his hands lying on the desk. About an hour later, he was awakened by needle-like pains in his hands and nose. It seems he had relaxed so well the entire weight of his head rested on the end of his nose, which lay flattened upon his hands.

One of the many qualifications helpful to the mate on those early steamboats was the ability to mingle with the deckhands. A fluent vocabulary of cuss words was also an asset. Once the mate saw that the freight was stored properly and the boat had started on its voyage, his responsibilities were minimal until a docking occurred, and he spent a great deal of his time with the deckhands, spinning yarns and playing cards with them. The minute the boat docked, however, he had to become a bundle of dynamite, raging and cursing the men as they unloaded and loaded the cargo. The men didn't take the profanity too seriously, however, because they knew it was primarily for the benefit of the passengers and onlookers. In fact, the more vehement his jargon, the more the deckhands respected him. They thought of a good mate as a stalwart confederate whom they highly respected.

The deckhands were the laborers of the boat. All loading and unloading of cargo was done by them, as was pulling the craft when a cordelle was laid, or any other work that had to be done. Roustabouts were probably paid more that most common laborers of the time, but they had to be strong. If the cargo included animals, it was usually the duty of the deckhands not only to load them but to care for them. Sometimes that could be a major problem. Once, a stubborn mule refused to load. After much coaxing with no success, some of the deckhands were ordered to carry the animal aboard and carry it aboard they did, flying hooves and all. They also were masterful at loading cotton bales. At some landings, the bank was quite steep, steep enough that when a bale of cotton was placed on the bank end of the gangplank, it would slide quickly to the boat deck. A deckhand, holding the bale with a cotton hook, would run behind the parcel and control its speed and direction. Occasionally, rather than guiding it with his hook, a daring roustabout would ride a bale down. The bales didn't always slide straight, however, and, if not guided, could catch one of the cables that supported the gangplank. When that happened, any rider aboard the bale would find himself tossed into the river. Such actions were not looked upon favorably by the mate and the errant deckhand would usually be punished, often with a beating. The majority of deckhands were black.

Another important duty of the deckhands was to sing the lead line, informing the pilot of the river's depth. It was an ability expected of all of them. If the pilot signaled with the whistle that he wanted the lead called on a certain side or on both sides, it was a deckhand's job to start calling it until they told him to stop. A lead line is a rope thirty to thirty-two feet long that is weighted at one end. Leather strips are fastened to the rope at six-foot intervals. At the six-foot mark, a single strip is attached, followed by two strips at the twelve-foot mark. Three strips are fastened at eighteen feet; and at twenty-four feet a leather piece with a hole in it is bound. The depth was not called in feet, but with terms such as "mark twain," made famous by Samuel Clemens. Mark twain was the call for twelve feet; mark three, pronounced "thi-ree," was the the call for eighteen feet; and mark four, the call for twenty-four feet. There were also calls for depths between the markers. A depth of ten and a half feet was called as quarter-less twain, meaning the depth is a quarter of the way between the six-foot mark and mark twain. Quarter twain is a quarter of the way between mark twain and mark three. The quarter calls continued to the twenty-four-foot mark. All water deeper than twenty-four feet was called "no bottom." As important as using the correct terminology was the manner in which it was called or "sung." Even if he could not understand the words, due to wind, distance, et cetera, a riverman could tell the depth by the way the deckhand sang it. The shallower the water, the quicker the deckhand cut off the call. The deeper the water, the more the call was prolonged. Singing the lead line was utilized by rivermen long after the steamboats met their demise but began disappearing in the late 1950s and early 1960s because of the advancement of technology.

Black rivermen served in many positions. In a Batesville newspaper article, John Q. Wolf recalled some of the black steamboatmen of the Upper White River. Among the cooks mentioned was Gab Willis, a Batesville resident and an employee on the steamer *New Home*. Wolf described Willis as not only a good cook but a highly respected man and citizen. Additional black steamboat cooks mentioned were Hence Hawkins, Charles Bateman, Alex Criswell, Flan Burr, Sam Burr, and Grant Brown. Of other black rivermen, Wolf wrote:

> Among the cabin boys I remember were Chuck Berry, Sandy Miller, Gus Prior, Edgar Burr, Will Owens and Walter Owens.
>
> Dock McDearmon fired on several different boats and followed the trade for many years. It isn't every man who knows how to fire a boiler so as to keep up a good head of steam. Dock was a reliable, dependable fireman. I have seen him fire his boiler in the month of June when it was blazing hot, then climb onto an improvised scaffold right over the boiler—the hottest place on the boat—and go to sleep. Bill Harris fired on the *Home* for a time and occasionally Essie Powell or Arch Humphrey would assist him, but mainly there were deck hands. Will Smith, Joe Bell, Jess Harris, Jake Jones, and Stanford Burr were good firemen.
>
> As deck hands I remember Jim Davis, who was also called Jim Slocum and sometimes Jim Fewclothes. Others were Alex Harris, Bob Merriweather, the Valentine boys, William Neely, Perry Wahits, Ed Ketchers, Tom Nunnally, Will Hawkins, William McCurran, Sam Brown, Andrew Gray, Julius Dillard, Sam Woods, Pink Ripley, Eph Kimbrough, Granville McCoy, the McCauley boys, Tom Smiley, Bill Abram, Joe Woods, Henry Harris, Allen Dowell . . . Phil Rucker, Henry Abrams, Tom Pope and Mitch Hawkins.[15]

Wolf also mentioned two black deckhands who later took other steamboat positions: Bruce Smith, who became an engineer, and Dan Smith, who became a pilot.

Other black steamboatmen who worked on the White River steamboats *Woodson, Governor Eagle, Ozark Queen, Huff,* and the *Tom Hess* after Wolf quit the river were listed by Bob Merriweather and William Neeley. The list included Ted Meniken, Alex Galloway, Dave Finley, Frank Criss, George Criss, Will Criss, Bob Bone, Joe Pinkston, Henry Ripley, Bud Hurley, Newt Hurley, Jim Kindall, Henry Kendall, Will McCauley, Green McCauley, John Hooper, Jode Smith, Ed Brown, Hilliard Brown, John Lacy, Bill Williams, Jim Williams, Joe Dooms, Fred Osborne, John Herron, Will Herron, Pester Peeples, Henry Ivy, Stanfored Burr, Lewis Smith, Red Smith, Charlie Young, George Bass, Clin Martin, Dennis Taylor, Will Taylor, Button Taylor, Dick Hubbard, Heff McCauley, Charley Alexander, Johnnie McGinness, Clede McGinness, Henry Lee, Frank Rucker, Tom Smiley, Will Smiley, Rufe Taylor, Charlie Watkins, Shelby Tunstall, and Omar Roddy.[16]

Wolf, obviously, felt great respect for the black rivermen with whom he worked, as did many steamboatmen. He once commented:

> From the early days the Negro filled an important niche in steamboat life. . . . On the average there were about fifteen Negroes on each boat in the upper river trade. These included deck hands, firemen, cooks, and cabin boys. They were a happy, care-free lot and except when the boats were at landings receiving or discharging freight, or taking on cordwood, they had an easy time. During the daytime, when the boats were running they spent much time playing Seven-Up down on the boiler deck. . . .
>
> At night several of the boys would engage in shooting craps in the engine room. As I recall, Arch Humphrey, a heavy-set Negro, was the most successful crap-shooter of the *Home.* Most of the boys would take a drink, but they wouldn't get drunk. Arch Humphrey was the only one who would get unsteady on his feet.
>
> The deck hands of the several steamers entered heartily into the spirit of rivalry that existed between the boats. They were always loyal to the boat they worked on, whether it was a run-down, decrepit has-been, or a floating palace; whether it was large or small, swift running or slow poking, it made no difference. When two boats passed each other, the deck hands would gather along the gunwales and engage in a rollicking interchange of left-hand compliments for each other and for their respective boats—each boat always being held in profound contempt by the other boat's crew. They would indulge in the most glowing tributes to their own vessel—its wonderful performances, its liberal patronage by everybody, the lavish banquets served the crews three times a day, while making the most derogatory and uncomplimentary remarks about the other boat.
>
> In one of those colloquies between Mitch Hawkins and Abe Harris, Mitch was boasting about how many times his boat had been to Lead Hill, Arkansas, and Forsythe, Missouri, and Abe was discounting his claims about 75 per cent when a bystander asked Mitch how far he had ever been up White River. Mitch replied, "Ise been clean up to de mouf!"
>
> It was most interesting to note the dexterity with which some of the deck hands handled the cotton. They used short cotton hooks to pull the bales this way and that and to keep them rolling down from the top of the bank to the stage plank or gunwales. When the banks were wet and slippery, they often rode the bales down. I have seen Jim Davis (we called him Jim Fewclothes) ride many a bale down a slippery bank. At the top of the bank he would jump on a bale lying on its flat side, reach over and fasten his hook in the far edge. One of the boys would give the bale a shove and over the bank and away it would go with Jim aboard, clear to the river, without a mishap.
>
> The deck hands provided a good deal of musical entertainment. It is good to listen to them sing at any time, but it is a real treat to hear them, huddled up on the boiler deck of a steamboat, on a balmy night in May, singing plantation melodies, as they sang them in the 1880's, with banjo and guitar accompaniment. Passengers used to gather in groups or in doorways, to listen, and applaud. . . .[17]

No steamboat was successful in passing Elbow Shoals (mentioned earlier) until June of 1852 when Captain Childress departed from Jacksonport, Arkansas, and headed up the White River in command of the sixty-five ton steamboat *Yohogony*. A number of stops were made along the way to unload cargo and to take on wood to fire the boilers before the craft finally arrived at Dubuque. Because of the new channel recently cut in Elbow Shoals just above Dubuque, the steamboat's crew felt confident. Upon departure from the landing, Captain Childress, with Capt. D. H. Hardy serving as pilot, headed the *Yohogony* upstream, determined to succeed where others had failed in reaching Forsyth. There were a number of passengers aboard the vessel for the historic event and excitement among both crew and observers grew as they neared the shoal. While the newly cut channel was a vast improvement, the *Yohogony* still labored the entire day in its attempt to pass over the shoal but met with little success, even when a number of the passengers disembarked, to lighten the load, and watched the battle from the river's bank. With darkness approaching, the steamboat backed downstream where three hundred sacks of salt consigned for delivery to merchants in Forsyth were unloaded before the crew and passengers retired for the night. The unloading of cargo proved to be the "magic" needed, and the following day the *Yohogony* again challenged the shoal and prevailed to become the first steamboat to arrive at Forsyth. Two men, Jim and Tom Clarkston, were hired to haul the shipment of salt by ox wagons overland to the waiting merchants.

The *Yohogony*'s achievement was widely acclaimed. In reporting the event, the *White River Commercial* of Jacksonport stated: "A feat so rare, so hazardous and successful speaks well for the energy and skill of the officers of the boat. They are truly deserving of public favor."[18] The success of the *Yohogony* seemed to offer encouragement to other captains to travel to Forsyth, and commerce on the Upper White River increased dramatically. The renowned *Yohogony* continued to ply the White and was frequently mentioned in area newspapers, though its name was spelled in a variety of ways. On December 7, 1853, the *Memphis Daily Appeal* reported: "The Youghiogheny came in yesterday bringing 58 bales of cotton to different consignees. No manifest. She leaves

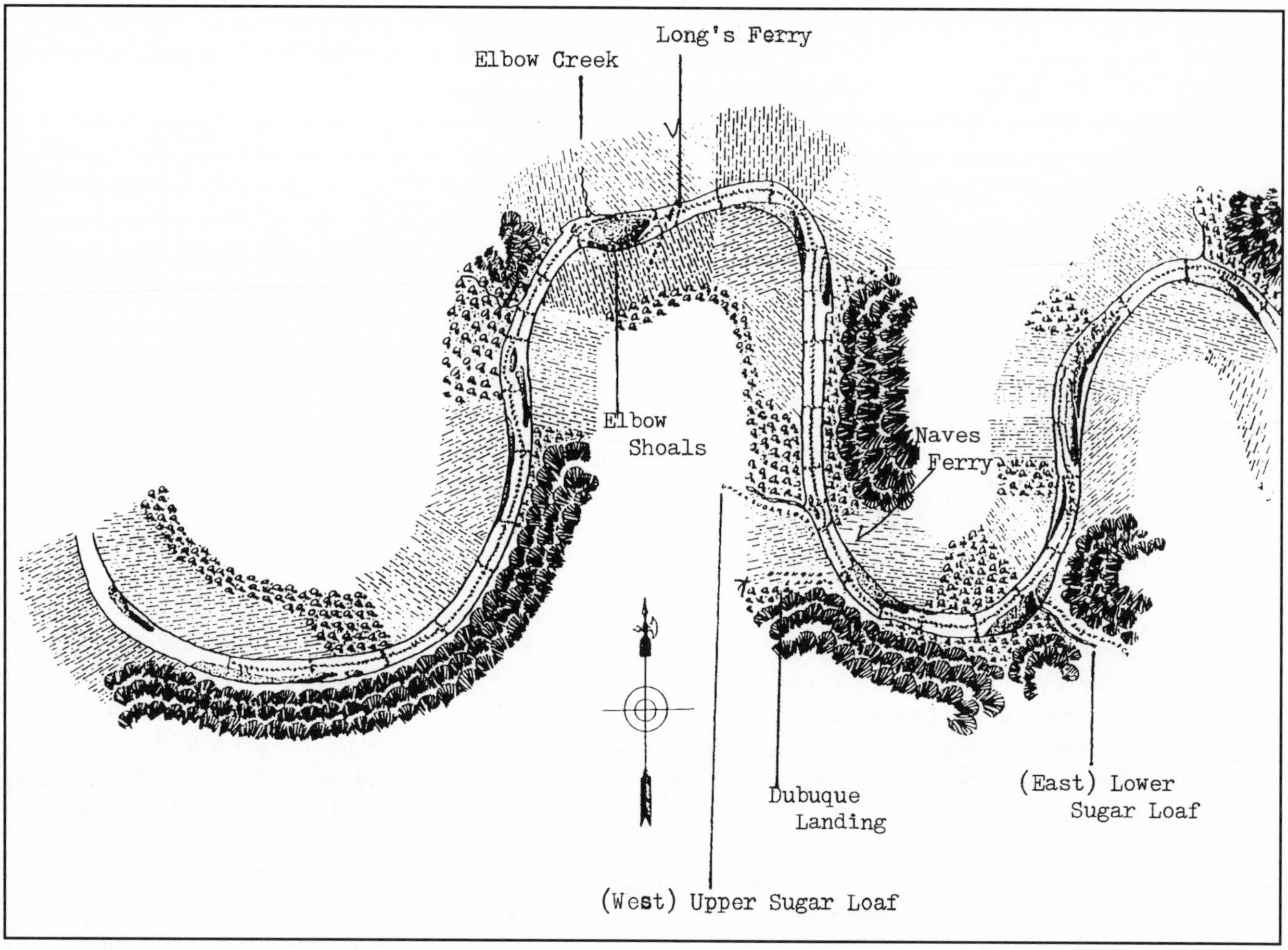

April 4, 1888, U.S. Army Corps of Engineers map, White River, Elbow Shoals and Dubuque area. It was made under the direction of H. S. Taber, Captain, U.S. Army Corps of Engineers, by Jas. C. Long and Chas. E. Taft, Asst. Engineers.

Courtesy of the U.S. Army Corps of Engineers office, Little Rock, Arkansas.

Wednesday for Jacksonport. This will be her last trip in the trade. She goes to Red River. We learn from Mr. D. H. Hardy, pilot of the *Youghiogheny,* that the *Julia Dean* is raised and will be around in about one week." It seems the luck of the *Yohogony* had run out, however, as it never made it to Red River, for on January 5, 1854, it sank about eight miles below Des Arc, Arkansas.

Just twelve months following the successful trip of the *Yohogony*, the steamer *Ben Lee,* in May of 1853, with Captain Wilson at its stern and J. D. Blackburn serving as clerk, traveled to Forsyth, taking only five hours to pass through the channel at Elbow Shoals. The *Ben Lee*'s next trip that spring was more difficult, however, and it fought the strong currents two days before conquering the high waters. The *Ben Lee* made four trips to Forsyth in 1853 and continued to run the Upper White in 1854 with Capt. W. C. Crawford in command in August of that year. In 1855 it was commanded by Captain Butler.

The *Mary L. Daugherty* was another frequent visitor to the Upper White. A ninety-five-ton side-wheeler, it made several trips to landings in northern Arkansas and southern Missouri, including Forsyth, during 1854 and 1855. The steamboat was built in Pittsburgh in 1853 by Capt. Silas Daugherty, one of its owners, at a cost of seven thousand dollars and ran primarily on the Upper White and the Black Rivers. Capt. J. C. Whiteside, another of its owners, also served at the helm of the *Mary L. Daugherty* for a while.

One of Arkansas's most famous steamboat owners, Capt. John D. Adams, ran a steamer named the *Jesse Lazear* to Forsyth on several occasions in 1856 and 1857, so, as is readily apparent, commerce on the Upper White River was steadily increasing. The *Jessie Lazear* was also a mail packet on the lower river in 1855.

Traffic remained busy on the Lower White as well during the 1850s. On December 20, 1854, the much heralded and long-awaited steamer of Capt. James C. McManus appeared at Memphis. Christened the *National,* its arrival was reported by a local reporter:

> At first sight she appeared to ride the waters like a nymph of the wave. Having grounded in and moored her lines amid the loud and continued plaudits and eager ejaculations of a curious throng, we, in keeping with the spirit and purpose of our position, sprang aboard and traversed the beautiful craft from stern to

stern—asked a number of questions and received a boat full of answers. We learned from Capt. "Mac" of the hurricane deck, and Steve of the desk, that she is 173 feet long, with 30 feet beam and four feet hold. She has two engines, with 18 inch cylinders, and seven feet stroke, and one of the best doctor engines ever built. She has three large, 42 inch boilers, 34 feet in length. She works a water-wheel 28 feet in diameter, with eight feet length of bucket. She has 32 staterooms, all provided with the most excellent accommodations, sufficient to serve in the main 75 passengers. The light, easy and unique structure—the style, taste and exquisite character of the painting and decorations, all blended together serve to render the *National* the flower among flowers, nymph among nymphs, and best among beauties. The flag swinging from her jackstaff, bearing the beautiful name *National* on a white field, with a shield representing the stars and stripes, our National emblem, is surmounted with the caption of liberty. The officers are well-known in our midst as gentlemen of worth, intelligence and high professional character: J. C. McManus, captain; S. D. Hancock, clerk; John Diamond, 2d clerk; J. M. Booker, mate; P. C. Montgomery, engineer; F. Montana, pilot; and Frank Goos, presiding at the Court of Bachus. The *National* leaves for New Orleans at nine o'clock.[19]

Though it briefly operated in the St. Louis trade in 1855, the elegant *National* was primarily a New Orleans to White River packet. It ran in the Black River to Pocahontas and in the White to Batesville, serving Jacksonport and all intermediate landings.

By mid-summer of 1855, all the steamers had left the White River for the dry season except the *Justice*. The *Memphis Daily Appeal* of July 31 of that year contained this item: "The *Justice,* last of the Mohicans, or rather the only boat left in the White River trade, will leave this port on her return trip Thursday next." On August 2, the newspaper printed an additional comment about the steamer: "Ho! for Jacksonport and Little Red River! Capt. Billy Underwood and his invincible little packet *Justice* leaves for the above this evening. She will leave after the close of the polls, which will give the Salt River folks a chance to go by way of boat. James Potter and F. D. Farley are her clerks. Go on the *Justice,* and if you are not pleased, the *Appeal* is a know nothing! All aboard at five P.M.!"

Frequent accidents continued to plague the steamboat business. The most tragic on the White was a fire aboard the *Caroline* on March 5, 1854. A beautiful side-wheeler of 103 tons, the *Caroline* was described as the "Belle of White River."[20] At the time of the accident, the White was above flood stage. The fire that erupted aboard the vessel spread quickly and consumed the craft in a matter of minutes. The misfortune occurred in a remote area of the river. The sixty-mile stretch of the White from Indian Bay to the river's mouth was a secluded area with not a house, cabin, or landing for the entire distance. The banks were simply woods, underbrush, and swampland. Forty-five people lost their lives in the *Caroline* tragedy, making the accident the greatest disaster to happen on the White. For years following the misfortune, travelers aboard other steamers seldom slept when the steamboat was passing through this section of the river at night.

There was a tale of tragedy that was passed from generation to generation by people living in the Clarendon, Arkansas, area that many felt was about the *Caroline*. The story told of a young steamboat pilot named Joe and his bride. The couple were honeymooning aboard a lovely side-wheeler cruising the White when a fire flared on the vessel. The steamer had reached Indian Bay near Clarendon and the flames were quickly engulfing the boat. Attempting to save the passengers, the captain shouted to Joe to "hold her just a little longer." Shortly, the captain shouted, "Joe, jump! Save yourself." It was too late, however, as the pilothouse collapsed and Joe could not escape. His bride survived, but her hair "turned white" and "she lost her reason." Her remaining years were spent in a mental institution where her thoughts remained in the past and she never realized she was growing older. Each time she was visited by her physician, she would report that Joe would be home from Memphis the following week and he would be so happy because she had delivered a baby the night before. Then, she would withdraw a doll from beneath her covers and lovingly lay it beside her. One day, the saddened widow told the doctor that Joe had visited her the previous evening and had said that he was coming home to stay. All that day and into the evening, she and her doll eagerly awaited his return. Maybe her wait was rewarded, for sometime during the night she died, the doll held tightly in her arms and a peaceful smile brightening her face.[21]

Business in the White River trade was dull in the fall of 1854. One Memphis reporter wrote in the *Memphis Daily Appeal:* "White River trade is small potatoes and few in the hill. From the last accounts up the river, it will be seen that the turtles are making regular trips, and are thought to be entitled to much credit for the interest they exhibit in towing their catfish neighbors over the sandbars."[22] Apparently the water was also at a low stage.

Quite a brawl occurred on the *Julia Dean* in October of 1854. The vessel left Memphis carrying one hundred Irish deck passengers who were en route downriver to work on the Mississippi levees. As the boat was traveling toward the mouth of White River, it became grounded some fifteen miles below Memphis and remained stuck for about twenty-four hours. To pass away the time, the deck passengers threw a party, with alcohol. The good-natured party degenerated into a general brawl. To overcome the inebriated deck passengers, the wily Captain Bateman persuaded about forty of the celebrants to go ashore by telling them that they had reached their destination. After the *Julia Dean* resumed its journey, the crew attempted to subdue the remaining deck passengers, but fighting erupted all over the vessel. Before the brawling Irishmen could be overcome, the male cabin passengers had to come to the aid of the crew. Although only one person was seriously injured in the affray, several hats were seen floating down the muddy Mississippi, showing the existence of a considerable amount of "head-knocking."

One of the largest steamboats to visit Jacksonport in 1855 was the *Ingomar*, piloted by Capt. Silas Daugherty and owned by Captain Brandenberg of Kentucky and Louis Hanover of Pocahontas. The *Ingomar* created quite a stir the first time it nosed into port at Jacksonport. In addition to a cargo of three thousand sacks of salt, it carried a large amount of sugar and molasses and was so heavily loaded that it took it eleven days to go from Jacksonport to Pocahontas on the Black River. The spacious steamer was a huge riverboat, 281 feet long and with a 37-foot beam and 44-foot floor. The vessel contained forty-two staterooms and was powered by five boilers. After its initial visit, the 730-ton *Ingomar* made only a few additional trips to Jacksonport.

The winter of 1856–57 was a particularly difficult one for the steamers traversing the White River. In January of 1857, a hard freeze made the river impassable, and the steamers *Louisa, J. Morrisett,* and *Editor* were frozen in some distance upriver. The experience so discouraged the master of the *Editor* that when it finally returned to Memphis, he withdrew it from the trade. The 391-ton *J. Morrisett* later struck a snag and sank just above Jacksonport. Through the years, the old hull of the side-wheeler served as a diving board for the young boys of the area.

In June of 1857, the White claimed the life of Col. John Ringgold, one of the most prominent citizens of Batesville and northern Arkansas. The accident happened while Colonel Ringgold was returning on the steamboat *Sam Hale* from Little Rock, where he had taken his daughter. Capt. John Adams, master, reported the details of the misfortune:

> As the boat was turning a bend ten miles below Clarendon, Capt. Adams and several other gentlemen walked down through the pantry on the larboard to the lower deck, to inspect some improvements, which had recently been made in the machinery of the boat, Col. Ringgold remaining in the cabin. They had scarcely reached the lower deck and walked aft, before, it seems Col. R. concluded to follow them which he did, speaking to the steward as he passed through the pantry. He reached the deck and was passing aft along the guards, when as the steward thinks, he either gave way in one of his ankles or tripped against a ring bolt and fell overboard, and struck off with apparent ease and self-confidence, swimming for the shore. Capt. Adams had the boat stopped almost immediately and Mr. Crawford threw a piece of timber and plank out to him, but though floating within ten feet of him he appeared not to notice them. In the meanwhile the life-boat was launched, but was too late to reach him before he sank, and he never arose. He sank within thirty feet of the shore.[23]

In late December of 1857, the steamboat *Comet* made its maiden voyage up White River. The new, comfortably furnished vessel was built at Red Wing, in the Minnesota Territory, the first boat to be constructed there. The steamer was under Capt. B. B. Branch, with Andrew Hoamer as clerk. The river failed to meet Captain Branch's expectations and after only the one trip in the White, he placed the boat in the St. Francis River trade.

The first steamboat to travel even farther up the White past Forsyth to the mouth of the James River in Missouri was the *Thomas P. Ray* in 1858. In the history of steam navigation on White River, this feat remained unexcelled, although it was equaled some eighteen years later by the *Batesville,* the third steamboat so named. The *Thomas P. Ray* was a shallow-draft boat, and on May 18, 1858, piloted by Hardin Shipp, it arrived at the mouth of the James with a load of cargo for Ozark merchants. For its downriver trip, the steamboat took on a shipment of cotton that had a final destination of Memphis. Its upper deck was gaily decorated with flags for the event, in celebration of its performance, and onlookers along the shore waved their approval as the *Thomas P. Ray* steamed by. The trip was marred by a tragedy when, on the first night out from the James River, the first mate and a deckhand were involved in a stabbing incident.

The *Thomas P. Ray* was something of a "hard luck" steamboat. A stern-wheeler of sixty-six tons gross, it was built in Brownsville, Pennsylvania, in 1852. It ran for a while in the Arkansas River, but the first mention of it in the White River is found in an article from the *Memphis Daily Appeal* of December 27, 1854, which read: "We learn from a young friend who has just returned to the city from a visit to Little Rock that he passed the *T. P. Ray* in White River, where she is waiting for a section of steam pipe to be sent from Memphis. It is thought that those soldiers who were badly scalded will recover. The five who were lost were probably blown overboard and drowned." It seems the accident was caused by a boiler explosion, a fairly common event on the boats because boilers were pushed to their limit in the attempts to conquer the rivers. Since the *T. P. Ray* was used in 1854 to haul government supplies and troops on the Arkansas River, it is probable that it was not engaged in the White River trade at the time of the accident, but was traveling to and from the Arkansas River by the cut-off.

Problems for the *Thomas P. Ray* continued when the steamboat was involved in two legal cases, both of which finally reached the Arkansas Supreme Court in 1857 and 1858.[24] In early 1856, it was purchased by Jesse Mooney, a steamboat operator in Marion County, Arkansas, on the Upper White. The previous master and owner, Capt. Oaty P. Dowell, had suffered severe financial difficulties, and two Jacksonport merchants named Pool and Watson filed claim for supplies, materials, and money, totaling $359.84, which they had furnished to Captain Dowell prior to January 7, 1856. A writ was obtained and the boat was seized by the Independence County sheriff. After obtaining ownership, Mooney and Capt. Francis A. Maffitt, the boat's master, executed a bond for the *Thomas P. Ray* and appealed the judgment to the circuit court, saying the case should be dropped because the steamboat was named defendant rather than the previous owner. Agreeing, the circuit court removed the case from the docket. Pool and Watson then appealed to the supreme court, and the case *Pool and Watson v Steamboat Ray* appeared before that tribunal, where the decision of the lower court was reversed and the case proceeded according to law. The second judgment found against the *Thomas P. Ray* occurred in October 1856 when George Case filed a complaint for $48.10, monies due Case for a half month's salary to "his boy, Flan," who served as cook on the boat, plus the cost of materials furnished to Captain Maffitt for repairs and equipment for the vessel.

Legal problems were not the only adversity faced by the steamboat *Thomas P. Ray* during this period. In the spring of 1856, the vessel was blown from its moorings during a storm at Batesville and sank in eight feet of water. It was severely damaged, as was the cargo, but the boat was quickly raised and repaired. In July of 1856, the *Batesville Independent Balance* reported: "We are pleased to learn that the steamer *Thomas P. Ray* will soon be in the trade again. She has been bought, since she was sunk at this place, by a company of gentlemen living above this place, has been thoroughly renovated, and will begin her trips again in a few weeks under the command of Capt. Maffitt. The *Ray* is said to have very powerful engineery, has a strong hull, and is just such a boat as can be relied upon for safety and expedition."

Jesse Mooney managed to keep the *Thomas P. Ray* running in the Upper White River trade, with Captain Maffitt as its master, during most of 1856. On November 22, 1856, the vessel was sold for twenty-five hundred dollars to George Pearson, also of Marion County. The deed, however, was not officially recorded until December 25, 1857. It appears Pearson was the last owner, and the *Thomas P. Ray* continued its regular trips along the river.

Delighted at its return to regular service, one area newspaper commented on February 27, 1857: "The *Thomas P. Ray* very unexpectedly made her appearance yesterday for the Upper White. We admire her pluck, and sincerely hope that she may straighten out her embarrassments and again take her place in the White River trade, and make regular trips to our landing."[25]

The little steamboat complied, making frequent trips to Batesville. It was there in late March of 1858, where it was loaded with salt, whiskey, and other products for Marion County customers upriver. During a boating season, the *Thomas P. Ray* carried over three thousand sacks of salt, hundreds of barrels of whiskey, and tons of other merchandise up the river.

By the late 1850s, steamboat service had greatly improved and the business was steadily growing. In the summer of 1858, the White River United States Mail Line was purchased from Captain Adams and Dean by Capt. Charles W. Coles. The mail boats made semi-weekly trips from Jacksonport to Napoleon, where they connected with the Memphis and Napoleon mail packets. While they received complaints, as mentioned earlier, their frequent arrivals were welcomed. With such growth in the steamboat industry came more competitive prices.

Freight costs from Memphis to Jacksonport at the time included the following:

Pound freights, per 100 lbs.	$ .50
Whiskey and water barrels, per barrel	1.25
Salt, per sack	.50
Flour, per barrel	.50
Cotton gins, each	8.00
Wheelbarrows, each	.25
Fanning mills	4.00
Straw cutters	.50
Corn shellers	.50 to .75
Pails, per doz.	.25
Chairs, in bundles, each	.25
Rockers	.25 to .50
Sofas, each	2.00 to 3.00
Divans	1.50 to 2.50
Pianos	8.00
Bedsteads	1.00 to 2.00
Testers	.50 to 2.00
Buggies	5.00
Barouches and carriages	7.00 to 10.00

Money, jewelry, and other valuables were carried for ¼ percent of value, and bill of lading to be signed for. Freight from Napoleon to Des Arc was thirty cents per one hundred pounds; freight from Des Arc to Memphis was fifty cents per one hundred pounds; and cotton was one dollar per bale. Passage from Napoleon to Des Arc was five dollars; from Des Arc to Memphis, eight dollars; from Memphis to Indian Bay, eight dollars; Memphis to Augusta, nine dollars; and from Memphis to Grand Glaize and Jacksonport, ten dollars.[26]

One of the numerous steamers plying the Lower White in 1858 was the *John Briggs,* a New Orleans to Jacksonport passenger packet with a freight capacity of three thousand bales of cotton or three hundred head of cattle. The new *Briggs* was a light-draft steamboat capable of carrying a good freight on four feet of water. Another large, light-draft boat in the river at that time was the *Return*. The steamer made regular trips from Memphis to Des Arc and Augusta on the White River, as well as to West Point and Searcy on the Little Red River. Leaving Memphis every Saturday evening "after the arrival of the cars" (railroad cars), the *Return* arrived at Des Arc on Monday evenings. On one trip in early December of 1858, it carried three hundred passengers to Memphis.

As noted, travel by steamboat was becoming increasingly popular. During January 1859, the steamers *Return,* with Captain Jones, and *Admiral,* with Captain Fleming, each made weekly trips from Memphis to Augusta on the White River, and to the West Point and Searcy landings on Little Red River. Along with the *Evansville,* Captain Baird, master, the three steamers brought over twelve hundred people to the White River Valley during the first three weeks of 1859. More than half of the passengers were newcomers to the area.

Misfortune struck the *Return* as it was steaming downriver on August 2, 1859. Just a short distance above De Valls Bluff, it smashed into a submerged snag. Striking the steamboat under the steps on the starboard bow, the object knocked a huge hole in the vessel's side, and it sank within ten minutes. Fortunately, there was no loss of life. As the boat collided with the hidden snag, Captain Fleming and the craft's officers promptly sounded the alarm, and Lemuel Dickens, the engineer, quickly released the steam from the boilers to prevent the scalding of those aboard the listing vessel. Apparently, the snag tore out one side of the *Return*'s bottom, for Dickens saw the doctor engine raise some eighteen inches, and the deck rise and fall as the snag raked aft. Working quickly and efficiently, the crew removed the ladies and children, then returned for the male passengers. All fifty travelers and their baggage were saved before the boat sank. The ship's papers and money were removed by the clerk, J. P. Booker, who carried them safely ashore.

Among the passengers on the *Return* was a physician who was traveling to Tennessee for a special visit. When the collision occurred, he was lying in his berth suffering from the "rigors of a chill." The impact knocked him to the floor, momentarily stopping his shaking. When the passengers reached the shore, the doctor demanded and received, through sundry efforts and badgering, a skiff for Clarendon. From there, he planned to take a stage to continue his journey. The disgruntled traveler's plans were again disrupted, however, when he missed his stage in Clarendon by several hours.

As the ill-fated *Return* sank beneath the waters of White River, the steamer careened to one side, its boilers rolling overboard into some forty feet of water and its tall smokestacks tumbling beneath the surface. After coming to rest, the *Return* lay near the right-hand shore, bow upstream, its stern in twenty-five feet of water and its bow in nine feet. Repeated soundings failed to locate the boilers in the deep water.

Captain Jones briefly replaced the *Return* with the *Tennessee Belle,* but later purchased the steamer *General Pike* for the White River trade. An excellent 248-ton, side-wheel vessel, the *General Pike* was hailed by its captain as a craft which would please all customers.

When the sleek *General Pike* left Memphis on its maiden voyage to White River, several gamblers or "slickers" were on board. While traveling down the Mississippi, the slickers filched a goodly amount of money from one of the passengers. Whether the money was lost by gambling or some "con" game is unclear; the report revealed only that the passenger "thought he had a sure thing in betting against their tricks." Fortunately, several passengers and the officers of the steamboat intervened and forced the slickers to return the money. Punishment for the offenders was the standard one previously mentioned. As the steamer proceeded on its journey, it stopped at isolated points along the river where the culprits were deposited singly to bemoan their fate. The *Des Arc* editor praised the officers of the *General Pike* for protecting their passengers "against the insidious wiles of these scamps who attempt to live by their wits."[27]

The *General Pike* again made the news in late May by performing a rescue mission. As the steamer passed Des Arc, the boat's crew rescued a family from a house where they had been trapped for some time by high waters. Bowers, the vessel's clerk, reported seeing farm animals that were dying all along the river, and high waters were causing greater damage than ever known. Again the *Des Arc* editor praised the steamboat: "The *General Pike* still wins high encomiums from the traveling community. Her passengers held a meeting and passed a series of highly complimentary resolutions, commending the boat and her officers to those who may wish to travel with comfort, pleasure and in safety."[28]

Also in 1859, the *Monongahela Belle,* Captain Gilchrist, master, arrived at the Batesville wharf carrying the largest load of freight ever transported above Jacksonport. This was the last appearance of the trim steamer at Batesville. After departing for Memphis with its record cargo, it struck a floating log and sank in the Mississippi River. Officers of the steamboat *Oakland,* en route from Memphis to Buffalo City, stated that the *Monongahela Belle* struck the log near St. Francis Island, some fifteen miles above Helena. Although the boat sank immediately, there were no lives lost; however, neither the cargo nor steamer could be saved.

As the villages along the White grew, citizens celebrated holidays and other special events with steamboat excursions. The editor of the *Des Arc Citizen* described one such trip:

> At 2 o'clock on the evening of the 25th ult., we took passage on the steamer *Evansville,* Capt. Baird, bound for Jacksonport. This craft having been thoroughly repaired and refitted for the Memphis and White River trade, presents superior inducements to travelers and shippers. Capt. Baird is a No. 1 commander, and one amongst the most independent in our knowledge. He is not of the class who have much to say, but of his capacity to do full justice to all who entrust business in his charge there can be no doubt or question. He has had long experience as a steamboatman and understands his business thoroughly. His financial and business capacity is inferior to no man in our knowledge.
>
> At Augusta, we were met with quite a throng of her citizens, and although it was late at night, had the pleasure of taking by the hand a number of her whole-souled and energetic people. The spirit of enterprise and the beautiful location of the town must eventually make it a place of importance, as soon as the country back of it is wrested from the hands of those who have so long held the lands "in durance vile" and prevented an industrious population from compelling the "forest to bloom as the rose."
>
> On Sunday morning we arrived at Jacksonport, and were pleased to meet with a large crowd of familiar faces. The business of this place has increased largely during the past year. The Upper White and Black river packets were receiving freight and passengers for the different points above. . . . The *Evansville* left Jacksonport on Sunday evening, and arrived at Searcy landing, on Little Red at 4 o'clock, on Monday morning. We were met at the landing by B. B. Bradley, Esq., who conveyed us to Searcy—3 miles—in a neat and comfortable two horse hack, where in company with Wm. T. Jones, Esq., of Brownsville, we were introduced to the estimable family of B. D. Turner, Esq., with whom we took breakfast, after which we wended our way to the "Searcy Inn," kept by our kind hearted, attentive friend, Rev. J. P. Kellum. . . .

After attending a concert and supper at the Searcy Female Institution, the editor departed the next day. His story continues:

> On Wednesday, in company with our friend, A. B. Hope, we journeyed from Searcy to West Point. This place has improved in population, business, &c., astonishingly during the past year. In a commercial point of view it possesses many advantages over the neighboring town of Searcy, and must, in a few years, at least, eclipse its older competitor. The navigation of Little Red river to West Point is good the year round—while boats can reach the Searcy landing—three miles from town—in high water. As soon

> as a good road is constructed to West Point from Searcy, the trade is compelled to concentrate at the head of constant navigation.
>
> On Thursday night we attended a party near West Point, at the newly erected residence of B. K. Rodgers, Esq., where we met an array of beauty and intelligence which was "delightful to look upon." The dancing was kept up until the "bright light of morn bedecked the eastern horizon." All were delighted with the fine array of "eatibles and drinkables" prepared for the occasion, and by common consent voted that B. K. should build a new residence every year. Success, say we, to enterprise and energy.
>
> On Friday night, in company with Capt. J. R. Jones of the steamer *Return,* and our townsman S. P. Catlin, Esq., together with a couple of young ladies in their charge, we took passage on the steamer *Admiral,* Capt. Pete Fleming, and were safely landed at Des Arc on the morning of January 1, 1859, well pleased with our holiday trip.[29]

As competition among the steamboats increased, the captains sought to gain patronage by favorable publicity from gifts to various community service organizations and churches. In early January of 1859, the new Methodist Church at Des Arc was the recipient of two chandeliers and four superior globe lamps from Capt. J. Riley Jones, master of the *Return.* To show their appreciation, a large congregation gathered to hear an interesting sermon by Rev. J. F. Carr. The new chandeliers and lamps added materially to the comfort of the audience, enabling them to "see for themselves" as the light shot forth brilliantly on the "inner walls" of God's building. After the sermon, Captain Jones was led to a seat near the pulpit to hear resolutions by the board of trustees commending him for his generosity. The highlight of their thanks to the captain was this short but very embellished speech by Miss E. Sanders:

> Sir: As the humble organ of my sex, I stand to express with beggared language our entire involvency to you for such unparalleled liberality to our Church. Our gratitude for such benevolence is all we can bestow; and we are sure you seek none other than this. We admire and applaud the soldier, the statesman, the poet, and the philosophers; but we love the philanthropist—as such we regard you; then sir, you have the best feeling of our hearts; by such acts as these you have a name and a fame that shall live after death;—the memory of this gift recorded on High. You, Sir, in obeying this impulse have yielded yourself to one of the most ennobling principles that can animate a being destined for immortality. You have our united wishes for your present and future good—and as you have dispersed darkness from our benighted Church and placed light therein, may you at this illuminated altar, find that light which will dispel eternal darkness, and light you to a Haven of rest.
>
> And, Sir, should this be the selected place for you to ascend the hymeneal altar, may these beautiful lamps reflect their golden light on one who will make earth a paradise to you.

The Des Arc editor congratulated Captain Jones for the polite patience he exhibited throughout the lengthy platitudes expressed by "those who live on land, especially of that particular kind of which the Captain was the happy recipient from our friends of the Methodist Episcopal Church in Des Arc."[30]

Misfortunes continued to plague the steamers traversing the White. Anxious moments occurred aboard the steamers *Return* and *Evansville* on Sunday evening, April 17, 1859, when the vessels collided a few miles below St. Charles. The *Return,* ascending the river, struck the descending *Evansville* with its bow near amidships. The steamers were turning "a short point" and were within less than fifty yards of each other before either knew the other was approaching. According to the *Des Arc Citizen,* the pilots were equally to blame for the mishap since neither whistled until the vessels were nearly together. While the *Evansville*'s larboard guard suffered a minor injury, damage to both steamboats was slight and each continued on its way.

A growing public interest for improved river transportation between Batesville and Jacksonport began to gain momentum. A large crowd of interested citizens gathered at Batesville in early September of 1859 to determine methods of improving the White. After the meeting convened, the Hon. D. C. Montgomery was appointed chairman, and W. H. Russell and Jesse Searcy, secretaries. A committee of ten prominent citizens was appointed to examine the practicality of removing navigational hazards from Batesville to Jacksonport. Serving on the committee were Capt. Franklin W. Desha, Edwin R. McGuire, W. B. Rutherford, Morgan Magness, John Ruddell, Hardin Hulsey, Henderson Simpson, C. P. Head, David S. Fraley, John W. Campbell, and John M. Engles. On September 17, the committee made a detailed tour to study the river between the two ports and, on October 11, released a comprehensive report on all the shoals. The committee recommended the purchase of a snagboat and an expenditure of up to fifteen thousand dollars to successfully improve river navigation between the two towns. The rapidly mushrooming internal strife within the nation, however, wrecked the good intentions of the committee, and, as far as is known, the plans for this particular river improvement were abandoned.

September 8, 1859, found a great deal of excitement in Des Arc as the splendid *E. M. Ryland* appeared at the river town's landing. The steamboat was entering the Memphis to Jacksonport run and arrived at Des Arc right on schedule. The local newspaper described the steamer:

> She is a neat, sidewheel craft, and carries as polite and tidy a crew as ever walked the deck of a steamer. She has a fine calliope on board and furnishes any amount of music to her passengers, as well as to those along shore. The *Ryland* arrived at our landing last evening on her return trip to Memphis. By invitation from Capt. Johnson (Benjamin) and his officers, a large crowd of our citizens visited the boat, and were received with that politeness and attention which will long be remembered. The young, the gay, and the beautiful were there, and they moved in the graceful mazes of dance. We were reminded of earlier years and the bewitching snares that twine around the hearts of the young. The *Ryland* will leave Memphis again Tuesday, arriving here tomorrow week, which will hereafter be her regular day.[31]

The steamer became a favorite of Des Arc. Whether the *E. M. Ryland* was the first steamboat on the White River with a calliope on board is uncertain, but the musical instrument soon became one of the wonders of river travel. Bill Cush gave the following description of a calliope to the *Fort Smith Herald* in early 1859:

> At Pine Bluff, there was a circus steamboat with a calliope aboard. Just about dark, it struck up the tune "The girl I left Behind Me," and never did I hear such music! The high notes seem to mount to the very stars, and the low ones to rumble to the bowels of the earth. The performer plays with great enthusiasm. He stands enveloped in the rolling clouds of steam, and keeps both his ears stopped with cork. The great advantage of the instrument over all others, and over even the fullest bands, is its complete independence of surrounding tumult. All the clangor of Pine Bluff—the barking of her dogs—the lowing of all her cows—the neighing of all her horses—the whooping of all her fowls—all were appropriated as an accompaniment, and as far as they went, answered a fine part. It was furious music! Thirty miles up and down the river, the Negroes danced to it. Colonel Roane who lives opposite town, came down to the sand bar, and cut the pigeon wing in the sand as gaily as he did on the night of his wedding. Major Rector said he never saw him dance so well! All the varmints of the bottoms heard it—coons and opossums paused in their night rambles, and listened. Hogs awoke from their beds, etc.[32]

Unquestionably, players of these wonderful instruments were great entertainers and relished playing to the crowd along the shore. Whether one loved or hated it, the calliope was an instrument difficult to ignore. It was music one could feel.

A new, small steamer arrived in the Lower White River in 1859 to ply the mail and passenger line between Clarendon and Des Arc. Described as the prettiest little steamer afloat, the *Charm* was eighty-three feet long, had a three-foot hold, two seven-inch cylinders of fifteen-inch stroke, and displaced eighty-three tons. Owned by Chidoster, Rapley, and Company, the boat was under the command of Capt. H. B. Hendrix. By special arrangement utilizing the *Charm,* transportation service was offered from Fort Smith to Memphis, via Des Arc, in the amazingly short time of four days, or from Des Arc to Memphis in twenty-four hours. The trip involved traveling by stage, steamboat, and railroad. Passengers received one night's sleep on the steamer *Charm,* which connected with the stages to Des Arc, De Valls Bluff, and Clarendon. Fort Smith travelers could take the semi-weekly mail stage from Fort Smith to Des Arc, where they would ride aboard the steamboat *Charm* to Clarendon, then travel by stage to Madison and board a railroad car for the remaining trip to Memphis. The *Charm* left Des Arc every Sunday and Thursday.

Steamboating in the Upper White River remained busy during 1859 and ended on a happy economic note. The *Mary Patterson,* Capt. Morgan Bateman, master, arrived at the Batesville wharf in late November, heavily laden with freight for Batesville and above. Before leaving for Sylamore, a number of the local belles and beaux boarded the trim craft for an excursion to Mount Olive.

Capt. Morgan Magness Bateman, son of Capt. Beniah Bateman. He started his steamboat career as a pilot on the Julia Dean, *of which he assumed command in 1854. Captain Bateman owned and ran the* Mary Patterson, *which was built at Grand Glaize, Arkansas, in early 1859. It was sunk early in the Civil War to impede the ascension of Federal boats up the river. The* Mary Patterson, *a 105-ton vessel, made several trips to Forsyth, Missouri, and was once marooned there for several months due to low water. After the war, Captain Bateman was master of many fine steamboats, including the* Harry Dean, *a vessel of 264 tons. The finest boat of which he was captain was the elegant* R. P. Walt. *Captain Bateman died April 23, 1870.*

Courtesy of the University of Arkansas, Little Rock, Archives and Special Collections.

The genial captain and his officers made the voyage a memorable one for the members of the delighted party. After returning the happy excursionists, Captain Bateman turned the prow of the *Mary Patterson* upriver toward Calico Rock. When he descended the river, Captain Bateman briefly stopped at Batesville, then left for Augusta, reiterating his intentions of keeping his steamboat in the Upper White River trade.

The hearts of the Batesville citizens were also gladdened by the arrival of the elegant steamer *Iatan* on December 10, 1859. Capt. Samuel Taylor, master of the beautiful 421-ton side-wheeler, immediately issued an invitation to the young folks to attend a dance in the vessel's fine cabin. When darkness arrived, many turned out to accept the kind captain's offer, and the river echoed to the delightful sounds of music, happy chatter, and laughter. At the conclusion of the dance, Captain Taylor feted his guests with delicious refreshments, after which the recipients gave enthusiastic thanks to the officers for the enjoyable evening. Reputedly, the *Iatan* was the largest boat to come to Batesville and was one of the favorites.

The *Mary Patterson* and the *Admiral* closed 1859 with a bang. Under the command of Captain Baird, the *Admiral* was steaming down the river on the morning of December 23 when it unexpectedly collided with Captain Bateman's boat near the head of Big Island, some four miles below St. Charles. Both vessels injured their bows, and several persons aboard the *Mary Patterson* were severely bruised, but the steamers were sufficiently safe to continue their trip.

Steamers navigating the waters of the White, Black, and Little Red Rivers during 1859 and 1860 included the *Sam Hale,* the *Fortune,* the *Charm,* the *Return,* the *William Campbell,* the *Badger State,* the *Audubon,* the *Evansville,* the *Pocahontas,* the *John Briggs,* the *Grand Glaize,* the *Europa,* the *City of Knoxville,* the *Oakland,* the *Nebraska,* the *Medora,* the *Monongahela Belle,* the *Mary Patterson,* the *Maysville,* the *William H. Langley,* the *Tennessee Belle,* the *Editor,* the *E. M. Ryland,* the *General Pike,* the *Admiral,* the *Iatan,* the *Interchange,* the *Crescent,* the *St. Francis,* the *St. Francis No. 2,* the *Belvidere,* the *Favorite,* the *Novelty,* the *A. W. Quarrier,* the *Arkansas Traveler,* the *Louisiana Belle,* the *Frontier City,* the *S. H. Tucker,* the *Rose Douglas,* the *Hazel Dell,* the *Masonic Gem,* the *Tahlequah,* the *Acacia Cottage,* the *Kanawha Valley,* the *New Moon,* the *Izetta,* the *Golden State,* and the *Daniel B. Miller,* a New Orleans steamboat. Some of the steamboats were only in the river for a short time.

Though usually busy, the *Mary Patterson* was out of service during much of the fall season of 1860 and early 1861 because it was immobilized by low water at Forsyth. In February, a slight rise in the river allowed Captain Bateman and the *Mary Patterson* to descend the White from Forsyth to the Coker farm near the mouth of East Sugar Loaf Creek in northern Arkansas. Another rise permitted Captain Bateman to continue to Bull Bottom Shoals in Marion County, but it was not until late March that he could return with the *Mary Patterson* to Batesville. The crew grew restless during the long stay at Forsyth, and their inactivity resulted in at least one tragedy when Jim Massey, the engineer on the steamboat, killed Berry Ellison, the Taney County sheriff. Captain Bateman served as pilot on the mailboat *Kanawha Valley* on the Lower White for part of the time the Mary Patterson was stranded upriver.

Another steamboat that may have ascended the White River as far as Forsyth that year was the *Louisiana Belle.* The *Louisiana Belle,* an eighty-nine-ton stern-wheeler, was a trading craft. Well stocked with wares of various kinds, the trader stopped at any point to sell or barter merchandise. The trading boat was comparable to a wagon peddler who paused at farmhouses along roads to service customers, thereby providing a vital service to families isolated from villages by long distances or poor transportation.

As the decade closed, the first golden era of White River steamboating had arrived, and the magnificent steamers with their elegance and comforts were truly the marvels of the river. The arrival of a steamboat was always an occasion for celebration, with the popular captains entertaining with sumptuous feasts, dancing, and other entertainment. To the citizens of the small towns and villages along the river, the steamboats were the acme of refinement with their finely carpeted cabins, their musical bands and calliopes, and their tables laid with shining silver, fine china, and linen. Those tables were loaded with delicacies of food and drink, including such tropical treats as oranges, bananas, and lemons, and such seafoods as fresh shrimp, crab, and oysters. During the season, fresh venison and other regional game was sometimes featured. Needless to say, the steamer captain was "King of the River," and his elegant steamboat was the "Queen."

It is a forgotten era, the day of plantation gentlemen and Southern belles, the day of steamboat journeys to Memphis, of bridal tours to New Orleans, Cincinnati, Louisville, and St. Louis. It was a time when a planter would venture to market with his cotton, often accompanied by his family, to revel for a few weeks in the pleasures of the city. It was a time when exchanges of visits between river towns such as Buffalo City, Batesville, Augusta, and Jacksonport were adventures taken with eager anticipation and relived again and again when completed. It is no wonder the arrival of a large steamer was an occasion for merriment and joy. All too soon, such merriment would end as the nation became engulfed in civil strife that left little time for gaiety.

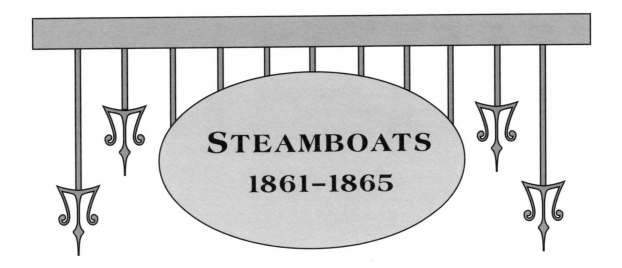

STEAMBOATS 1861–1865

As steamboating on the White River entered 1861, a change was made in the command of the popular steamer *General Pike.* When the packet arrived at Des Arc during the first week in January, the new master, Capt. Riley Jones, was in command, with Capt. Pete Fleming as clerk. The *General Pike* left Memphis each Saturday evening, arriving at Des Arc on Monday, and its first return trip of the year was the largest cargo that had left White River for some time. The *Masonic Gem* and the *Hazel Dell* were not so lucky, as both were moored at the Memphis levee awaiting some business. Due to the slow trade, Captain Pillsbury of the *Masonic Gem* decided to leave the Memphis run and start regular trips between Jacksonport, Batesville, and Buffalo City.

The fine New Orleans packet *Iatan,* Captain Eaton in charge, also opened the new year with great expectations. The steamer was the only one in the river from New Orleans, having forced the withdrawal of its competition. Reportedly the largest boat to travel the White River, the *Iatan* carried over three thousand bales of cotton to New Orleans on one of its early trips in 1861.

The splendid steamer *Admiral,* Captain Thomasson commanding, was also enjoying a period of prosperity by transporting huge cargoes of freight and passengers. A rivalry between the *Admiral* and the *Golden State* grew with each passing week, and on January 11, 1861, a Des Arc newspaper reported: "The *Admiral* is now a regular Thursday boat, leaving Memphis on Thursday evening. Between her and the *Golden State* a fierce rivalry has sprung up. They both leave Memphis at the same time, and race all the way up. They are both crack boats."[1]

On January 31, 1861, the *Admiral* arrived at Des Arc with a large load of freight and passengers after having a "No. one" trip highlighted by passing its arch rival at the mouth of the White. When the *Golden State* landed at Des Arc on that same day, on board were "the handsomest lot of passengers to have the good fortune of gracing the cabin of a White River boat in many a day."[2] Those on the sleek *Golden State* had enjoyed themselves with rollicking music and joyful dance. Perhaps it was well they could experience laughter, for the menacing clouds of war were hovering over the South, and soon their happiness would turn to despair. On this trip, however, the passengers had reason for their exhilaration, as they had witnessed a thrilling encounter between their boat and the fleet steamer *Admiral.* Both steamboats had left Memphis at the same time and had gone racing down the river with their flags waving on their masts and black smoke streaming from their twin smokestacks.

Some dispute arose over the race. It was the custom among steamboatmen that a pair of horns, or antlers, was a sign of speed, and the fastest boat proudly displayed them. When another boat challenged and won, the defeated captain was honor bound to surrender the horns to the victor. Those aboard the *Admiral* thought their boat had won the competition down the Mississippi and wrote the following letter to the *Des Arc Constitutional Union* newspaper:

> Steamer *Admiral,*
>
> Jan. 30, 1861
>
> To Captain Hicks King of the *Golden State*
>
> Dear Sir: We have learned that it is a custom among steamboatmen, that whenever one boat, wearing a pair of horns, seeks a trial of speed with another boat in the same trade and becomes beaten, she is in honor bound to decline the horns to the successful boat. Your boat evidently sought a trial of speed last night, in descending the Mississippi River, with the steamer *Admiral,* Capt.

Elias Thomasson, and was fairly beaten by her. Therefore you will no doubt hand the nice pair you have on display over to her.

Very respectfully yours, etc.
Signed 37 passengers of *Admiral*[3]

So, the buckhorns of the *Golden State,* the time-honored symbol of swiftness, were claimed for the *Admiral* by its passengers. The passengers of the *Golden State* disagreed. There was a race, they said, but the ladies aboard the *Golden State* became frightened and asked the captain to stop. The gallant Captain King yielded to the cries of the fair sex and allowed the *Admiral* to pass. In order that all along the river might know the truth, this rebuttal, from passengers on the *Golden State,* was published one week later in the newspaper:

Steamer *Golden State,* Jan. 31, 1861

We, the undersigned passengers on the steamer during her trip from Memphis to her White River destination last week, having seen a card from the passengers on board the steamer *Admiral,* in your last issue, in which it is stated that the last named boat proved herself a faster craft than the *Golden State,* on a trial race between, at the time when we were present, and on account of which the *Admiral* claims the buckhorns from Capt. King's boat; take occasion to say here that while we believe the passengers on Capt. Thomasson's boat think there was a race, and that their favorite showed a superiority over the *Golden State* in swiftness, we know the boat upon which we were traveling did not attempt to run by the *Admiral* in a race, because her commander was requested by the ladies aboard not to do so, which he most respectively yielded by having the flues opened and the steam let off, and allowing the *Admiral* to pass.

Please allow us to express our sincere thanks and kind regards to Capt. King, the gentlemanly Captain Russell in the office, and other officers, for the pleasant and safe trip, and we, without hesitation, recommend the *Golden State* to the people of White River as the safest and most reliable boat in the line; her officers ever ready, with good accommodations, to add to the comfort of all aboard.

Respectfully yours, etc.
Signed by 76 passengers.[4]

In March of 1861, there were several steamboats operating in the White River, but the approaching civil strife was beginning to cause apprehension and uncertainty among the steamboat captains. The web of war seemed poised and ready to ensnare the vessels of the valley.

These were the last days of the old South—days of brass bands and flag waving, days of expounding the virtues and glories of war, days of gallantries, of gay farewell parties, and of mirth and merriment. Typical of the tempo of the times was the excursion trip aboard the *Admiral,* as described in the March 22, 1861, edition of the *Des Arc Constitutional Union:*

Captain Baird, now owner and commander of the steamer *Admiral,* on her last trip from Memphis to her White River destinations, tendered a pleasure excursion to his friends along the way, on that occasion. His fine steamer arrived at our wharf Monday evening, with flags flying, and brass band playing the much celebrated and popular air of "Dixie's Land." The excursionists already aboard were joined here by a large party of Des Arc ladies and gentlemen, when the boat shoved out for Augusta, West Point and Searcy; and the hospitable preparations which the captain and his gentlemanly officers had prepared for their friends were stormed in hearty earnest. Dancing, mirth and merriment reigned supreme in the midst of "fair women" and the rougher sex until the "wee small hours ayant the twal." Accessions of beautiful ladies and their gallant escorts were made to the party at each point 'til the boat became literally crowded with the moving numbers of the dance. The kindness and politeness of Capt. Baird, Mssrs. Campbell, Wigginton, and other officers of the *Admiral* will long be remembered pleasantly by all who were on board, and we but reflect their sentiment when we wish her and her gentlemanly crew a long and successful existence in White River.

Such gaiety was in sharp contrast to what lay ahead for the White River Valley during the upcoming war years. During the winter of 1860–61, through the newspapers brought by the steamboats, citizens of the region kept close watch on the dramatic developments of the North-South conflict. The Southern states were seceding, and the border areas, including Missouri and Arkansas, were under increasing pressure to select a side.

For many months, while the legislative powers pondered their decision, voluntary military groups of various types were forming. A county group in the Jacksonport area called the Jackson Guards was one of them. May 5, 1861, was a memorable day in the busy river town of Jacksonport; the small village sent the 118 young men of the Jackson Guards to fight for the Confederacy. Their departure was actually one day before Arkansas officially voted to secede from the Union. The Jackson County volunteers became Company G of the First Arkansas Regiment in the Confederate Army. It was the first company to leave the state for active duty in the war and saw continuous action through the four years of the war until its surrender in 1865.

Most of the members of the Jackson Guards were sons of the area's most affluent citizens. The young men knew nothing of war and naively thought they should take trunks of dress suits with them. They were advised by their commander, Captain Pickett, to take only one suit, a woolen top shirt, and two suits of underwear, leaving behind all fancy clothes.

The citizens of Jacksonport and the surrounding area assembled in the Presbyterian Church to bid a poignant farewell to Company G. Attended by her maids of honor, Miss Mary Tom Caldwell, granddaughter of Capt. Thomas T. Tunstall, presented the company with an exquisite silk flag that had been made and embroidered by the women of Jacksonport. The weather outside was frightful, but even such stormy elements could not diminish the beauty of the presentation. After the ceremony, the detachment proudly filed from the church to board the steamer *Mary Patterson,* which stood waiting to transport the group to Memphis. About an hour prior to their departure, bright sunshine broke through the storm clouds, lightening the spirits of all. Amid fond farewells and sad goodbyes, the steamboat slowly rounded out from the wharf, a wharf crowded with proud parents, wives, relatives, and friends eagerly seeking one last glimpse of their loved ones. With twin ribbons of smoke curling from its towering chimneys, and its stern wheel churning the waters behind it, the *Mary Patterson* gently passed from sight. So began an unforgettable trip to war, a journey from which many never returned.

Also on board the *Mary Patterson* for this memorable trip was an Italian band from New Orleans that had been stranded in Jacksonport. The musicians entertained the youthful company until the steamboat arrived in Memphis.

On its way down the White, the *Mary Patterson* stopped at the Grand Glaize landing where another volunteer military group, the Glaize Rifles, wearing bright new uniforms, lined the riverbank to greet and bid farewell to the Jackson County group.

Just a week prior to the arrival of the *Mary Patterson* at Grand Glaize, an incident had occurred there that reflected the general anxiety felt by many citizens of the White River Valley. A stranger, who gave his name as Bill Stone, had appeared in the village. The man refused, however, to provide any other information about himself or his purpose for being there, and the people of the community decided he was a Union spy and should be hung. Though R. J. Shelley, proprietor of a local hotel, intervened and saved Stone's life, the newcomer was not allowed to go free. Instead, he was crated up in a large cage and addressed to Abraham Lincoln. Prior to caging him, someone suggested he should be "marked," so one half of his beard and head were shaved clean. While on exhibition in his box awaiting the next boat's arrival, he served as an object of terror to the children of the town.

The *Mary Patterson,* loaded with the Confederate volunteers, happened to be the next boat. The Jackson Guards were delighted to hear that a Yankee spy was ready to be shipped to Lincoln. With spirited enthusiasm, some of them rushed up the street and rolled the cage to the riverbank as though it were a bale of cotton. A tall, angular old lady whose son was about to depart for the war cried out, "Roll him in the river, roll him in the river!"[5] Bill Stone, or whoever he was, had a long trip. The "wild young men" heading for war treated the man to taunts and threats the entire length of the journey. At Memphis, Stone was offered his freedom, but since the port was such a Southern location, he refused to leave his box and was taken as far as Cairo, Illinois.

The *Mary Patterson,* commanded by its owner, Capt. Morgan Bateman, ran for the Confederate States. One of its missions was on May 18, 1861, when the steamboat traveled to Pocahontas on the Black River to pick up seventy-five tons of lead and twelve tons of powder for troops in Tennessee.

Another military group, the Augusta Guards, departed by steamboat in June to join the Confederacy. They became Company D in a cavalry regiment called the First Arkansas Mounted Rifles. With material furnished by the merchants of the village, the women of Augusta gathered during late spring to make the gray uniforms and to knit socks for the company. The women also practiced the use of firearms so that they might defend themselves and their homes if necessary while the men were away. In her book *Fight and Survive!* Lady Elizabeth Watson Luker quoted a description of the Augusta Guards' departure given by Mrs. Eugene Goodwin: "The picture of that last parting, as the boat rounded the bend, the boys' caps and handkerchiefs waving, some singing, some shouting, stands out in bold relief and refuses to be effaced after forty years."[6]

The week prior to the departure of the Augusta Guards, Jacksonport was deluged by unorganized volunteers. News of the invasion of Arkansas by Union troops that were on their way to Pocahontas had reached the area about two o'clock on Sunday morning. By half past ten on Monday morning, over three thousand men arrived in Jacksonport and insisted on going to the scene of the conflict. Many had traveled a great distance; some of them had to swim rivers while holding their muskets and gunpowder over their heads. All were eager to defend the South. It was decided that only three thousand of the best equipped should go, and the steamers *Admiral, Cadet,* and *Belvidere,* laying at Jacksonport, were brought into service to transport the impromptu army. The steamboats traveled up the Black River to the mouth of Strawberry River where they met the *Mary Patterson* and received word that the news of the invasion was premature and incorrect. The volunteers were returned to Jacksonport where they disbanded.

Other White River steamboats began carrying Confederate soldiers and supplies. On June 6, 1861, the *A. W. Quarrier* left Clarendon with troops for the northern part of Arkansas, going via the St. Francis River. Later that day, the *Kanawha Valley* passed Des Arc en route to Black River with a thousand guns and two twelve-pounder cannon.

In early July, the side-wheeler *Sovereign,* the *Mary Patterson,* and the *Admiral* traveled to Camp Pillow, forty miles above Memphis, to move Col. T. C. Hindman's Confederate command to Pittman's Ferry on Current River near the Arkansas-Missouri line. The command was transported as follows: five companies on the *Admiral* (including Colonel Hindman and his staff), six companies on the *Sovereign,* and three on the *Mary Patterson.* One of the officers on the 336-ton *Sovereign* was Capt. E. H. Fletcher, commander of Company O. Captain Fletcher wrote of the trip:

> Although our boat measured 237 feet in length, we came up the White River (proverbially one of the narrowest and most crooked rivers on the continent) without any trouble whatever. During all this time we had but two cases of sickness on board . . . and they were put on the hospital boat *(Conway).* The other companies had from 15 to 20 cases apiece. (An epidemic of measles was playing havoc with the troops.) We arrived at Jacksonport on Sunday morning, when we had a most enthusiastic reception from the people of the town and vicinity. Here our troubles commenced. The mouth of Black River comes in a mile above the town and a large bar right in the mouth was the cause of an hour's delay. Nevertheless in spite of bars, snags, the narrowness and extreme crookedness of the little stream, the *Sovereign* worked her way up to Powhatan, a town situated about 50 miles by water below Pocahontas. Meanwhile Col. H. had deserted the *Admiral* above

> Jacksonport, when an accident rendered her unfit for service, and gone on up in advance of the smaller boats. The *Sovereign* arrived at Powhatan Wednesday night when we determined to await the arrival of the smaller boats that had taken up the other troops. On yesterday (Thursday) the little "Tom Sugg" (something like the "Ben McCulloch") came down and my company and Capt. Talliaferro's were ordered to take passage. We got off from Powhatan yesterday morning and passed Pocahontas this morning about six. Cleburne's Regiment is at Pittman's Ferry on this (Current) river, which Ferry is very near the line. Hindman's encampment is at Perkin's Ferry, six miles below Cleburne by the river. . . .[7]

Leaving Memphis on Saturday, July 6, aboard the steamer *Ohio Belle,* Col. Patrick Cleburne's regiment had arrived at Pittman's Ferry just a few days before the troops of Colonel Hindman's. The 406-ton side-wheeler and its passengers received warm welcomes from the towns along their route, including Helena and Laconia. At Laconia, the *Ohio Belle* passengers were not only greeted with lovely ladies and rollicking music, but were supplied with wagonloads of vegetables and barrels of milk, beef, mutton, pork, and chicken. On Monday night, the steamer reached Clarendon and a dance was proposed. Soon the parlor of the hotel was crowded with "tinkling feet keeping time to merry music" until time to leave. The ladies accompanied the soldiers to the riverbank, where they waved a long farewell in the faint light of dawn. Cleburne's troops enjoyed similar festivities all along the way until they reached their encampment in northern Arkansas.

On September 11, 1861, the *Des Arc Semi-Weekly Citizen* reported the arrival of eight Federal prisoners transported on the steamer *J. J. Cadot.* A Lieutenant Fulton was in charge. Six of them had been under the command of Captain Chrisman. The two others were from Ellsworth's original Zouaves, and one of them was still wearing his uniform of red pants and blue jacket. On his head could be seen "Bloody 12th." The prisoners were taken from Des Arc to Little Rock by land.

In the *Des Arc Semi-Weekly Citizen* of September 25, 1861, appeared the following letter:

> Steamer *Cadot,* September 23, 1861
>
> We the undersigned passengers and soldiers on the downward trip of the Steamer *Cadot* from Pocahontas to Des Arc, feel it our duty to express our gratitude to Captain Timms and the officers of his boat for their careful and kind attention to us while on the trip, and more especially to Mr. and Mrs. Timms for their untiring attention to the sick, in trying to make us as comfortable as possible. The ladies did not cease to wait on the sick at any time during the trip. What we say to them is not half that they merit.

The conflict between the states brought increasing problems for the White River mail boats. Established in July 1855, the White River mail line had faithfully served the area to the best of its ability since its inception. As the war progressed, the *Des Arc Semi-Weekly Citizen* publisher, most assuredly a Southerner, sarcastically wrote:

> We wish to call attention to the fact that Lincoln's government no longer pays Capt. Coles for delivering the mails on White River. The rump government has bursted up emphatically, so far as mail facilities are concerned in this region. We still hear of daily lines of stages from Little Rock to Batesville, but we shouldn't wonder that Lincoln patronized certain portions of Pulaski County for some time to come. The *Kanawha Valley* and *Sam Hale* are good boats, and as they are now carrying the mail with only a hope that the Southern Confederacy will remunerate them for it, we believe it to be the duty of the public to see that they are sustained. Steamboats cannot run without ready cash to pay their expenses. All Capt. Coles asks, at present, is a patronage sufficient to the running expenses of his boats. Unless this is done by travelers and merchants, our mails will be reduced to once a week, or perhaps once in two weeks.[8]

Without doubt, the mail contracts were one of the biggest sources of income for the steamers receiving them, as they assured operating capital for the boats to run regularly throughout the year. For example, Captain Coles's contract in 1858 for delivering the mail from Napoleon to Jacksonport had been for sixteen thousand dollars, plus an additional eighty-seven hundred dollars for transporting it from Jacksonport to Pocahontas on the Black River.

Disaster hit the *Kanawha Valley* on August 5, 1861, while en route to Memphis. Fire broke out in its hull at five o'clock in the morning and threatened to consume the entire vessel. The pilot immediately ran the burning steamboat into shallow water near a sandbar some 150 yards from shore. Meanwhile, the officers awoke the passengers, but flames blocked their escape to the lower deck. Determined to save the ladies and children, the men dropped them overboard from the boiler deck. Tears flowed freely as fathers and husbands forced their loved ones into the water. Crew members were waiting below offering words of encouragement. Fortunately, all aboard reached safety on the sandbar where first aid was rendered and shelters erected for protection against the elements. Help eventually arrived from the steamer *H. D. Mears.* Personal losses were less than one thousand dollars, and the steamboat, not severely damaged, was resting securely on the bar where it was well protected from breaking or bending.

As heavy fighting drew closer, many steamboats began leaving the river, but the old faithful ones in the Lower White remained busy delivering mail and transporting troops and supplies. Information on steamboat activity in the Upper White River was becoming scarce; however, at least one steamer, the *New Moon,* was still traveling above Batesville. On August 21, 1861, the *New Moon,* Captain John Dearing, master, arrived at Memphis with thirty huge kettles and a steam engine, which were being taken to a saltpeter cave sixty miles above Jacksonport. Messrs. Brinkley and Jones of Commerce, Mississippi, had bought the cave for twenty-five thousand dollars and were manufacturing gunpowder for the Confederacy. Jo Carlton, a Jacksonport merchant, was also involved in the saltpeter business. In February of 1862, Carlton reported to the *Jacksonport Herald* that he shipped about a ton and a half of saltpeter every week to Nashville, and he soon expected to ship two or three tons per week.

The demands of war began to strain the economy of the White River Valley, and the prices of basic necessities started to rise. In an effort to control such price increases, Col. Solon Borland, commander of the Confederate forces in upper Arkansas, issued an order November 29, 1861, from his Pocahontas headquarters, banning speculation and hoarding for profit. The colonel asserted that certain persons were trying to monopolize and traffic in the necessities, citing examples of sharp price rises in the basic commodities. One illustration was the cost of salt jumping from two to five dollars per barrel up to twenty dollars per barrel. Persons violating the directive were to be arrested and the articles seized and sold at fair prices, deducting from their value the expense of seizure and disposal.

There was immediate opposition to Colonel Borland's order, and a clamor arose for its withdrawal, but the adamant colonel stood pat. News of the squabble finally reached Little Rock, and a counter-proposal was issued by Gov. H. M. Rector. Colonel Borland did not relent easily, however. Refusing the challenge to his authority, Colonel Borland seized a loaded steamboat at Grand Glaize that was, allegedly, in violation of his directive. His action added fuel to an already hot issue. The *Little Rock Daily State Journal* wrote: "We learn a steamer well laden with products of lawful traffic, winding her way down White River for the Confederate port of Memphis, was seized at Grand Glaize, in Jackson County, a few days ago under Col. Borland's general orders, and is now held as a prize, or something of that kind. Really, this despotic and arbitrary interference with the lawful commerce of the country is getting to be a most terrible nuisance and unless desisted from will bring the country to ruin!"[9]

The incident brought these comments from the *Pocahontas Herald:* "We are sorry to see the conflict going on between the State and Confederate authorities about the blockade laid on exports by the colonel commanding the district. Unless there is some interference from Richmond, we fear there will be some trouble in the matter."[10]

Opposition continued to mushroom until it was asserted that the entire press of Arkansas, with the exception of two newspapers, considered the action illegal and a dangerous stretch of military power. The growing distress was quickly relayed to Confederate headquarters in Richmond, where the secretary of war hastily revoked the proclamation and general order of Borland, proclaiming that it was unlawful and without the approval of the War Department. Borland was relieved of his command and told to report to Maj. Gen. A. S. Johns. Less than a month after the controversial order, the steamboats were again moving freely on the river.

In February of 1862, the Confederate mail steamers shifted the upper terminus of their run from Jacksonport to De Valls Bluff. Responding to the battle along the Arkansas-Missouri border, the *S. H. Tucker* and the *Cambridge* were still transporting Confederate troops to Pocahontas. In late February, they conveyed the Seventh Arkansas Infantry Regiment on what turned out to be the final trip for the *Cambridge*.

Commanded by Col. G. W. LeMoyne, the regiment assembled at Little Rock to move by land to Pocahontas, but an epidemic of measles struck the unit, so the sick were placed on the *S. H. Tucker* and the rest of the unit left on foot. Inclement weather and illness forced Colonel LeMoyne to abandon the march and head for the White River to await a steamboat. The regiment wagon train was sent ahead, while the men marched to the river. About six miles above Des Arc, Colonel LeMoyne hailed the steamboat *Cambridge,* which was en route from Jacksonport to Memphis. Calamity struck the steamer and its military passengers the following evening, February 23, 1862, when the vessel collided with a log that jabbed a hole in its side. The steamboat sank in less than four minutes. As the *Cambridge* submerged, it careened and rolled over on about ninety soldiers who had become frightened and jumped overboard. The boat came to rest with about ten inches of its hurricane deck above the water; the sick were placed on that deck. Among those in the water, only one life was lost. Others who remained on the boat were not so fortunate. Sixteen soldiers, two slaves, five crew members, and an unknown number of additional passengers perished. The steamboat was totally destroyed, but the *S. H. Tucker* picked up the survivors and took them to Pocahontas.

The arrival of Union troops in the upper White River Valley drove most of the few remaining packets there to the lower river. Several steamboats continued to play a part in the battle strategy of both the Confederate and the Union military throughout the conflict.

From the beginning of the war, the Confederate concept of holding the rivers was primarily to do so from the banks, as the rivers in Europe were held, while the Union idea was amphibious.

In March of 1862, Gen. S. R. Curtis, who had few accomplishments during the Civil War, defeated the Confederates resoundingly at Pea Ridge in northern Arkansas. He then cut across Arkansas. Among the targets of General Curtis's drive south in April of 1862 were the saltpeter mines near Yellville and Talbert's Ferry. From Talbert's Ferry, Curtis moved toward Batesville, arriving there on May 3. His cavalry continued on to Jacksonport. Their occupation brought the steady procession of steamboats on the White River down to a small trickle.

In the May 9, 1862, edition of the *Traveler,* a Union publication, editor George Hand made some interesting comments about Jacksonport and conditions there during the Union occupation:

> Jacksonport on White River is, or has been, decidedly a commercial point; at present however it presents a doleful appearance. Most of the inhabitants have left. . . . Considerable cotton and sugar is to be found here. What disposition is to be made of it, we presume the General knows. Flour sells at 14 dollars a hundred lbs.; coffee, scarce as secesh soldiers, at one dollar a pound; liquor, four dollars a quart; bacon, .30 per pound; cotton prints .30 a yard; calf boots, twenty dollars. Our troops look and probably feel sweet, at least they have had full rations of

Empire City, *one of a fleet of steamers that transported supplies to Union troops stationed on White River during the Civil War.*

From the Orville Gillett Collection, courtesy of the Arkansas History Commission and the University of Arkansas, Little Rock, Archives and Special Collections.

> sugar and molasses. Fish are abundant in the river here, and are daily sold in the streets at reasonable prices. Water. Singularly enough, all the cisterns in this place are owned by widow women. Moreover the widows are very sparing of their water.[11]

In an attempt to deter the Union forces, on June 5, 1862, Joseph Fry, commander of the Confederate gunboat *Maurepas,* informed General Hindman that he had destroyed 659 bales of cotton and eighty-one hogsheads of sugar at Jacksonport, but had found it impossible to get a local force to cooperate with him further. Low water forced Commander Fry to take the 399-ton gunboat, formerly the steamer *Grosse Tete,* to Des Arc.

Shortly after his arrival in May, Union general Curtis requested naval support and communications be sent up the White River. His message was passed along with orders to use every effort to supply the army in that quarter.

The original plan was to assist General Curtis with two gunboats and three Ellet rams. Because of arguments over command of the Ellet rams, the scheme was altered. The final expedition consisted of the gunboats *St. Louis, Lexington, Conestoga,* and *Mound City* commanded by Comdr. A. H. Kilty, plus two transports carrying the Forty-sixth Indiana. On June 17, the expedition ran into enemy pickets near St. Charles, Arkansas. The troops were landed and the boats moved up to clear the waterway where Lt. John W. Dunnington of the Confederate navy had sunk the Hollins gunboat *Maurepas* and two transports, the *Mary Patterson* and the *Eliza J.,* to create a blockade. The Confederates had also placed guns on the bluff ashore near the blockade point.

There were only 114 men to handle the Confederate artillery, but Commander Kilty did not know this, nor did he know the positions of the guns. Although Col. G. N. Fitch of the Indiana regiment wished to encircle the artillery by land, Kilty refused him permission to do so until naval fire had been tried. It was a costly mistake. Early in the fighting, a shot from a rifled forty-two-pounder pierced the front of *Mound City*'s casemate and went through the steam drum. A frightful explosion followed, and the men in the casemate were cooked alive. Those who escaped overboard were killed in the water by Confederate sharpshooters. At roll call the following morning, only 25 of the 175 in the crew answered. The survivors went wild and plundered the boat, including the effects of those dying. Kilty was among the severely scalded and, for a while, it was uncertain if he would live.

The *Conestoga* towed the helpless ironclad downstream while Colonel Fitch signaled the other boats to cease fire and carried on the fight with bayonet, capturing all remaining Confederates alive. The convoy sent to assist General Curtis never reached him.

U.S. gunboat St. Louis *took part in the Battle of St. Charles on White River and the Battle of Arkansas Post on Arkansas River, helping free both rivers of Rebel boats so that Federal troops could be supplied by water.*

Photo from the U.S. War Department, courtesy of the General Staff, National Archives, and the University of Arkansas, Little Rock, Archives and Special Collections.

U.S. gunboat Lexington *took part in the Battle of St. Charles on White River in 1862 and the Battle of Arkansas Post on the Arkansas River during the Civil War. Commanded by Captain Bache, the* Lexington, *along with the tinclads* Cricket *and* Marmora, *went to the mouth of the Little Red River in August 1863. While the* Lexington *and* Marmora *waited, the* Cricket *went up Little Red and captured the steamers* Tom Suggs *and* Kaskaskia, *the last two Confederate steamboats on the White River.*

Photo from the U.S. Bureau of Ships, courtesy of National Archives and the University of Arkansas, Little Rock, Archives and Special Collections.

Golden Era *was 180 x 33 x 4.5 feet and was used as a Federal transport in the White River during the Civil War. Commanded by Capt. Robert G. Osborne, the boat was with the fleet that fought the Battle of St. Charles, June 17, 1862, in which* Mary Patterson, Eliza G., *and* Maurepas *were scuttled to prevent the fleet from advancing upriver. Gunboat in rear is not identified.*

From the Downs Collection, courtesy of the University of Arkansas, Little Rock, Archives and Special Collections.

The tide was turning for Curtis, and conditions were becoming desperate for his troops by June 25 of 1862. On that day, he wrote from Jacksonport that his stock was starving and that no more forage or beef could be obtained in his former position west of Black and White Rivers. Reinforcements and supplies were needed immediately. General Grant tried sending the *Lexington* and the *Conestoga* up the White on June 28, but in addition to the sunken boat obstructions, the water had fallen too low for them to get through, bringing a halt to transport of troops. Without the gunboat protection from guerrillas and light artillery along the riverbank, the transports could not operate on the river.

Meanwhile, Confederate general Hindman had placed five thousand men under Gen. Albert Rust to resist General Curtis, and the command was gathering on the White River near Clarendon. Curtis's fifteen thousand troops were literally stranded at Jacksonport with no subsistence other that what could be confiscated there. After several skirmishes, he and his men made a final departure from the area in July.

With the loss of the *Mary Patterson,* Capt. Morgan Bateman began recruiting for the Confederate army and served as captain of a company he organized in Jacksonport on October 1, 1862. The group became Company E of Col. Archibald Dobbin's First Cavalry Regiment and was stationed in eastern Arkansas, primarily on Crowley's Ridge, until 1864, when it was transferred to Col. Thomas J. Morgan's Cavalry Regiment in southern Arkansas.

Guerrilla activity was a major annoyance for the Federal steamboats throughout the conflict. During the summer of 1862, the chief engineer of the gunboat *Lexington* was killed when he was shot through the head by a sniper. Just prior to the death of the engineer, a Rebel was captured who had been following the Federal vessels along the shore for about thirty miles, firing on them at every opportunity. Found on the rifleman was a letter of authority from General Hindman directing him to watch the Federal boats and pick off officers whenever he could. The man was, at first, confined aboard the transport *White Cloud,* but following the death of Huber, the *Lexington* engineer, the guerrilla was placed aboard the *Lexington* and fastened on the wheelhouse in such a position that he could be seen plainly from the shore.

Though several shots were fired in his direction while he was tied there, none hit him. He was later taken down and placed in confinement on the *Lexington* until proper military disposition of him could be made. Firemen on the *Lexington* were also wounded during this period, and the *Golden Era* was fired upon several times though no injuries resulted.

The White River remained low through August, so the Union gunboats *Benton, Mound City,* and *General Bragg,* with four of the Ellet rams, were sent downstream under the general command of Lt. Comdr. S. L. Phelps to "thumb a nose" at Vicksburg.[12]

The importance of the rivers to the strategy of battle was recognized by many in the military. A request was made by Union officers for a number of small-draft steamboats to maintain control of the tributaries of the Mississippi, including the White, during the dry season. A half dozen such vessels were purchased in August of 1862 and were plated with boiler iron to repel musket balls. Most of the boats also had mounted six twenty-four-pounder howitzers and could carry a contingent of sharpshooters behind their iron. Best of all, their draft was only about twenty-two inches. The howitzers were removable if very shallow water was encountered.

As the fighting progressed, new vessels appeared in the White. The conflict brought steamboat captains to the river who were eager for the Federal transport trade but who were unfamiliar with the White River. Experiencing difficulty in navigating the unknown shoals, sandbars, and submerged obstacles, many of them met with disastrous results.

Recognizing the importance of a speedy and reliable supply of war materials and troops, the Federals tried to hire experienced White River pilots to steer their transports, but they found few who were willing to accept their offers. Capt. Enos Lamb, great-grandfather of John P. Morrow Jr. of Batesville, was offered one thousand dollars per trip to pilot one of the vessels up the river. A skilled captain on steamboats in the Mississippi River system, Lamb had come to Jacksonport in 1850 and knew the White well.

U.S. gunboat Benton *saw limited service on White River during the Civil War in August of 1862 due to low water.*

Photo from U.S. Army Signal Corps, courtesy of the National Archives and University of Arkansas, Little Rock, Archives and Special Collections.

U.S. tinclad No. 6, *the* Cricket. *This boat captured the last two Confederate boats on White River and its tributaries. They were the* Tom Suggs *and* Kaskaskia, *which had gone up Little Red River to escape Federal gunboats but were captured at the Searcy landing in August 1863. The* Lexington *and the* Marmora *waited at the mouth while the* Cricket *made the capture. The boat was commanded by Capt. George M. Bache on this expedition.*

Courtesy of the University of Arkansas, Little Rock, Archives and Special Collections.

After refusing to pilot for the Union army, Captain Lamb fled the area, fearful of being forced to perform the service.

By September of 1863, the Union troops and gunboats had driven the Confederates from the White River and controlled all traffic on the waterway. Among the last Confederate boats to be captured by the Union was the *Tenas,* formerly the *Tom Suggs,* which had transported Confederates to camps on the Current River. The little 41-ton vessel was seized on Little Red River on August 14, 1863, by the *Cricket,* a 178-ton stern-wheeler with much greater firepower. Steamboats were plying only the lower river, primarily to serve the Union forces, and on October 11, the steamers *Lebanon, Thomas T. Patten, Dacotah,* and *Altoment* were at De Valls Bluff. At that time, too, the *Sallie List* had just arrived at Memphis from De Valls Bluff with 327 prisoners from Little Rock for transfer to the *Hawkeye State* for shipment to Federal military prisons. Because it had a railroad line to Little Rock, De Valls Bluff became an important transfer point, and steamboats from Memphis made frequent trips to this railroad connection.

Those steamboats that continued to traverse the White during the war were in constant danger of attacks by Confederate guerrillas. When the *Rose Hambleton* arrived at Memphis on November 4, 1863, the captain reported that partisans had fired upon his boat when about five miles below Des Arc. A rifle ball passed through the body of the boat's mate just below the shoulder blade, seriously wounding him. Several days later, the *Ella* was attacked while carrying Federal troops to Jacksonport. Guerrillas fired from the dense foliage along the riverbank, wounding a captain and a major of a cavalry unit aboard. The attack on the *Ella* did not seem to dampen the spirits of those on board, however, for when the boat docked at Jacksonport, a party was held in the cabin of the steamer. Lady Elizabeth Watson Luker in her book *Fight and Survive!* described the festivities for the Yankee officers as the classic steamboat party. Following is a quote from one of the participants: ". . . between the Captain, the Boat, the steward, the scenery, songs, yarns, fun and a court martial whereat the whiskey was most impartially tried and NOT found wanting, we had the greatest time we ever saw on a steamboat."[13]

In addition to the gunboats and ironclads mentioned earlier, other steamboats in the White River in 1863 were the *Gillium,* the *Emma No. 2,* the *Creole Belle,* the *Robert Hamilton,* the *Crescent City,* the *H. A. Homeyer,* the *Q. Lloyd,* the *Pocahontas,* the *Des Moines City,* the *J. S. Pringle,* the *Bertha,* the *Progress,* the *William Wallace,* the *America,* the *Mill Boy,* the *Florence,* the *W. R. Glasgow,* the *Arago,* and the *Dove.*

By early 1864, Col. Robert R. Livingston, commander of the Northeastern District of Arkansas, was having difficulty delivering supplies to the Union forces in Batesville. Guerrilla activity was so prevalent at some points that he had to clear the area before the cargo boats could pass safely. Low water was also adding to the colonel's dilemma, preventing the larger vessels from ascending to Batesville.

Several steamboats, including the *Ella,* had become regular weekly packets from Memphis to Helena to De Valls Bluff. One of the *Ella*'s chief competitors was the *Des Arc,* owned and mastered by Captain Chenoweth.

On March 22, 1864, the *Des Arc* caught fire under somewhat mysterious circumstances at De Valls Bluff. A beautiful 276-ton side-wheeler, the boat was built at Paducah in 1862 and was 210 feet long. It was one of the best packets on the White. The *Des Arc* had been used in the Mississippi as a Federal troop transport, but when its current owner took the oath, it was placed in service in the White River. Because it had hauled Union soldiers, the *Des Arc* was rather unpopular with the planters along the river, and, desirous of making friends, the officers of the steamboat often permitted the young people to dance on board when the boat was at a landing or traveling between several landings.

The burning of the *Des Arc* occurred following such a party. The local legend of the fire involved Capt. Jim Fargus, who had served in Company C of the Eighteenth Arkansas Regiment but was severely wounded in the early days of the war and was disabled, preventing his further service. He returned to the Fargus plantation, situated on a long sweeping bend of the White River a few miles below Augusta, where he again became a cotton farmer. To be allowed to maintain his cotton business, Fargus had to take the oath of allegiance, an act he said was like sticking a knife into his heart.

According to the story, Fargus and a few of his friends decided to board the *Des Arc* to join in the festivities there. In the first cabin,

Steamboats docked at Des Arc during the Civil War, about 1863. Among those moored are the Pocahontas, *the* Ella, *and the* Emma No. 2. *The latter ran in White River after the cessation of hostilities.*

Courtesy of the University of Arkansas, Little Rock, Archives and Special Collections.

Steamboat Des Arc, *shown at De Valls Bluff, on White River, about early 1864. The boat later burned at De Valls Bluff but was scuttled to prevent total destruction.* Photo courtesy of Wilson Powell.

they ran into an acquaintance who lived near the mouth of Taylor's Bayou. Fargus spoke cordially to his friend, who responded by making a snide remark about a lady named Ann Lanier, also on board. Fargus asserted that he and the young woman were only friends, but he was answered with an another insult. Fargus begged that his old acquaintance not do anything which would spoil their friendship. The young man persisted in his assault, accusing Fargus of coming between Ann Lanier and him. Finally, Fargus punched his tormentor in the mouth and walked away with his erstwhile friend's threats ringing in his ears. With blood spurting from his mouth, the jealous young man shouted that not a single bale of cotton on the boat would reach Memphis.

The young people danced in the main cabin until late that night while the boat made several landings. By the time it reached De Valls Bluff, the steamer carried several hundred bales of cotton. The captain told the party aboard that there would be a two-hour stop at De Valls Bluff, but to continue dancing if they desired. Eventually, the bell on the hurricane deck rang its signal to depart and black smoke began curling up from the chimneys. Pilot Chester Smith prepared to disengage his boat, as the young people disembarking there departed. Fargus's tormentor was nowhere to be found.

The *Des Arc* had barely left the wharf when fire was discovered in the cotton. The crew fought bravely, but wind fanned the flames and in a few minutes the steamer was a floating furnace. The story says that men and women leaped overboard, with many of them drowning. Others were supposedly trapped in the fiery vessel and burned to death.

There was no evidence that Fargus's rival set the fire, but he was never seen again in Arkansas. Ann Lanier asked Fargus if he believed that his former friend was guilty and Fargus replied a firm yes. Fargus then proposed marriage to Miss Lanier, placed his arm around her waist, and they walked away.[14]

Probably the most authentic version of the *Des Arc* disaster is found in the *Memphis Daily Bulletin* of March 26, 1864. This report states that while loading at De Valls Bluff on March 22, fire was discovered at 9 A.M. in the *Des Arc* hold between its wheelhouses. The hatches were immediately closed, a hole cut in the deck over the fire, and a steady stream of water poured into the hold. The alarm was given. There was much anxiety because there were a number of other boats heavily laden with freight also at the landing. None had up steam except the *Arago,* which was grounded next to the burning *Des Arc.* U.S. gunboat *No. 25,* Capt. G. B. Loyd, commander, pulled the steamer *Arago* free, and it retired to a safer place. Capt. John Finney had wanted to run the *Arago* beside the *Des Arc* to remove the cotton on its deck, but was ordered aside by Captain Loyd.

Meanwhile, the flames broke through the hold, so it was decided that scuttling was the only way to save the burning boat. This was done, and it began to take on water. Gunboat *No. 25* towed the flaming steamer across the river to prevent the other boats and the large amount of supplies from catching fire. All passengers, baggage, money, and books were removed, and the cotton on deck was jettisoned. However, the large amount of cargo in the hold prevented the boat from sinking fast enough, and the flames were spreading upward. Captain Loyd ordered all crew members from the deck and fired six thirty-two-pounder balls into the hull, but to no avail. Flames soon enveloped the upper decks, and the *Des Arc* was consumed by the fire. Much praise was given for the heroic and indefatigable exertions of the captains and crews, since their actions saved a tremendous amount of public and private property.

Owners of the *Des Arc* were listed as Ogden and Champion of Columbus, Ohio, contradicting an earlier report that Capt. J. R. Chenoweth had purchased the boat. Perhaps he had sold it to the partnership. Although valued at sixty thousand dollars, the steamboat was insured for only twenty-thousand dollars and had cost her current owners fifty thousand dollars. Following the war, the *Des Arc* was raised, refurbished, and returned to service.

On March 26, 1864, the U.S. gunboat *Naumkeag* left De Valls Bluff with the transports *Q. Lloyd* and *Celeste,* which were loaded with army stores for the Union troops at Batesville. The steamboats arrived safely at the mouth of the Little Red River that evening and, early the next morning, neared Augusta. Shortly before the convoy passed Augusta, a body of guerrillas left the village and hid behind a pile of driftwood and logs. When the boats came within range, the guerrilla band fired upon the convoy and a soldier aboard one steamer was wounded in the knee. A stiff westerly breeze prevented the steamboats from stopping to give battle, but broadsides were fired from the gunboat, killing and wounding several of the ambushers. A later dispatch from the *Naumkeag* stated, "The river is very narrow here and it would have been impossible to have kept our craft from being badly damaged had we checked our speed."[15]

Not satisfied with their efforts at Augusta, the Confederate guerrillas rallied again after the convoy passed Grand Glaize, where the boats were attacked by about 150 partisans coolly standing in the open and firing their weapons. One Rebel was immediately picked off by a gunboat sharpshooter, but it took the firing of some thirty-two rounds that felled about one-fourth of the attackers to finally disperse the guerrillas. The only damage inflicted on the steamboats was the wounding of a pilot on the *Q. Lloyd.* Later, a black woman came to the riverbank, saying that the Rebels had admitted their defeat but were preparing to attack

The steamboat Des Arc *on fire near De Valls Bluff during the Civil War. Gunboat* No. 25 *is hovering nearby.* Des Arc *was two hundred feet long and thirty feet wide and one of the superb White River steamboats. Its construction was started in 1860 at Paducah by A. L. Davis, who failed to complete it. Capt. Hicks King finished the job.* Des Arc *arrived at Memphis in late 1862, but the war prevented its entering the White River then, so it ran in the Louisville and Memphis trade. It was later brought to the White River where it partially burnt. The steamboat was rebuilt at a cost of fifty thousand dollars and placed in the Vicksburg trade until 1866, then was bought by Martin and R. P. Walt for White River. They sold it to the Elliots, who ran it in White River until it was dismantled in 1871.*

Courtesy of the University of Arkansas, Little Rock, Archives and Special Collections.

U.S. gunboat No. 25 *on White River near DeValls Bluff in late 1863 or early 1864. Because of Confederate guerilla attacks, gunboats such as this had to escort the transports up the river.*

Courtesy of the University of Arkansas, Little Rock, Archives and Special Collections.

again. This, however, proved untrue, and the convoy safely reached Jacksonport at sundown. The following morning the steamers departed for Batesville, but after a few miles, found the river unnavigable, so returned and anchored at the confluence of the Black and White Rivers. A messenger was dispatched to Batesville with instructions to send a wagon train to meet the convoy at a point nine miles up Black River. After the rendezvous, the boats returned to Jacksonport; however, by that time the river had risen and the seventy-ton *Celeste* again left for Batesville. The boat arrived back at Jacksonport on April 4, and the entire convoy reached De Valls Bluff on April 7.

While the convoy was on its trip, the transport *Dove,* with U.S. gunboat *No. 25* as its escort, ascended the White River to Augusta but found such a hot reception that it was forced to flee after only one day there. Aboard the *Dove* were 50 men of the Eighth Missouri Cavalry, under Capt. J. J. Matthews, and 275 members of the Third Minnesota Infantry. All were under the command of Colonel Andrews of the Third Minnesota. A large contingent of the servicemen were sent ashore to surround the town. Two Rebels were captured, but the prisoners refused to reveal the whereabouts of the balance of their troop. Shortly, however, the Federal band was informed by some blacks about the position and strength of the Confederate camp and headed for the site.

Seven miles from Augusta, the advance group of Federals came upon General McRae, accompanied by a provision wagon and 7 men who were reconnoitering Rebel forces. Thirteen miles from Augusta, the 175 infantry and 30 cavalrymen from the *Dove* charged the Confederate complex only to find it empty. As dusk approached, the Federal troops were pulled back for return to the steamboat, where the remainder of their group stood guard over the vessel. Six miles from Augusta, the band was attacked from the rear. The Federal forces reformed and fired upon their assailants, "emptying many saddles." The Confederates fell back two hundred yards and formed a new line with larger numbers. Fighting continued for over two hours. With darkness near and their ammunition almost gone, the Union troops headed for Augusta as the Confederate forces followed them at a distance. Upon their arrival aboard the *Dove,* the transport hastily steamed down the river while the gunboat remained to receive two stragglers and to exchange some final shots at the Rebels before its departure.[16]

With the White River controlled by Federal forces, steamboats continued to ply the White above Des Arc through most of May of 1864, though many traveled only with an escort or in convoys. In early May, the *Sunny South,* the *Celeste,* and the *Sir William Wallace,* accompanied by U.S. gunboat *No. 37,* arrived at Jacksonport. After being serenaded by the First Nebraska band, the officers and

A group of steamboats anchored at Des Arc during the Civil War in 1863 or 1864. At that time there was an army depot at the river town.
Courtesy of the University of Arkansas, Little Rock, Archives and Special Collections.

crew of the gunboat "were loath to part with so excellent an institution."[17] But leave they did, as did Union colonel Livingston and his troops on May 26, when everything was hastily loaded on seven transports, including the steamer *Tycoon,* to flee from Confederate general Shelby and his troops. Shelby had been sent into northern Arkansas to prevent the frequent navigation of the White River by Union forces and to organize the more or less independent commands located in the area. On board the seven transports for descent of the river were equipment, animals, sick and dismounted men, and some refugee families who were Union sympathizers and had arrived in Jacksonport with Union troops that had been fighting in the northern part of the state.

The steamboats ran aground on Reed's Bar opposite Grand Glaize the afternoon of the May 27 and had to be unloaded, one at a time, to get them over the bar, then reloaded for the remaining trip downriver. While time was of the essence, there was no way to hurry the back-breaking work of lifting the cargo from the boats in the dark, nor the slow, careful maneuvering of each of the vessels over the bar, nor the carrying of the unloaded equipment and goods across the loose sand to the new position of the steamers. Sunrise found the steamboats downriver from Grand Glaize, just a couple of hours ahead of Shelby and his forces.

On June 11, 1864, a group of Union army officers visited De Valls Bluff on an inspection tour. The crew of U.S. gunboat *No. 51,* formerly the *Fairy,* hosted Major General Sickles, General Steele, and members of their staffs until late into the night. The gunboat then traveled down the White to the mooring of the *Kate Hart,* where the Union commanders spent the remainder of the night. The return trip to Little Rock was made by rail. The meeting was, perhaps in part, a strategic planning one.

Later that month, General Steele, from his command post in Little Rock, decided to extend the right wing of his forces farther up the Arkansas River and requested that Ledyard Phelps, the district naval commander, convoy his transports down the White from De Valls Bluff and up the Arkansas. The *Tyler,* the *Naumkaeg,* and the *Fawn,* all under Lt. Comdr. G. M. Bache, were ordered up the White. At the time, the *Naumkaeg* and the *Fawn,* along with the *Queen City,* were between Clarendon and St. Charles. The *Lexington* was at White River Station at the mouth of the White. The steamboats had barely received their orders before word came that Gen. Joseph Shelby, coming down the left bank of the White, had anticipated Steele's move and was circling around that right wing with twenty-five hundred raiding cavalry and five guns.

First contact of the steamboats with Shelby's troops came on

U.S. tinclad No. 2, *the* Marmora, *did escort duty on White River during the Civil War. It was also a patrol boat.*

Courtesy of the University of Arkansas, Little Rock, Archives and Special Collections.

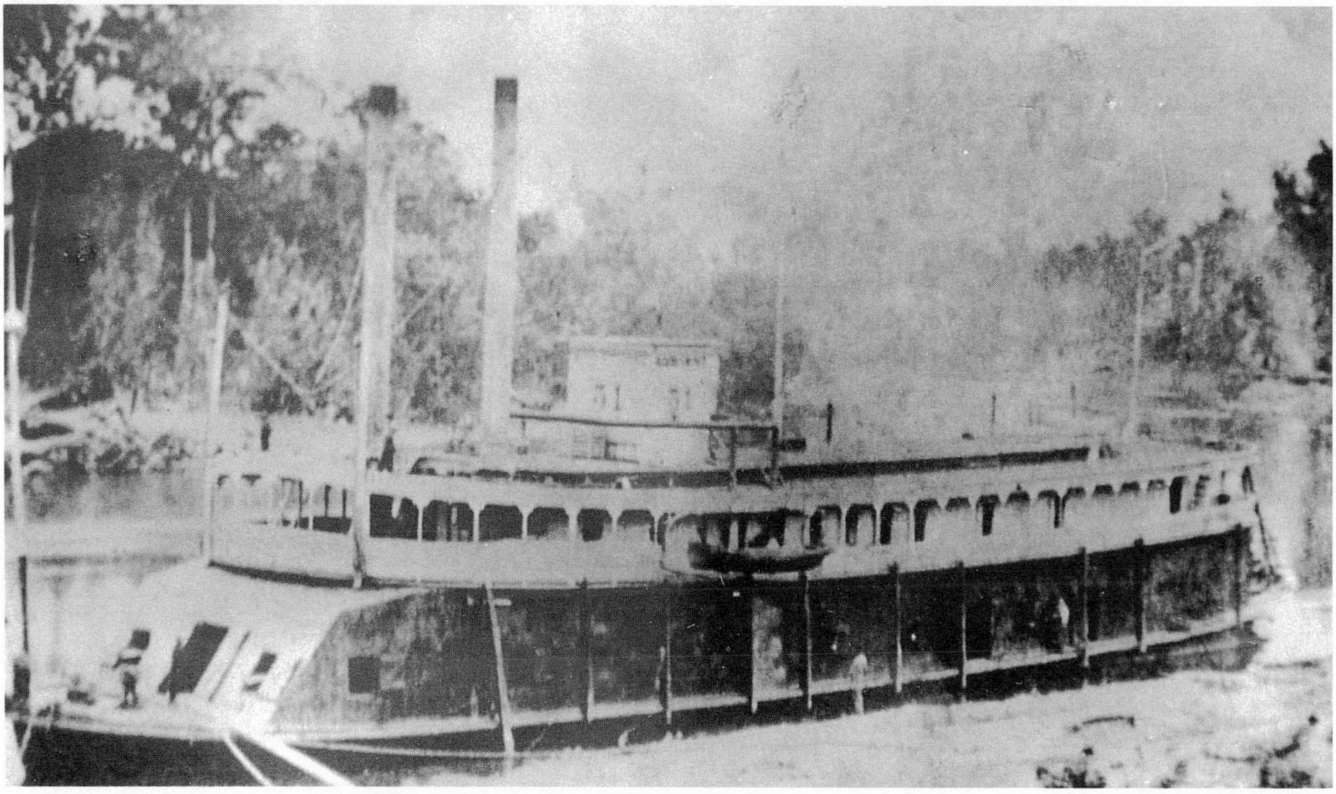

U.S. tinclad No. 51, *the* Fairy, *was one of the gunboats that the Federals operated on White and Arkansas Rivers during the Civil War. The craft was 157 x 31.5 x 4.7 feet. A group of Federal officers, including General Steele and staff, were guests on the boat on June 11, 1864. They were received by General Sickles and staff at DeValls Bluff and, after a long conference, were taken downriver on the boat to the steamer* Kate Hart, *Capt. John J. Edson, master, where they were quartered for the night. They returned by rail to Little Rock.*

Courtesy of the University of Arkansas, Little Rock, Archives and Special Collections.

June 22 at White River Station when fifty-six men of the Twelfth Iowa situated in a stockade were rushed by a wing of three hundred Confederate cavalry. The *Lexington* drove them off. Two days later, Shelby himself saw the *Queen City* near Clarendon and decided to try a night surprise attack. Between three and four o'clock in the morning, guns fired on the tinclad, making immediate hits in the engine. Two ensigns aboard the *Queen City* panicked, resulting in no effective return of enemy fire being made by the Federal forces. Hickey, the Union commander, told his men they had the choice of trying to swim for freedom or being taken prisoner, as he was going to surrender.

Lieutenant Commander Bache was upstream with the *Tyler, Naumkeag,* and *Fawn,* having just picked up the transports. At nine in the morning, on his way down the White, he received news of the *Queen City* disaster. Hoping to at least save the ship's equipment, he sent the transports back upriver and hurried on with his warships. Before he reached the *Queen City,* however, Shelby had blown up the steamer. When the gunboats arrived, Shelby's troops were still stationed around the bend where they had maneuvered the steamboat, and the Confederate commander decided to make a fight of it. The result was the usual one between field batteries and gunboats. The *Tyler* positioned below the Confederates while the other two vessels remained above, placing the land troops in a crossfire. Deciding he could do no more damage, Shelby withdrew his forces a distance of two miles. He also left one of his guns and most of his dead behind.

Guerrilla action along the White became bolder, forcing most steamboats to travel only in convoys. On July 7, the steamers *Lilly Martin, Kate Hart, Prairie State, Argonaut, B. M. Runyan, Canton,* and *Pike* arrived at Memphis from De Valls Bluff. Although accompanied by three gunboats, a daring band of Rebels had fired upon the boats near St. Charles causing minor damage. Aboard the *Pike* were many refugees that a Memphis reporter described as the most deplorable ever seen. Several had died of disease and exposure during the trip.

One of the river's favorite vessels fell prey to a guerrilla attack in early September of 1864. While ascending the river under the protection of U.S. gunboat *No. 30,* the 277-ton *Commercial* was attacked at Gregory's Island by a force estimated at from one hundred to three hundred Rebels. Concealed behind a levee, the Confederates poured rifle fire into the unsuspecting boat as it neared the ambush point. Fifty musket balls struck the sidewheeler, killing one person and wounding five others. As the frightened passengers and crew of the *Commercial* scurried for shelter, the gunboat opened fire and the shots from the heavier cannon sent the guerrillas fleeing down the levee. In spite of such attacks, Capt. John J. Edson, master, and the *Commercial* continued to carry freight and passengers in the river, even after being released from government service.

In a rather amusing encounter, guerrilla forces also struck the *Eclipse* in mid-October of 1864 as it was descending the White. When the boat was near Clarendon, a band of about thirty guerrillas ambushed the vessel around 8 P.M. Striking quickly, the

U.S. gunboat Tyler *saw escort service on the White and Arkansas Rivers during the Civil War.*

Courtesy of the University of Arkansas, Little Rock, Archives and Special Collections.

attackers covered the unsuspecting steamboat with volleys of musket fire, hitting it about forty times. No one was injured, but activity on the boat was fast and furious for a few moments. The mate, who was on the hurricane deck when the shooting erupted, quickly started for the lower decks. In his haste, he stumbled over the bell rope, causing it to ring sharply. Thinking this was a sign of surrender, the jubilant guerrillas rushed down the riverbank yelling, "Come ashore, you damned Yankees! Come ashore, you damned Yankees!"[18]

The "damned Yankees," however, refused to cooperate and quickly turned the *Eclipse* back toward St. Charles, leaving the shouting Rebels brandishing their muskets on the riverbank. Even though a handful of flattened bullets was picked up in the pilothouse following the battle, the pilot, miraculously, had escaped unharmed. While returning to St. Charles, one of the steamer's heavily-laden barges sank, but its freight was saved. A gunboat was sent to chastise the Rebels, but they were long gone by the time the craft reached the battle scene. In October of 1864, Federal troops evacuated St. Charles.

Although not booming, commercial steamboat activity on the White River did continue during all of 1864. Adding to the problem of military and guerrilla actions on the river, however, was the lack of business. The shipment of private freight on the De Valls Bluff to Little Rock railroad was prohibited by the Union military, and the Arkansas River was also unnavigable, so there was no way to send freight to Little Rock during much of 1864. Despite such difficulties, some steamboats did survive in the trade during the period, including the *Fanny Ogden,* Captain Townsend, master, the steamer *M. S. Mepham,* Capt. A. W. Shaw in command, and the *Emma No. 2,* commanded by Capt. David Willard. Each of these boats carried cargo and passengers from Memphis to the White River.

In addition to those just mentioned from 1864, regular packets in the White River during January of 1865 included the *William Wallace,* Capt. Alcoke; the *Sunny South,* Capt. Fulton; the *Kate Hart,* Capt. John B. Davis; the *Curlew,* Capt. Elthorpe; the *Rose Hambleton;*

U.S. tinclad No. 26, *the* Queen City, *was sunk in June 1864, by Confederate troops at Clarendon, Arkansas. It was one of the few boats lost by Federals while running on White River.*

Courtesy of the University of Arkansas, Little Rock, Archives and Special Collections.

and the *May Duke*. Frequent steamers were the *War Eagle,* the *Albert Pearce,* and the *Ella*. Boats making intermittent trips included the *Liberty No. 2,* the *Citizen,* the *St. Cloud,* with Capt. John D. Elliott, the *Belle Peoria,* the *Lady,* the *Mattie,* and the *W. Butler*.

Providing worthy competition for all of the above were the steamers of Capt. John J. Edson, the *Rebecca* and the *Rowena*. The *Rowena,* formerly of the Memphis-Cincinnati run, was a beautiful vessel that was 180 feet long, 35.5 feet wide, had three boilers, and displaced 341 tons. The *Rowena* reached Memphis on January 19, 1865, headed for the White River, and received the following recommendation:

> The *Rowena*—This favorite and fleet boat came down, bound for White River, with a good trip and will leave for Helena and Duval's Bluff at four P.M. precisely. The great success of her new commander, Capt. John J. Edson, while in command of the *Commercial* is sufficient to insure him the largest patronage in his new enterprise. There is not a more successful and more reliable steamboatman afloat, and his experience in White River stamps him as the right man in the right place . . . The *Rowena* will be the regular Memphis and White River packet.[19]

The enterprising Captain Edson quickly obtained permission from the Union commander to run without interruption in the trade. Dubbed the "Queen of White River boats," the *Rowena* was also designated as a regular mail and dispatch boat.[20] Pilots of the vessel were Captains Kinman and Rhodes, with John H. Moore and Billy Fields serving as clerks. Caterer Monogham was described as spreading a table superior in variety and excellence to any heretofore available on a Mississippi River steamboat.

On February 6, 1865, the popular *Fanny Ogden* left Memphis for De Valls Bluff and returned to the Mississippi port on the thirteenth. The steamer's performance was remarkable in its seven day journey, during which it traveled over seven hundred miles, handled 780 tons of freight, and embarked and disembarked 1,487 infantry and cavalry troops, 342 horses, and one hundred beef cattle.

A hot rivalry quickly developed between the *Fanny Ogden* and the *Rowena*. A race between the two steamers occurred in February of 1865 from Helena to Memphis, resulting in a dispute between the officers and friends of each vessel. Those of the *Fanny Ogden* claimed victory by two or three hours, a feat Captain Edson of the *Rowena* flatly denied. Captain Edson said the *Fanny Ogden* left thirty-one minutes ahead of the *Rowena* and did not come into port until his boat rounded the bend below the city. Regardless of the true outcome, Captain Edson was jubilant and invited a select group to a gala party aboard the *Rowena*. The appearance of many prominent military figures at the festivity was the only indication of the tragic struggle still raging between the states. Fair ladies and courtly gentlemen danced to fine music, dined on delicious specialties, and held lively discussions until nearly daybreak. The event served as a welcome break from the harsh realities of war.

The *Fannie Ogden* was pressed into government service in late February 1865 but was released from that duty sixteen days later. The steamers *John. D. Perry, David Tatum, Sunny South, Belle Peoria, Silver Wave,* and *Commercial* were also commandeered by the Federal forces and used for military transportation between De Valls Bluff and the mouth of White River.

Two strong Memphis and White River steamboat lines emerged in 1865—that under the stewardship of Capt. John Edson with his steamers, *Rowena* and *Rebecca,* and the line under the auspices of Hart and Company of Memphis, which operated the *Commercial* and the *Tycoon.* Captain Wilson served as master of the *Commercial,* and Capt. John B. Davis held command of the *Tycoon.* The publisher of the *Memphis Daily Bulletin* was enthused over the rivalry, which produced immediate results. On April 15 of that year, he wrote: "The opposition between the lines of the Memphis and White River packets, formed by the *Rowena* and *Rebecca,* and that of the *Commercial* and *Tycoon,* has caused a reduction in the fare to De Valls Bluff to ten dollars. The former rate was twenty-five dollars. Opposition is good; keep it up!"

In addition to lower rates and enhanced accommodations, the competitors sought to reduce the travel time between the two ports as well. The fleet *Rebecca,* Capt. Joe Banfil, master, ran from De Valls Bluff to Memphis in the amazing time of twenty-eight hours. The feat briefly made the vessel the champion White River packet, but the *Rowena* quickly broke that record. The competition continued, and on April 15, 1865, the *Tycoon* established a new record. Capt. John B. Davis and the *Tycoon* left Memphis at 6:10 P.M. on the fifteenth and arrived at the mouth of White River at 5:45 A.M. the following morning and at De Valls Bluff at 7:00 P.M. that evening. The *Tycoon* had made the trip in twenty-four hours and fifty minutes and passed the *Rowena* at the foot of President's Island. Captain Davis lost forty minutes discharging government freight and forty minutes at the mouth of the White, so the actual running time of the *Tycoon* was twenty-three hours and ten minutes, about three hours and thirty minutes faster than that of the *Rowena.* Not to be outdone, later that spring the *Rowena* bested the time set by the *Tycoon* by two hours and ten minutes to again claim the record.

The death of a popular White River steamboatman, Capt. J. M. Gilchrist, saddened the entire White River Valley on March 28, 1865. Captain Gilchrist of Jacksonport, but formerly of Memphis and Cincinnati, died of a spinal disease aboard the steamer *Sam Young* after an illness of only two or three days. The captain had once owned and commanded the *Monongahela Belle* and the *Interchange.* Steamboat flags along the White were flown at half-mast on March 29, reflecting the deep respect that fellow steamboatmen felt for Captain Gilchrist.

As the end of the Civil War approached, commerce was opened in the Upper White River and in the Black River to

The Rowena *was built in 1864. The boat was 180 x 35 x 6 feet and grossed 341 tons. Brought to the White River in 1865, it ran from Memphis to De Valls Bluff, Jacksonport, and Batesville, Arkansas. In October 1867, it was snagged and lost near Helena, Arkansas, on the Mississippi River.*

Courtesy of the University of Arkansas, Little Rock, Archives and Special Collections.

Pocahontas and above. Though still hampered by Federal restrictions, damage from guerrilla harassment was no longer a threat to the steamboats, permitting navigation to Batesville and to Buffalo City. To capitalize on the reopening of this once lucrative trade, Capt. David Gibson extended the regular trips of the *Rowena* to Batesville, with stops at Des Arc, Augusta, Jacksonport, and intermediate points. Since the area had long been without steamboat service, a lively trade was expected.

Although the steamboats could run unhampered to Batesville, the commerce of the area failed to meet the expectations of the captains. Trade was very limited and cotton not as plentiful as supposed. The long years of conflict had stripped the region, leaving most of the inhabitants destitute. Despite the lack of freight, though, there was much travel between Batesville and Memphis, and troop movements were especially heavy in July and August.

The end of fighting brought the return of several of the old familiar steamboat captains to the White. Among them was Capt. Morgan M. Bateman, who was paroled at Jacksonport on June 5 and within a few weeks was hired by Capt. Martin Walt as master of the *Cleona*.

The end of the war also brought the return of excursion parties, and the gracious hospitality of the steamboat captains provided the White River Valley inhabitants with an opportunity for gaiety almost forgotten during the long years of strife.

With the close of 1865, the long, bitter days of the country's struggle ended, and the first few months of peace were approached with caution. Although some troops were still stationed along the river, the steamboats were allowed to pass freely without molestation. As the reconstruction process slowly gained momentum, the people worked to rebuild their lives and regain their pre-war serenity and prosperity.

Steamboat Osage, *built at Castle Rock, Missouri, in 1864 for the Osage River trade, but entered the Memphis to Jacksonport commerce in late 1865. The* Osage *ran to Jacksonport until spring of 1866, returned in November 1869, and ran regularly from Augusta to Pocahontas, on Black River, until sold in July 1870 to the Memphis and Little Rock Railroad to run between Clarendon and DeValls Bluff. In April 1871, the boat ran from DeValls Bluff to Jacksonport for Railroad Packet Company Line, which folded in November 1871, and then the boat left White River.*

Photo courtesy of the Missouri Historical Society and the Printery, Clinton, Missouri, and the University of Arkansas, Little Rock, Archives and Special Collections.

STEAMBOATS 1866–1900

In the Reconstruction period following the Civil War, steamboat activity remained unrestricted in the White River, and an influx of steamers appeared there to replenish the shortages of materials and supplies caused by the bitter years of fighting and the resultant absence of commerce. Although many of the returning soldiers, both Union and Confederate, found their homes ruined, their businesses destroyed, and/or were without money or jobs, their ingenuity was soon manifested. Broken family ties were mended, defunct commercial enterprises were rejuvenated, and trade along the river increased. The entire region echoed with the whistles of a rapidly increasing number of steamboats.

Among the boats advertised in early 1866 were the St. Louis and White River packets *J. S. McCune,* Capt. James H. Duffer, master, and the *Albert Pearce,* Capt. J. F. Luker in charge. The St. Louis, De Valls Bluff, Des Arc, Jacksonport, and Little Red River Packet Company advertised the *Goldfinch,* Captain Gere in command, and the *Minnie,* commanded by Captain Shaw. Running in the Memphis, White, and Little Red River trade were the steamer *Lady,* Capt. J. P. Boughner commanding, and the *Justice,* with Capt. Abner Baird walking the hurricane deck. Also in the Memphis and White River trade were the *Commercial,* Capt. William J. (Billy) Ashford, master, and the *Harry Dean,* Capt. Morgan Bateman in charge. In March of 1866, the *Harry Dean,* a 235-ton sternwheeler, arrived at Jacksonport to transport a company of black troops to De Valls Bluff to be mustered out of the Union army.

Also mentioned in early 1866 was the *Osage,* described as a regular Memphis, White, and Little Red River packet. The *Osage,* a 147-ton side-wheeler, immediately drew compliments for its ability to carry large cargoes with efficiency. Built by its owner, Captain Lambert, who was also a ship's carpenter, it was initially utilized in the Osage River trade in Missouri, but the completion of the Pacific Railroad destroyed that market, and Captain Lambert brought his boat to the White River.

Also making an immediate bid for popularity was the steamer *J. S. McCune,* which entered the St. Louis and White River trade in June of 1866. Built for twenty-one thousand dollars at Brownsville, Pennsylvania, in July 1862, the 226-ton side-wheeler was originally named the *Brilliant.* It was sold to the federal government in August 1862 and ran as a tinclad until sold to Captains Espy and Duffer in August 1865, when it was renamed the *J. S. McCune.* The trim craft was 157 feet long, had a 31-foot beam, a 4.5-foot hold, and an elegantly furnished cabin.

After arriving at Jacksonport on Tuesday morning, March 27, 1866, Captain Duffer of the *J. S. McCune* extended a general invitation to all citizens for an excursion trip to Batesville. The word spread quickly and the captain's kind offer was accepted by fifty-three men and women who, after the war years of deprivation, eagerly anticipated an enjoyable trip. The group walked gaily up the stage plank as they waved goodbyes to those unfortunate friends who had to stay behind. At twelve o'clock, the last bell sounded and the boat pulled away from the Jacksonport wharf with one of the happiest groups of pleasure seekers ever to be witnessed. Following a delicious dinner, the tables were moved aside and the lively strains of music from the boat's band filled the air. Dancing continued during the entire trip with only an occasional intermission for additional treats. Upon arriving at Batesville, the genial Captain Duffer invited local residents to join the festivities, and a large number of the Batesville "lads and lassies" infused new life into the party aboard the steamer.[1] With the break of day, the Batesville participants departed, but the celebration was not over.

After pausing for breakfast, the dancing resumed and continued until the *J. S. McCune* again docked at Jacksonport. Almost overshadowed by the party was the announcement by Captain Duffer about his large cargo of freight for the various mercantile firms of Batesville and Jacksonport. The captain promised to run directly from St. Louis to Jacksonport, making the round trip every fifteen days, to afford direct shipments to merchants trading with St. Louis firms.

The *J. S. McCune* was not the only steamboat catering to the desires of the river towns for excursions. The *Jacksonport Herald* reported that the *Justice* arrived with a party of pleasure seekers from Grand Glaize, and farther down the river, the *Commercial* was entertaining the Des Arc citizens.

Cargo business was picking up in the White River, too. On April 7, 1866, the little steamboat *Justice* arrived at Batesville loaded to the guards with freight for E. R. McGuire and Son. The immense cargo was said to be the largest brought to the upper river port since the war. The *Justice* continued running from Memphis to Batesville and often above to Buffalo City.

Also entering the Memphis and White River trade during the first six months of 1866 was the very light draft *Petrolia,* a 100-ton stern-wheel steamboat dubbed as "capable of going through in double-quick time."[2] The steamboat became a regular in the White River trade.

As commerce continued to improve, more and more steamboats flocked to the White. Louisville and New Orleans packet owners bid for parts of the lucrative business. Capt. Pink Varable and associates of Louisville placed the steamers *Cora S.* and *Mercury* in the trade, and from New Orleans came the *Lady Franklin.* Captain Finkbine, commander of the *Lady Franklin,* vowed to run semi-monthly, providing travelers and shippers through passage to New Orleans.

Another addition to the White River trade was the rather colorful steamer *Cherokee,* Capt. W. W. Alexander, master, which arrived at Batesville in November of 1866 with a good load of freight. Owned by Captains Alexander and Bateman, who ran it to Batesville as often as the water permitted, the *Cherokee* took out 142 bales of cotton. Although the boat wasn't very large, it is doubtful it deserved the comment made by a Memphis editor who said: "The *Cherokee,* a canal boat with a stovepipe chimney and a tea kettle boiler, came in yesterday with a cargo comprising of ten bales of cotton and an empty whiskey jug. She is from one of the Arkansas Bayous. Our contemporaries were much disappointed at finding the whiskey jug empty. The *Cherokee* is awaiting the return of the *Robert E. Lee,* with which steamer she proposes to have a race on the down trip."[3]

As 1866 ended, the *J. S. McCune* and the *Agnes* were making regular trips from St. Louis to the White River, while the *Des Arc* and *Commercial* were on schedule from Memphis. The *Cora S.* and *Mercury* were serving the area from Louisville, and the *Lady Franklin, John D. Perry,* and *Harry Dean* were the regular packets from New Orleans. Serving the Upper White and Black Rivers regularly were the *Fairy Queen,* the *Zouave,* and the *J. R. Hoyle.*

Steamboating entered 1867 with the *Des Arc* continuing to receive praise from Des Arc citizens, who called it a model of perfection whose officers were of superior mold. Commander Ashford had been replaced by Capt. John D. Elliott, whose efficiency was lauded. Capt. J. Lee Finnie was in the office, while Major Green agreeably performed the duties of express agent. Not to be overlooked was the excellent table set in the main cabin by Shoemaker.

One of the disasters occurring in the White River during 1867 was the wreck of the Louisville packet *Mercury.* The 184-ton vessel was under the command of Capt. George Dickinson when it became lost during a storm. While steaming down the flood-covered Lower White, the pilot entered the cut-off to the Arkansas River by mistake. Realizing his error, he turned back, but just as the stern-wheeler was turning the bend, it struck a snag and quickly filled with water. Panic swept through the heavily loaded steamboat and about twenty persons lost their lives. The chaos was further heightened by the thrashing and braying of 250 mules which were dumped overboard when the boat careened. All the animals perished. Due to the flood conditions and the freezing weather, chances for escape were few. A large number of those passengers and crew who survived were badly frost-bitten from being in the cold water. As bales of cotton slid from the rolling *Mercury,* seven men swam to the floating bales where they sought safety. While gliding down the wind-swept river, they all lodged on the same drift, which provided a momentary haven from the swirling waters. Seemingly safe, at least from immediate drowning, four of the men were killed when a tree was blown down, striking the drift on which they were lodged.

Occasional altercations were always a part of life on the steamers and were dealt with swiftly by the captains. In 1867, the *Rowena* was in the service of the Memphis and White River Packet Company, running with the *Commercial.* The barkeeper and the night watchman of the *Rowena* "indulged in a game of fisticuffs" and were put ashore by a disgusted Captain Davis.[4] A few weeks later, as the *Rowena* arrived at Memphis with a light freight but a huge passenger list, two of the black employees quarreled and one cut his opponent across the abdomen, exposing his intestines. The seriously wounded man was sent to a hospital, but little hope was held for his recovery.

The keen competition among the steamboats in the White River was shown by the desire of each to bring out the first bale of new cotton each season. As an added inducement, various prizes were offered by the captains. In the 1867 season, Captain Ashford, of the *Commercial,* emerged victorious. The first bale, from a Clarendon planter, was obtained by giving a prize of two barrels of pork, one barrel of whiskey, and two barrels of meal, plus the market value of the cotton. The officers of the *Norman,* a Louisville steamer, offered more than Captain Ashford, but the Memphis influence was too strong, so the bale was placed aboard the *Commercial.*

Due to financial difficulties, the New Orleans and White River packet *John D. Perry* was sold by Captain Baird to Capt. Patrick

Henry Wheat, a veteran White River steamboatman. After a complete overhaul, the craft was in perfect repair and was described as one of the best cotton boats available. To further ensure its success, Captain Wheat staffed the *John D. Perry* with well-known, experienced officers. The highly-respected Capt. Morgan Bateman of Independence County was appointed master, and Capt. Wilmot Gibbes of Sulphur Rock was made head clerk. Pilots were Silas Daugherty and Henry Klange, residents of Jacksonport.

Captain Bateman created considerable excitement when he brought the *John D. Perry* to Jacksonport on its first trip of the new cotton season in August 1867. When the beautiful steamboat puffed into port, a large crowd was gathered to greet the popular captain and his crew. As the huge riverboat slowly landed, the air was filled with festive music provided by the local brass band. After the stage plank swung into place, the passengers came ashore in a holiday spirit. The gala activities left no doubt that the *John D. Perry* was the toast of Jacksonport. The local editor urged all planters to patronize the *John D. Perry* so that when the boat departed for New Orleans on Sunday morning, it would be "loaded to the guards with cotton. She deserves it! Let her have it!"[5]

Misfortune befell the popular steamer *Commercial* in October of 1867, when it became grounded at the head of Little Island, some forty-seven miles from the mouth of the White. After most of its freight was transferred to a lighter, the engines were started and the grounded vessel jerked free; but it plunged into a snag, knocking a hole in its side. The steamboat careened to one side, but luckily the water was not over the guards. By working quickly, the crew stopped the leak and pumped the water from the hull. Meanwhile, the *Rowena* came alongside and took the damaged freight from the crippled vessel. After removing the cargo from the lighter and the passengers from the *Commercial,* the *Rowena* left for Memphis with the *Commercial* limping behind.

Proving the old adage that misfortunes never come singly, disaster again struck the Davis packet line a few weeks later when, opposite Helena, the *Rowena* struck a snag and sank in eight feet of water. Although the passengers and crew were saved, the craft was a total lost. The boat was valued at thirty-two thousand dollars but was insured for only twenty thousand dollars. The mishap was caused by the wreck of the *General Brown,* which had sunk there about twenty-five years previously and had been turned over in the channel by high waters. Though the *Rowena* could not be saved, its furnishings were salvaged and safely packed in boxes.

The resiliency of Captain Davis was quickly manifested when, within a week, he had chartered the *Guidon* until a permanent replacement for the *Rowena* could be found. Staffed by the former officers and crew of the lost vessel, the *Guidon* was scheduled to leave Memphis for the White River each Tuesday.

Another fine steamboat fell prey to the hazards of navigation in 1867. On December 6, while en route from Jacksonport to New Orleans with 1,032 bales of cotton, ten tons of freight, and a few passengers, the *J. S. McCune* ran aground at Little Island. After the crew dislodged the boat, the journey was resumed, but fire broke out on the unfortunate steamer as it neared Prairie Landing. The flames quickly enveloped the entire vessel; however, by working quickly, the crew safely evacuated all the passengers. Unfortunately, the brave steward remained too long on the hapless craft and perished in the raging flames, but the officers and other crew members escaped safely. After burning to the water's edge, the hull sank. The owner valued the *J. S. McCune* at sixteen thousand dollars but carried only ten thousand dollars insurance.

Before the year ended, an additional steamboat met disaster. The steamer *Little Rock* sank near Clarendon. While ascending the White, the sturdy stern-wheeler struck a snag and soon filled with water. The boat was heavily laden with lime that, upon mixing with the water, formed slacked lime, creating significant heat. The vessel soon caught fire. The pilot immediately steered the boat to the shoreline before it sank. All of the passengers were picked up by the *Ozark,* the first boat to the scene following the accident.

With the arrival of 1868, Captain Davis made several changes in his packet line, including the introduction of the *Liberty No. 2* to replace the lost *Rowena.* The *Liberty No. 2* had cabin facilities for two hundred passengers and was elegantly furnished. The staterooms were large enough to accommodate six ladies, each "dressed with all the present duplex, elleptic extension, non-breakable, elite frill, with two Saratoga trunks each, and 42 band boxes." High praise was heaped upon the *Liberty No. 2,* its crew, and Captain Davis. The steamboat was proclaimed to be one of the fastest in the river. While Captain Davis stayed in Memphis to supervise his packet line, Capt. G. W. Brooks was placed in charge of the *Liberty No. 2,* with Capt. E. C. Morton as clerk and a popular young man named Milt Harry serving as his assistant. In mid-January of 1868, Captain Morton retired, and Harry was placed in charge of the office. Milt Harry went on to become quite a steamboatman, living up to his popularity and the people's expectations of him.

In late January of 1868, the route of the *F. W. Brooks* was changed from regular runs in the Little Red River to runs in the Black and Upper White trade. The larger boats had experienced difficulty running regularly above West Point, but, even so, the removal of the *F. W. Brooks* from the Little Red River left those people living in Searcy more than a little distressed. The dissatisfied owner of the *White County Weekly Record* commented: "This having but one steamer in our river per week is altogether out of the question. True, the creek is rather small, but none too much for the mammoth *Liberty* to show its dimensions at our landing. Being accustomed to semi-weekly, and at times tri-weekly and daily boats, we feel discontented, yes, fractious, when of that luxury we are deprived."[6]

The *Liberty No. 2* was, indeed, a bit large for the Little Red River, being 225 feet long with a 35-foot beam and powered by three boilers. An even larger steamboat made at least one trip up this tributary of the White in early April of 1868. When the *Commercial* was removed for repairs, the 414-ton side-wheeler *St. Patrick* arrived to take its place. After the *St. Patrick* returned to Memphis from its first voyage, the editor of the *Memphis Avalanche* reported: "The advent of the *St. Patrick* up White River astonished the natives, as it is the largest steamboat that ever attempted to go up Little Red, though she successfully made the turns in that crooked stream and came out without a scratch, which reflects credit upon her pilots, who are experienced in their profession."[7] (Perhaps the scribe had forgotten that the *St. Patrick* made trips up White River during the Civil War.)

The *St. Patrick*'s tenure on the Little Red River was short, for within days, the *Commercial* was repaired and returned to the trade. Upon the *Commercial*'s reentry, the *St. Patrick* departed for Louisville.

Although barely mentioned by the Memphis newspapers, and understandably so, the Louisville boats were making regular trips to White River and were, apparently, receiving a good share of the business. The *Tempest* touched at Memphis on March 12, 1868, en route to Louisville from White River; and the *Norman*, bound for the White, touched at the Mississippi River port on April 1 of that year. On April 4, the steamer *Tempest* was again on its way from White River to Louisville.

To combat the increasing threat of the Ohio River steamboats to the Memphis and White River Packet Company, Capt. John B. Davis left for Louisville to arrange for through bills of lading for freight over the Memphis and Louisville railroad. Through this action, he hoped to squeeze the Louisville packets from White River. While the move may have affected some commerce, it did not eliminate Louisville steamers in the White.

The publisher of the *Memphis Avalanche* hailed the attempt by Captain Davis. The low esteem that the citizens of Memphis had for the Louisville packets is clearly shown in this paragraph from the *Avalanche:* "The *Tempest* passed up for Louisville yesterday at an early hour. She put off ten bales of cotton and had three bales for Louisville, but she was well loaded with cord wood. It is expected that our neighbor on the Ohio will soon cultivate a large trade with the people along White River in the latter article. It will be more acceptable to the Louisvillians than the rifle whiskey that they ship to the residents of Arkansas."[8]

As spring approached, the stern-wheel steamboat *Natoma* from Pittsburgh arrived in Memphis and left a short time later for the White River and a journey up the Black River. *Natoma* had on board a party of Pennsylvanians who were there to explore "the wilds of Arkansas," a trip that was long remembered by all those aboard. The *Natoma* remained in the White River trade for several years.

In preparation for the fall business, Captain Davis of the Memphis and White River Packet Company purchased the superb side-wheel passenger packet *Mayflower*. Built for forty thousand dollars in 1867, it was a new boat with all the latest improvements. Captain Davis also bought the *F. W. Brooks* for four thousand dollars and, after a complete renovation, planned to run it in the Upper White and Black River trade in conjunction with his large steamers.

On August 28, 1868, the elegant *Mayflower* left Memphis for its first trip up White River. A Memphis reporter wrote that people along the river would see one of the finest steamers that ever floated the bosom of the old White. He felt the steamboat was the best and most elegantly furnished in the trade.

The Memphis and White River Packet Company now had steamboats leaving Memphis for Jacksonport every Tuesday, Thursday, and Saturday afternoon at five o'clock. The steamers connected with the Little Rock railroad at De Valls Bluff and the *F. W. Brooks* at Jacksonport. The line carried c.o.d. shipments without charge for collection, thereby underbidding other lines for cargo.

The *Mayflower* had an unusual mishap in October of 1868. The elegant steamer backed into an obstacle which tore away part of its afterguard and dropped a few head of cattle overboard. For a while, the deckhands had to act as cowboys while they rounded up the swimming cattle. After all of the animals were safely retrieved, Captain Ashford proceeded downriver.

Disaster struck another of the Memphis and White River packets when the little *F. W. Brooks* sank on October 18. It was a total loss to Captain Davis's line. A former Arkansas River boat, the *Argos*, replaced the *F. W. Brooks*. Capt. W. H. Sebree had purchased the craft at an auction for the bargain price of $1,125. Just four months previously, the boat was priced at $3,500. In November of 1868, Captain Elliott purchased one-fourth interest in the *Argos* for $600, and Captain Sebree left for Jacksonport to run the vessel in the Upper White tributaries in conjunction with the Davis steamboats.

Always catering to the wishes of his patrons, the enterprising Captain Davis initiated another change in White River steamboat services when he announced a modification in dining service aboard his steamers. The development was announced in the *Memphis Daily Appeal* on November 28, 1868: "Another improvement is about to be inaugurated upon the Memphis and White River packets. We allude to the restaurant style of living. This has been tried effectively upon our St. Louis packets and has given entire satisfaction. It will also be a success in the White River line. No people in the South travel as much as those who live along White River and any saving of expense is an object during the previously hard times. The *Mayflower* is now being changed for the new order of things, and the *Commercial* and *Liberty* will soon do likewise."

The newspaper failed to specify just how the passengers received a savings. Perhaps they could travel a little cheaper by foregoing a few meals. Or, possibly, travelers who elected to order from a menu were given a cheaper fare. The line planned to have the restaurant system of dining established by December 22.

The end of 1868 saw several steamboats vying for the White River trade. Included in the struggle during this difficult Reconstruction period were the Memphis and White River packets *Mayflower, Liberty No. 2, Commercial,* and *Des Arc;* the New Orleans steamer *John D. Perry;* the St. Louis packet *Laura;* and the Louisville vessels *Argonaut, Tempest,* and *Norman*. Among the smaller steamers serving the Upper White and the Black River and connecting with the larger steamboats at Augusta and Jacksonport were the *Argos, Fairy Queen,* and *R. P. Converse*.

Commerce in the White River in the aftermath of the Civil War did not pick up as quickly as steamboatmen there hoped. In 1869, faced with declining revenues, Capt. John B. Davis and the owners of the Memphis and White River Packet Company reached a compromise with an independent steamboatman, Capt. John D. Elliott, whereby each agreed to withdraw one steamer. Under the new arrangement, Captain Elliott's *Des Arc* was to leave Memphis on Tuesdays and Davis's *Mayflower* on Saturdays, each carrying the mail. Both steamboats connected with the Little Rock train at De Valls Bluff and the upper river packets at Augusta and Jacksonport. The Davis vessels *Liberty No. 2* and *Commercial* were laid up pending new business arrangements. In late January, Captain Davis sold the *Mayflower* to Phelps, McCullough, and Company of New Orleans, and the elegant steamer was placed in the Red River trade. Captain Davis then reactivated the *Liberty No. 2* in White River, but found the competition too tough and, in early June of 1869, dissolved his Memphis and White River Packet Line. His mail contract and all other interests in the White River trade were sold to Capt. John D. Adams, superintendent of the Memphis and Arkansas River Packet Company. The action marked the reestablishment of another pre–Civil War steamboatman in the White River.

Captain Adams had emerged penniless from the war, but with the backing of his old friends, the steamboat builder James Rees and Thompson Dean, Captain Adams had purchased several steamboats and had reentered the Arkansas River trade. In November 1868, the Memphis and Arkansas River Packet Company had been formed. After the Davis purchase in 1869, the company established a White River branch line. Trying to monopolize the trade, Captain Adams quickly purchased one-half interest in the steamer *Des Arc,* which was still being run by the Elliott Independent Line.

While the Memphis packets struggled, the New Orleans steamer *John D. Perry* was having a banner season. On January 2, 1869, the *North Arkansas Times* of Batesville reported: "The *John D. Perry*, the large and handsome New Orleans steamer under the command of her gallant owner, Pat Wheat, arrived on Thursday morning. She took a trip upriver for cotton and returned last night. No more gallant a craft runs than the *Perry,* or more accomplished steamboatman than Capt. Wheat runs White River, and we are glad to learn that the boat is doing a flourishing business. The *Perry* is making regular trips in the New Orleans and White River trade and is deserving of the patronage of all our merchants and shippers."

The *Perry* returned again to Batesville later in the month, heavily loaded with freight. It continued in the trade until May 6, 1869, when disaster befell the splendid vessel. After arriving at De Valls Bluff, Captain Wheat docked the *John D. Perry* and secured it for the night. The boat was supposedly safe from all river hazards, but the dreaded fire alarm was sounded by the night watchman about midnight. Flames of unknown origin were discovered in the ladies' cabin and quickly enveloped the boat. Though the crew fought the fire bravely, their efforts were futile, and the doomed steamboat was destroyed. After burning, the hull sank and broke into two pieces. A saddened Captain Wheat watched the water cover the remains of his cherished vessel as the magnificent *John D. Perry,* once the pride of Jacksonport, assumed its niche in the annals of White River history. The misfortune was a severe loss to Captain Wheat's business.

Capt. John D. Adams, one of Arkansas's steamboat tycoons. He had mail contracts on the White and Arkansas Rivers in the 1850s. After the Civil War, he organized the Memphis and Arkansas River Packet Company, which put several fine steamers in the Arkansas and White Rivers. Captain Adams later branched out to the Mississippi, where his company ran many superb boats. The Kate Adams 1, 2, *and* 3 *were named after his wife.*

Courtesy of the University of Arkansas, Little Rock, Archives and Special Collections.

Favorable boating conditions during the spring of 1869 permitted several steamboats to ascend the White to Batesville and above. In mid-May, among the boats appearing at the Batesville landing was the *Laura,* a steamer belonging to Capt. Morgan M. Bateman. The *Laura* had undergone extensive repairs in Memphis in January of 1869, as the boilers were "out of kilter and her chimneys had the Grecian bend in the worst way," according to the *Memphis Daily Appeal.*[9] Falling victim to the trade war existing in the White River, the *Laura* was later sold by a U.S. marshall for $2,510. Captain Bateman's debts to the crew alone amounted to about $1,700. In referring to the sale, a local scribe wrote that the boat was as cheap as a Memphis alderman. Capt. George Cheek, purchaser of the *Laura,* planned to repair the boat and put it in the ferry trade.

Also appearing in the White during 1869 was the beautiful

Legal Tender, *built in 1867 at New Albany, Indiana. This beautiful boat was 200 x 33.5 x 5.5 feet and displaced 539 gross tons. In early 1869, Capt. John D. Elliott and associates purchased it for the Memphis and White River trade for twenty thousand dollars, and it ran regularly from Memphis to Jacksonport, Arkansas, for several years.* Legal Tender *was a big favorite with the shippers. In the cotton season of 1872, it made twenty-four trips carrying out 11,190 bales of cotton. This compared to 7,127 bales on twenty-two trips by the rival* R. P. Walt. *The boat was sold in early 1876 to Capts. Ed Nowland and John N. Harbin of the Memphis and Arkansas River Packet Company. It ran from Memphis to Little Rock and Pine Bluff until April 15, 1876, when it struck a snag some forty miles below Pine Bluff and sank, a total loss.*

Courtesy of the University of Arkansas, Little Rock, Archives and Special Collections.

side-wheeler *Legal Tender.* Capt. John D. Elliott and associates had purchased the superb steamer for twenty thousand dollars. The spacious boat displaced 539 tons and was among the largest in the White.

A dramatic contrast in size to the *Legal Tender* was the little thirty-three-ton *Malta,* which also entered the White River trade in 1869. A stern-wheeler with one engine, the steamboat headed for the Upper White "to make a subsistence for her officers and crew, consisting of two men." The *Malta* ran in the Black River from Pocahontas, Arkansas, to Poplar Bluff, Missouri, and as far as it could go up the Current River in Missouri. In 1870, it was purchased for two thousand dollars by Levi Hecht, a Pocahontas merchant. Shortly thereafter, the boat descended the river with a load of corn and bacon products from the Current River farmers. During the season, the *Malta* plied the Current to Doniphan, Missouri, sometimes with only five inches of water on the shoaliest bars. Mentioned frequently by newsmen, the little vessel made the news again when its colorful owner challenged the fleet steamer *Robert E. Lee* to a race. Hecht suggested that the steamboats race from Pocahontas to Poplar Bluff, a distance of two hundred miles, for fifty thousand dollars. The *Arkansas Gazette* editor was amused by the challenge and wrote, "This is a chance for betting men! Bring on your steamboats!"[10] The race had no chance to occur, for the little *Malta* sank on September 20, 1870, in the Current River, some thirteen miles above Doniphan.

Among the steamboatmen building new vessels for the White River in 1869 was Capt. Charles W. Coles. Christened the *Batesville,* the steamer was built in Pittsburgh and was designed expressly for the Black River trade. Captain Coles traveled to Pittsburgh to supervise its construction. The *Batesville* was double decked and had a hull 120 feet long, with a 26-foot beam and a 4.25-foot hold. Supplied with lever engines of 3.5-foot stroke, the boat contained two double flue boilers, 18 feet long and 34 inches in diameter. Other equipment included a doctor engine

Capt. Charles W. Coles, steamboat captain and agent for packet lines with regular runs between Jacksonport and St. Louis, Memphis, and New Orleans, with the steamers John D. Perry, Agnes, Liberty 2, Mayflower, *and the U.S. mail packet* Commercial.

Courtesy of the University of Arkansas, Little Rock, Archives and Special Collections.

and a double-geared steam capstan. Captain Coles was the master of the *Batesville,* while Capt. Albert Smith, brother-in-law of Coles, served as its clerk. The Batesville publisher stated that the people felt honored at having another steamboat named after their town, and a "high old time could be looked for when she arrived."

The staunch *Commercial* was again put into service in the White River in 1869, when Capt. John B. Davis formed the Merchants and Planters Independent White River Mail Line. Captain Davis stated that his new line would serve Augusta, Searcy, West Point, De Valls Bluff, Clarendon, Indian Bay, and all intermediate landings. His passenger rate from Memphis to Clarendon and points below was $8.00; to De Valls Bluff, $10.00; to Little Rock, $15.00; to Des Arc, $11.00; and to Augusta, West Point, and Searcy, $12.00. The freight charge for cotton per bale to Memphis was $1.25, and to New Orleans, $2.25. Pound freight to Des Arc and below was $.30 per one hundred pounds, with rates to West Point, Searcy, and Augusta at $.35 per one hundred pounds. Dry barrel rates to the above were $.35 and $.50 per barrel, respectively, with wet barrels (whiskey, pork, etc.) costing $1.00 and $2.00, respectively.

The popular *Commercial* thrived in the trade and the *Memphis Daily Appeal* reported: "The Old Reliable is again on the warpath. Today she departs for her ancient hunting grounds on White River and will make the woods along the stream echo with her well-known war-hoop. Capt. John B. Davis and the *Commercial* are familiar names, not only to a reporter, but to the denizens along the most beautiful river in the South. She connects with trains for White, and makes all way landings. Jimmy Thompson and Charley Sharpe are her well-known clerks."[11]

Early November of 1869 brought a new steamboat to the White, as well as the return of another old friend. The *Mary Boyd,* Capt. Reuben Haynes, master, was a Memphis and Arkansas River packet that ran intermittently in both the Arkansas and the White. The *Mary Boyd* was described by a Memphis reporter as "the most complete of her class afloat."[12] Its cabins were elegantly embellished and furnished with the latest style of furniture. The carpets were rich and the tableware was pure china and silver. Its staterooms were large and fitted with taste, the beds all on springs. The steamer was 158 feet long, with a 33-foot beam and a 4.5-foot hold. The vessel had three boilers, each 20 feet long and 18 inches in diameter.

The old favorite returning to the White in 1869 was the *Liberty No. 2,* now commanded by Capt. Patrick H. Wheat, who had been the owner of the burned *John D. Perry.* The *Liberty No. 2* had undergone repairs, including a new hull, costing over ten thousand dollars. The steamer became a regular mail packet for the Merchants and Planters Independent White River Mail Line.

White River became dangerously low in November of 1869, making navigation extremely difficult. The *Liberty No. 2* ran aground on November 17 at Little Island, and the next day the new *Mary Boyd* became lodged at Scrub Grass Bar, eighteen miles above the mouth of the river. The large *Natoma* plied only between Memphis and the mouth of the White during this period, declining to enter the White because of the low stage of the water.

The *Natoma* and Capt. W. J. Ashford, master, suffered some legal problems during the summer of 1869. In July, one of the passengers boarding the *Natoma* at Little Rock on the Arkansas River was a Reverend White and his wife. Reverend White was a black member of the Arkansas legislature from Helena. Upon boarding, Reverend White asked for a berth for his wife in the ladies' cabin, but his request was refused. The representative was told that there was a place below for "colored" ladies of distinction, but that no Negro on earth could have a room in the cabin of the *Natoma* while he commanded. Reverend White replied that he had helped to pass the public carrier law in the legislature especially for the benefit of Captain Ashford, since the captain had refused White cabin passage in 1865.[13] Representative White went on to sue Captain Ashford for ten thousand dollars. Settlement of the case is unsure, but indications are that White lost the suit.

The question of accommodations for black passengers was not settled quickly, and Reverend White seems to have been one of the foremost crusaders for equality. The *Arkansas Gazette* of January 21, 1870, commented about another suit Reverend White filed for five thousand dollars against the steamer *Liberty No. 2* because he was forced to eat in the pantry instead of at the table with white passengers. In reporting the case, the *Arkansas Gazette* commented that it certainly felt White was entitled to damages since, under the Fifteenth Amendment, no white person had the right to refuse to eat, drink, or sleep with a Negro, regardless of sex or condition. The newspaper also commented that the confrontation would "undoubtedly cause trouble."

The *Arkansas Gazette* of May 28, 1878, reported a decision in the U.S. Court at Pittsburgh concerning accommodations for black passengers aboard steamboats. The trial evidently resulted in the disagreement of two juries, after which Judge Ketcham "laid down the law in such plain manner that the steamboatmen need not err." The judge stated that "colored" passengers on steamboats were entitled to the same treatment as white people, but that there was no need for them to eat at the same table or sleep in the same stateroom if they were provided with facilities of equal value in a space apart from the accommodations provided for white people. A steamboat captain, said the judge, has the right to make the rules and regulations for the management of his own boat. With such "equal treatment," the *Gazette* writer felt "all trouble and dissatisfaction could be avoided" as the "duty of each party is set forth."

Steamboats regularly traversing the Upper White and Black Rivers during 1869 were the *Fairy Queen,* the *Osage,* and the *Argos.* The *Argos* made scheduled trips from Jacksonport to Batesville, Buffalo City, and Talbert's Ferry. The new steamer *Batesville,* Capt. Charles Coles, master, also made spasmodic trips to the upper region.

With the advent of 1870 came the arrival of a spectacular new White River steamboat belonging to the Memphis and Arkansas River Packet Company. The *R. P. Walt* arrived in Memphis on January 20, 1870, and created quite a stir. A Memphis reporter described the *R. P. Walt* and its arrival in the port:

> The new steamer *R. P. Walt* made her appearance at our landing yesterday forenoon . . . a handsome coalition was spread among her capacious cabins, and a number of prominent citizens gathered around the festive board to enjoy it. Wine was distributed freely, and many toasts were drank to the success of the new vessel as well as her namesake. The *Walt* is really a handsome steamer . . . A magnificent three-square grand piano, costing $800, graces her ladies salon. Her ware is pure silver and china, and was made expressly for the boat. Her hull, which is 202 feet long, 34½ feet beam, and with a depth of 5½ feet, is constructed

The R. P. Walt *was a truly elegant steamer built by the Memphis and Arkansas River Packet Company for their White River Line. Capt. John D. Adams was president of the company. The* R. P. Walt *was 202 x 34.5 x 6 feet and had four boilers. Its forty-three staterooms were lavishly furnished, but the ten set aside for the women were the most beautiful. The cabin contained sofas and love seats, and an imported piano. This sleek steamer arrived at Memphis on January 20, 1870. Prior to its maiden voyage in White River, a lavish party was held in its capacious cabins, where wine flowed freely for the many prominent citizens attending. After the public reception, the* R. P. Walt *departed for White River. Receptions were held at every town and landing along the river as far as Batesville. Capt. Morgan Magness Batesman was captain of this boat when he died. The steamer was destroyed in an ice jam at Memphis in December 1872.*

Courtesy of the University of Arkansas, Little Rock, Archives and Special Collections.

> of the very best material and is staunch as any steamer afloat. Her machinery, all new, comprises a battery of 4 boilers, 38 inches diameter and 22 feet long, the cylinders being 19 inches in diameter, with 7 feet length of stroke, working a pair of water wheels 28 feet in diameter, with 10 feet length of bucket. She has a capacity for 700 tons, and trims on 27 inches of water light, with water in her boilers and fuel aboard.[14]

The crew of the *R. P. Walt* included Capt. Adriance Storm, commander; C. G. Smither, William Willis, and E. W. Walworth, clerks; Billy and Jim Kinman, pilots; and table caterer, Garrett. The handsomely arranged bar was owned by Dan Cunningham and Joe Welter.

Capt. Donald Wright of the *Waterways Journal* of St. Louis gave these additional details about the elaborate *R. P. Walt* when he published a picture of it in 1959:

> Hundreds saw her 43 staterooms lavishly furnished, but the most beautiful of all were the 10 staterooms set aside for women. Each was fitted like a room in a fine hotel. Most of their furnishings were imported. The cabin floor was covered with fine carpets and the one in the ladies cabin was finer than ever seen on a Memphis packet. There the visitors saw an imported French piano, with deep upholstered chairs, sofas and love seats. The cabin was separated from the main one by long silk portieres. The piano was a gift from R. P. Walt for whom the steamer was named.
>
> On top of the *Walt's* pilothouse was a bale of cotton made of some sort of metal that glittered like gold.[15]

After the public reception, the *R. P. Walt* was loaded with freight, and the following morning the magnificent steamer departed on its maiden trip up White River. Receptions were held at each landing where it stopped. Fortunately, the White was at a stage high enough for the large steamboat to travel as far as Batesville, 300.9 miles above the mouth of the river. The *R. P. Walt* gained a reputation for being the best low-water boat to ever ply the White River when, in 1870, it easily carried two hundred tons of freight on three feet of water over Bland's Bar below Augusta.

The beginning of this new decade found the well-liked Milt Harry now serving as master of a steamboat. The *Fairy Queen,* which had undergone repairs at the Memphis docks, resumed its service in White River in February 1870, under the command of Captain Harry. The popularity of the little steamer and its able master is reflected in this item from the *Memphis Daily Appeal:*

> The gay and dashing *Fairy Queen,* the pride of Black River and the handsomest fairy ever seen along the banks of old White, is now at the landing and leaves today for De Valls Bluff, Augusta, Jacksonport, Pocahontas and all landings on Little Red and Black rivers. She is handsome as a bride, gay as a lark, stylish as a maiden with a Grecian band and Japanese switch; and take her all in all, she is a perfect love of a packet. We won't attempt a description, but let her astonish her old friends into a fit of ecstasy without premonition. Capt. Milt Harry, her popular master, may well feel proud of his beautiful steamer."[16]

Death once again struck to thin the ranks of the veteran White River steamboat captains when Capt. Morgan Magness Bateman died on the morning of April 23, 1870, after a short illness. At the onset of his illness, he was master of the beautiful *R. P. Walt.* Captain Bateman was a pioneer steamboatman and had built and commanded some of the best boats in the White. He was well-known throughout Arkansas, having operated steamboats on both the White and Arkansas Rivers. He was described as a quiet, unobtrusive, and peaceful citizen who was loved and respected by all who knew him. Boats in the area displayed their flags at half-mast upon announcement of his death.

Life on the White went on. Crews changed, boats were bought and sold, steamboats left the river and new ones appeared, but the industry remained busy, some individuals faring better than others. On March 11, 1870, the large *Seminole* landed at New Orleans with a cargo of 360,000 pounds of bulk pork of remarkably fine quality from the White River Valley. The cargo was bought immediately, causing a *Picayune* reporter to note that the planters on White River had turned their attention to raising meats as well as cotton. He predicted that they would find it quite profitable.

One of the most impressive vessels entering the White River trade in 1870 was the *Pat Cleburne,* a steamboat that could accommodate 124 passengers. As travelers entered the main cabin on the steamer, they walked on carpet costing ten dollars per yard and were surrounded by beautifully upholstered furniture. The cabin featured a two thousand dollar solid-silver water service consisting of urn, tray, and goblets that were engraved with the boat's name. Another highlight of the room was a seven octave DeCamp piano for the entertainment of the passengers. In the ladies' cabin, the furniture was of rosewood, trimmed with satin damask. The gentlemen's cabin contained thirty staterooms, and the ladies' cabin, fourteen, including four bridal chambers. Mattresses in the cabins were "Jenny Lind" spring mattresses. In the rear of the ladies' cabin was a recess where "moonlight and flowers and the fickle goddess of love" were supposed to reign. From this spot, a stairway led down to the nursery, also handsomely furnished, which contained berths and staterooms for sixteen people. The chambermaid's room was located here also, as were the ladies' closets and stationary marble washstands with hot and cold water pipes leading to them. Similar to all first-class side-wheel steamers, the barber shop was located on the starboard guard. The larboard guard was the location of a large pantry. The texas deck contained the captain's room, the officers' hall, ten staterooms for officers, and a cabin for "colored people." This cabin accommodated thirty passengers with berths and staterooms and could "comfortably stow away an equal number in cots." The black passengers were also served meals here in the same manner as in the main cabin below.[17]

Officers on the *Pat Cleburne* on its first trip up White River were Reese Pritchard, master; John Harbin, first clerk; Emmett Strange, second clerk; Jim Nichols and Isaiah Hamilton, pilots; Pate Waggoner and Charles Renford, engineers; Walter McDonald, first mate; and Garrett Sullivan, steward.

Steamboat Pat Cleburne. *Built by Capt. John D. Adams of the Memphis and Arkansas River Packet Company for service in White River, it was 192.25 feet long, 33 feet wide, had a 5.5-foot hold, and was 13.5 feet between decks. Freight capacity was five hundred tons or two thousand bales of cotton. The steamer contained thirty staterooms for men and fourteen for ladies, with ten in the texas for the crew, and a cabin for black passengers. After a few trips in White River, it was placed in the Arkansas and on April 17, 1870, was voted the most popular boat in both rivers. The vessel returned to the White River trade in late 1872, running until early 1873, when it was sold to the Lee Line.*

Courtesy of the University of Arkansas, Little Rock, Archives and Special Collections.

After only a few trips in the White in 1870, the *Pat Cleburne* was placed in the Arkansas River trade. The steamboat was switched between the White and the Arkansas throughout most of its career. In 1871, it was voted the most popular steamboat in the Arkansas and White Rivers in a contest conducted at the Women's Episcopal Fair at Little Rock. On April 17, 1871, the ladies presented a beautiful silk flag to Captain Pritchard in an impressive ceremony aboard the boat. A large crowd assembled in the main cabin for the presentation. The banner was made of heavy silk bordered with fancy fringe and featured alternate red and white stripes with a blue ground in the left corner on which was painted the Arkansas coat of arms and the words "regnant populi." Fay Hempstead, a Little Rock historian, made the presentation for the ladies, after which, several toasts were drunk to the *Pat Cleburne* and its gallant crew. Following the ceremony, the guests moved to the landing and watched the lovely steamer back out and steam upriver with its new flag waving at the masthead. It then turned around and came racing back with black smoke streaming from its twin chimneys, colors flying, crew singing, and a general waving of handkerchiefs to those on the riverbank. This graceful departure at Little Rock was, perhaps, the *Pat Cleburne*'s finest moment and the peak of its popularity.

As previously mentioned, reliable pilots for the steamboats were always in great demand, particularly those experienced in and knowledgeable of the White. In 1870, lack of pilot familiarity with the river caused the packets from Louisville several problems. Regular White River pilots, realizing the plight of these boats, began asking ten dollars per day for transit tripping. The wages for pilots on the regular packets ranged from $150 to $175 per month, but the Arkansas River pilots in 1870 drew $200 monthly. To meet the threat of the higher wages, thereby keeping their pilots, the White River boat owners advanced their pilot wages to $250 per month. Some of the more experienced were even paid up to $600.

In late November of 1870, another of the old White River steamboat captains succumbed. Capt. Samuel Taylor, described as the oldest steamboatman on the river, died at his home in Des Arc. Captain Taylor commanded many Memphis and New Orleans boats, including the *Julia Dean* and the *Crescent,* which he made into a floating hotel and wharf boat at Jacksonport before the Civil War.

By the end of 1870, wild game again became a part of the freight from the White River. When the *Legal Tender* arrived in Memphis in late November, it had sixty deer and ten saddles of venison hanging on its hurricane deck. The *R. P. Walt* arrived a short time later and a reporter described its load:

> In addition to the huge load of cotton brought from White River by the *R. P. Walt* yesterday, she had an immense lot of all kinds of game, comprising every known variety that inhabits the wilds of Arkansas. The boat's boiler deck was artistically garnished with alternate strings of quail, ducks, and geese, while countless numbers of deer, bear, oppossums and other wild varmits were hung thick and close under the roof of the boiler. It was said, also, that several slaughtered bear, coons, ground hogs and alligators were chuked in among the cotton bales by the mate to keep the pile straight and level. Every game wagon in town was busy several hours distributing these slaughtered, bleeding hecatombs of animals made up from the denizens of the swamps by the huntsmen of Arkansas.[18]

Within the first two weeks of 1871, misfortune struck the Black River mail line of Capt. Milt Harry. While on an upriver trip, his *Petrolia No. 2* struck a snag at Bulpissle Point, one mile from Blakely's woodyard and fifteen miles below Pocahontas. The vessel went down almost immediately. As the boat was sinking, several of the deckhands loaded some of the cargo into a yawl and left. Sid Daer, the second engineer, followed the crewmen and ordered them to return their plunder, but his demand was disregarded. To prevent their escape, he fired a load of buckshot, striking one of the men in the arms and legs, and the erstwhile deckhands returned the yawl to the sunken steamboat. The man's wounds were dressed and he was taken to Jacksonport for medical attention, but his condition gradually worsened and he died. The engineer was detained for a hearing. The cargo from the *Petrolia No. 2* was recovered, but a large rise in the river completely destroyed the boat.

Business along the White boomed in early 1871, with most of the steamboats finding profitable cargoes. In early February, the *Seminole* steamed into New Orleans with 1,823 bales of White River cotton, carried at a cost of $3.00 per bale. Shortly thereafter, the rate advanced to $3.50 from Jacksonport, and to $3.50 or $4.00 per bale from the Upper White and Black Rivers. The *Jennie Howell,* a new entry into the New Orleans and White River trade, left Jacksonport carrying nearly 2,000 bales at the advanced rate.

Following one trip, Captain Coles of the *Batesville* stated that there was plenty of cotton along the banks and the owners were anxious to ship to market. The unlucky *Batesville* continued to be plagued with accidents, however. When it arrived at Memphis from Black River on March 3, 1871, its chimneys had to be repaired because they had been knocked down after running under an overhanging tree. Despite such problems, Captain Coles managed to obtain good cargoes and, later in March, took the *Batesville* to Buffalo City to pick up 475 bales of cotton which he reshipped at Jacksonport. He then departed for Pocahontas on the Black River to obtain 405 bales from that area.

Spring of 1871 brought a sad moment when the popular old *Des Arc* was dismantled so that its machinery could be used in a new steamer. The career of the *Des Arc* had been a long, successful one, and it had proven a faithful servant for its various owners. Although nearly twelve years old, the *Des Arc* had never experienced a serious accident except when it burned at De Valls Bluff. The boat's construction was begun in 1860 at Paducah by Capt. A. L. Davis, who failed to complete it, but Capt. Hicks King finished the job. Almost destroyed by the fire at De Valls Bluff during the Civil War, the wreck lay at the port until 1864 when it was taken to St. Louis by Peter Kehos and Dan Able and rebuilt at a cost of nearly fifty thousand dollars. The machinery of the *W. L. Ewing* was placed in the *Des Arc* at that time. The *Des Arc* prospered in the Vicksburg trade until sold in 1866 to Capts. Martin Walt and R. P. Walt for forty thousand dollars worth of steamboat stock. After making money for months for the Walts, it was sold for thirty thousand dollars to the Elliotts, the owners at the time of its dismantlement. It was especially successful in the White River trade, and few steamers were so faithful for so long.

As the *Des Arc* faded from the scene, the unpredictable Capt. John B. Davis bounced back into steamboating in the White River. Operating the steamers *Osage* and *Sally V* as his line of packets between Jacksonport and De Valls Bluff, he attempted to establish a new era in White River steamboating. With the proposed schedule of his vessels, Captain Davis would enable travelers to go from Memphis to Jacksonport in about twenty-four hours. The *Osage* left Memphis under the command of Captain Davis as the pioneer packet in the new venture. It was to make three weekly trips, starting from De Valls Bluff each Monday, Wednesday, and Friday. As soon as business justified, the *Sally V* was to be added, giving the region a daily line of communication with Memphis. From his long years of operating in the White River, Captain Davis was well-known to the business community and citizens, so his latest business venture was forecast to be successful. The *Sally V* had Capt. James Rice as commander, with Charles Sharpe as clerk. Charles Smithers served as clerk of the *Osage*.

Both the *Sally V* and the *Osage* were making trips by July 1 of 1871. Mail was delivered to all points between De Valls Bluff and Augusta five times per week, to Jacksonport three times weekly, up the Little Red River to the Searcy landing twice each week, and from De Valls Bluff to the mouth of the White twice each week. Captain Davis's motto was "Rapidity and Regularity."[19] Unfortunately, by fall the competition once again forced Captain Davis from the White.

Capt. Albert G. Cravens, who had suffered the loss of his keelboat *John F. Allen,* was now serving as pilot of the steamboat *Argos* when the craft made a trip to Buffalo City in June of 1871. One of the roustabouts on the *Argos* was shot and badly wounded on that trip in the Upper White. The *Argos* became one of the casualties of the competition in the river during 1871. The staunch little

The steamboat Jennie Howell, *built for Capt. Pat H. Wheat for the New Orleans, White, and Arkansas River trade. In early 1871, the boat left Jacksonport with nearly two thousand bales of cotton. In October 1872, Capt. William J. (Billy) Ashford obtained the steamer and started the White River Accommodation Line from Jacksonport to Memphis. It was damaged near Helena in December 1872 but was raised and was in service on the Arkansas River in January of 1873.*

From the Downs Collection, courtesy of the University of Arkansas, Little Rock, Archives and Special Collections.

steamer was owned by Thomas Cox until his death, when it was sold at public auction at Batesville by U.S. marshall R. S. Bates for the paltry sum of $525. Reportedly purchased by a man from Little Rock, the *Argos* sank at the mouth of Poke Bayou at Batesville and was not raised.

Commerce in the White continued to improve during all of 1871, with an increasing number of steamboats running in the river. During the cotton season that year, the *Legal Tender* and the *R. P. Walt,* alone, carried out over sixty thousand bales of cotton from the White River Valley.

An elegant new steamer, the *Emma C. Elliott,* made its appearance in the White in January of 1872. Built by Captain Elliott to compete with the fine packets of the Adams line, the steamboat was named after one of his daughters. The beautiful side-wheeler ranked among the most ornate on the western rivers and was truly a palatial steamboat. Constructed at a cost of sixty thousand dollars, the boat was a marvel everywhere it docked. It was furnished in the most elegant manner and had a piano that was imported from France. Old rivermen later said that the *Emma C. Elliott* had one of the most beautiful whistles and bells of any packet. As you may remember from earlier text, the bell of the steamer was cast at Louisville, and Captain Elliott supposedly threw one thousand silver dollars into the pot, giving the bell a beautiful mellow tone and making it the finest of any steamboat on the Mississippi. The largest in the White River at the time, the steamboat was 215 feet long, had a 38-foot beam, a 7-foot hold, and a capacity of nine hundred tons.

Perhaps Captain Adams thought he could not compete with the Elliotts, as the *Arkansas Gazette* announced on January 12, 1872, that the Memphis and Arkansas River Packet Company had withdrawn from the trade and sold the *R. P. Walt* to the Elliotts. The *Emma C. Elliott* proved too big for the White, and after only a few trips, Captain Elliott replaced it with the *R. P. Walt* and withdrew it from the White River trade.

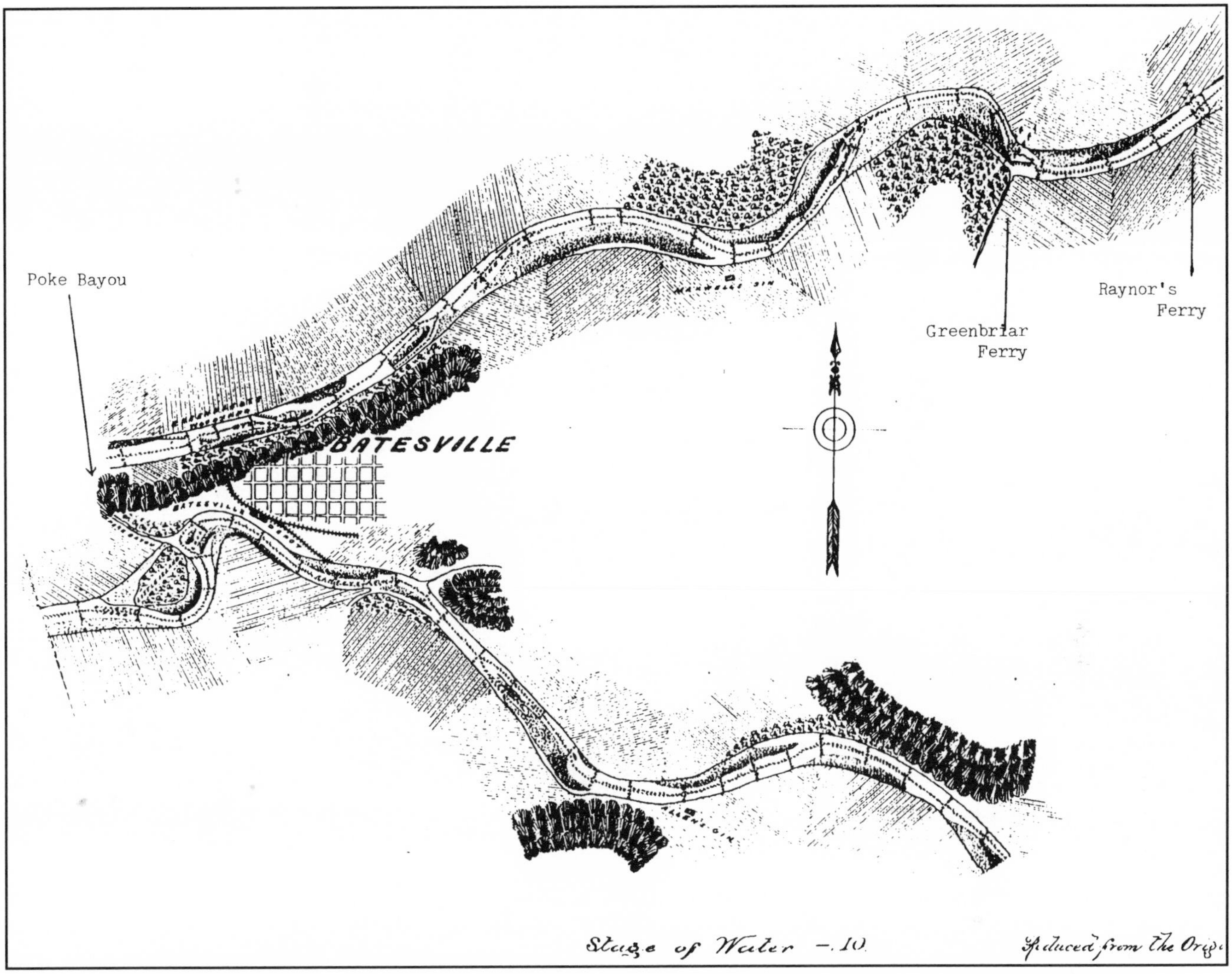

April 4, 1888, U.S. Army Corps of Engineers map, White River, Batesville area. It was made under the direction of H. S. Taber, Captain, U.S. Army Corps of Engineers, by Jas. C. Long and Chas. E. Taft, Asst. Engineers.

Courtesy of the U.S. Army Corps of Engineers office, Little Rock, Arkansas.

In 1872, a historic decision made by the residents of Jacksonport vitally affected the growth of the bustling little city. When the St. Louis, Iron Mountain, and Southern Railroad officials sought a right-of-way to Jacksonport, their request was denied, and understandably so, since the citizens were proud of the town's reputation as a river port and wanted no part in supporting the railroad. The decision proved to be the "kiss of death" for the growth of Jacksonport. The railroad officials rerouted the line through Newport, some three miles below Jacksonport, and Newport was destined to grow, while Jacksonport grew smaller. As the steamboat trade declined, so did the once thriving river port.

The coming of the railroad eventually spelled the end for steamboating in the White River, but initially, its building provided the steamers with plentiful cargo. The beautiful vessels carried the material and manpower needed to construct the railroads that would one day bring their demise.

On May 21, 1872, the steamer *Colossal* arrived at Memphis with a barge load of rolling stock headed for the White River. It was the first of many boats to haul railroad supplies up the White. Scarcely a week later, the *North Missouri* passed Augusta laden with railroad iron and two locomotives from Belmont. When about fourteen miles above Augusta, the vessel sank in deep water, but a St. Louis wrecking crew recovered the locomotives and tenders.

The end of 1872 brought bad boating conditions. The White was quite low and several boats became stranded or were damaged. The *Thomas H. Allen,* Captain Ashford, master, left De Valls Bluff one Sunday night around eight o'clock. When it was about five miles above the town, the steamer struck a snag, tearing a hole in its hull approximately six feet long and two feet wide. The *Thomas H. Allen* rapidly filled and soon sank, going down stern foremost. Fortunately it lay close by the shore at the time, so much so that when it sank it careened over on one side and lay against the bank. The water covered its stern up to the hurricane deck, while the bow was in shoal water. The pastry cook and

Steamboat Emma C. Elliott. *Built in 1871 by Capt. John D. Elliott for the Memphis and White River trade, the boat was 215 x 38 x 7 feet with a nine-hundred-ton freight capacity. Named for one of the captain's daughters, the* Elliott *was said to have a most beautifully toned whistle and bell. In fact, the bell was said to be more beautiful than any other built, and supposedly Captain Elliott tossed one thousand silver dollars into the metal as it was being cast, to make it so. The steamer cost sixty thousand dollars and was elegantly furnished. It ran in January and February of 1872 from Memphis to Jacksonport, Arkansas, making eight trips and carrying 3,747 bales of cotton and freight and passengers. The steamer was sold to the Anchor Line in 1873 to run between Memphis and St. Louis, on the Mississippi River.*

Photo courtesy of Capt. William H. Tippit, Hernando, Mississippi, and the University of Arkansas, Little Rock, Archives and Special Collections.

second cook were reported missing and assumed drowned. Many of the crew and passengers jumped overboard but were able to reach land safely. The *Batesville* passed the scene of the disaster a few hours afterward and took the passengers and crew to De Valls Bluff; the *Mary Boyd,* coming down just behind the *Batesville,* took all of the furniture off the boat and as much freight as possible and delivered it to De Valls Bluff. Though attempts were made to raise the *Thomas H. Allen,* the steamer remained where it sank, with the water at the stern over the railing of the hurricane roof and its bow in twelve feet of water. During the salvaging, a hole was cut in the cabin roof to remove the piano. One was also cut in the hold of the steamboat, leading wreckers to later believe the bottom of the steamer was gone. They raised it a foot or two several times, but it quickly sank after each trial. Almost all of the bridge material was removed and a large amount of the freight. When one of the divers went into the engine room, he found the clock stopped at 9:15, the time of the mishap. The boat proved to be a total loss.

The steamboats were hampered not only by low water in December of 1872 but also by weather. The last week of that year was particularly disastrous for the vessels at Memphis and other ports along the Mississippi and White Rivers. Prolonged low temperatures produced ice floes that threatened many steamboats moored at Memphis. During the late hours of December 26 and the following morning, the ice jammed into the steamers docked there with such force that some were reduced to a jumbled mass of splinters. The heavy chunks of ice totally destroyed the luxurious *R. P. Walt,* the *Belle of Pike,* the *Helen Brooks,* the *Laura,* the *Summer Coon,* and the *Undine* and damaged the *City of Augusta,* the *Pat Cleburne,* the *Andy Baum,* the *Arlington,* the *St. Francis,* the *Nellie Thomas,* and the *West Wind.* The *Celeste,* moored above the dry docks, was carried past the city and out of sight by the crunching mass of ice. The *R. P. Walt* was jammed into the bank with such force that its hull was twisted and broken into all sorts of shapes. The *City of Augusta* was also severely damaged when its starboard guard was pushed under the larboard wheel of the twisted *R. P. Walt*. Both the *R. P. Walt* and the *City of Augusta* were owned by the Elliotts and associates, so the loss fell heavily on them.

The advent of 1873 brought little change from Mother Nature, as the extremely cold weather continued into January of that year. The White River was frozen solid, with ice almost twelve inches thick in many places. The steamer *Dardanelle,* Capt. R. L. Haynes, master, was stranded at Calory Depot, a short distance below De Valls Bluff, by heavy ice gorges above and below it. The *John Howard,* a large New Orleans steamboat, was laid up by the ice at Crocketts Bluff. Happily, within a week, moderating temperatures finally melted the ice enough for normal river navigation to resume.

There was always plenty of excitement on the steamboats, and 1873 was no exception. While on a trip to Jacksonport in January, the stork visited the Elliott line's *City of Augusta* twice within twelve hours, once with the delivery of a baby girl and once with a baby boy. The girl, appropriately, was named Augusta, but the name of the boy was not given. Perhaps he was called Milt in honor of the boat's well-liked captain, Milt R. Harry. On that same trip of the *Augusta,* the steamer was puffing along near Indian Bay when it came upon the *Legal Tender* fast aground. During an attempt to dislodge the stranded steamboat, several of the crew of the *City of Augusta* assembled on the forecastle to watch. As the *Legal Tender* swung around, a taut hawser broke and struck the watchman and a deckhand, breaking the jaw of the former and the right arm of the latter. Notwithstanding births to its passengers and injuries to its crew members, the beautiful steamboat churned on its way upriver to Jacksonport.

Ice again plagued the White River steamboats in early February of 1873. When the *Pat Cleburne* arrived at Memphis on February 5, Captain Ashford reported that the Little Red River was frozen over and the White was covered with ice at Des Arc. Considerable ice was also reported between Des Arc and the mouth of the river, and the steamer encountered heavy floes in the Mississippi. When twenty or thirty miles below Memphis, the crew of the *Pat Cleburne* saw a deer floating in the middle of the river on a huge cake of ice. Wishing to rescue the trapped animal, Captain Ashford

Steamboat John Howard, *a New Orleans boat that served the White and Arkansas Rivers during the 1870s and early 1880, was 185 feet long, 36 feet wide, and had a 5-foot hold. It ran from New Orleans to as far as Batesville on the White and to Little Rock on the Arkansas. In 1864, Capt. P. C. Montgomery was the master, while in 1877, Capt. E. R. Perry was in charge. Capt. Henry Klank, of Jacksonport, was pilot much of the time. In October of 1879, while pulling over a shoal a short distance below Augusta on White River, the hawser broke, killing the mate.*

Courtesy of the University of Arkansas, Little Rock, Archives and Special Collections.

brought the steamboat to within twenty feet of the ice chunk, but the deer became frightened and plunged into the cold water and was thrust under by the ice.

By the middle of February, rains had cleared the ice and White River was again in optimum boating condition. The waterway was busy with steamers traveling to Batesville and above. Particularly active carrying out cotton from the Upper White were the *Batesville,* the *Jessie,* and the little *Maysville.* All three made several trips to Buffalo City. The *Maysville* was a Jacksonport to Buffalo City packet, and the *Batesville* ran from Memphis to Pocahontas and up White River as far as it could go. During the first six months of the year, the *Jessie,* Captain Spencer, master, was a regular between Jacksonport and Batesville with occasional trips to landings above Batesville. On one trip, the *Jessie* made the downriver trip from the Buffalo River in the amazing time of seven hours.

In June 1873, the popular Capt. Milt Harry chartered the *Jessie* and had Capt. Albert G. Cravens serving as its clerk. Captain Harry planned to make regular weekly trips between Batesville and the mouth of the White, where the small steamer would connect with the larger *A. J. White* from Memphis.

Another small steamboat, the *Ranger,* made its appearance on the Upper White in 1873. The *Ranger* hailed from Forsyth, Missouri, and was, supposedly, even tinier than the well-known little *Malta.* A *Batesville Republican* commented: "The *Ranger* is the name of a snorting steamer that landed in Polk Bayou this week near the bridge. She hails from Forsythe, Missouri, and the Captain confirms that she can make the trip when White River is at its lowest stage. Our reporter wanted to go aboard the *Ranger*, but the Captain, who was in his glory, declined to let him for fear he would sink the boat! Its either a joke on the reporter, Wm. H. Baynes, or the steamer."[20] The *Ranger* had two barges in tow on its maiden voyage down the White, an asset that, according to the *Arkansas Gazette,* would do much toward "lightening her over the shoals."[21]

Even with the threat of being put ashore on an island if caught, confidence artists were still alive and well on the steamers traversing White River. The appearance of rail transportation added a new dimension to the problem. In April of 1873, two passengers en route from Memphis to De Valls Bluff aboard the *Legal Tender* became victims of a confidence operation. While on the boat, the men purchased railroad tickets from De Valls Bluff to Little Rock. When they boarded the train, however, they found, to their dismay, the tickets were fraudulent. The *Arkansas Gazette* warned river travelers to be wary of this latest deception.

As 1873 closed, there were hints of the impact the newly built railroad lines would have upon steamboat towns. Since the advent of rail, Pocahontas had lost some of its prestige as the head of navigation on Black River. The *Weekly Observer* there commented: "On Tuesday last our town was somewhat enlivened by the arrival of the steamer *Ella* from Memphis . . . The *Ella* expects to remain in the trade as long as she can get support, and as the roads to the railroads are getting almost impassable, our merchants will do well to patronize the river."[22]

Though commerce on the White was still busy, trade on the river was gradually diminishing, and several communities were starting to notice some changes, particularly Jacksonport. For citizens there, the situation would only worsen.

The Memphis and Arkansas River Packet Company was reorganized by 1874, and its White River line was abandoned. With this company's departure, the Elliott line became the dominant one in White River steamboating, having three fine steamers in service: the *City of Augusta,* the *Legal Tender,* and the *Bannock City,* a recent addition under command of Capt. Milt Harry.

The year 1874 brought problems for even the successful Elliott line, however. In March, the *Bannock City* lost valuable travel time for the installation of new chimneys, its old ones having been damaged beyond repair. A short time later, the rigging of the *Legal Tender* became entangled in the limbs of a tall tree while the boat was at a landing on the White. Deckhand James Andrews climbed some sixty feet up the tree to free the rigging, but sustained severe injuries when he lost his balance and fell. Less than a week following this accident, the Elliott line received an almost fatal blow when the Shelby County sheriff attached the *Legal Tender,* the *City of Augusta,* and the *Bannock City* to satisfy a court judgment against the sureties of the defaulting county tax assessor. When the Elliotts refused to furnish bond for the impounded boats, the sheriff ordered them moored above the mouth of Wolf River at Memphis. Undaunted by the misfortune, Capts. William and John D. Elliott chartered the side-wheel steamer *George W. Cheek* and left for Jacksonport and Pocahontas for "business as usual." The *George W. Creek* traveled the White and Black Rivers until early May of 1874.

The spring of 1874 was a trying time for other steamers, too, with the *Ella* having its share of woes. When the boat arrived at the Pocahantas landing in April, Randolph County sheriff Fisher presented Capt. A. L. Cummings with a bill from Messrs. Harlin and Pine of Chicago for property allegedly taken from a house on the Black River shore a short distance below Pocahantas. The materials were the remains of the wreck of the *Bluff City* and had been stored in the building. Captain Cummings refused to pay the bill, so a writ was served upon him for burglary. After much haggling, a satisfactory settlement was reached. The publisher of the local *Weekly Observer* wrote that the property was only "borrowed."[23] The *Ella* had run into some tree limbs and knocked down its chimneys and needed the appropriated property to get out of the river. Evidently, the settlement enabled the owners of the *Bluff City* to put the boat in operational order again because it reappeared on the Black shortly after the payment.

John Q. Wolf wrote of another White River steamboat misfortune that occurred in 1874:

> The *Trader,* a Memphis boat, came up White River in 1874 with freight for Buffalo City and a good lot of passengers. It was an ideal time to make such a trip, for the trees were putting on their leaves, and the woods were aflame with redbud and dogwood, while many of the hillsides were covered with fragrant wild pink honeysuckle. The river at Batesville showed a good boating stage, but by the time the *Trader* reached North Fork the

> water was getting thin. After passing over the shoal just above the mouth of North Fork, one of the shallowest on the river, and going on to Shipp's Ferry, six miles above, the Captain decided to turn back. Consequently the boat's prow was pointed downstream. It was dark when the boat got back to North Fork shoal and the pilot thought it unsafe to try to take his boat through the shoal in the dark. He therefore gave orders to tie up until the next morning, and he eased the boat over to the long gravel bar on the right bank of the river and went to bed. At five o'clock the next morning the boat was high and dry on the gravel bar and thirty feet from the water. And that was not the worst of it, for the long drought of 1874 set in right then and the helpless *Trader* sat there on the treeless gravel waste for thirteen long weary monotonous months before there was sufficient rise to go out. . . .[24]

Steamers were sometimes sites of political gatherings, with candidates for regional and state offices utilizing the crafts as a platform for their political posturing. On October 1, 1874, the *Arkansas Gazette* announced that the residents of Jacksonport had been visited the prior day, September 30, by A. H. Garland, a candidate for governor. The steamer *Batesville* had been secured for an excursion to Newport to pick up the candidate, touted as the "next governor of Arkansas." The boat, crowded with "Jacksonport's fairest sons and daughters," arrived at the Newport landing about 4:00 P.M. Garland and entourage were given a hearty welcome and joined the Jacksonport passengers for the return trip to their city, a ride of about one hour duration. About 8:00 that evening, the group was escorted to the only hotel in Jacksonport, where a reception was held prior to a public address at the courthouse about an hour later. The event seemed to be a huge success, with the *Gazette* reporter commenting, "Never did a mortal man receive a heartier welcome."

As 1875 began, the ever popular Capt. Milt Harry was receiving new accolades for his side-wheel steamer *Quickstep*. The *Quickstep* was in for repairs shortly after its initial appearance, however, so Captain Harry chartered the 241-ton *George W. Cheek* to temporarily take its place. The *Quickstep* soon returned to service and became a favorite on the river.

Insufficient business and low water levels in the White caused several of the steamboatmen to move their vessels to another market or to dry dock for portions of 1875. One such steamer was the *Batesville*. On August 17, Captain Smith arrived at Memphis with the *Batesville* loaded with thirty-five hundred sacks of wheat bound for St. Louis. After laying up long enough to clean out its boilers in Memphis, the steamer left for the Missouri port where the vessel was placed in dry dock to receive a complete overhaul. When in good order, the *Batesville* was to serve the Milt Harry White River Line in connection with Captain Harry's latest acquisition, the *Ruth*. After spending four thousand dollars for renovation of the steamer, the *Batesville* left St. Louis in September with a full cargo bound for White River.

Autumn of 1875 brought two new steamboats to the White, the *Arch P. Green* from Cincinnati and the small stern-wheeler *Duck* from the Ohio River. Both were placed in the Upper White River. The *Arch P. Green*, an Elliott enterprise commanded by Capt. Alex C. Elliott, was built especially for the upper river trade. Constructed of good timber, it was a trim 110 feet long with a 22-foot beam and carried two engines with 3.5-foot stroke. It had cotton guards and a cabin for passengers. Serving as chief clerk on the steamer was Capt. Charles Woodbury, a gentleman who was recognized along the Western waters for his integrity, courtesy, and prompt attention to business. Captain Woodbury had served with the Memphis and Cincinnati Packet Company prior to coming to the White River.

Only one sinking was reported during the last three months of 1875. While running between Jacksonport and Batesville, the small steamer *Duck* struck a snag and sank near Jacksonport. The steamboat was later raised, repaired, and returned to operation.

Another White River steamboat to receive major repairs during 1875 was the *Ella*. Dry docked at Paducah, the *Ella* was overhauled from "pilot-house to keelson." The hull of the vessel was doubled and strengthened, it received new cylinder timbers, and its wheel was raised and enlarged to add one mile per hour to its speed. In addition to all the machinery being repaired and improved, the steamboat received a new pair of chimneys. New floors were also placed in the vessel, and its cabins and staterooms were fashionably decorated and furnished. The final touch was a fresh covering of snow white paint to its exterior.[25]

In 1876, the *Ella* again became active in the White River trade. In January, it ascended the White to Mayfield's gin, four miles above Calico Rock and some twenty-eight miles below Buffalo Shoals. The *Ella* came out on a falling river, rubbing gravel all the way and losing eighteen hours by being grounded. It then ascended Black River to Pocahontas, taking 30 bales of cotton from the steamer *Bluff City*, which had sunk just four miles below Lauratown. Later in the month, the *Ella* arrived at Memphis with 432 bales of cotton and laid up at the port for a while.

Trade in the Upper White River was flourishing. According to the *Memphis Public Ledger*, there were large amounts of corn and cattle, as well as cotton, awaiting shipment to market. At one point, over twenty thousand bushels of corn were loaded. The price for hauling cotton from the Upper White was currently \$3.50 per bale to Memphis and \$4.50 to New Orleans. The price from Black River to Memphis was \$2.50 per bale. Hard ash and hackberry wood in any quantity was selling along White River at \$1.50 to \$1.75 per cord, so the area was quite prosperous for the times. Interestingly, wages for pilots had dropped from their post-war days. White River pilots in 1876 drew \$100 monthly, while those in the Arkansas River were paid \$125.

In the spring of 1876, Capt. Milt Harry's line of Memphis and White River boats was consolidated with the Elliott line, forming a new company called the Milt Harry Memphis and White River United States Mail Line. Newspapermen along the White, always impressed by Captain Harry, lauded the move. With perseverance, Capt. Milt Harry had gained the upper hand over the Elliots, his primary rivals, and they were soon squeezed from the river. The Elliots sold their fine steamboat *Legal Tender* to Capt. Ed Nowland

The Arch P. Green, *an Elliott steamboat that entered White River trade in September of 1872, was 110 feet long and 22 feet wide. Commanded by Capt. Alex C. Elliott, the* Green *had Capt. Charles B. Woodbury serving as its clerk. In 1876, Captain Woodbury bought the boat and ran it until it sank in 1880 at Goose Neck Shoals some five miles below Batesville. Photo shows vessel moored at Wild Haws Landing near the present town of Guion, Arkansas.*

Courtesy of the University of Arkansas, Little Rock, Archives and Special Collections.

and John N. Harbin of the Memphis and Arkansas River Packet Company. Unfortunately, the beautiful side-wheeler struck a snag at Rowser's cut-off in the Arkansas River and sank about midnight on April 15, 1876. No lives were lost, but one of the deckhands was scalded on his face when a barrel of lime blew up. The boat settled to the river bottom about one-half mile below Swan Lake with six or seven feet of water over its larboard guards. Most of the freight was saved, but the magnificent *Legal Tender* was a total loss.

After additional reorganization, Captain Harry kept only two steamboats in his line, the *City of Augusta,* which he commanded, and the *Ruth,* Captain Postal, master.

In the Upper White, the independent steamboat *Batesville* remained faithful in its service to that portion of the river during all of 1876, with trips as often as water permitted. A *North Arkansas Times* reporter from Batesville described a trip he took on the steamer that year above Buffalo City:

On the evening of the 7th . . . we boarded the steamer *Batesville* at our wharf, when she loosed cable and steered for the mountains Hepsidam. . . .

Having been such a great while since a boat went higher than Talbert's Ferry, everybody above that point seemed almost crazy with excitement and joy upon our arrival. We went as far as Debuque in Boone County, this state, some twenty miles below Forsythe, Missouri. This, I presume, is the first time a steamer has been to this point since those patched breeches federals surrendered to Lee. The "Gray backs" of these mountains, being so far carried away by the sight of a steamer, would follow along the riverbank in sight of us for five or six miles, when becoming very much fatigued, they would make and beat a hasty retreat, amid the cheers of the boat's happy and lively crew. I thought we had some as "green" people down in our neck of the woods as anywhere on the face of the globe, but up in and about Debuque they can give our boys sixteen in the game and beat 'em so bad at "acting up greeny," that they won't know what their dad's names were before they married. While we were at a woodyard, taking on wood and freight, a lot of these mountaineers came aboard to see the "elephant," when some Christian friend, in order to make the show as interesting as possible to them 'neers, opened a tune on the boat's calliope . . . that caused, to the surprise and heartfelt sympathy of the boat's crew, a general stampede among the pioneers, frightening one of them so badly that he jumped into the river and waded out, instead of going out on the stage plank, and the last heard of him he was fifty miles from the woodyard, still wading over rocks, snakes and lizards, as fast as his legs would carry him, and shouting to the top of his voice, "Old Gabriel's down at the woodyard with a lot of devils, blowing his horn for sinners to get from these diggins!" We presume, ere now, he has reached the Centennial grounds and delivered the news to Barnum.

The farmers in this section all seem busy pitching their crops, and seem to have plenty of meat and bread, and some to spare, as the *Batesville* took on large quantities of wheat and bacon. She also took on a box of rich minerals, consisting of lead, zinc, copper, etc., to be forwarded to the Centennial.

Upon the whole, Mr. Editor, with the exception of the boat running into rocks, and striking some huge boulders, which made everybody feel bald headed, we had a very pleasant time, and no doubt had much fun, if not more, as we expect to have at the Centennial next May. In conclusion, we would say to those wishing to take a few days recreation to see beautiful mountain scenery, and natural mountaineers without any embellishments, take a trip on a steamer to Debuque.[26]

When the *Arch P. Green,* one of the Elliot steamboats, returned from repairs in Cincinnati in the fall of 1876, the steamer was under the command of Capt. Charles B. Woodbury, its former clerk, who had obtained ownership. It was the beginning of a long career for him as an Upper White River steamboat owner.

As the steamboat owners made plans for the fall boating season of 1876, Capt. Albert B. Smith from Batesville sent word from Louisville that he was building a new low-water boat to run with the *Batesville.* Capt. Ed. C. Postal also notified the public that he was building a stern-wheeler at Pittsburgh that he had christened the *Hard Cash.* The announcement by Captain Postal was history repeating itself. Another steamboat captain was challenging his former boss for a share of the commerce. Captain Postal chartered the *Ella* to run until his new boat was completed. He also hired the *Trader,* Capt. W. R. Todd, master, to run the upper rivers and connect with his large boat at Jacksonport.

On October 1, 1876, Capt. James Rees brought the new steamer *Hard Cash* to Memphis, where numerous steamboatmen and other interested citizens visited it. The boat was 168 feet long, had a 35-foot beam with a 4.5-foot hold, was powered by three

Steamboat Hard Cash. *Built in 1876 by Capt. Ed Postal for the Memphis and White River trade, the craft was 168 x 35 x 4.25 feet. It had a full-length cabin featuring Brussels carpeting, brocaded furniture, and a Chickering piano. All staterooms were grandly furnished, with a large mirror in the ladies' cabin. The freedmens' cabin was also beautifully fitted, offering first-class accommodations. The* Hard Cash *had a long, successful career, running between Memphis and Jacksonport, until sold to Capt. T. P. Leathers for ten thousand dollars in November 1883, to serve in the Vicksburg and Yazoo River trade.*

Courtesy of the University of Arkansas, Little Rock, Archives and Special Collections.

steel boilers 22 feet long and 38 inches in diameter, and had engines of 15-inch cylinders with 5-foot stroke. Its full length cabin was fitted with beautiful Brussels carpets covering the floor and had brocaded furniture, a Chickering piano, and a large mirror in the ladies' cabin. All staterooms were furnished in grand style. Aft of the cabin was a recess for nurses. A tastefully arranged "Freedman's bureau," or cabin for black people, also had first-class accommodations. The most superb silverware and china were parts of a well-equipped pantry. A Memphis reporter described the *Hard Cash* as the best boat ever built for the trade.[27]

To meet the challenge, Captain Harry chartered the *Batesville* and withdrew the *Ruth* for extensive renovation. It was hoped the *Ruth*, rejuvenated and shining, would be ready for the fall business. Apparently the ambitious captain was preparing to fight more than one adversary, as a reporter of the *Memphis Public Ledger* stated: "Commodore Harry, proprietor of the Memphis and White River line of packets, is preparing to give the railroad companies a lively fight for the coming season. He is one who believes that freight ought to be, and can be transported cheaper by water, where the track costs nothing, than by rail, where it costs millions to construct it, to say nothing of repairs. Acting on this idea, the commodore is repairing his steamers and getting ready to renew his old fight."[28]

The steamer *Batesville* received a running mate in the fall of 1876 with the appearance of the *Alberta*. The vessel was named for the daughter of its master, Capt. Albert B. Smith.

In late 1876, the *Batesville*, Captain Smith serving as master, fought the swift rapids and climbed the shoals of the Upper White to Forsyth, Missouri, then steamed beyond to the mouth of Bull Creek. With Capt. Will C. Shipp as pilot, the vessel brought out two thousand bushels of wheat, returning without mishap. As mentioned previously, the *Thomas P. Ray*, piloted by Hardin Shipp, brother of Captain Shipp, had gone some fifty miles farther up the White to the mouth of the James River in 1858. Not to be outdone, Capt. Will Shipp later took the *Batesville*, with young Edwin T. B. Warner in the pilothouse, to the mouth of the James, equaling the feat of the *Thomas P. Ray*. As far as is known, these are the only steamboats to make that hazardous trip.

The importance of the upper river packets is shown in the report made by Captain Woodbury of the *Arch P. Green* concerning cargo. From September 22, 1875, to January 20, 1877, the busy little packet made thirty trips from Newport to Batesville and returned, transporting 12,224 packages of miscellaneous freight and 2,953 bales of cotton. A combined total of 6,160 bales were shipped on the *Arch P. Green* and the *Alberta*, of which 893 were for Memphis, 2,298 for New Orleans, 2,940 for St. Louis, and 29 for other places.[29]

In early 1877, plans were formulated for the annual Mardi Gras at Jacksonport. A special excursion from Batesville to the festivities was scheduled, with Capt. Milt Harry and the *Ruth* taking parties from the Lower White at a reduced rate of $2.50 for the round trip. Due to the large numbers expected to attend, the *Batesville* was also scheduled for the excursion on the Lower White. The *Alberta* was scheduled to transport those wishing to attend from Batesville and the Upper White, and the *McArthur* was to care for those attending from the Black River. All were carried at half fare. Other steamboats, including the *Winnie* and the *City of Augusta*, provided excursion passage to the Mardi Gras celebration in later years.

With eager anticipation, citizens of the towns along the White River prepared for the big event in Jacksonport in 1877. Simon Adler of Batesville sold a large shipment of costumes for the masquerade ball. The Batesville Cornet Band rehearsed in preparation for the dance, as did the steamer *Ruth*'s string band, also scheduled to play at the festivities. The gala lived up to all expectations. On February 12, 1877, the King of the Carnival was brought from Newport to Jacksonport by water, escorted by several steamboats currently in the White River trade. Included in the water parade were the steamers *Ruth, Alberta, Batesville, Arch P. Green, Trader, McArthur, Music,* and *Duck*, followed by scows and flatboats.

The group from Batesville left on the *Alberta* and included the members of the Batesville Cornet Band. After leaving Ramsey's Ferry at 12:30, dinner was announced and Captain Smith and his wife provided a sumptuous feast for their guests. None of the passengers had any fear of danger as the popular Capt. Billy Shipp was at the helm. The party arrived at Jacksonport and was lodged for the night. The activities of the following day were described by Frank Denton of the *Batesville Guard:*

> Tuesday morn being Mardi Gras Day, everybody and the rest of mankind seemed to have arose early to see if Rex was coming. After waiting until about noon, and the King had not yet come, the steamers *Batesville* and *Alberta*, after getting a large cargo of human beings, hauled in the stage plank and departed for Newport to await the coming of the King. When the boat landed at the elevator, the King came ashore, with his staff and many followers. No one knew from whence he came, as he was certainly not on the boat when we left Jacksonport. However, King Peter Bee, the first of the House of Jackson, was there, and all of his royal subjects paid homage to the Royal King of the Carnival. . . .[30]

The king and his court boarded the *Ruth*, and the steamboats left for Jacksonport in a gala procession. This was, perhaps, the historic old river town's finest hour and its last truly big celebration. It was certainly the largest congregation of steamboats at the Jacksonport wharf. With eight steamboats moored at the landing and hundreds of visitors roaming its streets, the town was at the height of its glory and oblivious of the slow decline that was gnawing away at its population. Frank Denton's report continued: "After marching round about and receiving his subjects, the troops and horsemen and footmen of the Carnival dispersed to attend a masquerade ball, to trip the light fantastic to the music of the Batesville Cornet Band and the string band of the steamer *Ruth*, furnished by Admiral Milt Harry, of the House of Hamlet. Everything went off merrily, nothing to mar the feelings of the most polite. While in Jacksonport, we met with many old friends. . . ."[31]

Many White River Valley residents also attended the Mardi Gras festivities in New Orleans or Memphis each year, traveling to the larger cities via steamboats that usually offered a special excursion rate for the celebration.

Batesville held its own Mardi Gras carnival in 1879, organized by the "Bats and Owls, an Oriental Fraternal Lodge." Among other activities, the event included a parade that started at the steamboat wharf, a concert by the Batesville Cornet Band and two balls. The "Jacksi" club of Jacksonport was invited to participate.[32]

While commerce was busy on the Lower White, the increasing competition from the railroads there made several of the steamboat captains turn more and more to the upper river trade. On March 1, 1877, the *Batesville Guard* contained an advertisement stating the *Alberta,* Captain Smith, master, and the *Batesville,* Capt. Will C. Shipp in charge, would be regular Newport to Batesville, Sylamore, Calico Rock, Buffalo City, Talbert's Ferry, Dubuque, and Forsyth packets. Also mentioned was Captain Woodbury's boat serving as a Newport, Batesville, Mt. Olive, and Buffalo City packet.

The *Ruth,* commanded by Captain Harry, arrived at the Searcy landing in late March, despite low water. It was the first steamboat to arrive there since the previous August. Cordially welcomed, the steamer left with almost five hundred bales of cotton and the hope of the merchants for enough water to resume weekly trips. To the delight of area residents, Searcy was served by both the *Ruth* and the *Hard Cash* when water permitted during the spring of 1877. The publisher of the *White County Record* expressed the satisfaction felt by the community: "The waters are up, hence we have two steamers within two miles of Searcy every week. It is really pleasant to hear the joyful sounds of steamboat whistles. There is more music in them than in locomotives, and steamers are much more pleasant to look at, and a vast deal more pleasant to travel on. . . ."[33]

With a particularly wet spring, in May of 1877, the *Alberta* traveled to Hensley's Ferry, twenty miles above Forsyth, as well as up the Buffalo River to the Big Eddie. The steamer arrived in Batesville with forty-seven bales of cotton, seventeen hundred bushels of wheat, five hogshead of tobacco, one box of tobacco weighing 450 pounds, one bale of wool, one bale of hides, 20,000 pounds of flour, 14,300 pounds of bacon, and 900 pounds of lard. The cargo was typical of the diversity of products hauled by the Upper White boats.

One of the first walkouts by steamboat personnel on the Upper White occurred in September of 1877, when the deckhands of the *Alberta* struck for higher wages. Dissatisfied with the twenty dollar monthly pay for working four days per week, they called for a raise. Resolution of the strike was not mentioned; however, the *Alberta* lost little traveling time on the White during that month.[34]

Always striving to please his shippers, Captain Smith, of the *Alberta,* built a large warehouse at his new landing at the foot of Spring Street in Batesville. Here he stored and handled, free of charge, all freight consigned to him. Since the upper river shippers were frequently forced to pay a commission for the storage and handling of their freight, this was a substantial savings for them.

The *Alberta* was a favorite in Batesville and was mentioned repeatedly in the local newspaper. In September of 1877, the *Batesville Guard* gave the following report of a trip on the steamer:

> The little steamer *Alberta* turned loose all her whistles on Tuesday morning about eight o'clock, thereby announcing her readiness to leave, and her ability to scream louder than a young widow over the death of an old husband, leaving behind $100,000 for someone to buy craps and hair pins with. Capt. Albert Smith tapped the big bell and her handsome pilots, Charley and Hard (Shipp) turned her bow downstream, and away she went like a United States Marshall after an illicit distiller. She had 18 passengers aboard, nothing remarkable as to number, but my sakes, the quality! Capt. Smith and his lump of domestic tranquility, with Than Kinman to help, entertained all on board. We felt as if we were enroute for the Turkish side of the Balkans to receive the Order of Osmanli from the Sultan in person. . . . Batesville owes her present prosperity to the industry of the farmers of this and surrounding counties, and to Capt. Albert Smith, who has afforded them facilities of sending everything to market during the past summer, while the river has been as dry as an old topper in a busted saloon. . . ."[35]

The *Alberta* was again in the news in December of 1877, when it returned from a trip to Trimble's Landing, forty-one miles above Buffalo City. The steamer was loaded with 305 sacks of wheat, 100 sacks of cottonseed, 321 bales of cotton, and a great deal of miscellaneous freight, as well as a large passenger list. The steamboat lost some time at Talbert's Ferry in trying to load a large lot of hogs. After many vain attempts to lug the swine aboard, and with the water level falling rapidly, the captain decided to refuse the shipment and headed downriver while he still could.

One of the new steamboats in White River in the fall of 1877 was the 80-ton *Milt Harry.* The stern-wheeler, named for the commodore, was built at Cincinnati by Capt. Pete McArthur. It was one of the most complete little steamers afloat, fitted in handsome style. The steamer was 115 feet 8 inches long, with a 23.5-foot beam and 3.5-foot hold, and had all new machinery, consisting of two boilers, 36 inches in diameter and 18 inches long, with two flues. Of light draft, the snow white *Milt Harry* was designed to carry 150 tons of freight.

As another year of steamboating on White River drew to a close, business was booming on the upper river and remained fairly busy on the lower river. The railroad was taking its toll, however. Increasing amounts of cotton were being shipped by rail from White River country. During the past three years, the St. Louis, the Cincinnati, and the Louisville packets had completely withdrawn from the trade until business opportunities changed. The gradual decline of steamboat patronage on White River was being felt more and more by the boat owners.

Although the railroad was dipping into the transport business

The steamboat Milt Harry *was built in 1877 for Capt. Pete McArthur for the Black River trade. The vessel was 115.5 x 23.5 x 3.5 feet and displaced eighty net tons. It ran from Jacksonport to Pocahontas and above on the Black, and to Buffalo City on the Upper White. It is shown here at an unknown spot on Black River. The steamer burned above Batesville in February 1885.*

Courtesy of the University of Arkansas, Little Rock, Archives and Special Collections.

on the Lower White, when 1878 arrived, commerce remained brisk on the upper reaches of the river where there were fewer rail lines. The *Alberta,* Capt. Will C. Shipp in charge, arrived at Batesville, on January 3 of that year, heavily laden with freight from Talbert's Ferry. Later that month, the steamer docked at Batesville with 411 bales of cotton, one hundred sacks of cotton-seed, one thousand bushels of wheat, one thousand pounds of dried fruit, and one thousand dozen eggs from the same Marion county landing. A local reporter stated that the crew certainly had plenty of ham and eggs and peach rolls! On March 20, 1878, the *Alberta* returned again with a large amount of freight from Elbow Bend, a landing some fifty miles below Forsyth, near the infamous Elbow Shoals. Included in that cargo were 326 bales of cotton billed through to St. Louis, the largest shipment ever sent there at one time from the Upper White. The *Arch P. Green,* the *Winnie,* and the *C. B. Warner* were also plying the river between Newport, Batesville, Calico Rock, Buffalo City, and other upper river points. The *City of Augusta,* the *Hard Cash,* and the *Ruth* were serving as Memphis packets on the lower river.

Capt. Milt Harry's new steamer, *Josie Harry,* named for his wife, was completed in late August of 1878. Designed to enter the Memphis and White River trade, the vessel drew a great deal of attention. The *Pittsburgh Commercial Gazette* gave these details of the steamboat:

> . . . she is pronounced by all who have given her an examination to be one of the finest and most complete steamers built here for a number of years. She is furnished in elegant style; is supplied with all the latest appliances and improvements and is in every respect an A No. 1 boat. Length 175 feet, beam 36 feet, hold 5 feet, 13 feet between decks, with cotton guards. The hull was built by L. M. and W. F. Speer, of Belle Vernon, and is pronounced an excellent job; engines by James Rees; cylinders 19 inches in diameter, 6 feet stroke; with the indispensible Rees cut-off; 3 steel boilers, 40 inches in diameter, 26 feet long, the work of J. Thorn and Company; cabin, by Wm. Buston; 12 feet length of state-rooms on a side, (24 staterooms, total) with nursery in the rear; the staterooms are of unusually large size, are fitted in first class style, everything being new and of the best quality. The texas is large enough to accommodate officers and crew, and like the main cabin, is fitted up in elegant style, carpeted with Brussel's carpet,

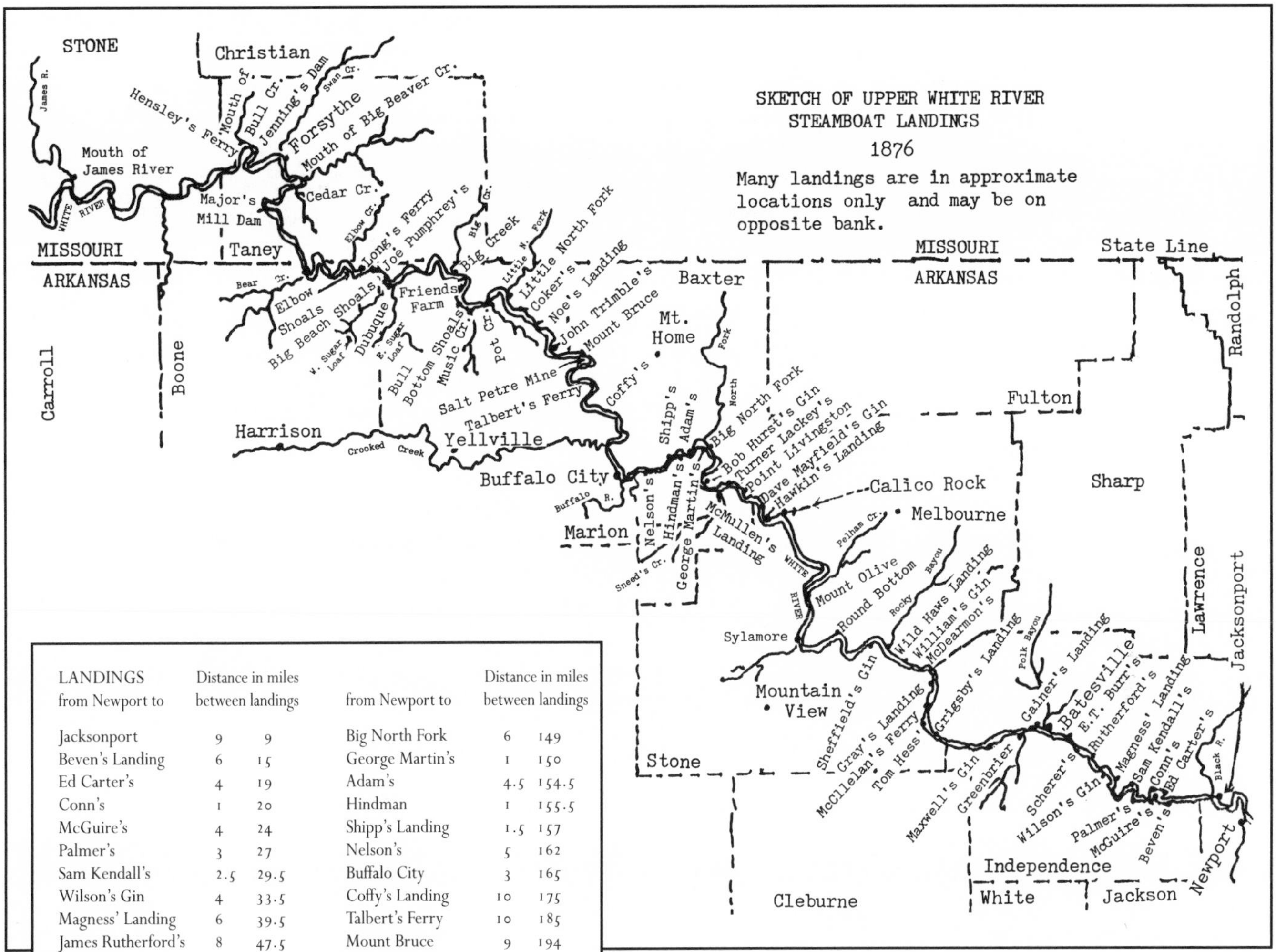

LANDINGS from Newport to	Distance in miles between landings		from Newport to	Distance in miles between landings	
Jacksonport	9	9	Big North Fork	6	149
Beven's Landing	6	15	George Martin's	1	150
Ed Carter's	4	19	Adam's	4.5	154.5
Conn's	1	20	Hindman	1	155.5
McGuire's	4	24	Shipp's Landing	1.5	157
Palmer's	3	27	Nelson's	5	162
Sam Kendall's	2.5	29.5	Buffalo City	3	165
Wilson's Gin	4	33.5	Coffy's Landing	10	175
Magness' Landing	6	39.5	Talbert's Ferry	10	185
James Rutherford's	8	47.5	Mount Bruce	9	194
Scherer's	5	52.5	Salt Petre Mine	3	197
E. T. Burr's	2.5	55	John Trimble's	6	203
Batesville	2	57	Noe's Landing	8	211
Gainer's Landing	2	59	Coker's	8	219
Greenbrier	1	60	Little North Fork	2	221
Maxwell's Gin	3	63	Pot Creek	5	226
Grigsby's Landing	10	73	Music Creek	3	229
Tom Hess'	1.5	74.5	Bull Bottom Shoals	3	232
McClellan's Ferry	4	78.5	Friend's Farm	3	235
Gray's Landing	2	80.5	Big Creek	2	237
McDearmon's	1	81.5	Dubuque	17	254
William's Gin	3	84.5	Big Beach Shoals	3	257
Wild Haws Landing	5	89.5	Joe Pumphrey's	6	263
Sheffield's Gin	3	92.3	Long's Ferry	3	266
Round Bottom	5.5	98	Elbow Shoals	.5	266.5
Sylamore	6	104	Bear Creek	17.5	284
Mount Olive	6	110	Major Mill's Dam	9	293
Calico Rock	16	126	Cedar Creek	11	304
Hawkin's Landing	3	129	Mouth Big Beaver Creek	3	307
Dave Mayfield's Gin	4	133	Forsythe, Missouri	10	317
McMullen's Landing	2	135	Jenning's Dam	15	332
Point Livingston	3	138	Mouth Bull Creek	4	336
Turner Lackey's	2	140	Hensley's Ferry	1	337
Bob Hurst's Gin	3	143	Mouth James River	30	367

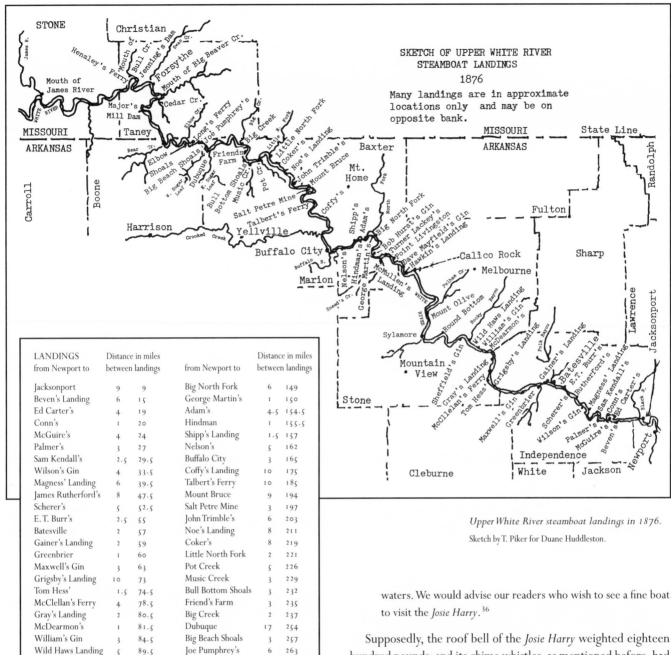

Upper White River steamboat landings in 1876.
Sketch by T. Piker for Duane Huddleston.

as is also the pilot house. She has two bridal chambers, fitted up and furnished elegantly and the ladies' cabin is supplied with an elegant upright Chickering piano. . . . The fine steamer is commanded by Capt. Milt R. Harry, a former Pittsburger, who has for a number of years been engaged in boating in southern waters. We would advise our readers who wish to see a fine boat to visit the *Josie Harry*.[36]

Supposedly, the roof bell of the *Josie Harry* weighted eighteen hundred pounds; and its chime whistles, as mentioned before, had five tones and could be heard fifty miles away. The palatial steamer displaced 482 tons, and its freight deck had a three thousand bale capacity.

Although Captain Harry planned to introduce his new vessel to Memphis and White River that fall, the *Josie Harry*'s arrival was delayed for several months due to an outbreak of yellow fever that raged unabated for weeks in Memphis. The well-known Capt. John D. Elliott succumbed to the indiscriminate killer on August 25, 1878. The ranks of the old captains were further thinned when Capt. Milt Harry's father, Capt. W. C. Harry, fell victim to the disease. Commanding the steamer *Ruth* at the time, the elder Captain Harry fled plague-ridden Memphis and took the boat to Augusta, but he was unable to avoid the ravaging illness. He died aboard the *Ruth* while it was moored at Augusta.

During the epidemic, Captain Postal and the *Hard Cash* made infrequent trips from St. Louis to White River until early November, when he returned to his regular Memphis/White River schedule. Capt. Milt Harry kept the magnificent new *Josie Harry* in the Ohio River until November also, then began to run it regularly in the White River trade.

With its arrival, in late November of 1878, the *Josie Harry* immediately made its mark on the White River commerce. On November 28, the magnificent steamer arrived in Memphis with the largest shipment of cotton ever carried by a steamboat from the White to that Mississippi port. The luxurious craft was loaded with 1,933 bales and, with additional water, could have carried over 2,000 bales.

Apparently yellow fever did not touch the Upper White and Black River ports during the early fall months, but navigation there was hampered by low water. The small *C. B. Warner,* however, continued to ply the Upper White to Calico Rock and above, proving to the shippers there that the vessel was one of the best low-water boats in the river. Captain Smith's *Winnie* kept running between Newport and Batesville during the period of low water. Pleased to have its service, a *Batesville Guard* reporter wrote: "The *Winnie* came up Sunday a little behind time. Hard Shipp, the pilot, reports the water at a very low stage and says it takes close work to bring a boat through, but still the *Winnie* is bound to come. That's right, boys! Bring her through or bust her bottom out!"[37]

Capt. Charles B. Woodbury was seriously ill at his home in Dayton, Kentucky, in late September of 1878. Although his illness was not explained, perhaps he, too, had an encounter with yellow fever. Capt. Byron Woodbury, his brother, assumed command of the *Arch P. Green* and quickly showed that he was an excellent steamboatman by making the quickest round trip of the season between Batesville and Newport, with a run of twenty-eight hours. Not to be outdone, one week later that record was shattered by Capt. Will C. Shipp, pilot of the *Winnie,* with the help of Captain Gibbes, who, reportedly, pushed the steamboat over the shoals with a pole.

Following Capt. Charles B. Woodbury's recovery, he returned to Batesville, where he purchased the warehouses of W. E. Maxfield, stating that he planned to build a substantial wharf on the riverbank. Captain Woodbury also offered handling and storage of freight shipments free of charge, matching the service offered by Capt. Albert B. Smith and the *Alberta.*

No sinkings were reported during the last months of 1878, but a tragedy occurred aboard the *Winnie* near McGuire's landing. Timothy Foley, a deckhand, was handling a coil of rope when he lost his footing and tumbled into the icy river. All efforts to rescue him were in vain, but his body was recovered a few days later on a shoal below McGuire's. Capt. Wilmot Gibbes stated that Foley had worked on the *Winnie* since it was built and was a steady sober man. He was survived by his mother in Iowa.

Other new boats in the White as 1878 drew to a close were the *Red Wing,* Capt. John B. Davis at the helm, and the New Orleans steamer *Florence Meyer,* a vessel that proved to be a punctual packet throughout the season. Capable of carrying a large cargo, the *Florence Meyer* proceeded to make many trips in the Lower White, when water level permitted, during 1879 and 1880. Ice on the river brought traffic to a halt until the middle of January 1879, with several steamboats frozen in at various ports along the White.

Although the villages and towns along White River were linked together by the steamboats, rivalries often existed between them, with the hot competition between the steamboat captains adding to the fun. An incident that occurred in late April of 1879 reflected that rivalry. The church members of Augusta held a bazaar to raise money and, to aid the project, Captain Postal of the *Hard Cash* presented a beautifully decorated pyramid cake baked by the steamer's steward, Richard Brannon. Capt. Milt Harry, whose wife was from Augusta, also donated a lovely ornate cake to the cause. During the spirited bidding at the bazaar, the epicurean delight from the *Hard Cash* sold for $87.50 while the *Josie Harry* cake added only $4.50 to the coffers of the church. That is quite a wide disparity and could be a mistake, but a Memphis reporter surmised that the difference was due to the great admiration the people of Augusta felt for Captain Postal. An added influence might have been that Captain Harry was a resident of Jacksonport, not Augusta.

Already hard pressed by the increasing railroad competition, steam navigation received another setback when a government tax was placed on the industry. Needless to say, the new levy was very unpopular with the steamboat captains. A reporter for the *Memphis Public Ledger* quoted portions of a speech that was written by Capt. Stacker Lee and presented by Capt. Milt Harry at a convention of steamboatmen: ". . . showing the whereofs of boats carrying freights at cheap rates, heavy insurance, and the bare faced cussedness of the newfangled government tax tacked on to the poor steamboatmen, who can't afford to pay lobbyists to represent them in Congress."[38]

Races between the steamers remained a popular activity. On May 2, 1879, Capt. Albert Smith and the *Alberta* raced the *Arch P. Green,* under the command of Capt. Charles Woodbury, from Newport to Batesville. A passenger on the *Alberta* described the encounter:

> Leaving Newport . . . the steamer *Alberta* was boarded. . . . Just before starting, the *Arch P. Green,* a tough little steamer, steamed out ahead and glided off like a trout, throwing continuous rainbows from the clear water. Everyone, but a poor blind man on board, saw that a race would be the result, and a one-eyed man, whose last eye was badly affected saw with half-an-eye that it would be a struggle! The *Alberta* gave chase! The passengers crowded to the bow of the boat and looked on with eager interest. The deck hands shouted and yelled, "I'm walkin' on ye. Git outen the way!" and numberless other little reminders that the river was slipping under the boat. The *Green* was not easily caught. Steam didn't puff from her "scape pipe," but came out in a continuous blast. The *Alberta* was all a bustle. . . . The engine throbbed and the boat quivered. The *Green* still steamed with determination, and one . . . could almost imagine that it was an enormous goose stretching

The steamboat Florence Meyer, *a New Orleans packet that ran on both the Arkansas and White Rivers in the late 1870s and 1880s. It was 246 net tons. It docked at Batesville, Arkansas, on February 2, 1880, with 300 tons of freight and returned on March 9 with 450 tons, reputedly the largest trip ever made from New Orleans to Batesville. It sank September 24, 1880, twelve miles above Natchez on the Mississippi River while en route to White River. Five lives were lost. Capt. James Nichols was master.*

Courtesy of the University of Arkansas, Little Rock, Archives and Special Collections.

out its neck in a mighty effort to distance a pursuer. A change came. The distance between the two racers grew less. Closer and closer, and the waves that beat back into the *Alberta*'s face were split and hurled aside, frothing and foaming. Every iron nerve was now strained. Less and less grew the foaming and agitated watery space. You could now read the boat's name, painted in small letters on the stern. Mightier quivering efforts. The boats were alongside, and the *Alberta* whistled for the river. The *Green* answered and moved aside. But the race was not over after the *Alberta* had passed. The *Green* was irrepressible, and crowded the seeming victor. By this time the boats had arrived at Jacksonport, where the *Alberta* took on a lot of freight. The *Green* stopped only for a few minutes, and steamed away. When the *Alberta* left, the *Green* was out of sight, not a difficult feat to accomplish, as the river is so crooked that it almost comes around and touches itself, and, in fact, an old man on board said that many years ago it crossed itself, but then an act of territorial legislature abolished such capriciousness. . . . The speed was not diminished, but with a determination to win, the clear ripples of the water were split with the same forces characterizing the race. Rounding a bend, the *Green* was in sight. She had stopped to put off freight. The race again became exciting, and for a distance of twenty-five miles the distance between the boats did not seem to change. The *Alberta* gained, but so slowly that it was like watching the hour hand of a clock. In shallow water the *Green* would dart ahead, but where the water was deep the *Alberta* gained. Finally, the *Alberta* reduced the distance to within a few yards. A heavy wind blew down the stream, which, in addition to the swift current, formed no mean obstacle. . . . The race was so close that the arrival at Batesville was almost simultaneous.[39]

In June 1879, the fleet *Alberta* set a new speed record by making a Newport/Batesville/Newport round trip in fourteen hours and ten minutes. Everyone aboard was quite proud, and pilots Jesse Daugherty and Ed Warner celebrated the feat by outfitting the pilothouse with carpeting and curtains.

During the late summer of 1879, a yellow fever epidemic again ravished Memphis, causing the White River packets to flee to other ports. The *Hard Cash* and the *Josie Harry* went to St. Louis and made only infrequent trips to White River during the outbreak. On August 8, the steamer *Trader,* Capt. Oscar Postal, master, started to White River on a trading expedition but was turned back. It was rumored that the captain was incarcerated for violating quarantine orders. With the arrival of cooler weather in October, the yellow fever epidemic abated, and the boats were permitted to return to the Memphis levee.

Falling water hampered navigation during most of September 1879. On September 12, the *Winnie* started upriver, only to break its lines while jumping a shoal at McGuire's. The steamer could go no farther, so its freight was unloaded and it returned to Newport. About three weeks later, the *John Howard,* a New Orleans to Batesville packet, broke its hawser while dragging over a shoal below Augusta. A piece of the broken cable struck the mate, killing him instantly. During the long siege of low water, only the *C. B. Warner* continued to make regular weekly trips. The steamboat logged nineteen journeys to and from Batesville and carried 1,332 bales of cotton, 88 bales of hides, sixty-two sacks of wool, and forty-seven packages of miscellaneous merchandise.

Improvement of the Upper White River channel was made in September of 1879 when J. D. McKown, U.S. engineer, and his assistant, T. P. Schrader, traveled to Buffalo City, where work was to be done on the shoals there. Construction of rock wing dams was scheduled to be completed in about two months. McKown stated that he felt the appropriation of ten thousand dollars would not only cover the work at Buffalo Shoals but also allow some work to be done below that point. About seventy-five men were expected to be employed to complete the project. The engineering party was under the auspices of Major Benyard of the Memphis district.

The *Jennie Stinson,* owned by Pete Boche, entered the Upper White trade in late December and planned to run regularly between Batesville and Buffalo City. Since the *C. B. Warner* and the *Alberta* were already serving the area, competition became keen.

Much to the delight of Memphis traders, business had improved on the lower river. The *Memphis Public Ledger* commented: "The hard money and old reliable packet *Hard Cash* came in last evening from White River with the largest trip of the season, and wins the horns and blue ribbon trip from the *Ouachita Belle,* beating her by several bales. She had 1,260 bales of cotton and 150 packages of sundries. As she stood out in the river, she presented a beautiful sight, cotton piled up to her hurricane roof. It reminded us of the antebellum days to see her coming into port. . . ."[40]

Capt. Milt Harry's elegant *Josie Harry* refused to be beaten by the *Hard Cash.* Capt. Jim Kinman brought the vessel out of White River just two weeks later with 1,262 bales, beating the *Hard Cash* record by 2 bales.

During the first weeks of 1880, the Memphis steamers *Hard Cash* and *Josie Harry* continued to serve their patrons diligently, as did the New Orleans packets *Florence Meyer* and *John Howard.* On February 29, the *New Orleans Times* reported the departure of the *Florence Meyer,* bound for Batesville loaded flat, carrying twenty-five thousand sacks of salt and a log of general merchandise that included boots and shoes, dry goods, hardware, coffee, sugar, and molasses. This was felt to be the largest cargo to have gone from New Orleans to White River for the past year. Unfortunately, the *Florence Meyer* never returned to the clear waters of White River after the spring season of 1880. On September 24, 1880, the steamer sank twelve miles above Natchez, Mississippi. The disaster claimed the lives of five crew members and resulted in the total loss of the vessel and cargo.

Capt. John Thompson Warner, owner and commander of the steamers Duck, C. B. Warner, Tom Hess, *and* Ralph E. Warner, *which was named after his son, whose picture was placed on the vessel's stationery. Captain Warner was the first of the famous Warner family steamboat captains.*

Courtesy of the University of Arkansas, Little Rock, Archives and Special Collections.

Running on schedule in the Upper White and Black Rivers were the *Jennie Stinson,* the *C. B. Warner,* the *Winnie,* the *Alberta,* the *Arch P. Green,* the *Milt Harry,* the *J. M. McArthur,* and perhaps other occasional visitors not mentioned.

On February 10, 1880, the *Arch P. Green* also met with disaster. The steamer took on 242 bales of cotton in Batesville, as well as several passengers, before the mooring line was hauled in and the vessel's bow turned toward Newport. Upon reaching Goose Neck Shoal about five miles below Batesville, the steamboat suddenly became unmanageable. Despite every effort to bring it under control, the craft ran against a snag, knocking a hole in the starboard side about two feet from its bow. The impact shattered its timbers, swinging the stern around, and it quickly sank in ten feet of water. Rapid rescue action saved all of the passengers, but the freight was badly damaged. Captain Woodbury immediately announced that he would start building a new boat to serve his customers.

Another upper river boat was already under construction, the only steamer ever known to have been built in the northern Arkansas county of Boone. According to an undated newspaper article written by Paschal R. Guntharp and now housed at the Jacksonport Courthouse Museum, four residents of Boone County, John Farmer, Newt Milum, Isaac Linton, and Bill Pumphrey, each subscribed one thousand dollars and hired Capt. Thomas B. Stallings to build the *Lady Boone*. Later court records show the captain as the sole owner. On an old blank bill of lading, T. N. Milum was listed as clerk. Originally scheduled for completion by April 15, 1880, the steamer did not make its first appearance at Batesville until late January of 1881, when en route to Newport for inspection, a requirement exacted of all new steamboats by the Steamboat Inspection Series (now the Coast Guard). In his article, Guntharp gave the following account of the *Lady Boone:*

> She was built and launched at Dubuque, Arkansas, a prosperous little town on White River near what is now Long's Ferry, five miles north of Lead Hill. Dubuque has long since vanished. . . . It was once a famous steamboat landing and a center for horse racing in its hey day. . . . She was a small double-decker with high clearance rakes. On her side against a white background were the flaming words, "The Lady Boone." Tom Stallings was her master. Her equipment included block and tackles, cables, bars, a capstan, and other necessary aids in passing the shoals. The boiler and engine were not installed until the boat arrived at Batesville on her maiden trip, these being unessential to a float trip.
>
> It was an occasion of great joy to her owners when, after a three day celebration at Dubuque, the new craft in her gala dress of white, rounded the curves of the river for the first time, hailed by spectators along the way. It is reported that Captain Stallings tied up for a day and night at Calico Rock on this first trip and received visitors, among whom were men who were so impressed with the new boat that they became associates of Stallings in building a second boat some three years later, the *New Home,* at Calico Rock.[41]

The *Batesville Guard* commented upon the arrival of the *Lady Boone:* "The steamer *Lady Boone,* out of Upper White River, hove

Special Upper White River Packet, Steamer **LADY BOONE.**

T. B. STALLINGS, Master. J. N. MILUM, Clerk.

Shipped, in apparent good order and condition, by ____________________

on board the good Steamboat LADY BOONE, the articles described below, to be delivered without unavoidable delay, (the dangers of Navigation, Fire, Explosion and Collision only excepted,) on Wharf Boat or Landing, at the Port of ____________________

where carrier's responsibility shall cease, with privilege of Lightering, Storing, Towing and Re-shipping

unto ____________________ or assigns, he or they paying freight for said goods at the rate of ____________________

and Charges, $ __________

☞Boat not responsible for breakage of Castings or Glassware, Mud, Wet, Old Damage, Bagging or Ties, or for injured Cotton, or for leaking or breaking of Liquors, or decay of perishable articles, nor for unavoidable accidents to or escape of stock.

IN TESTIMONY WHEREOF, the Owner, Master, Clerk or Agent of said boat, hath affirmed to ______ Bills Lading, all of this tenor and date, one of which being accomplished, the others to stand void.

Dated at ____________________ this __________ day of __________ 188

R. & T. A. Ennis, Printers, St. Louis

MARKS.	ARTICLES. Condition and Cooperage excepted and contents unknown.	GROSS WEIGHT. Subject to Correction.	Charges. Not payable until Collected

Bill of Lading for the Lady Boone.

From the Duane Huddleston Collection.

Capt. Thomas Benton Stallings, known as the "Commodore of the Upper White River." Stallings came from a family of rivermen. He built the Lady Boone *at Dubuque in 1880. When it sank, he used its cabin on the* Home, *which burned November 3, 1887. In his honor, a U.S. Army Corps of Engineers snagboat, the* Tom Stallings, *bore his name. The* Tom Stallings *went out of service in 1953.*
Courtesy of the University of Arkansas, Little Rock, Archives and Special Collections.

into the Batesville port on Tuesday of this week with 146 bales of cotton, mostly belonging to the boat, and left for Newport for inspection. This is the first trip of the *Lady Boone,* and to say that she is a beauty does not half express it, and with her able commanders, the old reliable Capt. Tom Stallings on deck, and the very faithful Capt. Albert Cravens at the wheel, she will ply the river from Newport up. The *Lady Boone* is brand new and light draught, being 110 feet long, 22 feet beam, with 8 inch engines and 3 1/2 feet stroke, and a carrying capacity of 400 bales."[42]

The *Lady Boone* did a flourishing business traveling between Newport and the Upper White River ports. During its career, it was a faithful and prompt packet, carrying out cotton and cotton seed, grain, ore, bacon, flour, and other products from the region and returning upriver with sugar, salt, and various other merchandise needed by the area citizens. Cotton was still king in the upper river, with zinc and lead ores providing valuable additional cargo.

One of the many exciting moments aboard the *Lady Boone* occurred when a thunderstorm passed over the boat and lightning struck the foot of Richard Lancaster, a deckhand. The bolt tore off Lancaster's shoe and knocked him down, but he was not seriously harmed. The storm traveled another two miles, where a mule belonging to Squire Buercklin was also knocked down but suffered no serious injury. No other storm damage was reported.

The *Lady Boone* served the Upper White River faithfully, until the waning months of 1884, surviving one sinking in November 1882. A spot on the river that was always a challenge proved to be its downfall in 1884. Guntharp told of Captain Stalling's last trip with the boat:

> Her strenuous combat for three years against the rapids and rough weather had weakened her. . . . the captain once said to his crew, on starting from Newport to Dubuque; "Men, keep a skinned eye. We are heavy loaded and our line is old." . . . On arriving at the shoal below Bull Bottom, he plowed into the turbulent shallow which had been aggravated by a slight rise in the stream. His men were now on the bank with block and tackle. They had managed to cordelle her around Old Joe, the stubborn old boulder which always gave trouble.
>
> And then came the crash. The line broke, and the boat came driving back down stream sidewise, striking Old Joe broadside. With a mighty crash she pivoted and dangled for a moment, then swung around and collapsed against the second boulder. The engineer rushed from the engine room when the fire box broke and the flames licked at him. Captain Stallings leaped from his cabin, and the other men left their posts. All swam to land and from there watched the flames consume their treasured craft.[43]

Notwithstanding Guntharp's account of the end of the *Lady Boone,* it is believed that the fire was extinguished when it reached the waterline and the burnt wreck salvaged. The *Lead Hill Bugle* newspaper of September 20, 1884, stated that the *Lady Boone* was sold at a marshall's sale on the previous Monday and was bought by Samuel Heller. John Q. Wolf, who served as clerk on Captain Stalling's next boat, the *New Home,* later wrote that the *Lady Boone* was dismantled and the machinery put into the new vessel, which was built at Calico Rock in 1885.

A replacement for another old, faithful steamboat arrived in White River in the fall of 1880. Capt. Albert B. Smith had taken the *Alberta,* carrying the machinery of the *Arch P. Green,* to Louisville, where the equipment was placed on a new steamer, the *Alberta No. 2.* After numerous delays caused by low water and lack of wood, which forced Captain Smith to remain several days at Newport, the beautiful stern-wheeler *Alberta No. 2* arrived at Batesville. A local scribe hailed the steamboat as the best ever built for the Upper White River. It was described as having eight elegantly furnished staterooms with every comfort for the traveling public. The new vessel was 150 feet long, had a beam of 29 feet 6 inches, and was 10 feet 9 inches between decks. Equipped with two engines, rappet valves, 10-inch diameter and 3.5-foot stroke, it was driven by a wheel 13 feet in diameter with a bucket 19 feet long. Its one boiler, which was 20 feet long and 44 inches in diameter, contained lap-welded flues. Although it had a custom house tonnage of 257 tons and a carrying capacity of one thousand bales of cotton, the light-draft steamboat drew only 11.5 inches of water light. It cost Captain Smith the *Alberta No. 1,* valued at eight thousand dollars, plus seventy-five hundred dollars cash.

Serving in the Upper White River, the *Alberta No. 2* posed a threat to the other steamers trafficking there, steamers such as the *Lady*

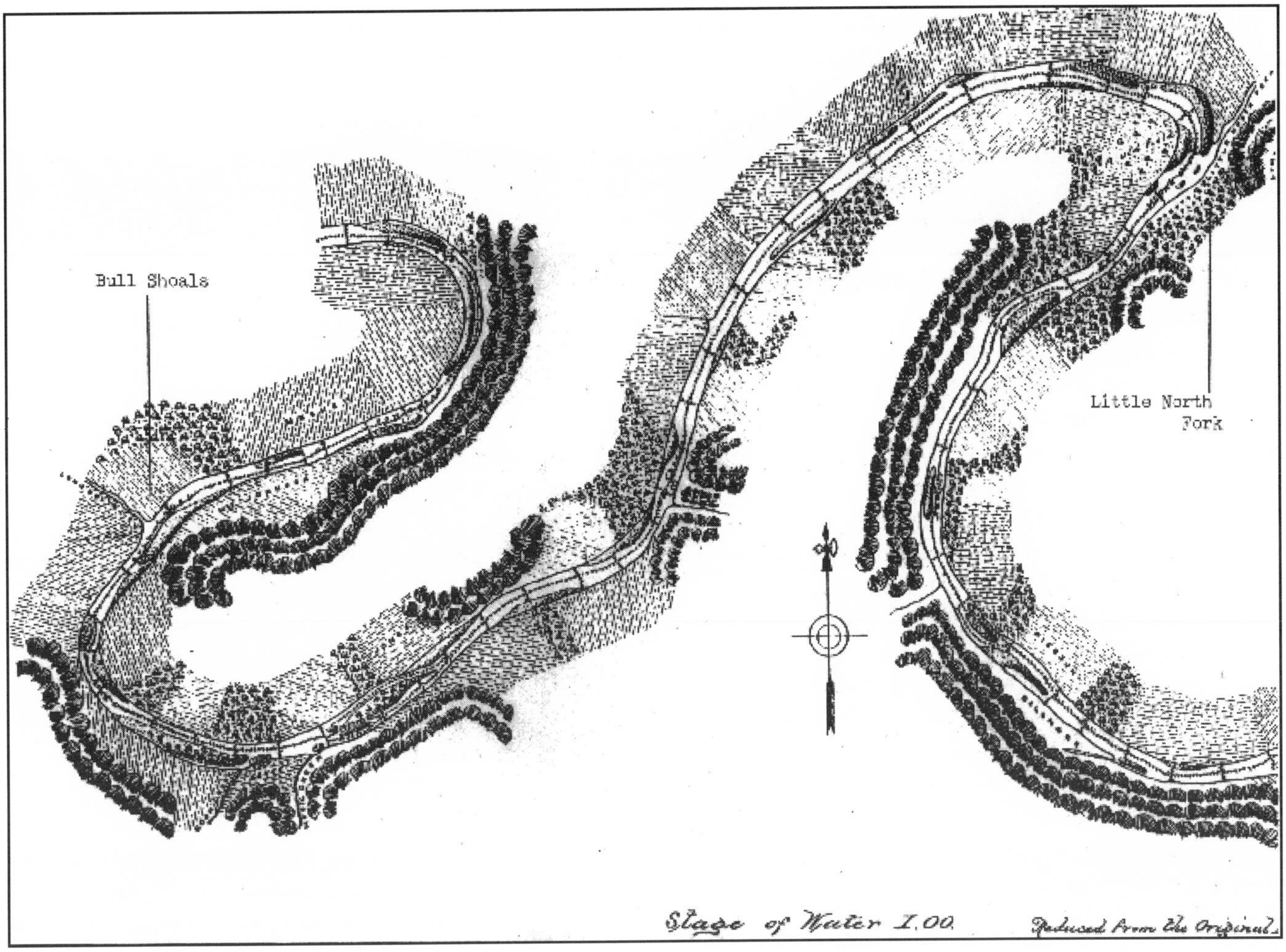

April 4, 1888, U.S. Army Corps of Engineers map, White River, Bull Shoals area. It was made under the direction of H. S. Taber, Captain, U.S. Army Corps of Engineers, by Jas. C. Long and Chas. E. Taft, Asst. Engineers.

Courtesy of the U.S. Army Corps of Engineers office, Little Rock, Arkansas.

Boone, prior to its sinking, and the *Whitewater,* mastered by Capt. Charles B. Woodbury. Captain Smith attempted to squeeze out his competitors by making a pact with the railroad officials at Newport whereby the rails would refuse to deliver unconsigned freight for the upper river merchants to any boats other than those of the Smith line. Highly incensed by the monopolistic actions of Captain Smith and the railroad officials, a meeting with Batesville merchants was called by Captain Woodbury. Since a concentrated effort was being made to obtain an extension of the railroad to Batesville, Frank D. Denton reported the assembly rather diplomatically in the *Batesville Guard,* hoping to avoid offending railroad officials:

> "River vs Mail"
>
> On last Monday evening, several of our businessmen came together in a meeting, made and signed a contract with Capt. Woodbury, of the steamer *Whitewater*, about as follows: The signers agreed to give the *Whitewater* all their carrying business for one year, with the privilege of two years, at the following rates; 50 cents per bale of cotton from this port to Newport, and pound freight 16⅔ cents per hundred, either way; and flour at 25 cents per barrel; these rates to be binding during the boating season for good freight trips, to take effect from and after date. This is a deduction of one-third on former rates. We understand the meeting and agreement was brought about by the reason of the railroad refusing to deliver un-consigned freight for the Upper White River to any boat other than the Smith Line *(Alberta* and *Winnie).* This is a contest in which we have no interest, direct or indirect; it is an action of the railroad, and we certainly consider that a man can and should ship as he may choose, and any action of our businessmen at this time, in the least hostile to the railroad, may be premature and injurious to the commerce of our town. At least we regard it so, for the channel that transports the cheapest will in the end be patronized, and it will be folly or foolish to think that any one town, or interest, will bring the railroad to any terms other than their own. Remember the world is an institution with many and various routes of trade, and when you don't like the one, you have the pleasure, as well as the right, to choose another line of travel.[44]

After the sinking of the New Orleans packet *Florence Meyer,* the *Red Cloud* and the *Bedford* provided the area with weekly packet service from the Crescent City to the Lower White. On March 5,

1881, the *Bedford* carried out 1,479 bales of cotton and 450 sacks of corn. The large vessel became quite popular and enjoyed a banner season, but did not return in the fall. The *Hard Cash* and the *Josie Harry* continued to run faithfully from Memphis to the Lower White River. Those steamboats serving the Upper White and/or Black River patrons were the *Alberta No. 2, Whitewater, C. B. Warner, Jennie Stinson, J. M. McArthur, Milt Harry, Lady Boone, Wild Boy,* and possibly the *Trader.*

In October 1881, the New Orleans steamer *Cherokee,* Capt. P. J. O'Reilly in command, arrived at Newport, starting what proved to be a lucrative career. Scheduled to leave Jackson County semi-monthly, the packet carried cotton and freight to New Orleans for $1.50 per bale and 50 cents per hundred pounds, respectively. In November of 1882, the *Cherokee* obtained an interesting cargo at Newport consisting of twelve hundred bales of cotton and eighty tons of manganese. Mined near Batesville, the ore was consigned to Newcastle on the Tyne, in England, where it was to be used in the manufacture of Bessemer steel.

As the year ended, the railroads were making greater inroads into the commerce formerly carried by the steamboats. The upper river steamers were now being threatened by an extension of the railroad from Newport to Batesville. The steamboat captains, however, were unwilling to concede any part of their business, and the bitter fight gained momentum.

The spring rains of 1882 provided an optimum boating stage, and the steamers churned up and down the river with increasing frequency. Most of the regulars from 1881 were still busy in the river.

An incident occurred aboard the *Whitewater* in April 1882 that became the topic of the day up and down the river. The incensed editor of the *Batesville Guard* printed the details:

"MASHER"

"In the Meshes of the Law—A Brutish Outrage"

On last Friday, two warrants were sworn out before Esquire Peete, against one . . . charging him with slander, the other . . . with the grave charge of assault with intent to commit rape. These warrants were sworn out by a young lady from Toledo, Ohio. . . . it was shown that the lady was en route to this place to visit a married sister, and the attempt was made aboard the steamer *Whitewater,* on or about the 29 of April last, after the boat had left Jacksonport. The main scene is said to have occurred near McGuire's Landing, and the proof is that after repeated advances and repulses, the gentleman(?) of wealth followed the lady into her stateroom and locked the door, laid hands upon her and thrust her upon the bed, then and there attempted his fiendish design. The evidence is, the young lady used every endeavor to force him to desist, when fortunately for the young lady, a violent rap at the door by Capt. Byron Woodbury . . . caused ——— to desist. The plain statement of the lady upon the stand, her manner of testifying, her conduct before the court, are indelible evidence that an outrage was attempted upon her person. And a still worse feature of this case is, that two deckhands were brought upon the stand by the defendant to swear away the lady's virtue. Upon evidence of Sheriff Case . . . one of the deckhands . . . was . . . arrested . . . for perjury. . . . His sworn testimony was at variance with what he

The steamboat White Water *was built in 1880 by Capt. Charles B. Woodbury for the Upper White River trade. The boat was 133 x 24 x 3.75 feet and displaced 167 gross tons. It was sold in June 1883 to Capt. Joe Ward for service in Rio Grande River. It was last owned by Columbia Transportation Company of Texas.*

Courtesy of J. Randolph Smith, son of Travis L. Smith Sr., owner of Columbia Transportation Company, and the University of Arkansas, Little Rock, Archives and Special Collections.

stated to these gentlemen. . . . The reason for his evidence in behalf of ——— and against the lady, can be surmised.

The state was ably represented by Governor Baxter and Messrs. Coleman and Yancey. The defense was ably handled by Messrs. Butler and Neil. The trial lasted from Monday to yesterday, when the decision was that the evidence fully warranted the court in holding the defendant over on a bond of $1,500 to answer at the next circuit court. The case of slander was withdrawn for the present, but no doubt will be brought up at the circuit court next January.

Many false rumors regarding this lady have been silently afloat, arising from the conduct of ——— towards her at the time and on the boat mentioned. At the trial this lady's virtue was vindicated, her chastity established to the satisfaction of everyone, and her conduct commended by every person who was present in the courtroom and heard her testify.[45]

The steamboats operated rather uneventfully until early January of 1883, when the *Hard Cash* experienced trouble. Just a few miles up Little Red River, it struck a huge overhanging tree that knocked down its chimneys and damaged its roof. Hasty repairs were made, and the steamer returned to White River and attempted to limp upstream to Augusta but was forced to return to Memphis. Following major refurbishing, the *Hard Cash* resumed its regular schedule in September.

Misfortune befell Capt. Albert B. Smith on November 17, 1883, when he lost his cherished steamer *Alberta No. 2*. The vessel had just left Jacksonport en route to Newport when a fire of unknown origin was discovered burning near the recess. Since the steamboat was loaded with four hundred bales of cotton and about four hundred sacks of cottonseed, an attempt was made to land it and unload the cargo, but the effort proved unsuccessful. Capt. John T. Warner, pilot, bravely remained at the wheel until the fiery inferno finally forced him to jump through the opening in the front of the pilothouse. The heroic engineer stayed in the engine room until communications with Captain Warner were severed, then he also jumped overboard. The gallant Captain Smith refused to leave until fire consumed the tiller ropes, which rendered the craft inoperative, and the captain, too, plunged into the water. The young watchman, Daniel Van Curen, fought the fire until the very last; in fact, he tarried too long and perished in the burning holocaust. The victim had been on the boat only a few days, having worked on the recently completed railroad to Batesville. The cargo of the doomed steamer was insured, but Captain Smith carried no insurance on the boat, valued at twelve thousand dollars. The captain stated he would draw the *Winnie* from the lower river trade and place it in the Upper White.

November 23, 1883, saw the arrival, at Memphis, of the sparkling new *Chickasaw,* Capt. Ed Postal's answer to the *Josie Harry,* which belonged to his old friend, former boss, and long-time competitor, Capt. Milt R. Harry. The *Chickasaw* was built at a cost of sixty-five thousand dollars, under the supervision of Capt. James Rees, its owner and a major stockholder in the

Steamboat Cherokee. *Built at Cincinnati in 1873, the boat entered New Orleans and Jacksonport trade in October 1881, running semi-monthly. Commanded by Capt. P. J. O'Reilly, the* Cherokee *was 210.2 x 38.8 x 6.6 feet and rated at 474 net and 688 gross tons. The boat was at Batesville on November 14, 1882, with Capt. Billy Joyce as pilot. It ran in White River until spring 1883, and perhaps later.*

Courtesy of Capt. William H. Tippitt, Hernando, Mississippi, and the University of Arkansas, Little Rock, Archives and Special Collections.

Memphis and White River Packet Company. The palatial steamboat was 190 feet long, 38 feet wide, had a 7-foot hold, and could carry 1,650 bales of cotton. Its cabins and staterooms were decorated with the finest and latest decor. All its accommodations were superior. Equipped with all new machinery, it had the latest marine improvements, including the famed electric lights, which were hailed as a great convenience to the pilots in navigating the many bends of White River. The steamer proved to be the last large passenger and freight steamboat to be constructed exclusively for White River patrons.

The *Chickasaw* left Memphis on November 15, 1883, for its maiden trip up White River. Pilots for the trip were Capts. Ed Warner and Hugh Nixon. Captain Warner later described that journey:

> . . . And how well I remember the first trip! I'd never been on a steamboat with electric lights. They bothered me. They were so bright they hurt my eyes. You know steamboats used to never make a landing from the mouth of White River until they reached Indian Bay. That was because on each side were dense forests, almost a wilderness, with low embankments and not a place to land. . . . Then the whole country . . . was the home of many wild animals, such as panther, wild cats, bear and besides snakes. Good gracious! I've seen snakes hanging from tree limbs and them seen to be eight or ten feet long. . . . The first night we came up White River, with the *Chickasaw* flashing her electric lights, it created a panic with the beasts of the forest. Several places where the channel ran close to the shore, I'd see the lantern-like eyes of some wild animal shining from a limb of a tree. I'd turn that light on him, and man alive, what a racket the creature made getting away, and when it thought it was a safe distance away, it would let out a scream like a wild note from a calliope. Of course, nothing but a catamount or panther made such unearthly screams. . . .
>
> But getting back to that first trip of the *Chickasaw*. Of course, she had been widely discussed in advance. Farmers, merchants, bankers, and everybody wanted to get a glimpse of the new packet. . . . No one knew a thing about the electric lights. That

The Chickasaw, *shown in 1883 with twenty-two hundred bales of White River cotton. Built in 1883 for the Memphis White River Packet Company under Capt. Ed Postal, it ran regularly for eight years from Memphis to Newport and, occasionally, Batesville. Built by James Rees and Son of Pittsburgh, the boat cost sixty-five thousand dollars and measured 190 x 38 x 7 feet. Equipped with elegant staterooms and cabins, it was the first boat to run in White River with electric lights. Pilot on its maiden voyage was Capt. Ed Warner, who vividly recalled the excitement caused when the steamer's light shone along the riverbank. Worshipers in a church saw the light and thought the world was coming to an end.*

Courtesy of Wilson Powell.

was a secret of Captain Postal. He wanted to surprise them, and by ginger, he did!

After we left Indian Bay the population along the river began to thicken. I knew where everybody lived, black and white, rich and poor. By the time we had reached civilization, I had caught on how to handle the searchlight. So, when approaching a farmhouse, village, landing or town, I'd play the searchlight on the houses, and I'm telling you, it liked to have started a panic!

The first place I saw after leaving Indian Bay, was a Negro church. I switched on the searchlight, then trained it on the church. I never saw so many people running from a place of worship as fast in my life. They tumbled over each other. . . . But presently the preacher looked up toward us, as we slowed down and came into the landing easy-like. Then there seemed to be more people rising from their knees than I'd seen drop to them. . . . Captain Postal called to them from the hurricane deck not to be frightened.

"It's our new electric lights. I want all of you to come on board and see it. Preacher," he urged, "bring the congregation along." And they came.

. . . all along the trip there was excitement. No one knew what it was when they saw the light flashing against the sky. I was told that in certain settlements, both black and whites prayed, believing that it meant the end of the world.[46]

Receptions were held at many landings along the White en route to Jacksonport. Captain Warner stated, that, of all the boats on which he served, the *Chickasaw* was his favorite. Although the steamer did not go to Batesville on its maiden trip, in future years, Captain Postal proudly took his new vessel there whenever possible.

An old favorite steamboat, the *Hard Cash,* made its farewell journey in the White River during November of 1883, arriving at Memphis on the twenty-sixth. With the purchase of the *Chickasaw,* Captain Postal had sold the *Hard Cash* to Capt. T. P. Leathers for ten thousand dollars. During its long months of faithful service, the staunch vessel had made three hundred trips to the area and had diligently served the towns and small cities along the White. The new owner placed the *Hard Cash* in the Vicksburg and Yazoo River trade.

The farmers and plantation owners along the White had prospered during the fall of 1883, having experienced the greatest cotton growing season on record. Capt. Edwin Tucker Burr Warner later described the abundance: "There were no acreage restrictions and every farmer, big or little, grew all he wanted to. I'll tell you they rolled in wealth that fall and winter. Why that fall when picking started, I've seen Negroes on the streets of Jacksonport and Augusta with the fronts of their vests covered with ten dollar bills. That was usually on Saturday nights after being paid for their week's picking. Of course, some didn't keep it very long. There was always a crap game somewhere along the river front, where the Negro was enticed by some dusky damsel and lost his money, either at the card or crap table."[47]

The end of 1883 brought the end of another old White River favorite. On December 24, the *Josie Harry* was puffing upriver toward Memphis, carrying a White River cargo of 664 bales of cotton and one thousand sacks of cottonseed, when it caught fire about twenty miles below Memphis. Despite the valiant efforts of Captain Harry and the crew, the steamer could not be saved. B. F. McConnell, who lived near the site of the disaster, later described the misfortune to Joe Curtis:

> I was a very small boy that day. I remember I was in front of father's cotton gin. We had several bales of cotton on the landing ready for shipment. I heard the distress whistle of the *Josie Harry*. I saw her coming upriver, deep smoke almost hiding the boat. Burning bales of cotton were being thrown overboard. She landed in front of our house to let her crew and passengers come aboard. Flames soon enveloped the beautiful steamer, and her hull, drifting toward the middle of the river, sank. Father and Mother invited the passengers and crew to our house, where they were taken care of until the following day when the *Chickasaw* came along and picked them up and took them to Memphis.[48]

In January of 1884, Captain Harry announced he would run the *Milt Harry* both above and below De Valls Bluff, passing there four times weekly. The superb *Chickasaw* continued to serve the Lower White regularly in 1884; and in September, Captain Harry reentered the Memphis and White River trade with the new *Joe Peters*. The vessel was said to be the fastest stern-wheeler afloat and was scheduled to leave Memphis each Saturday.

Navigation was hampered by extremely low water in the Upper White during the fall season of 1884, delaying the arrival at Batesville of the *Alberta No. 3,* Capt. Albert B. Smith's new boat. Built by the Howards of Jeffersonville, Indiana, the steamboat was almost an exact replica of the *Alberta No. 2*. It measured 150 feet long, with a 30-foot beam, and had two boilers. The *Alberta No. 3* replaced the *Winnie* in the upper river, and that vessel was sent to the St. Francis River. The *Lady Boone* was busy in the Upper White during all of 1884 until its sinking that fall.

The Goodrich steamer *Wild Boy* served the patrons on the Black and Current Rivers. A freight boat that displaced only thirty-nine tons, the *Wild Boy* was one of the smallest in the White River system. In December 1884, the steamer *Hope* also entered the Black River trade, and the *Milt Harry* made several trips there, so competition was stiff on this tributary of the White. A bit of excitement happened aboard the *Milt Harry* while the steamer was in the Black River in December. During an exhilarating Christmas party aboard the vessel, the barkeeper shot off one of his toes.[49] That would certainly be a Christmas to remember!

The completion of the railroad to Batesville, in 1883, had detracted more and more of the Newport to Batesville trade away from the steamboats, causing the abandonment of daily steamer trips between the ports. Of course, the vessels were still running between the two towns, primarily to haul cotton for connection with the Memphis steamboats and to carry their freight bound for the upper river; but their trips were becoming fewer, and attention was focused more and more on the Upper White. The extension of the railroad also forced the upper river steamers to shift their base of operations from Newport to Batesville.

Capt. Charles Woodbury introduced a new packet to the Upper White in November of 1884. The *John F. Allen* arrived from Cincinnati on November 28 with a heavy cargo for Batesville merchants. Although considerably smaller than the *Alberta No. 3,* the new boat was well built and of beautiful design. It was 130.2 feet long, had a 24-foot beam with a 4.2-foot hold, and displaced 133.9 net tons. The steamer suffered a mishap during its first two weeks of operation in the upper river when it ran into some rocks while steaming upriver between Buffalo City and McBee's Landing, in Marion County. After casting off two hundred bales of cotton, Captain Woodbury dislodged the vessel and, fortunately, the new steamboat suffered only minor damage.

As 1885 began, the *Milt Harry,* the *John F. Allen,* and the *Alberta No. 3* were regulars on the Upper White, while the *Chickasaw* and the *Joe Peters* were running on schedule from Memphis in the lower river. It appears the *Cherokee* also made a few trips from New Orleans to Lower White River ports in 1885.

Due to low water, Captain McArthur and the *Milt Harry* were stranded at Buffalo City for quite a period as 1885 began. The trapped vessel finally left the Marion County landing in early February, but perhaps it would have been better if it had remained there. Less than a month later, the steamer caught fire and burned near Batesville. The flames spread so rapidly that Captain McArthur and his crew barely escaped. Another fine steamboat departed White River.

At least one steamboat captain was still fervently interested in adding competition to the Lower White trade. Capt. Milt Harry acquired the nine-year-old, elegant side-wheeler *De Smet* to serve as a Memphis/White River packet; and, on October 17, 1885, brought his new purchase to Memphis, headed for White River. The beautiful old steamboat had a twenty-five hundred bale freight capacity and was declared as good as new, having performed little service during the last five years.

With the entrance of the *De Smet* into the trade, there were, once again, three Memphis boats serving White River patrons. The *Chickasaw,* Captain Postal commanding, left on Wednesdays,

The De Smet *was built by Capt. Joseph La Barge in the winter of 1871–1872. It was 486.6 gross tons and was 188 x 34 x 5.5 feet with three boilers, each 38 inches in diameter and 22 feet long. The cylinders were 17.5 inches in diameter with a 5-foot stroke. Named for Father De Smet, a famed Jesuit missionary among the Indians of the Missouri River Valley, it burned April 12, 1886, near Newport.*

Courtesy of Wilson Powell.

while the *De Smet* was opposed as a Saturday packet by Captain Smith's *Alberta No. 3,* which was now traversing the lower river.

A new addition to the Upper White in the fall of 1885 was the *New Home,* built at Calico Rock for Capt. Thomas B. Stallings. As previously mentioned, the machinery of the ill-fated *Lady Boone* had been installed in the *New Home.* The steamboat proved to be an able competitor for the Upper White River trade.

With commerce on the lower river less and less dependable, the local steamboat captains concentrated more and more on the upper river. Since cotton was still the major crop there, the area was a natural market for the steamboats. Ginning usually started in September and terminated in the late fall, at which time the seasonal rains brought the White to good boating stage. Because the first boat to arrive at the upper landings usually obtained the unconsigned freight, each captain tried to beat his opposition up the river. On January 1, 1886, the primary contenders on the Upper White River were Captain Smith, commander of the *Alberta No. 3;* Captain Stallings, master of the *New Home;* and Captain Woodbury, owner of the *John F. Allen.* John Q. Wolf, clerk of the *New Home,* described a competition involving the three captains:

> In late January, 1886, the river was frozen over. Three steamboats, the *Alberta No. 3,* the *John F. Allen,* and the *Home,* were lying at the wharf at Batesville anxiously waiting for a thaw. Much freight, destined for upriver points, had accumulated there, and much cotton was lying on the banks above, awaiting shipment. The three boats had everything in readiness for a quick dash. Presently the weather moderated and a warm rain set in, and the ice began to break up as the river started rising. Late in the afternoon Capt. Tom Stallings, master of the *Home,* being a bit more daring than were his rivals . . . decided he would steal a march on the others by pushing up the river a few miles, although he knew it meant battling the floating ice which filled the river every foot of the way. The *Home* fought her way through the ice to the Marcella Landing, twenty miles above. It was midnight, and Captain Stallings concluded it would be perfectly safe to tie up his boat for the rest of the night, since he had a good twenty miles start on his competitors. He ordered everybody to bed except the night watchman, instructing them to be ready at five o'clock the next morning. He gave the night watchman strict orders to have everybody up and ready to go by daylight. He also charged him to keep a sharp lookout down the river; to keep his eyes and ears open, and if he saw a light such as steamboats are required to carry at the masthead while running at night, or if he heard a boat whistle, to report to him at once and to rouse up the other officers and crew. The night watchman listened carefully to the instructions and assured Captain Stallings he would take good care of the situation. So the Captain, feeling pretty certain that neither Captain Smith nor Captain Woodbury would risk their boats at night in a heavy flow of ice, turned into bed about one A.M., congratulating himself on his strategy.
>
> About two hours later Captain Stallings was awakened by the familiar noise and clamor of a passing steamboat. Opening his window he looked out and saw a beautiful sight, though one he did not relish. The *Alberta No. 3,* the largest and fastest of the three, was driving past the helpless *Home* under full steam. He rushed about like mad, giving the alarm to officers and crew, and soon had everybody awake except the night watchman. His relaxation was so complete and restful that the commotion caused by the passing steamer had not disturbed his peaceful slumbers. Captain Stallings located him in the steward's room, reposing comfortably on two chairs, and snoring with great vigor and eloquence. It seemed a pity to break up a situation so comfortable and free from corroding care, but business is business, so the irate captain kicked the chairs from under him, precipitating him to the floor. He sat up, rubbed his eyes, and inquired if there had been a collision. He "resigned" the next day and his resignation was accepted without prolonged debate.
>
> Half an hour after the *Alberta* passed, the lights of the *John F. Allen* were seen in the distance, and she soon passed the *Home,* as the latter was trying desperately to accumulate a head of steam. Before the *Home* reached Buffalo City, she met the *Alberta No. 3* returning with a full load of cotton.[50]

Although Captain Smith was first up the river, his advantage was short lived, for on the next trip, the pilot backed the *Alberta No. 3* into the bank a few miles above Calico Rock, breaking one of its drive shafts. Captain Smith returned to Newport with only one shaft of the steamer working and never again placed the boat in the extreme upper river trade.

During the spring of 1886, the U.S. Army Corps of Engineers resumed work on improving the Upper White River. Working under the supervision of Captain Tabor, work started at Buffalo Shoals and moved downriver to meet improvements made the previous year. The goal was to establish a low-water channel to Buffalo City and a medium channel over the shoals.

The spring rains brought a rise in the river, and trips above Buffalo City were resumed. Unfortunately, there were a few collisions along the way. One occurred in Marion County in early April of 1886. Although relatively minor, the accident resulted in a confrontation between the crews of the two vessels. W. B. Flippin Jr., an eyewitness to the skirmish, recorded the altercation:

> The steamer *Home* arrived at McBee's Landing on last Thursday with eight tons of freight. The "boss" boat for the Upper White River went on to Lead Hill with 200 barrels of salt, the first boat that has made the trip this year. . . . The steamer *John F. Allen* arrived at McBee's Landing also, with as much freight as an Irish peddler could carry in a grip-sack. She ran against the *Home* and tore part of her guard away, at which crisis all hands went in "family prayer." Your correspondent went out of bullet range as quickly as possible. After the row was settled, and the *Allen* crew had got a coon-skin and wiped off their chins and pulled down their vests, I emerged from my hiding place in time to shout, "peace on earth, good will to men," as the boats rounded out.[51]

The trip seems to have been a particularly exciting one for the *Home,* or perhaps a normal one. On that same journey, there were some anxious moments before the steamboat reached Lead Hill; at least for clerk John Q. Wolf, who wrote:

> Bull Creek, fifteen miles above McBee's Landing was the most difficult the Steamer *Home* encountered while I was clerk. The level of the water dropped down abruptly some fifteen feet within a mile. There was ample water in the channel, but the current was so swift and strong that the *Home* could not stem the tide. She had climbed over the famous Buffalo Shoals the evening before with 600 barrels of salt on board, without laying a line. We had put off 400 barrels of salt at McBee's and now had but 200 barrels on board, and she was stalled at Bull Creek. A line was laid and still she could not go over. We were allowed only 175 pounds of steam in her boilers, but the engineer, a dare-devil sort of a chap, ran the steam up to 225 pounds by wedging a block of wood in between the safety valve "pop-off" and the deck above, thus rendering the safety valve useless. The boilers became so heated that the engineer had to keep the doctor, or pump, running the whole time we were going over to keep the boiler supplied with water. The situation was so dangerous that when the boat chanced to come in close to the shore, I put out a plank and jumped off to Terra Firma![52]

The sharp rivalry between Captains Woodbury and Stallings continued until low water stopped the trips to Buffalo City and to McBee's Landing. The last notation of the 1886 spring boating season was found in the *Mountain Echo* newspaper of May 7, which stated: "The indomitable Capt. Stallings arrived this morning at McBee's Landing in command of his boat, the *Home,* with 50 tons of freight. The *Home* is the only boat which will come here on 20 inches of water."[53]

As the hot competition raged in the Upper White, the *Chickasaw,* Captain Postal in charge, and Capt. Milt Harry's *De Smet* competed rather uneventfully for the Lower White River trade between Memphis and the White River. Misfortune struck Captain Harry in early April 1886, however, when the *De Smet* collided with the railroad bridge near Newport. The accident tore away the wheelhouse, cookhouse, guards, and outriggers of the steamer. After the impact, fire finished the Memphis packet, leaving Captain Harry without a boat. He chartered a much smaller vessel, the *Freddy Robinson,* to temporarily replace the *De Smet.*

The work by the U.S. Army Corps of Engineers from Buffalo Shoals to Batesville was completed by December of 1886, and a two-foot channel existed between the two ports at extreme low water. Plans were formulated to carry it to deep water in the coming spring.

Little changed in steamboating in the White River during 1887, but one major misfortune marred the year. Fire of unknown origin was discovered burning in the cotton bales on the

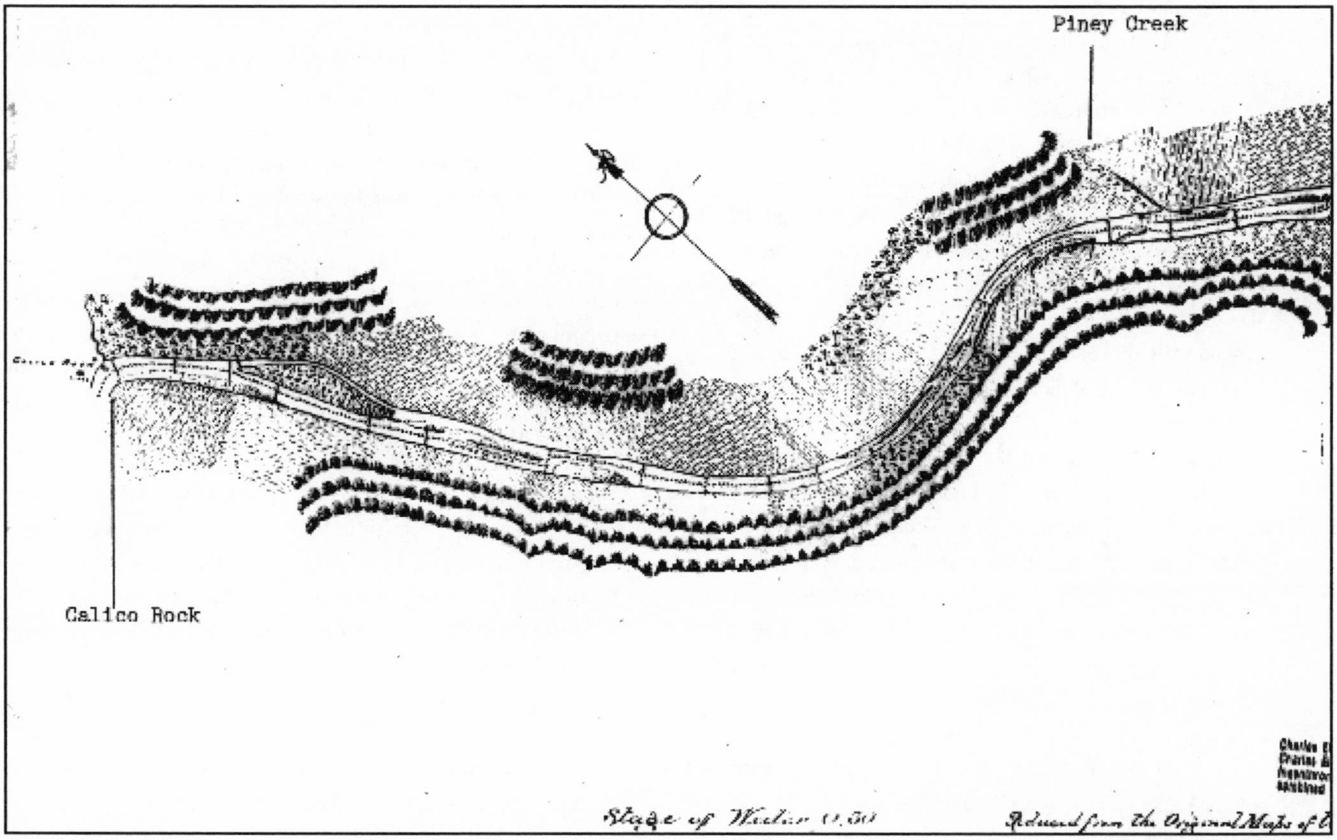

April 4, 1888, U.S. Army Corps of Engineers map, White River, Calico Rock area. It was made under the direction of H. S. Taber, Captain, U.S. Army Corps of Engineers, by Jas. C. Long and Chas. E. Taft, Asst. Engineers.

Courtesy of the U.S. Army Corps of Engineers office, Little Rock, Arkansas.

freight deck of the *Alberta No. 3* while it steamed down the White near Indian Bay on the morning of October 27, 1887. After the alarm was sounded, the passengers were quickly dispatched to safety, and the officers and crew valiantly tried to extinguish the rapidly spreading flames. Unfortunately, the fire ran rampant, enveloping the decks and forcing the crew to flee for their lives. After assembling on the riverbank, a roll call was made, and it was discovered that clerk Wilmot Gibbes was missing. The gallant captain was last seen in the office trying to save the books and other valuables, but his brave attempts cost him his life. Well known on the White, Mississippi, and Black Rivers, Captain Gibbes was truly a grand old man of steamboating.

The burning of the *Alberta No. 3* left only the *Chickasaw* in the Memphis and White River trade. Capt. Charles B. Woodbury purchased the *Dick Williams* at Evansville in September of 1887 in an effort to monopolize the upper river trade. His chief competitor, Captain Stallings, ran the *New Home* in the lower river trade during the summer low-water time and until late fall, when misfortune befell the boat. While on a trip on the Mississippi River on November 3, the steamboat caught fire and burned above Ferren. The disaster claimed no lives, but the *New Home,* the pride of Calico Rock, was lost, although its machinery was later recovered.

A new, small steamboat, the *Tom Hess,* built at Batesville, made its appearance in the upper river trade in the fall of 1887. Constructed by Capt. Edwin T. B. Warner and his younger brother, Capt. William T. Warner, the boat ran between Batesville and Newport, with occasional trips to Buffalo City and McBee's Landing. After he retired, Capt. Ed Warner wrote about the venture: "My brother Will and I went in together in 1886 and built a boat and called her the *Tom Hess* in honor of a friend who was a large planter and merchant, and he rendered us a little assistance in completing the boat. Mr. Hess naturally gave us all his business. In those days the boats paid all the railroad charges on freight bought and sold, and delivered hundreds of barrels of salt to their patrons and only settled after the cotton season closed. This condition, together with long, low water periods, and ice gorges, made it stronger than we could hold up—so we went busted."[54]

The boat was later owned and operated by Capt. John Warner, who proved fairly successful with the vessel. An entry in the Record of the *Tom Hess* in 1889 reflects the captain's pride in the steamboat:

> The steamer *Tom Hess* has, since the first day of December, handled 1127 bales of cotton, bringing 1043 bales to Batesville and 84 to Newport. During the same time, she handled 515 packages of merchandise and 53 passengers, besides towing three barge loads of cedar posts, etc., from Burr Eddy to the bar below Handford's mill.
>
> In handling this business the boat has run about 750 miles. For so small a boat to do this amount of work, it is evident that the officers and men having charge performed faithfully their work. Capt. C. M. Engles was in command a good part of the time. Willie Bishop, steersman, did good service. Mr. Ed. N. Frey, engineer, assisted by his brother George, had charge of the steaming department, and the distance traveled speaks for them. The gentlemanly and clever Ed Loewen rendered much valuable service for which I have to thank him.
>
> Much credit is due the sable-hued crew whose strong arms moved the bales, boxes, barrels, etc. . . . They consisted of Sanford Burr, Nanie Pinket, Zach Ross, Joe Wood, Alex Jeffery, and Capt. Dan Smith, all of whom performed faithfully their duties. To "Pap" Lee, the fireman, is due credit for duties well done. George English, the Cook, assisted by his wife, is entitled to praise for the faithful manner in which they fed the hungry crew and passengers. I hereby tender thanks to each member of this crew for services rendered.
>
> John T. Warner, Batesville, Dec. 27, 1889[55]

In the spring of 1888, the Upper White River rivalry was enlivened by the entrance into the trade above Buffalo City of the steamer *Ralph* under the command of Capt. Billy Shipp, its owner. Many years later, John Q. Wolf wrote about Captain Shipp: "Capt. Will C. Shipp . . . began his career by piloting keelboats. . . . He was reared on the upper river, and followed the river trade as master and pilot all his adult life. . . . It used to be facetiously said of Capt. Shipp, as indicating his thorough knowledge of the river, that if one should break off a small limb from a tree anywhere along its banks and show it to him, he could identify it at once and tell where it came from. In his long life, he spanned the entire history of steamboating on White river, its rise and its decline. . . . He was well known in every town from Forsyth, Mo., to the mouth of White River."[56]

Business in the Upper White was quite profitable during the 1887–88 boating season, and several captains made plans to enlarge their operations. Capt. Will C. Shipp left for Pittsburgh about April 15 to lengthen the *Ralph,* add electric lights, and make other improvements. Captain Smith notified the publisher of the *Mountain Echo* that the Memphis and White River Packet Company had purchased the steamer *General Charles H. Tompkins* and would place it in the trade as soon as the weather and water permitted. Although the *Tompkins* had a carrying capacity of eight hundred bales of cotton, it could run on only fifteen inches of water, a valuable asset for navigation of the Upper White.

The *General Charles H. Tompkins* enjoyed an impressive career in White River for the Memphis and White River Packet Company. During its tenure, the steamboat served in both the upper and the lower river, until November of 1891, and was highly respected the length of the White. It left an imposing record. During the last week of February 1891, the *General Charles H. Tompkins,* commanded by Capt. Thomas B. Stallings, made steamboat history when it traveled to the mouth of Bear Creek, some twenty miles below Forsyth, and returned to McBee's Landing with eight hundred bales of cotton. With the water at the guards, Captain Stallings then guided the steamer on to Batesville. As far as is known, this was the largest shipment ever carried from the extreme Upper White to Batesville. In March of 1891, Captain

Stallings, joined by Captain Postal, arrived at the Music Creek mines above Oakland, after having brought the *Tompkins* to McBee's Landing with a crusher for mine owner Joe S. Lemon. Other boats had refused to transport the huge piece of equipment on the present low water. To show his appreciation, owner Lemon offered all his future business to Captain Stallings and the sternwheeler. When plans were laid to transport the crusher to the Pangle farm on Jimmy's Creek, just above the present Bull Shoals dam, Mother Nature added a new dimension to the task with drastically falling water. The *General Charles H. Tompkins* was stranded at McBee's for almost a month. To save expenses, some of the deckhands were discharged and returned to Batesville. Hiring local help, the *Tompkins* eventually made it to Long's Ferry before returning to Batesville and below. In October 1891, the *Tompkins* was moved to the Lower White to replace the *Chickasaw,* which was in dry dock for repairs following a sinking. The service of the *Tompkins* in the lower river was unfortunately short this time, as the capable vessel sank in early November 1891 about two miles up the White River chute, where it struck a snag. Much of its freight floated off and was lost. The wreckage of the *General Charles H. Tompkins* was sold to a Mr. Sibley, who lived a short distance from where the steamer sank.

Capt. Charles Woodbury had also placed a new steamer in the upper river trade with the appearance of the *James P. Eagle* in January of 1889. The boat was quite beautiful and was painted a brilliant white, which led to its being given the nickname "White Eagle." The *James P. Eagle* was a dependable, productive packet on the Upper White until Captain Woodbury sold it in the fall of 1892 to Capt. Fred Inman of Pocahontas, and the craft was taken to Black River.

The U.S. Army Corps of Engineers continued their work to improve the Upper White channel, but their job was a frustrating one, often hampered by weather. Heavy spring rains in 1890 destroyed much of the government work just recently completed, filling the channel with new gravel bars. Rivermen agreed that a dredge boat was the tool most vitally needed and urged Captain Tabor, the U.S. Army Corps of Engineers' officer in charge of river improvements, to secure one. The results of the Corps' endeavors frequently met with mixed approval from local citizens.

In the spring of 1891, the U.S. snagboat *Henry Sheldon* traveled up the White with barges to construct two dikes at Earnheart's landing, some seven miles above Batesville. The dikes were completed several months later, but they proved worthless and had to be removed, bringing new rounds of scorn from area newspapers.

Throughout the years of steamboating on the White River, various steamboat captains took it upon themselves to remove navigational obstacles. In September of 1891, Captains Shipp and Cravens made a try. The two rivermen left McBee's Landing in a skiff carrying ten pounds of dynamite, which was used to remove obstructions in Buffalo Shoals and other points along the river. Their success was reported as astounding. When they arrived in Batesville following their labor, several people made contributions to further their work. An additional fifty pounds of dynamite was purchased, and more White River rocks and snags between McBee's Landing and Buffalo Shoals met their demise at the hands of the two steamboatmen.

During the summer of 1891, a movement was underway in the extreme upper reaches of the river to shift trade to Springfield, Missouri. The effort, while doomed to failure almost from its inception, affected steamboating in the Upper White for the next two years. As the counties of this region became more densely populated, there was a sharp increase in the marketable products produced there and a greater demand for imported goods and materials to the area. The number of steamboats plying the upper waters, and the efforts by the government to improve river transportation, caused certain business interests in Springfield to look closely at this possible new source of income. Plans were formulated to shift the trade toward Springfield, rather than downriver, and their aspirations materialized in April of 1891. The publisher of the *Springfield Democrat* praised their venture:

> For some time a number of businessmen of Springfield and North Arkansas have been maturing an enterprise for utilizing White River as a means of transportation. . . . Capt. S. Semonin of Batesville, an old riverman of twenty years experience, was the originator of the scheme, and through his zealous efforts the plan has been perfected. The company organized yesterday embraced the following prominent businessmen of Springfield and Arkansas: H. F. Fellows, of the Springfield Wagon Company; J. T. Keet, of the firm Keet and Roundtree; S. E. Cope, of Springfield Grocer Company; John McGregor, of the Springfield Hardward Company; D. D. Milligan, of the firm Milligan and Son; F. E. Headly, of the Headly Grocer Company; the Rogers and Baldwin Hardware Company; W. T. Bruer; A. J. Eisenmayer; J. Comer, a lumberman of Batesville; Capt. S. Semonin, of Batesville; W. C. Shipp, of Arkansas City, Ark.; J. S. Cowdrey, of Yellville, Ark.; Cox and Denton, of Gassville, Ark.; and W. C. McBee, of McBee's Landing, Ark.
>
> The plan is to operate on the Black and White Rivers in connection with the Gulf Railroad from Black Rock, on the former stream, to McBee's Landing near Batesville on the later. . . . The company is arranging for rates with the Gulf Railroad, and good terms can be secured it is claimed. This enterprise will open up 200 miles of the White River country, now almost shut out from the trade of Springfield. It will give the rich territory on the Arkansas border an outlet to Springfield for its varied products, and in turn open the region to the merchants and manufacturers of this place. . . . and the territory down the river will, through this enterprise, become tributary to Springfield instead of going to St. Louis. . . .
>
> All details for the contemplated transportation have been arranged, and the first boat of the new company will start from Black Rock to McBee's Landing tomorrow. This is one of the most important events for Springfield that has occurred for a long time. . . .[57]

U.S. snagboat Henry Sheldon *anchored at Sylamore on Upper White River, June 22, 1900.*
Courtesy of the University of Arkansas, Little Rock, Archives and Special Collections.

The new company was chartered as the Ralph Transportation Company with a capital stock of six thousand dollars. The company purchased the steamer *Ralph* from Capt. Will C. Shipp, and planned to keep it busy on the White and Black Rivers.

Due to the continued interest in the Upper White, a river convention was held at Batesville in May 1891. Delegates from nine Arkansas and two Missouri counties attended the opening session of the White River Convention. The primary objective of the meeting was discussion of the removal of obstructions to navigation in the river. Two senators and a representative also made speeches. Following the oratory, a permanent organization was formed to pursue improvement of navigation. In the afternoon, convention delegates, politicians, and local dignitaries boarded the steamer *Ralph* for an upriver inspection trip. The trip was not as harmonious as desired, however, with one participant later lamenting that four of the participants spent most of the day and night playing cards.

The affairs of the Ralph Transportation Company ran into difficulties when it was reported on July 19, 1891, that the enterprise was several hundred dollars in debt and that Captain Semonin had left. The boat was at Batesville, but the whereabouts of the captain was a mystery. What happened is unclear; however, auditors were hired to examine the company's business records, which were found in the express office at West Plains, Missouri. There was no explanation of how the records reached West Plains. After ten days, the examiners found that the alleged shortages or operating losses were about twenty-eight hundred dollars. Capt. Will C. Shipp took command of the *Ralph* in an attempt to recoup the losses and place the company on a sound financial basis. The Ralph Transportation Company continued to be plagued with problems and disagreements, however. A squabble over control of the steamboat *Ralph* occurred and eventually ended up in the federal court in Little Rock for settlement. By court order, the steamer was docked at Batesville, where it remained under the care of a watchman, until the fall of 1892. In September, the vessel was sold by the U.S. marshall at public auction in Little Rock for fifteen hundred dollars. Its purchaser was Capt. Ed C. Postal, who planned to run the *Ralph* in the lower river between De Valls Bluff and Indian Bay in connection with the Memphis and Little Rock Railroad.

While the Ralph Transportation Company did not succeed in

its attempt to divert trade to Springfield, another group of entrepreneurs organized for the same purpose. Led by Willard E. Winner, a well-known capitalist from Kansas City, the group, in late November 1891, formulated plans to build a railroad from the mouth of the Buffalo River through Yellville, Lead Hill, and Forsyth to Springfield. The line was to be called the Springfield, Yellville, and White River Railroad. Plans were also made to purchase a steamboat to transport freight from Batesville and the Upper White River to Buffalo City, where the cargo would be shipped by rail to Springfield. Long range plans called for the extension of the line to Memphis.

In late April of 1892, the steamer *Randall* arrived at Batesville, bound for Buffalo City. Owned by W. E. Winner and F. Q. Hadley, the steamboat was to serve two purposes: to run regularly between Batesville and Buffalo City carrying construction supplies and materials for building the railroad and to carry passengers and freight in competition with the other upper river boats.

The *Randall* was a nice, little, light-draft boat that was ninety feet long with a thirty-foot beam and had a carrying capacity of forty-four tons and thirty-two passengers. Built in 1889 at Sioux City, Iowa, it was well constructed, with plenty of power for good speed. Its cabin had twelve adequate staterooms. Under the command of Capt. Will C. Shipp, with Capt. Albert Cravens serving as pilot, the *Randall* was towing a heavily loaded barge on its initial appearance at Batesville. In addition to a number of wagons for Hinkle and Company, the barge carried numerous scrappers, wheelbarrows, shovels, and similar tools for railroad building. At Batesville, it took on lumber and other necessary materials for camp construction before leaving for Buffalo City. Among its passengers were six men who were to be construction foremen for the proposed railroad.

Following the first trip, Capt. William T. Warner became master, as well as the pilot of the *Randall,* on its semi-weekly trips to Buffalo City. Twenty-eight hours were required to make the upriver trip from Batesville, but the return journey was accomplished in twelve hours. While the *James P. Eagle,* under Capt. Charles B. Woodbury, was also still faithfully serving upper river patrons, the *Randall* became a favorite of W. R. Jones, publisher of the *Mountain Echo,* and was frequently mentioned in that newspaper.

As the ambitious plans of W. E. Winner and associates materialized, a town site for the southern terminus of the Springfield, Yellville, and White River Railroad was sought at the mouth of the Buffalo River. Efforts to locate the site and wharf for the steamer *Randall* on the Marion County side at the river's mouth proved unsuccessful. Winner then purchased acreage on the Baxter County side and proceeded to build his town. The new village was named Winnerva, perhaps suggestive of his nerve in attempting to build a railroad through the mountainous terrain of White River country. In addition to the railroad and steamboat

Steamboat Randall. *Photo is believed to have been taken in 1892 near Calico Rock, Arkansas, on the Upper White River. Packet belonged to promoters of the Springfield, Yellville, and White River Railroad being built from the mouth of Buffalo River toward Yellville, Arkansas. The money panic of 1893 forced stoppage of work on the railroad and the steamboat left the river.*

Photo courtesy of Audrey Brooks, Calico Rock, Arkansas, and the University of Arkansas, Little Rock, Archives and Special Collections.

Steamboats J. A. Woodson *and* Randall *on a gravel bar believed to be at Nellie's Apron in the Upper White River near the mouth of the Buffalo River. The* Randall *was bought by Winner and Hadley in 1892 to haul supplies for the Springfield, Yellville, and White River Railroad. Built in 1889 at Sioux City, Iowa, it was ninety feet long, thirty feet wide, and could carry forty-four tons and thirty-two passengers. It ran between Batesville and Buffalo City, with many trips to McBee's Landing. C. P. Pond was in charge of the* Randall, *and Capt. Will Warner of Batesville was master of the vessel much of the time. Capt. Charles Woodbury was master of the* Woodson.

Courtesy of the University of Arkansas, Little Rock, Archives and Special Collections.

commerce, the town's promoters hoped to attract the large numbers of rafts that were carrying timber and mineral resources from the White River Valley.

On August 26, 1892, the foundation for a large store building was laid at Winnerva. Work at the site progressed as rapidly as materials were obtained, and three new houses were started during the week of September 2, while the mercantile structure was near completion. By the end of 1893, however, construction on the railroad halted. Almost seven miles of roadbed had been completed, but a shortage of funds curtailed work and finally stopped construction entirely. When activities ceased, the steamer *Randall* disappeared from the river, and the Winnerva and White River Transportation Company became extinct. All building in Winnerva stopped, and the little town withered and died. A total of seven or eight buildings had been erected at the site, including a three story hotel that was later used by construction crews when they built what became known as the White River Division of the Missouri Pacific Railroad. By the late 1930s, all of the structures at Winnerva had disappeared.

Steamboat activity on the Lower White had dwindled miserably. In the spring of 1893, there were no boats from Memphis serving the White River. It was the first time in approximately fifty years that a Memphis steamer had not traveled to the region regularly. While there were future trips, and traffic on the lower river did pick up again, the days of the elegantly furnished passenger packets were over. Most of the boats that later ran in the Lower White were small ones whose trips became fewer and fewer, until they, like those on all of the White, finally disappeared altogether.

Bitter weather conditions and ice again caused problems in January of 1893, and most of the steamers lay idle at Batesville during that period. Despite such hazards, however, Captain Woodbury, who had leased the *J. A. Woodson,* left Batesville to assist the *A. R. Bragg,* which had sunk at the head of Padgett's Island, several miles below Batesville. Constructed at Newport in 1890, the *A. R. Bragg* ran mostly in the Black River. The steamer was repaired and later returned to the trade. Its last service was in 1903 and 1904 when it ran from Black Rock on the Black River to Newport on the White.

The *J. A. Woodson* was a stiff competitor for the Upper White River trade, and Captain Woodbury did his best to cater to his

The A. R. Bragg *loaded with cotton. Built at Newport, Arkansas, in 1890 by Inman-Decker Packet Company, it measured 115.6 x 26.8 x 4.7 feet, displaced 162 net tons, and was the largest steamboat built at Newport. Its last service was in 1903 and 1904, running from Black Rock (on Black River) to Newport (on White River).*

patrons. An undated clipping that described an excursion trip aboard the *J. A. Woodson* was found in the scrapbook of the mother of Mrs. Mary Fitshugh Spragins, a past president of the Independence County Historical Society. It reads:

> To make a trip up White River for the purpose of enjoying its magnificent scenery, on one of the several steamboats that ply the waters of the upper river the greater part of the year, is the cherished desire of everyone who has ever lived in Batesville, or visited the place for any length of time. Acting on this impulse, a party of about 25 young ladies and gentlemen boarded the splendid Steamer *Woodson* on Thursday of last week, bound for McBee's Landing, about 120 miles above Batesville. . . .
>
> Mr. and Mrs. Glenn and their children, and Mr. and Mrs. J. C. Fitzhugh were also members of the party as far as the Glenn farm, where they have a delightful summer residence. . . .
>
> Captain Woodbury extended the party a hearty welcome for which this genial steamboatman is famous from one end of the river to the other. The *Woodson* is the largest, fastest, and by far the best equipped boat on the river for passenger service. The accommodations for the party were both ample and comfortable during the entire trip. . . .
>
> At three o'clock the big steamboat swung loose from Batesville Landing and turned her prow up the river. A big rise was coming down and the boat had to fight a strong current all the way to McBee's. Yet she made an average of five miles per hour, and, with a double crew, ran night and day. The river is most beautiful, however, at low water. Then the stream is as clear as a spring branch, and one, from the deck of a steamboat, can see the rocks and gravel on the bottom of the river from one shore to the other, and count the fish as they scud away from the prow of the approaching boat. The river was too high, however, for that on this trip, and the water was very muddy.
>
> Late in the afternoon a rainstorm drove everyone from the decks to the cabins, and it became so cool that fires were lighted in the stoves. When darkness came on, the electric lights were brought into requisition—the first that ever shown on the upper White River, and the boat proceeded without interruption.
>
> At the Glenn farm, Mr. Glenn and his jolly party were landed in a driving rain and darkness absolutely Egyptian in its density. But the gin close by furnished friendly shelter, and by the aid of a lantern and a buggy they had taken up on the steamboat, they were finally able to reach the house. . . . Then, with no more landings to make, the boat fought the current all the rest of the night which mate Teeters declared to be the worst he had ever spent on a steamboat.

The J. A. Woodson *at Col. V. Y. Cook's Landing, a few miles below Oil Trough, to take on a load of cotton from the Cook Plantation. Built in 1881, the* Woodson *was 142 feet long, 30 feet wide, with a 3.7-foot hold, and displaced 220 tons empty. The* Woodson *frequently ascended the river to McBee's Landing, near Cotter, and went as far above as Lead Hill. It was run in White River from 1891 to 1896 by Captain Woodbury.*

Courtesy of the University of Arkansas, Little Rock, Archives and Special Collections.

But the passengers all slept well, despite the storm, and daylight found us at Sylamore. How the party did eat! . . . The most eloquent tribute we can pay to the *Woodson* table is to say it kept the liberal and thoughtful master hustling all the time to provide for his hungry passengers.

The rain, which did not cease until noon, did not prevent our enjoying the beautiful scenery of this southern Hudson. The magnificent mountains and the tall cliffs, assuming picturesque shapes from different points of view and painted in many fantastic colors by the contact of the rain for ages with the acres and minerals contained in their scant soil, supplied interesting entertainment during the whole trip.

We shall make no attempt here to describe the beauty and grandeur of the scenery of the Upper White River. . . .

At midnight Friday the boat reached Buffalo City, where she lay until daylight to take on and discharge some freight. There we found Hon. J. C. Smith of Baxter, with Fred Hanzer of Little Rock, and a Mr. Micks of Chicago, awaiting a boat for Batesville. These gentlemen had been looking for investments among the zinc mining claims of Marion County and were very favorably impressed with the outlook there. Mr. and Mrs. Seawell, of Yellville also embarked there, having been waiting for a boat for several days to start on an extended trip to Chicago, New York and Washington. . . .

At noon Saturday the boat reached McBee's, the objective port of the trip. The afternoon was spent in discharging the freight, and at dark we dropped back to Buffalo City, where we lay up for the night. Soon after daylight Sunday, the big boat swung out into the middle of the river to catch the full force of the current, and we started homeward at a gait of fifteen miles per hour and arrived at Batesville at four o'clock in the afternoon, having stopped several times for wood and passengers. Altogether it was a delightful trip. Much of the scenery was viewed from the splendid outlook of the pilot house, the excellent and affable young pilots Dick Prater and Charley Teeters, taking pleasure in pointing out objects of interest and answering innumerable questions asked them. Down in the engine room, Engineers Graham and Calloway were equally polite and attentive in explaining the operation of the machinery, and Mate Teeter never missed an opportunity to contribute to the pleasure of the passengers. . . . The entire party will long bear in it pleasant remembrance, and cordially unite in wishing the *Woodson* and its genial captain a prosperous business and good fortune.

J. A. Woodson *on an excursion trip. Exact date and place of photograph is unknown. The late Capt. Charles Warner stated that the pilot on the trip was his father, Capt. Will Warner, and the master was Capt. Charles B. Woodbury.*

Courtesy of the University of Arkansas, Little Rock, Archives and Special Collections.

Another new steamboat in the Upper White during 1893 was the *Oakland.* Built by Capt. Will Warner, the *Oakland* was a neat little steamer that had been completed in October of 1892. It received high praise from local newsmen.

The business interests of W. C. McBee at McBee's Landing continued to grow, and in June 1893 he started construction of a steamboat. By building a boat capable of easily ascending the White to Lead Hill and above, McBee hoped to obtain a major portion of the trade of that region. Capt. Albert G. Cravens and E. B. Johnson, who had acquired some fame as a boat builder, were hired to construct the vessel. Upon completion, the builders announced that the new steamboat would carry a nice load of freight and several passengers on eight inches of water. To increase the hauling capacity, a barge named *Sandy* was built for towing behind the steamer. The *Myrtle,* named for one of McBee's daughters, left McBee's Landing in October 1893 on its maiden voyage to Batesville for inspection. Unlike some vessels assembled along the White, the *Myrtle* was built entirely at McBee's Landing, complete with machinery. The little steamboat had a freight capacity of thirty tons.

Pilot Cravens described the *Myrtle*'s first trip to W. R. Jones, of the *Mountain Echo:*

Mr. Editor: I intended writing up the first trip of the steamboat *Myrtle* every day since our arrival up to Buffalo City; but have been sick-a-bed ever since, and am now dictating this from McBee's Landing, where I am flat of my back with La Grippe and Pnewmonia.

Our dropping down the river to the foot of Buffalo Shoals was a feat unprecedented in the navigation of White River. The river was lower than for many years, and the oldest residents familiar with its different stages, declare it only five inches higher than the very lowest stage that she has ever known to mark. We were 15 days in going from this Landing to the foot of Buffalo Shoals—we took our time—clearing a channel sufficient for passage by removing loose boulders, gravel, debris and by blasting through the higher rocks of the roughest places, using over 100 pounds of dynamite—finally landing below the shoals without accident or injury to the boat or crew, and in as good condition as when we left.

We left Buffalo City and in three days were in Batesville. After passing Nelson's Landing we commenced taking on cargo along the route. We could have carried a great many bales of cotton had we had along the "Sandy," our barge, whose capacity is 200 bales.

Batesville having been reached and the object of the trip the inspection of the boat, we rested three days interviewing and shaking hands in that social little city of our many and long time friends; and where the Memphis Custom House Officers . . . ran up, interviewing us and thoroughly inspecting the new steamer *Myrtle* of McBee's Landing, Marion County, Arkansas. The inspectors pronounced her all "O.K." in every sense of the word in every department.

The inspector peeked and nosed around about and through the boat; and with our little pump, tested our boiler which has attracted so much attention and criticism, up to 600 pounds pressure. When that degree was reached, the inspector very politely asked our engineer how much steam pressure he wanted. Our engineer answered that 175 pounds was all needed . . . for all purposes on the steamer *Myrtle*. The inspector give him . . . five pounds extra, making it 180 pounds; and would have given as much more if we had requested it. They passed high compliments on the machinery and the make up of the boat.

We left Batesville with 30 tons of freight for miscellaneous points up the river and finally in two days, on very low water upstream, landed at Buffalo City, the fastest time I've ever known a steamer to make the distance.

We came through the Rapids blowing off upon entering, and still blowing off upon our exit, within ten minutes of the watch. The crew was all down sick when we reached Buffalo City, so we laid up to recuperate and get medical attention. . . .[58]

The *Myrtle* proved to be a fine upper river boat and was frequently alluded to by W. R. Jones in the *Mountain Echo*. Unfortunately, its career was fairly short. After running in the Black River trade during the fall and winter of 1884, it was in White River headed for McBee's Landing to haul cotton to Batesville when disaster hit. Under the command of Captain Stallings, the boat reached Oil Trough late in the evening on March 1, 1895, and was tied up just above the post office for the night. As the cook was preparing breakfast the next morning, he had an accident and the room caught fire. Within a few minutes, the entire steamer was in flames, with the crew barely escaping unharmed. The little vessel was totally destroyed.

Dissatisfaction over the expenditure of river improvement funds remained a constant problem, and it became apparent that all parties could not be satisfied. In an argument with the publisher of the *Batesville Guard*, W. R. Jones of the *Mountain Echo* asserted that Captain Taber of the U.S. Army Corps of Engineers was wrong to use most of the appropriation on work below Batesville, and that they were not justified in demanding the spending of the balance ($18,000) there.[59]

Steamboating in 1894 remained quite active on the Upper White and spasmodic on the lower river through most of the year. One steamer on the Lower White, the *Rex*, provided a river excursion in May 1894. Professor T. I. Doan of De Valls Bluff chartered the boat to entertain the students of the high school. Under the command of William Shipp, the *Rex* was beautifully decorated for the occasion. Over two hundred pupils, parents, and friends enjoyed Professor Doan's hospitality, which included music provided by Nelson's String and Brass Band. According to the *Gazette* report, the trip was a "howling success" and Professor Doan captured the hearts of his students.[60]

Three steamers were churning the waters of the extreme upper river: the *J. A. Woodson*, Capt. Charles B. Woodbury, master; the *Ralph E. Warner*, Capt. John T. Warner commanding; and the *Myrtle*, with Capt. John Shipp in charge and Capt. Albert G. Cravens as pilot. In the first few weeks of the year, the boats carried away approximately fifty thousand dollars worth of Marion County cotton. The whistles of the steamboats could be heard daily on that portion of the White.

Wishing to own another steamboat, Capt. Will T. Warner engaged E. B. Johnson to construct one especially adapted to the upper river trade. The boat was completed by fall, and Captain Warner took his new vessel on a test run. It proved to be well built, durable, and quite an elegant little steamboat. Captain Warner was completely satisfied and gave his mother the honor of naming the craft. Quite appropriately, she christened the steamer the *Dauntless*.

The *Dauntless*, a beautiful little stern-wheeler of 73.49 tons, lived up to the expectations of its captain and became a stalwart regular on the Upper White. It often ran during times of low water when even the best of its competitors were unable to travel. Though water conditions were quite low, the faithful steamer was still churning the waters on June 7, 1895, when it left Batesville towing a barge loaded with two carloads of mining equipment.

Unwilling to be outdone by Capt. Will Warner and the *Dauntless*, Captain Woodbury was determined to keep running the *J. A. Woodson* to McBee's Landing during the summer months of low water. After jumping many shoals with great difficulty, he finally reached Sneed's Creek, some ten miles above Calico Rock, but could proceed no farther. The disappointed captain tied his steamboat to the bank and sent five passengers and seven deckhands back to Batesville in a yawl. Two other passengers and several deckhands remained with Captain Woodbury on the stranded *J. A. Woodson*.

Another little boat built specifically for upper river travel appeared in the White in the late summer of 1895. Fulfilling a lifelong goal to own his own steamboat, Capt. Albert Cravens, along with G. J. Angelly, built the steamer *T. E. Morrison*. The vessel was indeed small, measuring only fifty-four feet long and ten feet wide, but it was capable of accommodating sixteen passengers and carrying fifteen tons of freight. Its builders claimed the *T. E. Morrison* could run on six inches of water. All reports described it as a dandy that could travel to Buffalo City on the lowest water ever known.

The development of the zinc mines along the Buffalo River resulted in frequent requests from the mine owners to the U.S. Army Corps of Engineers to make the stream navigable for small steamboats in order to provide easier transportation of the ore from the mountainous area. The requests were, initially, unheeded, but they did draw attention to this White River tributary and the ore market which existed there.

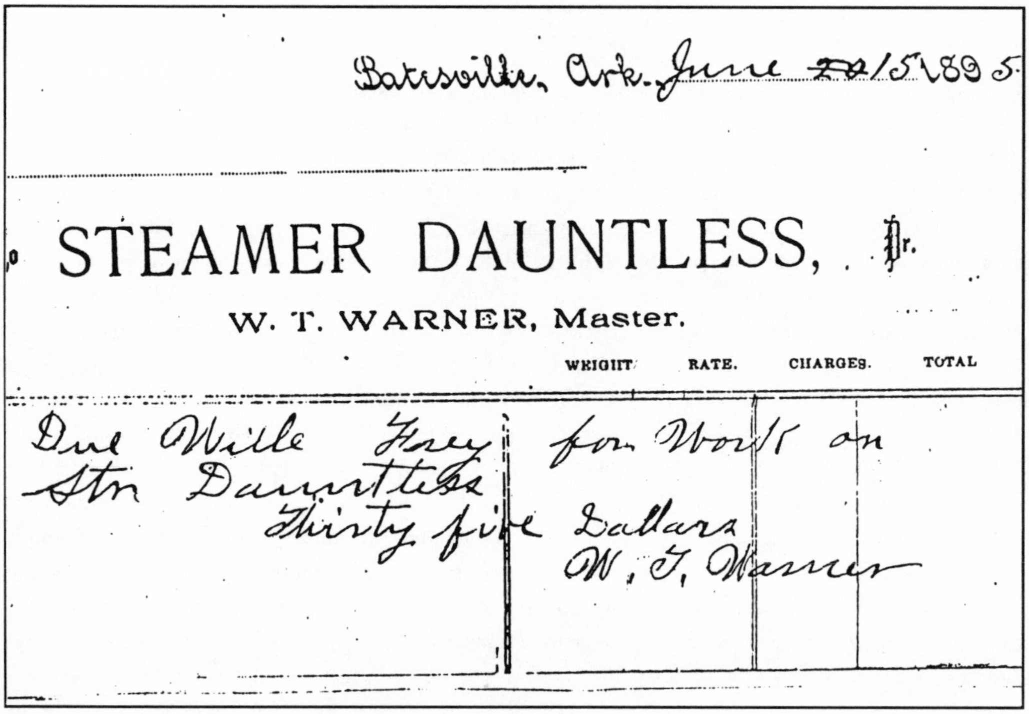
Batesville, Ark. June ~~20~~ 15 1895

STEAMER DAUNTLESS, Dr.

W. T. WARNER, Master.

WEIGHT	RATE.	CHARGES.	TOTAL

Due Wille Frey for Work on Str Dauntless
Thirty five Dollars
W. T. Warner

Bill of Lading for the Dauntless.
From the Wilson Powell Collection.

On Easter Sunday in April of 1896, Capt. Albert Cravens contributed to that attention when he turned the bow of the *T. E. Morrison* up the Buffalo River and made a successful trip of several miles. The boat was carrying a group of excursionists. To say that the success of the limited trip was exciting to Captain Cravens would be a serious understatement. The enthusiastic captain notified W. R. Jones of the *Mountain Echo* that he would soon take the superb little vessel about eighty-five miles up the Buffalo River to win a one hundred dollar bonus. Whether Captain Cravens attempted the long voyage is unknown, but no record could be found of his tackling the river again.

The spirit of adventure burned deeply within the steamboat captains, and, although all were friends, they were also fiercely competitive. When news of the success of Captain Cravens reached Capt. Will T. Warner, the desire to excel Cravens's feat was intense. Fortunately for Captain Warner, an opportunity soon presented itself. The officials of the Morning Star Mine at Rush, Arkansas, contracted with Captain Warner to make a test run with the *Dauntless* to see if the Buffalo River could be proven navigable. On the trip, Captain Warner was to take some machinery and passengers to the mouth of Rush Creek.

Among the passengers on the steamer were Captain Warner's wife and his niece, Leone McGuire. The daughter of Mollie and Will McGuire, Leone was visiting in the Warner home at Batesville when the Buffalo River trip developed. Realizing the importance of the trip, Mrs. Warner wanted her niece to experience the adventure and took the girl on the boat without the permission of her mother. In defense of her actions, the captain's wife wrote her sister: "Dear Sis: This is such a temptation for Leone that she can't resist it. The boat is going up the Buffalo River and it is such a nice trip, she is crazy to go. So don't be mad at her. Will wants us to go and this will be about the last trip that I can go, as it is getting so warm. Now look here, Sis, don't get mad at us. I will take good care of her, and when we come back, I will come over and keep house for you and let you and Will go whenever you want to. . . ."[61] At the time of the trip, Capt. Will Warner was thirty-one years old and his wife was about twenty-six.

The account of the adventuresome trip was recorded in one short paragraph in the May 1, 1896, edition of the *Mountain Echo:*

> Forty miles up Buffalo River are the mouths of Rush and Clabber creeks. Heretofore, it had been considered one of the impossibilities for a steamboat to go up the Buffalo River on any stage of water, but last week, Capt. Will Warner of the *Dauntless,* having some freight and passengers for the Morning Star determined to do the impossible, and so, without accident, he made the run with the staunch little steamer *Dauntless* 40 miles up the limpid and virgin stream, awakening with steam whistle the silent echoes of those uncovered mountains of zinc. The water was about average stage and he proposes to make another trip up the Buffalo hereafter.[62]

From this description, one wonders why other boats had not been navigating the Buffalo River, since the journey of the *Dauntless* sounded fairly uncomplicated. Other narratives, however, recounted a more difficult trip.

Many years later, Walter L. Isom, who was a passenger of the *Dauntless* on the Buffalo River trip, clearly remembered the difficulties encountered in ascending the various shoals and rapids between the mouth of the Buffalo and Rush Creek. When Isom was a young man of twenty-one, he was working with Bob Trimble on a farm on Cow Creek, some three miles from the mouth of the Buffalo. As the young men worked along the bottoms, they heard a steamboat's whistle pierce the quiet of the river valley. They raced to the edge of the Buffalo, where they saw the steamer *Dauntless* puffing slowly up the swift waters of the river. In open-mouth amazement, they watched the boat glide nearer and nearer. When it was quite close, Captain Warner shouted to the observers on shore and asked if they wished to "take a little boat ride." It took only a brief consultation between them before the young men accepted the invitation and climbed aboard the steamboat. A few other watchful natives also joined the adventure as the *Dauntless* crept toward its destination.

Progress up the Buffalo was extremely slow, with the steamer having to stop frequently so that the crew could chop away overhanging tree branches that would catch on the smokestacks of the vessel. The crew became quite adept in wielding an ax. Shoals along the river's path presented another problem. When each shoal was reached, the crew would lay a line to some distant tree on the riverbank and attach the other end to the capstan on the bow of the steamer. "It was operated like a windlass," stated Isom. "Six or eight men would insert poles in the device and turn it so as to reel in the line, thereby pulling the boat over the shoal."[63]

Progress was so slow that, although Walter Isom and Bob Trimble boarded the boat one day, they did not arrive at the mouth of Rush Creek until during the second day of the trip. Upon reaching his destination, Captain Warner supervised the unloading of the cargo, then immediately headed the *Dauntless* toward the mouth of the Buffalo and the deeper waters of White River.

The extraordinary feat by Capt. Will T. Warner again raised the demand to improve the Buffalo River for navigation. This time, some positive results were obtained. A survey of portions of the river was made by the U.S. Army Corps of Engineers. The study covered the Buffalo from where it enters White River to the mouth of Rush Creek, the exact route of the *Dauntless.* The distance was computed to be 24.2 miles, with the river falling an average of 3.161 feet per mile. It was determined that navigation was possible only by constructing five locks and dams costing $750,000. After reading the report, Captain Sibert, the officer in charge of the U. S. Army Corps of Engineers improvements on the Upper White, recommended that the commerce on the Buffalo did not justify such expenditures. His findings ended the hopes of significant steamboat navigation on the Buffalo River.

The navigational feat of Captain Warner and the *Dauntless* stands unequaled in Buffalo River history. While other steamboats sometimes traveled up the Buffalo as far as "Gin Eddy," a point about one and one-half miles from the river's mouth where the farmers brought their cotton for downriver shipment to market, no other boat even approached the achievement of the *Dauntless.*

Unfortunately, the famous little *Dauntless* caught fire and burned on November 10, 1896, about ten miles below Batesville; thus the boat was removed from the trade. Since the *J. A. Woodson* had been returned to its owners by Capt. Charles Woodbury, all the steamboats that had been plying the extreme Upper White were gone. In the short space of eighteen months, the *Myrtle,* the *Ralph E. Warner,* the *Dauntless,* the *T. E. Morrison,* and the *J. A. Woodson* had vanished from the region. Their departure was strongly felt by the citizens of the area.

While we have been discussing, primarily, steamboat traffic in the upper river during 1895 and 1896, there were several vessels trafficking in the Lower White. Included among them were the *S. P. Pond,* the *Mary F. Carter,* the *Rex,* the *Ralph,* the *G. W Lyons,* the *Luella Brown,* the *Emma,* the *G. M. Sivley,* and the *L. E. Patton.* A number of boats were also in the Black River. Among them were the *Moark,* the *Krata,* the *Portia,* the *G. M. Sivley,* and the *Black Diamond.*

As mentioned, this period was particularly disastrous for the steamboats traveling the Upper White, and many of the familiar vessels were gone. To ease this shortage, two new steamboats entered the trade in the fall of 1896. The *Tycoon,* built by the Morrison Tie Company, and the *Ozark Queen,* constructed at Ramsey's Ferry in Batesville by Capt. Charles B. Woodbury, appeared upon the scene.

Of all the captains who ran steamboats on the Upper White River, Captain Woodbury was one of the best liked and most competent. After arriving in the region in 1875, the captain was captivated by the magnificence and beauty of the area, and he served it faithfully until his death.

The *Ozark Queen* was the last steamboat to be built for the passenger and freight trade above Batesville. Its tremendous struggle against the river hazards, the competition from other boats, and the increasing threat of the railroad typified the last days of steam packets in the Upper White River. The launching of the *Ozark Queen* was described in a clipping in the scrapbook of Mrs. Mary Fitzhugh Spragins:

> Five o'clock, P.M., Saturday, September 12, was the time set for the launching of Capt. Woodbury's new steamer, the *Ozark Queen,* and at that hour a large portion of the city's population had gathered at the dock below Ramsey's Ferry. They came in buggies, on bicycles, and on foot, and were scattered about in groups, picnic fashion, on the rising bank back of the dock. While waiting for the final preparations to be made for the launching of the *Queen,* most of those availed themselves of the opportunity of taking a look at the splendid equipment and neat arrangement on the *Tycoon,* which presented a pretty and graceful appearance at her moorings just below the *Queen*'s dock. At shortly after five o'clock, Mr. Teeter gave the word all was ready. Capt. Woodbury and little Miss June Glenn stepped up to the bow, and the latter recited the christening words:
>
> I christen thee *Ozark Queen,*
> Glide smoothly to thy home
> On the beautiful White.
> Float lightly, speed swiftly and safely.
> Long live the *Queen*!
>
> At the conclusion of these words, she broke a bottle of pure and sparkling White River water across the bow. Then the temporary supports were thrown from under the keel and the large hull started, but was stopped by some pieces of scantling on the banks of earth that projected above the level of the ways. After about

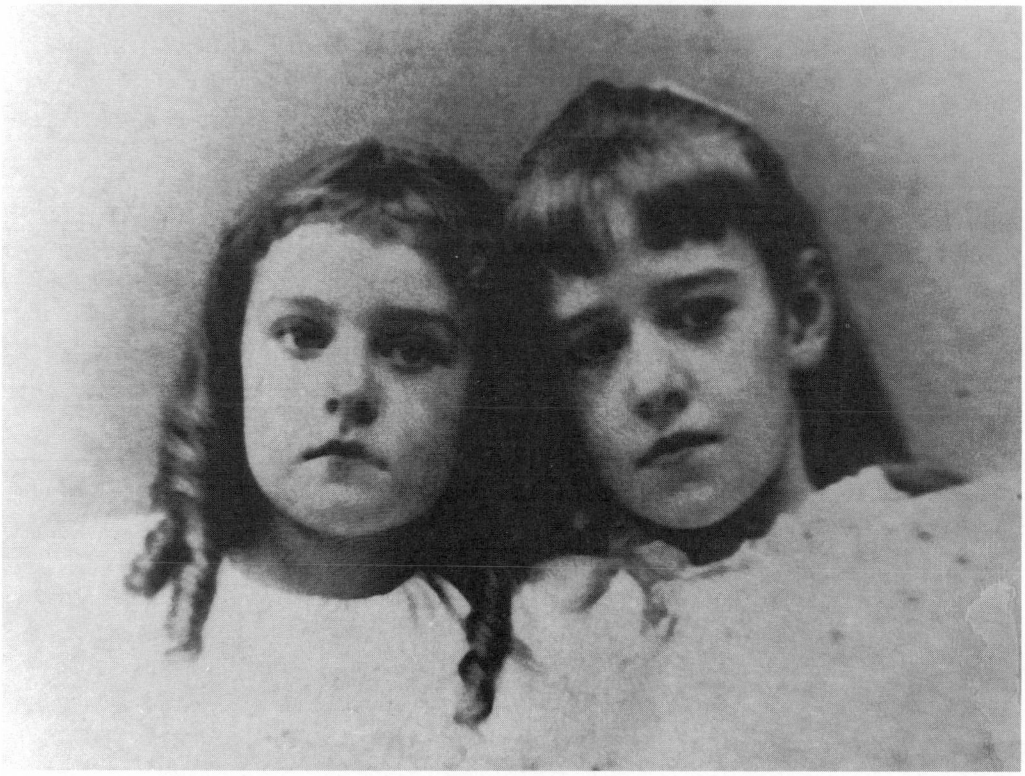

Left, *little Miss June Glenn, later Mrs. Charles McClue of Little Rock. She christened the steamer* Ozark Queen *at Batesville in 1896. The other girl in photo became Mrs. Hinkle of Batesville.*

Courtesy of the University of Arkansas, Little Rock, Archives and Special Collections.

> 30 or 40 minutes of work by Teeter and his force, these obstructions were overcome, and at 6:50, amid the cheers and good wishes of the assembled spectators, the *Ozark Queen* glided smoothly and gracefully to her home on the bosom of the beautiful White.

The small girl who so happily christened the *Ozark Queen* later became Mrs. Charles McClue of Little Rock, Arkansas. In an interview in 1970, this gracious, charming lady reflected upon the event: "The boat settled majestically on the clear, beautiful stream as if it had always belonged there. This occasion was a happy experience for my childish heart and the memory of it I shall cherish always!" When asked to recall personal experiences aboard the *Ozark Queen,* Mrs. McClue fondly reminisced:

> The following years gave me many pleasant trips up and down the White River on the *Ozark Queen* with my beloved friends Capt. and Mrs. Woodbury. One episode which stands out in my memory was one night after blowing the whistle for a ferry line or cable to be lowered; our wheel was badly damaged because the line was not lowered enough, and all hands on board worked fast and furiously to repair the damage and be on our way.
>
> Another near tragedy was in trying to get around Buffalo Shoals one night; I heard crashes and splintering boards on the side of the engine room and saw sparks fly out of the side of the boat. During such times of anxiety, Captain Woodbury always left me in the care of the boat's pilot.
>
> On one occasion, when we were grounded in shallow water and had been struggling for quite some time, I was sitting on a high stool in the pilot room, and I asked the pilot to let me turn the wheel. This he did, and almost at once the boat slid out into deeper water. I was too happy for words that I had accomplished such a feat! Of course, I didn't know that the pilot's hand had been on the wheel also, but everyone on board congratulated me! What a thrill!
>
> At times we were making trips during stormy weather, but never a fear did I have as long as I knew Cap'n was there. These memories take me back to some of the happiest days of my childhood!

Captain Woodbury's boat was an instant success, securing good trips of freight and passengers. Residents along the Upper White River eagerly anticipated its arrival. Mrs. Minnie B. Johnson, nee Huddleston, recalled the excitement that accompanied the coming of the *Queen:*

> When I was a young girl on Papa's farm on the old Denton Ferry road, we could hear the steamboats distinctly as they rounded the bend and whistled for McBee's Landing. Before the sound could fade way, us kids would yell, "The *Queen*'s a comin! The *Queen*'s a comin! Steamboat's here!" Then, we would race like scared rabbits through the woods to see who could be the first to reach the river. I guess we looked like little maniacs running through the brush with our arms waving and our hair flying, but the arrival of a steamboat was a big event for us. When we reached the river, we would line up to watch the passengers come off the boat, and the deckhands unload the freight.

The *Ozark Queen* vied with the *Tycoon,* Capt. Dick Prater, master, and the *Josie Sivley* for the Upper White trade during the 1896–97 boating season. Captain Woodbury's boat was the largest of the three, being 133 feet long, 25.6 feet wide, and with a 4-foot hold.

Batesville landing is the site of this picture of the Ozark Queen. *It was built at Batesville and christened on September 12, 1896. Built by Capt. Chas. B. Woodbury, the vessel was 133 x 25.6 x 4 feet, and its tonnage was 135 net and 310 gross.*

Photo courtesy of Wilson Powell.

It displaced 135 net tons and 210 gross tons. The *Tycoon* was much smaller, displacing only 64.5 tons net. The *Ozark Queen* made by far the most trips upriver and, therefore, carried more passengers. Nine trips were made by the steamer from Newport to McBee's Landing, eleven to Buffalo City, one to the rapids, and one from Batesville to Sylamore, carrying a total of 260 passengers. By comparison, the *Tycoon* carried only 50 passengers on nineteen reported trips. There was no report for the *Josie Sivley.*

The crew of the *Ozark Queen* included Charley Teeter, pilot; James J. Graham and Hopkins, engineers; and Carl Teeter, mate. The cabin and kitchen were under the supervision of Mrs. Woodbury, the captain's wife.

Trade had once again picked up on the Lower White. Regular packets plying the lower river included the *Rex,* the *A. R. Bragg,* and the *Mary F. Carter.* Several smaller lumber-camp boats, such as the *Saltzman, Emma,* and *Louisa,* were also traveling between the various landings on that portion of the White. The *J. A. Woodson* was now running between Newport and Black and Current River ports, as was the *G. M. Sivley.* Other steamers operating in the Black included the *Tycoon,* the *A. R. Bragg,* the *Portia,* the *Krata,* the *Black Diamond,* the *Arthur,* the *Louisa,* and the *Moark.*

Although trade was dull in early 1898, the Lower White was once again served with a frequent steamboat to Memphis. The *New Mattie,* a 131-ton stern-wheeler, was owned by Capt. William J. Ashford, the primary stockholder in the Memphis and White River Packet Company. This was the first packet from the Tennessee port to White River in two years. Capt. Ed Warner served as pilot on the *New Mattie* and later fondly related some of his experiences on it to Joe Curtis, reporter for the *Memphis Commercial Appeal:*

> I reckon it was about 35 years ago when Captain Ashford and associates bought the sternwheel boat named *New Mattie.* He put her in service between Memphis and White River points. I'll never forget how that boat looked the first time I saw her. She was the craziest thing that was ever on the Mississippi River. . . . She resembled a half moon with its tips hanging down. What caused her to have that queer shape was a hump in her hurricane deck and I never knew whether she was built that way or what happened to cause the hump to be so prominent in her make-up.
>
> The first day she arrived at Memphis, there were a number of Negroes lined up at the top of the levee. They watched her come into the wharf, then one big black fellow we knew as "Slough Foot" arose, brushed the dirt off his trousers and walking away remarked,"Humph, she ain't nothing but Humped Back *Mattie,*" and that name followed her through her career.
>
> There was another unusual thing about the *New Mattie.* Her rudders were built aft of her water-wheel eight feet. But don't overlook that Capt. Ashford didn't pass up her appearance. He laughed about her time and again. So, after one cotton season, he took her to the marine ways at Mound City, Illinois, and had her rebuilt into one of the prettiest small packetboats that ever ran the White, Mississippi, or any other river.
>
> She made Captain Ashford a lot of money. But one trip she was overloaded with cotton, hit the embankment, and sank 12 miles from the mouth of White opposite Wild Goose Bayou. As far as I know, her hulk still lies buried in the mud.[64]

The *New Mattie* sank at 7:30 P.M. on February 17, 1900, after it started leaking badly. It was run onto a bar, but careened and sank in eighteen feet of water, afterwards breaking into two pieces

The Ozark Queen *carrying an excursion party up White River. The boat ran during boating seasons from Newport and Batesville to Buffalo City and McBee's Landing, with trips to Lead Hill and above when water permitted. Capt. Charles B. Woodbury was owner, and Capt. John T. Warner was one of the pilots.*
Photo courtesy of Wilson Powell.

aft of the boilers. At the time of the accident, the boat carried thirty-five passengers, 356 bales of cotton and one thousand sacks of cotton seed. All passengers were saved, but two deckhands perished, and 350 bales of cotton were lost. What was thought to be the wreckage of the *New Mattie* was found near Wild Goose Bayou in 1976.

The *Ozark Queen* and the *Tycoon* remained in keen competition for the Upper White commerce until 1899, when the burning of the *Tycoon* at Batesville on January 28, 1899, brought an end to that rivalry. The steamboat was owned by Capt. T. E. Morrison and was valued at eighty-three hundred dollars.

In early 1899, Captain Woodbury and other steamboat owners were encouraged by the passage of the River and Harbor Bill by Congress. The action provided for the implementation of Capt. William L. Sibert's plan to improve the Upper White River. An 1896 survey of the White had shown the distance between Batesville and Buffalo City to be 88.75 miles, with a drop of 1.56 feet per mile. To overcome the decrease in elevation, Captain Sibert had recommended the building of ten locks and dams at a cost of $1,600,000 to ensure year round navigation to Buffalo City. The bill also appropriated $160,000 to start the first lock and dam, which was to be located at Batesville. One lock was authorized annually until the ten were completed. Money was also provided for dredging and snagging operations. Area residents were delighted. It appeared there was still enough interest in steamboat navigation in the White River to warrant federal funds being allocated for improvement of the White. Though some of that plan was implemented, the balance of it was never completed, and the days of the steamboats were numbered. They were the victims of modernization.

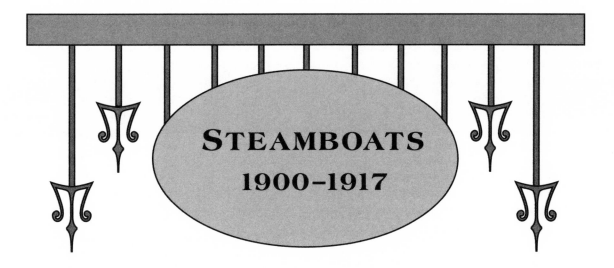

Steamboats 1900–1917

Bids for supplying materials for the construction of Lock and Dam No. 1 at Batesville were opened in Little Rock in July 1900, then forwarded to the Chief of Engineers in Washington for final approval. By the time construction started, the *Ozark Queen* was no longer alone in the Upper White River, though it still dominated the trade there.

The Memphis and White River Packet Company had purchased the *Ora Lee* from the Lee Company and renamed the steamboat *Orlando.* Although the vessel drew almost thirty inches of water, its owners hoped to run it some in the upper river. There are no records of the *Orlando* ever going above Calico Rock, however, so the steamer posed no real threat to the *Ozark Queen.* Though its upper river activity was limited, the *Orlando* became a favorite in the Lower White. Built in 1891 at Howard Shipyards in Jeffersonville, Indiana, the boat was 140 feet long, 32 feet wide, 4.5 feet deep, and displaced 189 net tons. Officers of the steamboat were Capt. R. G. (Gabe) Ashford, master; John Halley, clerk; W. B. McGee, second clerk; J. E. Hall, mate; Harry Graham and Thomas Fletcher, engineers; and W. Charles (Chess) Wilcox and Edwin Tucker Burr Warner, pilots.

A regular packet between Memphis and Newport, the *Orlando* also occasionally provided excursion trips for Newport citizens. One such junket was promoted by the *Newport Daily Independent:*

> Capt. Ashford's son, R. G., will have charge of the *Orlando* on this trip as his father has business in West Point and other places this week. The round trip of the *Orlando* excursion up White River will be one dollar, which includes meals; children half fare. Those carrying lunches will be charged fifty cents.
>
> Parties desiring to go to Memphis on the *Orlando* for the reunion can make the trip at a very light expense. Seven dollars will be charged for the round trip, which includes meals and berth and the privilege of using a state room for the four days which the *Orlando* will remain in Memphis.[1]

There is no doubt that the *Orlando* was a favorite of Capt. William J. Ashford's son, who reminisced about the boat in 1950 to Joe Curtis of the *Memphis Commercial Appeal:* "I always thought the *Orlando* was the prettiest packet that was ever on the White. She had a beautiful whistle and very pretty, soft-toned big bell on her hurricane deck. And when it came to traveling, she never allowed any boat of her size to throw water in her face. She was a very pretty steamboat, and the people along White River actually loved her!"[2]

Joe Curtis reported another story about the *Orlando,* related by Capt. Gabe Ashford about Chess Wilcox, one of the pilots:

> It was Chess' habit to wire his sweetheart when the *Orlando* departed Memphis stating she would arrive at Newport about her usual time, which was at nine at night. And you could lay your last dollar she'd be there too. And you could make another same bet that the sweetheart would be waiting at the landing with her fast trotting horse and buggy. After the boat tied up, Chess and his pretty girl went driving until time to clear port.
>
> I recall one trip up White River when the water was very low. We reached Utley Dread, a bad place in the river between Augusta and Newport. It was supper time and the meal was served in the main cabin. Chess was in a hurry to keep his date and forgot to ring a slow bell, so when the *Orlando* hit the shallow water, she ran away from the reef and went into some willows reaching up to the pilot house, knocking her smokestacks down, one of her escapes, and the railing on one side of the hurricane roof.

> It required several hours to get her in condition to continue up river. When she arrived at Newport at three the next morning, Chess' girl and beautiful turnout was not in sight. She waited there until almost midnight before deciding her Romeo would not be there to meet her. Then she turned her buggy around, gave her horse his head, and went home.
>
> Well, the only damage to the *Orlando* was two new smoke-stacks which had to be bought and were delivered the next day, put in place, and we resumed our usual schedule.[3]

Although the damage to the *Orlando* was relatively minor, no mention was made of the damage done to pilot Wilcox's courtship.

Business was brisk for the *Orlando*. From December 1900 to June 1, 1901, the steamboat logged twenty-three trips from Memphis to Newport, carrying 1,485 passengers. The *Orlando* was seemingly at its peak of popularity and financial success when its luck deserted it. The *Newport Daily Independent* newspaper recorded its demise:

> The steamboat *Orlando,* the pride of this port, belonging to the Memphis and White River Packet Company, struck a log Friday afternoon, July 5, twenty-six miles above De Valls Bluff, between Devil's Hill and Peach Orchard, going down in seven minutes after the collision.
>
> The *Orlando,* on account of low water, could not reach this port last week and turned back on her course at Bradford. The accident occurred between four and five o'clock in the afternoon, and it was thought at first that the engineer had gone down with the boat, but this proved groundless.
>
> No passengers were aboard, and though the freight loss was total, not a single employee of the boat was injured. The stern sank in eight feet of water, while the bow rests tilted in the air. After the sinking, the current twisted the boat around, making the aperture larger and badly breaking the hull. . . . Capt. W. J. Ashford is the principal stockholder of the Memphis and White River Packet Company and the loss will fall heavily on him.[4]

On the upper river, the Illinois Marble and Milling Company introduced the *Jessie Blair,* a light-draft vessel that was to make regular trips from Batesville to Buffalo City and other landings on the Upper White, as well as occasional trips up the Buffalo River. Brought to the White in 1900, the gasoline-powered boat ran in the upper river through most of 1901.

Steamboats General Joe Wheeler, Welcome, *and* Buck Elk *hauling supplies to build the railroad from Batesville up White River to Cotter, Arkansas. In photo, boats are near Calico Rock and construction work can be seen on bluff. The* Wheeler, *sixty-five net tons, was owned by Capts. Billy Joyce and Tom Stallings of Newport, while the* Welcome, *forty-five net tons, was owned by Capt. E. C. Ridell of Jacksonport. The* Buck Elk *was one of Capt. William L. Heckman's boats and was fifty-eight net tons. Date of photo was 1902.*

Courtesy of the University of Arkansas, Little Rock, Archives and Special Collections.

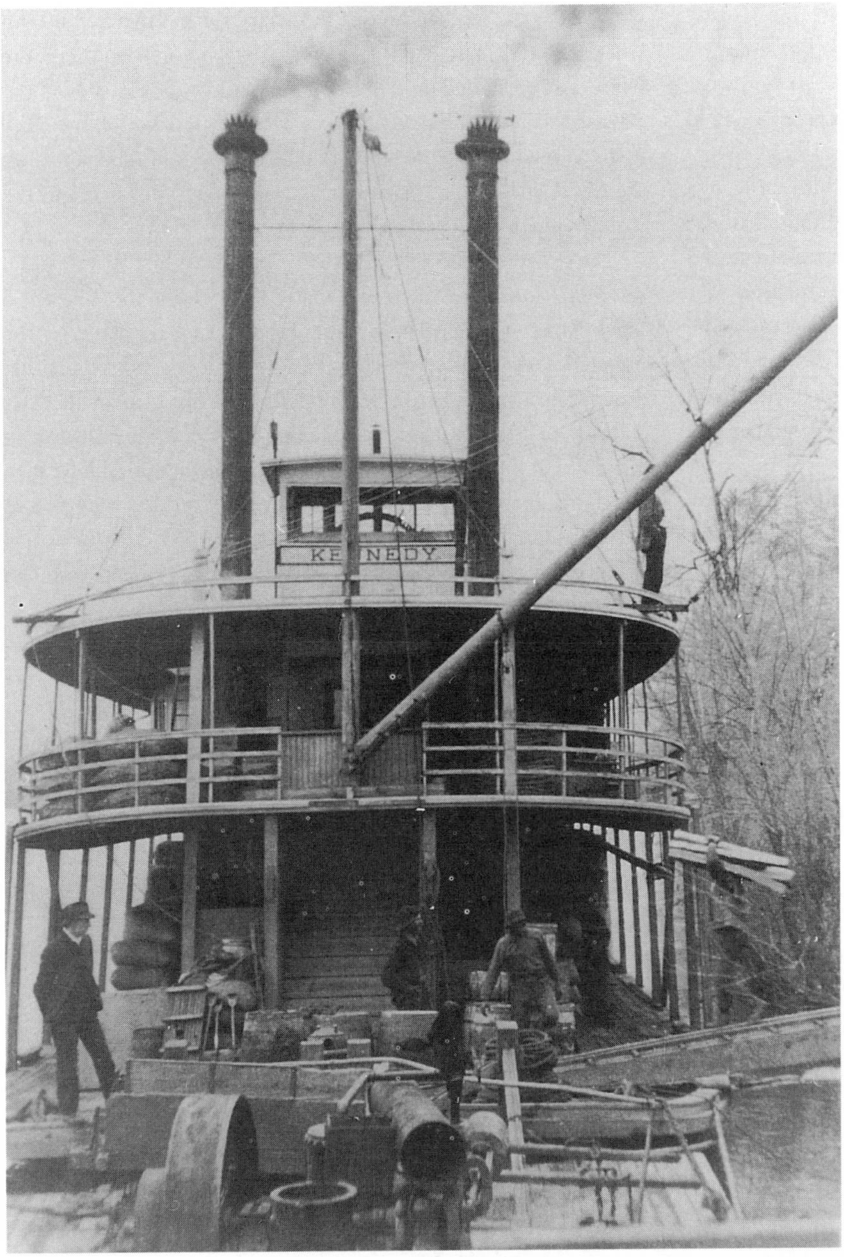

The steamboat Kennedy, *commanded by Capt. William M. Heckman, docks to take on wood at an unknown landing on White River. Pilot on the vessel was Capt. Ed B. Warner, who is standing outside the pilothouse. The boat transported supplies for construction of the White River division of the St. Louis, Iron Mountain, and Southern Railway.*

Photo courtesy of Capt. Charles H. Warner and Wilson Powell.

Other steamboats that plied the White River from May 31, 1900, to June 1, 1901, included the *A. R. Bragg,* the *C. E. Taylor,* the *Harry Waltz,* the *General Joe Wheeler,* the *Kennedy,* the *Quickstep,* the *Troubador,* the *Dea,* the *G. W. Lyons,* the *Grace Smith,* the *City of Peoria,* and the *Iverness.* Included on the Black and Current Rivers were the *Roy,* the *El Blanco,* and the *Lorna Doone.*

Steamboat Bill's column in the March 9, 1946, edition of the *Waterways Journal* contained an interesting story about the *Kennedy* and the *General Joe Wheeler.* At the turn of the century, the St. Louis and Hermann Packet Company secured a contract from the Missouri Pacific Railroad to transport almost all the materials needed to build the new railroad extension out of Batesville to Cotter and above. The company removed their steamer *Buck Elk* and two barges from the profitable Gasconade River trade in Missouri and placed them in White River. They also purchased an additional barge from Frank Blaske and the steamboat *Kennedy* from the Kennedy Brothers on the upper Mississippi. These, too, were placed in the White. Samuel M. Heckman was master of the *Buck Elk,* and Fred J. Heckman was placed in charge of the *Kennedy.*

William Heckman, also known as Steamboat Bill, spent some time on the White River during the winter months. One day Bill and Fred Heckman made a trip up the river on the *Kennedy* with Capt. Ed Warner at the wheel. While on their excursion, they heard a steamboat blow for a landing upriver. Fred Heckman questioned what made the sound. Captain Warner responded, "That is the steamer *Joe Wheeler* blowing a landing whistle. She is not much of a boat but she has the finest nickel-plated whistle on top of her pilot house that ever steam went through."

Steamboat Bill and his brother tried to acquire the whistle from the owner of the *Joe Wheeler,* but to no avail. Bill's parting words to his brother when he left the region in the spring, were "to get that whistle one way or another." Fate soon provided Fred Heckman with his opportunity.

The *General Joe Wheeler* was on a trip up the White carrying a dangerous cargo of blasting powder and baled hay. About halfway to its destination, the steamboat suffered a serious breakdown and had to go to the bank. Knowing the railroad needed its powder badly, the captain was in a quandary when the *Kennedy* came steaming along. The captain of the *Joe Wheeler* hailed the *Kennedy* and said, "Fred, you old Yankee, you have always traded square with us and if you will tow us up to our destination I will pay you anything within reason."

You can imagine Fred Heckman's answer. The master of the *Kennedy* replied, "In this case you cannot hire the *Kennedy* for money but that whistle talks. We will trade whistles, then tow you up where you want to go and then tow you back down empty to where you can get repairs."

The captain of the *General Joe Wheeler* moaned his response, "I have had many ups and downs in my day and in my last days this sorrow has to come upon me. I have lost some fine boats by burning and sinking but nothing has hurt me like this. Take the whistle, son; the South is used to giving up to the North and I knew that when that new fast-stepping boat came down here it boded no good for the *Ozark Queen,* the *Joe Wheeler* or even the *Quickstep.*"[5]

When the *Kennedy* returned to Hermann, Missouri, from White River, the famed whistle sounded its landing. Upon the sale of the *Kennedy,* the whistle was installed on the steamer *Lora.* When the *Lora* was sold, the new home of the whistle was the *Julius F. Silber.* In 1912, the whistle was moved to the steamer *Chester* when Steamboat Bill took charge of that vessel. After three years, he sold "the melodious monster," for twenty-five wagon wheels, to a Mr. Dresser at Leavenworth, Kansas. From there, the whistle was installed on the little towboat *Leavenworth.* Steamboat Bill later tried to repurchase the whistle, but his offers were turned down. Before he could decide if he should raise the ante, the towboat *Leavenworth* sank near Napoleon, Missouri, and the wonderful whistle was lost.

The exceptional dryness of 1901 along the White River caused problems for all of the steamboats. The comments of veteran Black River steamboatman Capt. Fred Inman, reported by the *Newport Daily Independent,* conveyed the seriousness of the situation: "Capt. Inman began steamboating on Black River in 1861 and says that the past season has been the worst for his business in all of that long period, worse even than the memorable year of 1874. The waters have been so low this season that it costs 100 per cent more to navigate than it does at a good stage of water; that is to say only one-half load can be hauled at present, and then a trip takes twice the time. . . ."[6]

Even with the drought, the *Joe Wheeler,* owned by Captain Riddell, made trips to the mills in the vicinity and received good loads on both the White and the Black Rivers. Captain Inman kept the Inman-Decker packets *A. R. Bragg* and *F. W. Tucker* running between Newport and Black River points and to Johnson's Landing on the Current River. The logging business was providing cargo for several steamboats, including the *Quickstep* with Capt. Billy Bishop, the *Harry Waltz* commanded by Capt. George Biolette, and the *Evening Star.* All were boats of the Kelly Lumber Company.

The mussel shell business was also drawing several steamboats to White River. Among them were the little *Eagle,* owned by Capts. Billy and Charles Warner, and the *Lotus,* commanded by Capt. Fred Kennedy. Captain Kennedy became involved in a dispute with the railroad just before Christmas 1901. Apparently, the

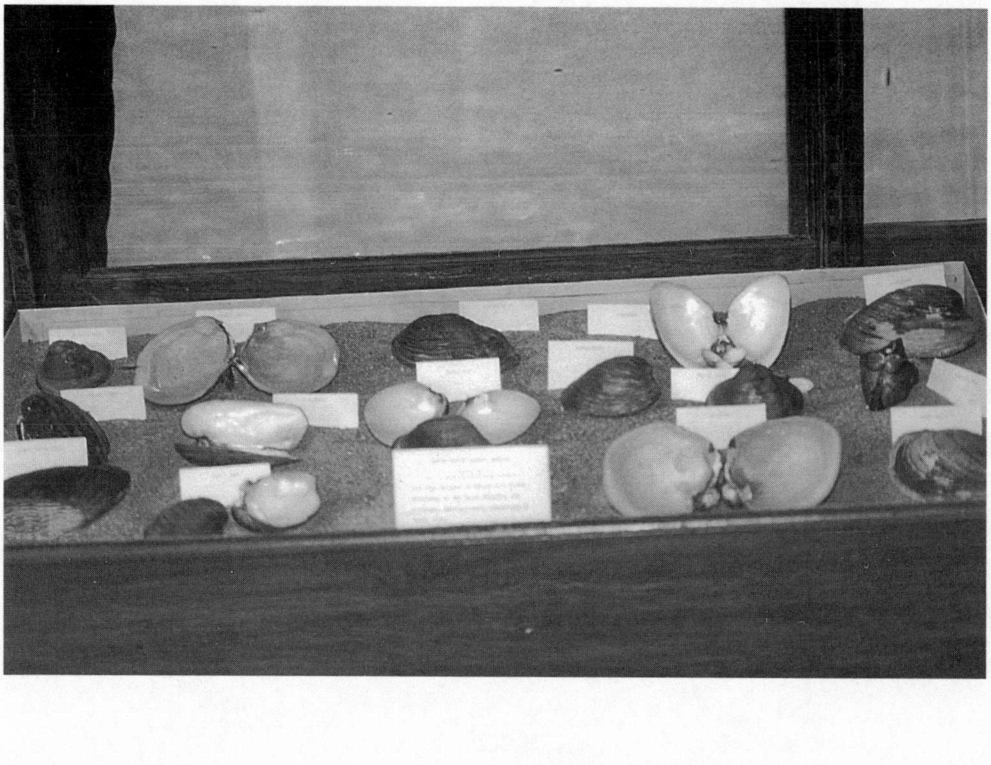

White River mussel shells donated to the museum by Mr. and Mrs. Arthur Stewart. The wide variety of shells were given nicknames by early settlers and rivermen. They are still identified by these names. Pictured front, left to right—first row, *Black Sand Shell, Pig Toe, Bluffer, Sand Shell;* second row, *Three Ridge, Cucumber, Butterfly, Niggerhead, Monkey Face;* third row, *Maple Leaf;* back row, *Pimple Back, Paper Shell, Pistol Grip, Grandma, and Mucket. The showcase is in Jacksonport Courthouse Museum.*

Photo by Sammie Rose.

Lotus had to tie up at a railroad bridge for several days because the structure was in such poor condition that it could not be opened for the steamboat to pass. The *Augusta Free Press* reported that Captain Kennedy received $250 from the railroad company for the inconvenience. Scarcely a month later, disaster befell the shell steamer. On January 20, 1902, a heavy sleet, followed by a driving rain that added more weight, toppled the *Lotus* some eight miles below Grand Glaize. After sinking near the bank, the helpless boat lay on its side with four feet of water in the engine room. The *Harry Waltz* was sent from Newport to help raise the submerged vessel, owned by Harvey Chalmers and Son of Amerstam, New York. The Chalmers business was reputedly the largest button factory in the world. Utilized for carrying shells, the *Lotus* was capable of towing two hundred tons and ran between Newport and the mussel beds downriver. It was built at Rock Island, Illinois, in 1893 and was seventy-six feet long with a sixteen-foot beam and a three-foot hold. Despite damage to its chimneys, the steamer was easily raised and arrived at Newport four days later.

On March 31, 1902, Captain Kennedy and the *Lotus* arrived at Newport from Grand Glaize with one of the largest shipments of shells ever brought to the port. Now a buyer for the Chalmers company, Captain Kennedy had worked in the mussel shell business in the upper Mississippi for many years but said, without hesitation, that the mussel beds between Newport on the White River and Black Rock on the Black River contained more shells than any area he had seen. The captain felt the continuous beds were a gold mine. Just a few days prior to the arrival of the *Lotus* at Newport in March, Captain Kennedy had sold a perfect twenty-eight-grain pearl to Walter Harris for $250.

Pearl buyers traveled from great distances to the White River during this time. Some of them camped along the river and spent their days digging and opening mussel shells. When the pearl business first started on the White, the shells were considered worthless and could be found in great heaps along the sandbars and riverbanks, not to mention those that were tossed back into the river. As a market developed for making buttons from the shells, however, harvest of them became the major business and the search for pearls was secondary. By 1926, there were few pearl hunters along the river, other than locals.

There were several different types of mussels found in White River, and some were more valuable than others. Realizing they could make good money selling the shells, and maybe find some pearls as well, many farmers devised an amazing array of rigs with which to raise the mussels from the riverbed. Probably the best known was the crowfoot bar. The crowfoot drag was made by twisting together two crossed wires about a foot in length and turning back the ends to form hooks. Six or eight of these were then suspended from an iron bar which was dragged over the mussel bed. When touched by one of the wire "fingers," the mussel closed its shell around the metal and was lifted to the surface, where the mussels were removed. A picture of a crowfoot boat can be seen in the photograph of the *Jacksonport Ferry*. While many of the shells were sold outside the White River Valley, the Newport Button Company also bought large quantities and was active in the button business for many years.

The period from July 1, 1901, to July 1, 1903, was an unusually busy one on the extreme upper river. Construction on Lock and Dam No. 1 at Batesville was completed, and work was started on No. 2, some ten miles above the city. The White River branch of the St. Louis, Iron Mountain, and Southern Railroad from Batesville to the new town of Cotter, in Baxter County, was under construction. Several boats joined the *Ozark Queen,* with Captain Woodbury still in command and Capt. John T. Warner as its pilot, in the Upper White trade. A number of the steamers were

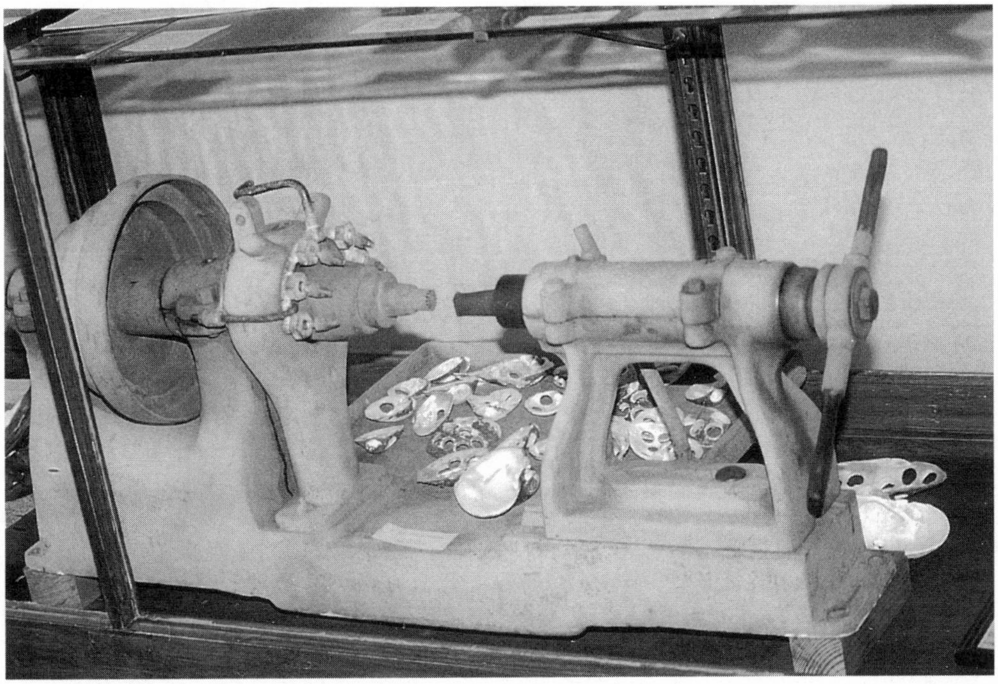

Button-cutting machine and cut mussel shells in the Jacksonport Courthouse Museum.

Photo by Sammie Rose.

Jacksonport Ferry *had an engine-powered, side paddle wheel plus cables for movement. It was commonly known as* Point Ferry *and was located where the Black River flows into the White. It was thought to have been called* Point *due to the fact that the land made a point where the rivers meet. In the foreground is a "crow-foot" boat used for musseling. The bar or "mule" mounted in its rear was dropped and dragged, serving as a rudder. The side bars were dragged through the feeding mussel beds; as the wires went through the open shells, they would close, attaching themselves to be lifted in. The shells were used to make buttons.*

Photo made in 1966 by Johnnie M. Gray.

engaged in hauling equipment and supplies for the building of the railroad. The *Cleveland* was being used to convey materials to build Lock and Dam No. 2. The gasoline-powered boat *Eureka* was also placed in the Upper White trade in 1902, having been repaired following sinking in the river below the cedar yard at Batesville. Capt. Charles Engles was its master.

The *Ozark Queen* continued to dominate the extreme upper river. In early March 1902, the steamer traveled the 125 miles to Oakland and returned with 382 bales of cotton. Prior to the building of the railroad, it was not uncommon for a steamboat to appear at Oakland, but the arrival of the *Ozark Queen* was the first time in a number of years that a boat had visited the region.

As with other steamboats in White River at the turn of the century, passengers aboard the *Ozark Queen* were many and varied. In an article appearing in the *Independence County Chronicle* in the summer of 1984, James R. Fair Jr. included excerpts from the journal of Junius R. Case, a young man from Mountain View, Arkansas, who was a clerk in the Bank of Batesville in 1902. Case's entries about a trip on the *Ozark Queen* paint a vivid picture of steamboat travel at that time:

March 5 Mr. Wolf asked that I might be allowed to go up river for Talley Lumber and Feed Co. and the request was granted so I'll go up the next trip of the *Ozark Queen*. . . .

March 6 . . . We left the landing at 5:15 and steamed up the river a few miles and stayed. Until dark the deck hands were out gathering driftwood for fuel. The weather is fine and we have a jolly lot of people aboard. There are 23 cabin passengers and we are pretty well crowded. Three of us must sleep in each stateroom. As soon as supper was over out came cards and poker chips and the game is now running for the night. I intend to spend most of my time in the pilot house. The river is falling rapidly and with our enormous load I guess we will move slowly.

March 7 At daylight were off again and we ate our breakfast of pork, eggs, biscuits and butter with a relish. But alas we were doomed to a bad day. At an early hour we stuck on the Lone Willow Shoal and didn't get off for five hours. So we didn't get much past Ross' Landing tonight. My, how the wind blows on the river!

March 8 . . . the river has fallen so rapidly that we have done little else than get on and off shoals. Four times we stuck, and only succeeded in getting to Wildhaw's landing by dark.

The gasoline-powered boat Eureka, *owned by Crawford and piloted by Capt. Charles Engles, moored at Batesville in 1902. Steamer in the background is the* Ozark Queen. *The* Eureka *ran to McBee's Landing in 1901 and 1902, carrying supplies for building the railroad up White River from Batesville to Cotter.*

Photo courtesy of Wilson Powell.

March 9 We arrived at Sylamore at 12 o'clock and were met by all the family . . . the little ones were very much taken with the steamboat, and Hubert decided at once that he would be a steamboat captain when he is a man. Charlie says he doesn't believe a larger boat could be builded. At four I told them good-bye as we steamed off up the river. We lay at a wood-yard above Mount Olive tonight.

March 10 We managed to get stuck on the Sneeds Creek shoal about noon and at bedtime we are still trying to get over. The river is still falling but I am in love with the scenery and the weather. . . .

March 11 Spend the entire day trying to get over . . . tomorrow we will turn back.

March 12 . . . Tonight we are back at Calico Rock . . .

March 13 . . . Stayed at Sylamore most of the day, loading cotton. Tonight we are at Wildhaw's landing.

March 14 We got an early start this morning and arrived here (Batesville) at 11 A.M.[7]

Despite the dangers of low water, Captain Woodbury kept the *Ozark Queen* running in the Upper White into June of 1902. The *Mountain Echo* reported: "The steamer *Ozark Queen* pulled her nozzle out of the bank at Buffalo City at one P.M. Thursday, and at three P.M. Friday landed at Batesville. . . . At Calico Rock, seventy-five Italians came aboard. There was a barge lashed to the boat, which proved to be very serviceable later on, because when we arrived at Batesville, it and the lower deck of the *Queen* were crowded with Greeks, Dagos, and Austrians who have been working at various camps on the railroad."[8] In addition to its regular cargo and passengers, the *Ozark Queen* frequently carried immigrants who had come to secure work constructing the railroad and the locks. It was not uncommon for the vessel to have fifty to seventy-five of them aboard.

The completion of Lock and Dam No. 1 was celebrated in Batesville on November 27, 1902, with a large banquet attended by numerous dignitaries. Climaxing the festivities was an excursion up White River to the site of Lock and Dam No. 2. Four hundred people climbed aboard the *Ozark Queen* and the *Cleveland* for the trip. On the return journey to Batesville, the celebrants called for a race between the steamboats. The two captains readily agreed, and at the starting signal, the crowded steamboats raced toward Batesville. Mile after mile sped by before the *Cleveland* finally inched ahead of the *Ozark Queen,* in spite of the determined efforts of Captain Woodbury and his crew. As the boats rounded the point above Batesville, the *Cleveland* remained in the lead and emerged victorious.

To the dismay of the officers in charge of Lock and Dam No. 1, and to the horror of Batesville citizens, just one week following the celebration, the abutment of the dam on the far side of the river gave way due to a heavy rise in the river. The water washed out around the abutment and cut away a large circle of rich land in Ramsey's field. The damage was repaired the next year and a new abutment was built.

Dam No. 1 backed White River up about nine miles, which then backed up the water in all the spring branches and creeks that emptied into the river. The winter of 1904–05 was particularly severe, causing all that back water to freeze over in January and again in February 1905. Poke Bayou at Batesville was about six feet deep above Neeley's Spring and was frozen hard. The ice provided area citizens with a sporting opportunity they didn't often have, and hundreds of them, old and young alike, participated in some ice-skating on the frozen tributaries.

Another ominous note for the steamboats appeared in the *Mountain Echo* of November 21, 1902: "The White River railroad ran its first train to Mount Olive, an ancient forgotten town on White River, about fifty miles this side of Batesville." The "iron horse" was moving deeper and deeper into the White River territory.

Perhaps the outcome of the *Ozark Queen*'s race with the *Cleveland* was also an omen of future events for Captain Woodbury and his steamboat, because 1903 proved disastrous for them. During the last week of December 1902, the *Ozark Queen* was returning from McBee's Landing with a cargo of four hundred bales of cotton and a huge amount of miscellaneous freight when it went aground at Lone Willow, a short distance above Lock No. 2. After working for hours to dislodge the heavily laden boat, Captain Woodbury let the fire in the boiler go out and awaited a rise in the river. It was a wait of six long weeks. Finally, in February 1903, the White rose enough to float the vessel free. The accident cost the captain some fifteen hundred dollars, a loss he could ill afford.

Undaunted, the hard-working old riverman worked furiously to recoup some of that loss, keeping the *Ozark Queen* busy plying the Upper White. The strain may have been too much for him. On March 13, 1903, the *Newport Daily Independent* newspaper reported that Captain Woodbury had become ill while on a trip upriver and was compelled to return to Batesville, where his condition worsened.

The late Walter Isom, who was working at the Buffalo City Landing at the time of Captain Woodbury's last trip recalled the docking of the *Ozark Queen* there: "When the *Queen* docked, poor Cap'n was awfully sick. He wanted to go on up to McBee's, but just couldn't make it. We unloaded the *Queen,* and she headed for Batesville. As I watched her round out, I knew that Cap'n would never make it back."[9]

As he lay fighting for his life, the fever-ridden Captain Woodbury must have realized his steamboating days were over, for he sold his prized *Ozark Queen* to the White River Transportation Company. On March 16, 1903, after nearly thirty years of service to the Upper White River patrons, Capt. Charles Woodbury died at his home in Batesville. His death was rather symbolic of the passing of steamboating in the White River, as the twin trails of railroad track were slowly crawling up the White River Valley to the new town of Cotter. Within just a few short years, these rails would choke off all steam packet trade and an adventurous era would draw to a close.

Cotter Railroad Bridge. This "draw bridge" carries the railroad across White River at Cotter, Arkansas. Built in 1903, it was placed on a large gear to swivel parallel with the river so steamboats could pass.

Photo by Sammie Rose.

Following the death of Captain Woodbury, the *Ozark Queen* continued to run in the Upper White during 1903, joined there by only the *Joe Wheeler.* The *Ozark Queen* and the *Joe Wheeler* stayed until the very last, but the inevitable happened and in mid-June of 1903, Capts. W. Shipp and T. Stallings made their final trip downriver from the Upper White. Each of the captains was probably reflecting upon his rich history on this portion of the White as he slowly steamed away from McBee's Landing and passed all the old familiar places on the downriver journey: Buffalo City and the mouth of the Buffalo River, Norfork, Calico Rock, Sylamore. Certainly, the era of steam packets in the Upper White River could not have been ushered out by two more appropriate captains.

Both the *Ozark Queen* and the *Joe Wheeler* were taken to Newport, where they were offered for sale. The *Ozark Queen* left immediately for points below on a shell purchasing trip for Magness and Handford. By September, the *Joe Wheeler* was hauling timber for the Kelly Lumber Company.

The final death knell for any hopes of the return of steam packets in the Upper White was sounded on August 24, 1903, when the whistle of a steam locomotive heralded the arrival of the first passenger train from Batesville to Cotter. With its coming, regular rail service was established and the haunting whistles of the steamboats were gone from the upper river forever, replaced by the lonesome wail of the locomotive.

While the building of the railroad spelled doom for the steamboats, most local citizens were fascinated by the new development. Elmo Ingenthron, a noted regional historian, told a story about people gathering regularly by the spot near Cotter where track was being laid and construction was under way for a railroad tunnel. On the side of the river opposite the tunnel was a bluff, and an old gentleman who was quite interested in the project stood contemplating the work. A young man came up to him and said, "Uncle Bill, when that train comes, it is going to go right through that hole over there where that tunnel is." The elderly man looked again at the undertaking, thought a moment, then replied, "Well now, I'll tell ye; they might get up enough speed to jump that river; but I don't believe they'll ever jump it; but if they do, I don't think they'll ever be able to hit that hole in the mountain."[10]

Typical of many built at the time, the railroad trestle crossing the White River at Cotter is on a turntable so that it could swivel parallel with the river when the steamboats came through, thereby avoiding damage to their smokestacks. It proved to be an unnecessary feature.

Steamboat lines operating in the Lower White River reorganized during 1903, and Rosedale, Mississippi, became the business terminal for some of those that ran as weekly packets. The *Jack Rabbit* and the *Susan* plied between Rosedale and Clarendon; the *A. R. Bragg* and the *F. W. Tucker* ran from Jacksonport to Augusta; the *City of Idaho* and the *Monarch* traveled from Newport to Clarendon; and the *George Pope* operated between Augusta and Little Red River. The only Memphis packet was the *City of Peoria,* which ran to Clarendon. Other boats making trips on the lower river in 1903 included the *Josie,* the *Mary Carter,* the *Current View,* the *Hosmer,* the *Russell Lord,* and the steamer *Ondine,* from Rock Island, Illinois.

The *City of Idaho,* Capt. I. E. Russell commanding, arrived at Newport in July of 1903 with one of the finest barge loads of mussel shells ever sold at that market. There were thirty-three tons in all, with a cost of seven to eight dollars per ton.

A gripping tragedy had occurred on board the *City of Idaho* in June when Capt. O. F. Kennedy was in command. While the boat was on a trip in the lower river, the captain's son, Henry Ward

In foreground is the Cotter Rainbow Bridge that carries Arkansas State Highway 62 traffic. In the background is the railroad bridge across White River and the tunnel shown in the very center of the bridge.
Photo by Sammie Rose.

City of Idaho *loading mussel shells to take to button factory. It displaced 74 net or 116 gross tons and was 88 x 21 x 3 feet. Built in Memphis in 1898, it was owned by F. L. Kennedy.*

Photo courtesy of the Jacksonport Courthouse Museum.

Kennedy, was playing in some loose shells. The shells shifted and threw him into the river some fourteen miles north of Augusta. Despite the efforts of the crew, young Kennedy drowned and the river was dredged for nine miles to find his body. Two large steamers were lashed together and churned the waters trying to dislodge the body from driftwood or willows, on which it was though to be caught. Perhaps the misfortune was the reason for Captain Kennedy's not being in command of the *City of Idaho* in July.

Steamboating was rather uneventful during the early months of 1904. At least one steamer again became involved in politics. In July, the *Joe Wheeler,* now under the command of Capt. W. A. Joyce, took several candidates on an excursion to Grand Glaize. When the vessel left Newport, it was decorated with bright streamers and banners proclaiming colorful campaign slogans. At Grand Glaize, the politicians disembarked to cast their campaign promises on all receptive ears. After an enjoyable afternoon, the campaigners boarded the *Joe Wheeler* and returned to Newport, arriving there about three and one-half hours later.

Small steamers still busily churned the Black River and made occasional trips up the Strawberry. Three Inman-Decker packets, the *Krata,* the *F. W. Tucker,* and the *Taylor,* were particularly active in the Black.

There was one steamboat that traveled above Batesville in 1904. The *Twins,* a boat eighty feet long and thirty-one feet wide, with a three-foot hold, made two or three trips from Batesville to Wyatt's Landing, carrying 120 tons of livestock and 20 tons of miscellaneous freight.

The *Twins* was conceived by Capt. William Thomas Warner and Tom and Teed Williams. It was the last steamboat constructed at Batesville. Using the salvaged machinery from the *Dauntless,* the boat was built at the old Warner home on the banks of Poke Bayou. It was designed for the cotton ferry service from above Gainor's Ferry to Batesville. Unfortunately, the venture proved unsuccessful. While the steamer stayed very busy during the cotton-ginning season, other times were quite slow, even with some excursion work. In the ferry service, five or six round trips per day could be made, but during an off day, only three trips or less might be called for. In April 1904, Warner sold his interest in the *Twins* to Tom and Teed Williams.

During the 1904–05 boating season, the Inman-Decker packet *A. R. Bragg* disappeared from the White and was replaced by the

The A. D. Allen *anchored at Lock and Dam No. 3 at Batesville in 1904. At this time the* Allen *was a commercial boat loaded with some mussel shells on the freight deck.*

Photo courtesy of Wilson Powell.

62-ton *George Pope*. Also in the river was the *A. D. Allen,* a commercial boat that carried shells and miscellaneous freight. Several tiny gasoline-powered boats, such as the *Cora Lee,* the *Bob West,* the *Little Abby,* the *J. Taylor,* and the *Peerless* appeared on the river, but the new steamboats were getting smaller and smaller. The largest boat plying the White was the *Susan,* a 198-ton steamer that made three trips between Rosedale and Clarendon. The second largest steamboat at that time was the *F. W. Tucker,* a vessel of some 99 net tons. The *F. W. Tucker* disappeared from the White in 1906. The Inman-Decker Packet Company replaced it with the *Minnehaha,* a smaller vessel that displaced only 45 tons.

The only navigation reported in Upper White River was a single trip made by the little *Myrtle Corey* from Cotter to the mouth of the White. The arrival of the tiny vessel at Calico Rock on its downward journey was described by the *Calico Rock Progress:* "The little steamer *Myrtle Corey* came down river from Cotter Tuesday evening and tied up overnight at the landing here. Steamboats have become so scarce in the upper river that even the arrival of this little craft drew a large portion of the population of the town to the riverbank to see the boat come round the bend, and extend a welcome to the captain and his jolly crew. Capt. Eddie is the owner of the boat and is taking her to Little Rock where she will be used to tow barges and other powerless craft."[11]

Notwithstanding the lack of steamboat activity in the Upper White, the U.S. Army Corps of Engineers maintained the river to Lock and Dam No. 2 above Batesville. Capt. John T. Warner, commander of the snagboat *Quapaw,* received orders for seven months of snagging operations. Three months were to be spent in White River from Lock No. 2 to Augusta, three months in Black River, and one month in Current River. The Corps of Engineers continued to improve the Upper White by forcing the construction companies to remove the rocks and other obstructions placed in the river during the building of the railroad to Cotter. The old upper river veteran Capt. Thomas B. Stallings, commanding the steamer *Twins,* was hired for the task. Captain Stallings employed a full force of men to dynamite all rocks too large to move and completed the job in three and one-half months.

Another old favorite was removed from the White in 1906 when misfortune struck the *Joe Wheeler* at Newport. Moored there while undergoing repairs, the steamer was unoccupied when the mishap occurred. About two o'clock in the morning, the strong current of an overflow broke its ropes and carried the steamboat

U.S. snagboat Quapaw, *with Capt. John T. Warner serving as master, helped keep the White River channel free of snags to improve travel. Note snag-puller at* right *of picture.*

Photo courtesy of Wilson Powell.

on one last trip down White River. It followed the river until one-half mile below town; then it plunged out into the bottomlands and wrecked in the woods. Valued at forty-five hundred dollars by owner Capt. W. A. Joyce, the *Joe Wheeler* was the oldest craft in operation in the White. The steamboat was a complete loss.

During the history of White River steamboating, many St. Louis boats plied the river to Jacksonport, but the railroads finally forced them from the region. One last futile attempt to revive this once lucrative White River trade was made in 1907 through the efforts of J. Wallace Byler. Byler was a salesman for the Peters Shoe Company of St. Louis and traveled through northern Arkansas for the St. Louis firm. He had been reared near White River in Izard County, Arkansas, and was married to Eugenia Butler, the daughter of Batesville judge J. W. Butler. The ingenious salesman devised a plan to sell a steamboat load of shoes to merchants in Newport, Batesville, Des Arc, and other towns along White River. Byler's mission was two-fold: to secure cheaper rates by shipping by water and to receive a large amount of publicity by attempting to revive the St. Louis and White River trade. Perhaps it was also the fulfillment of a boyhood dream, conceived while watching the steamboats travel the upper river and load and unload at the old Wild Haws Landing, near the present town of Guion.

Officials of the Peters Shoe Company agreed with Byler's plan and chartered the *Liberty*, owned by Capt. W. M. Sauvage and Hiram G. Adler. The steamer was built at Middleport, Ohio, in 1900 and measured 128.4 by 20.5 by 42 feet. Captain Sauvage was to be in command of the vessel on the trip, and Byler, now dubbed Commodore, was to be second in command. Capts. Austin Joyce and Robert Walters were hired to pilot the *Liberty* down the Mississippi to the White, where Capts. W. A. (Billy) Joyce and Will S. Shipp were to steer it up White River. At the time Billy and Austin Joyce were hired, Captain Sauvage did not know that they were related, but when they met in St. Louis, Captain Sauvage learned they were cousins. Their last meeting had been on the old steamer *Liberty* on White River over twenty years earlier.

On May 8, 1907, as the *Liberty* was being readied for the long journey, Captain Joyce accompanied Byler to inspect the boat. He then wrote to the *Newport Daily Independent:* "Accompanied by Commodore J. W. Byler, I visited the Steamer *Liberty,* a very nice sidewheel boat, loading under the auspices of the Peters Shoe Company, and is scheduled to leave Thursday noon. Providence permitting, and with nothing unusual to bar our welfare, we will reach the city of Newport Wednesday or Thursday, and the Commodore expects a royal reception at the hands of the citizens."[12]

The *Liberty* was liberally decorated with flags and bunting, as well as several banners promoting Peters Shoes. One such standard proclaimed, "FIRST CARGO CONSISTING EXCLUSIVELY OF SHOES EVER SHIPPED ON THE MISSISSIPPI," while another stated,

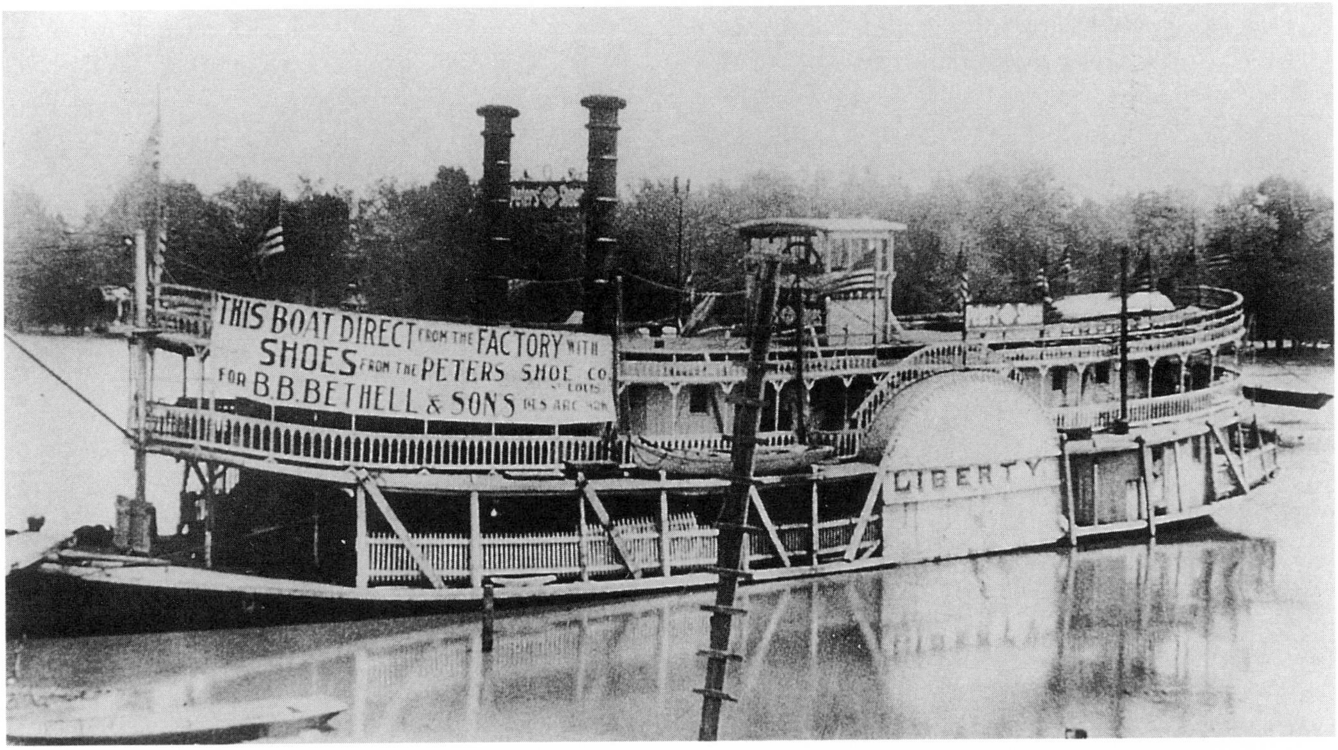

The steamboat Liberty *was the last St. Louis boat to journey to White River. It is shown here in 1907, loaded with shoes from the Peters Shoe Company of St. Louis. The trip was a promotional project of J. Wallace Byler, who hoped to renew the St. Louis and White River trade. Owned by Capt. W. M. Sauvage and Hiram G. Adler, the* Liberty *was piloted down the Mississippi by Capts. Austin Joyce and Robert Walters. At the mouth of the White, Capts. Billy Joyce and Will S. Shipp took over as pilots to steer it up White River.*

Photo courtesy of Ralph DuPae and the Murphy Library, University of Wisconsin, La Crosse.

"LOADED WITH PETERS SHOES FOR WHITE RIVER PORTS."[13] One photograph of the *Liberty* shows a sign specifically mentioning Des Arc, so banners may have been made for individual ports along the White where merchants had ordered some of the cargo.

As a further gesture of goodwill, all merchants who had purchased a shipment were asked to accompany the *Liberty* on its historic journey. Although few accepted, George M. Sink did board the steamer at Des Arc for the remainder of the trip.

The *Liberty* arrived at Memphis on May 13, 1907, where it was announced that the steamboat would stop at De Valls Bluff, Des Arc, Newport, and Batesville, as well as other landings on White River. Plans also called for a delegation from the Deep Water Ways Convention to meet the steamer at Newport. At the opening of the meeting on May 17, Newport mayor W. R. Thompson pleaded for the revitalization of the disappearing steamboat trade and lauded Byler's efforts. The mayor commented:

> One of the most . . . impressive illustrations . . . showing why the cause we are now advocating should not slumber, has been launched by an Arkansas boy—one who was born and reared at the Wild Haws landing—one who when a mere barefooted boy brought himself into notice by flagging a steamer to sell the captain an opossum—and one who grew to manhood within our midst. This man is today demonstrating to us and to the commercial world through the press, that navigation through our waters is not impossible. . . . This boat is now wending her way through the raging waters of the Mississippi and White rivers, en route to Newport to give aid and encouragement to the cause we are today advocating. . . .[14]

A reception reminiscent of the old Mardi Gras celebrations was planned for the *Liberty*. The Newport reception committee, visitors, and convention delegates were to board the steamboat *Miriam*, owned by Capt. W. A. Joyce, and travel downriver to meet the *Liberty*, after which the *Miriam* would escort the St. Louis boat back to Newport, followed by a parade of smaller craft.

By noon, a crowd was assembling at the Newport wharf where the *Miriam* was getting up steam in preparation to carry the dignitaries and others to meet the *Liberty*. The *Miriam* was filled to capacity with eager participants, leaving a large number of hopeful passengers on the riverbank due to lack of space. Original plans were for the *Miriam* to meet the *Liberty* near the White River bridge, but the St. Louis visitor made better time than anticipated, and the local steamboat had barely gotten underway when the *Liberty* rounded the curve just below the city. The gaily decorated *Miriam*, sporting one banner which read, "WELCOME TO COUSIN WALLACE," met the St. Louis vessel at the ferry just below town.

A bottle of champagne was broken over the prow of the *Liberty* upon its arrival, and a loving cup, concealed beneath an array of flowers, was presented to Wallace Byler. Commodore Byler and the officers of the *Liberty* were the toast of Newport. The *Liberty* officers were special guests at the Deep Water Ways Convention the following morning. During the session, Byler read a telegram from the Peters Shoe Company: "Extend to the Deep Water Ways Convention and people of Newport our greetings and express our hope that the initial trip of the *Liberty* will prove a stimulus to favorable action on the part of the government."[15]

While the festivities continued, cargo was unloaded from the steamer, and about noon Commodore Byler and the officers returned to the *Liberty* for their departure for Batesville. Hailed by many spectators all along the way to Batesville, the steamboat was greeted by a large crowd when it arrived there. Sight of the beautiful steamboat churning the water as it approached Batesville brought an ovation from the festive group ashore. After a short stay in Batesville, the *Liberty* headed back to Newport amid rousing goodbyes.

A holiday mood prevailed when the steamer again arrived at Newport, and excursions were planned for all of the next day. Once again, the White River echoed with the laughter and musical sounds of a steamboat party. The festivities subsided on a rather sour note, however, as shown by an item in the *Newport Weekly Independent:* "Charged with selling liquor without a license on the steamer *Liberty* during the excursion last Sunday, W. M. Sauvage, the owner, Robert Walters, clerk and mixologist, and Hiram Adler, who was said to be a guest on the steamer but assisted in selling liquors, were arrested last night by Constable A. M. Mallew and arraigned before Justice T. W. Shaver at two o'clock in the morning. The three pleaded guilty to the charge and were fined $50 and costs each."[16]

The *Liberty* never returned, and as it slowly passed from sight, local citizens witnessed the departure of the last commercial steamboat from St. Louis to travel White River.

A few weeks after the *Liberty*'s departure, one of the few surviving old-time White River steamboat captains died. On June 4, 1907, Capt. William J. (Billy) Ashford, commander and owner of several truly magnificent steamers, including the *R. P. Walt,* succumbed at his home in Memphis. He was seventy-two years old. With his passing, another link to a glorious period was irrevocably severed.

One former prominent White River steamboat owner and commander tried to reenter the White River trade in 1907. Capt. Ed C. Postal traveled to the towns and small cities along the river during August, trying to sell stock in a new company that would build a boat for weekly service from Augusta to the mouth of the White. Captain Postal hoped to eventually resume steamboat passenger and freight service to Memphis. On October 31, 1907, the *White River Journal* of Des Arc, reported the progress of the captain: "Capt. Postal was at our wharf with the steamer *Miriam* Tuesday morning. He states that he had been endeavoring to get a boat for the trade between Des Arc and Memphis for some time. As yet the *Miriam* is the only steamer he has been able to secure. It is a small boat and we predict that it is not large enough for the trade between here and Memphis. . . ."

The fond hopes of Captain Postal to again command a large steam packet in White River never materialized, nor did the stock company that he tried to organize. In 1911, Captain Postal purchased the steamer *Lightwood* and ran it in various trades. The *Lightwood* ran in White River in 1924, connecting with the *Harry Lee* at the mouth of the river, and was the last packet on White River. The steamboat burned December 31, 1925, at Rosedale, Mississippi. Capt. P. R. Joest was master at the time.

The timber industry provided several steamboats with business on the Black River. One of the most active was the *Pocahontas.* Built at Poplar Bluff, Missouri, in 1907, the boat ran until the late 1920s or early 1930s. Other smaller steamers continued plying the White, each seeking to survive in its own way. The *Miriam* and the *Leader* were engaged in hauling lumber and shells, as were several other little steamboats in the area.

In the spring of 1908, Capt. Billy Joyce chartered the *Miriam* to the Wright Carnival Company to convey the show to various river ports for six months. He remained pilot of the boat. The performers gave shows at Newport in early April, then left for Clarendon. The band aboard the steamer struck up lively tunes as the vessel passed towns along the way. Unfortunately, the gay atmosphere was only a prelude to disaster. Tragedy struck the carnival group and the *Miriam* in the Mississippi River, destroying the boat and snuffing out twelve lives. The catastrophe occurred on the widest stretch of the river eighteen miles above Helena during a violent storm. Captain Joyce was in the pilothouse when the turbulence hit. He made a run for the bank, but the hurricane force of the wind lifted the boat and blew it around. The vessel capsized when it hit the water, with the terrified passengers barely having time to climb upon the rail that was above the surface. The boilers were lost as the boat overturned, permitting the hull to float. Waves ten feet high dashed those who were clinging precariously to the hull. Some of them were knocked loose and lost before the eyes of their helpless friends. Engineer William Berry and a deckhand set out for the shore in a skiff, but waves enveloped the frail craft and both were drowned. For two hours, the dazed passengers clung desperately to their uncertain support as huge waves continued to break over them. Some could not last. A reporter from the *Newport Weekly Independent* described the death of one of the passengers: "Each moment the waves threatened to engulf them all. But when one woman, weakened by the strain and chilled by exposure, cried out for help, a heroic effort was made to give her needed aid, but too late came the rescuers, and before their very eyes Anna Golden of St. Louis released her hold, threw her hands upward in a last appeal and disappeared."[17]

Sinking lower and lower, the *Miriam* ran onto a sandbar just before dusk. The remaining passengers were beginning to lose hope of rescue when the little gasoline-powered boat *Home Run,* operated by T. E. Schaefer of Halbert Point, came to their rescue. Three trips were required to take the survivors to safety.

The demise of the *Miriam* ended Captain Joyce's career as a boat owner on White River. He served for a short while as a pilot on the steamer *Choctaw,* after which he moved with his family to Memphis.

With the continued decrease in freight and passenger traffic, the remaining steamboats turned more and more to the timber trade for survival. A number of the boats were controlled by

The Pocahontas *was built at Poplar Bluff, Missouri, in 1907 for Capt. G. W. Huff. It was 75 x 22 x 3 feet and had a net tonnage of thirty-five. The boat ran until the late 1920s or early 1930s. Its whistle had a beautiful tone and was later used in a mill in Newport, Arkansas.*

Photo courtesy of Wilson Powell.

lumber, tie, and cooperage companies. The *Rock City* was owned by the Zearing Lumber Company; the *G. W. Huff*, by the Mount Olive Stave Company; the *Jim Duffy*, by the A. Ford Tie Company; and the *J. B. Galloway* and the *Alda* were owned by the J. B. Galloway Company.

The steamboat *J. B. Galloway* was formerly the *A. Saltzman*, built at St. Joseph, Missouri, in 1899. Its hull was 75 by 16 by 3 feet, with a gross tonnage of 36. The *J. B. Galloway* operated in White River at least through the fall of 1904. The *Alda* was purchased by the Galloways during the fall of 1904. It was built at Booneville, Missouri, in 1891. Its hull was 121 by 21.2 by 4 feet, with a gross tonnage of 73.8. The steamer was listed as a passenger and freight carrier until the June 23, 1908, inspection at Clarendon, when the passenger's license was canceled and it was certified only as a towboat. During the 1901–10 season, the *Alda* made forty-nine trips from Clarendon to logging camps.

Typical of the timber boats was the *G. W. Huff*, Capt. John T. Warner, master. The *G. W. Huff* made 187 trips in Upper White River from July 1908 to May 1910, running 3,616 miles and carrying 13,682 tons of freight. This was the equivalent of 547 carloads, or eighteen trainloads of thirty cars each, a string of cars four and one-half miles long. The *G. W. Huff* was described by a Batesville reporter as one of the best of its size, and the reporter praised Captain Warner as the best-known and most efficient riverman in Arkansas.

As previously mentioned, harvesting mussels remained a major business for the lower river. In June of 1910, the *Mary C. Lucas* arrived in the White River and became quite active there. Owned by W. M. Corley, a shell and pearl buyer, the steamer had been in the Arkansas River trade. The *Mary C. Lucas* had an electric generator of its own and was used by Corley for hauling mussel shells to Newport. From 1910 through at least 1914, Corley ran several steamboats in the Lower White, including the *Lillian H.*, a vessel with a one-hundred-foot beam that was operated as both a Clarendon and Rosedale packet and as a pearling boat. Corley's shelling activities were welcomed by the local citizens. One reporter estimated that Corley probably put one thousand dollars per day into circulation for the products of the White.

The shell buyers often carried large sums of money, since they usually paid in cash. Possession of such currency added another dimension of danger to being a riverboat captain. A murder occurred on one of the shelling boats in June 1911. Captain Lamberst, of the riverboat *Niggerhead*, was killed and robbed of eight hundred dollars as he slept on his boat while it was tied up at Pepper's Lake. Two hundred armed citizens combed the area, searching with bloodhounds for the killer. Lamberst's employer, Henry F. Kath of New Boston, Illinois, offered a three hundred dollar reward for capture of the attacker. The captain was survived by his wife and five children of Mt. Carmel, Illinois.

The steamer *City of Muskogee* appeared in White River in 1917,

The Mary C. Lucas, *owned by the Inman Packet Company, was built in 1903. It was brought to White River in 1910 by W. M. Corley, a shell and pearl buyer. The boat had its own light plant and was 88.8 x 20.5 x 3.7 feet with a net tonnage of fifty-two.*

Photo courtesy of Wilson Powell.

Loading rice at Crocketts Bluff, Arkansas, on the White River in March 1917. The City of Muskogee *was built by the businessmen of Muskogee, Oklahoma, and vicinity to rejuvenate the dying steamboat trade on the upper Arkansas River. The boat was 127.6 x 28.5 x 4.3 feet.*

Preller photo, courtesy of Wilson Powell.

H. A. Preller Floating Photographers. Information on the boat states "Photographs, Copying, & Enlarging, Artistic Painting." The firm was from Columbus, Kentucky. Their charge was one dollar for half a day. A photo of the City of Muskogee *at Crocketts Bluff was made by Preller.*

Photo courtesy of Wilson Powell.

hauling rice and other cargo. Built by businessmen from Muskogee, Oklahoma, in an effort to rejuvenate steamboat trade on the upper Arkansas River, the craft made several trips in White River.

There was some boat traffic on the extreme Upper White River in Missouri during the early 1900s. In 1907, John P. Usher ran a riverboat out of the Branson landing to Forsyth. The sternwheeler *John P. Usher* was commanded by Capt. S. W. Haymes and Lieutenant McFarland. Unfortunately, on its maiden voyage to Forsyth, carrying a number of Branson citizens, the craft had difficulty on the return leg of the trip and was tied up at Bull Creek Shoal. The career of the *John P. Usher* seems to have been short. A more successful Forsyth to Branson boat appeared in 1908. With Captain Troutman in command and Hy McFarland as engineer, the gasoline-powered side-wheeler *Moark* made frequent excursion trips between Branson and Forsyth. Often the excursionists enjoyed live entertainment while on board. Due to the poor quality of existing roads, many local people also utilized the White as a mode of transportation both for themselves and for their freight. Records indicate the *Moark* hauled up to eight tons of freight from the Branson railroad site. The building of Powersite Dam in 1911 brought the *Moark*'s career to an end.

The arrival of the Missouri-Pacific Railroad in Branson and Hollister in 1905 presented another perspective to the economy there. Not only did the railroad carry a large amount of freight to the area, it also brought more and more visitors, and the era of tourism was born. Entrepreneurs, recognizing the potential of catering to these travelers, began building resorts along the river. Their efforts were further rewarded when, on February 4, 1911, Congress approved the construction of a dam on the White, three miles upriver from Forsyth. While the primary reason for the dam was the generation of electricity, the creation of Lake Taneycomo proved to be a long-term secondary benefit that added to the recreational attractiveness of the region.

One of the first people to realize the possibilities of river transportation along the newly formed lake was Hobart McQuarter. In 1916, McQuarter founded the Sammy Lane Boat Line and put in commercial gasoline-powered riverboats. At first, the boats were used primarily to haul heavy cargo and supplies. Soon, however, local citizens were using the boats as transportation from one river community to another. As the numbers of tourists visiting the area grew, The Sammy Lane boats worked with the Missouri-Pacific railroad to ferry train passengers from the depots in Hollister and Branson to resorts along the river.

The Sammy Lane Boat Line also became an official rural mail carrier, and mail was delivered by these boats to all the communities along the lake until July 1954. Local residents relied on the punctuality of the boats and were seldom disappointed. At Powersite, where the dam was built, a trip to the lakefront with

The Moark, *a gasoline-powered side-wheeler, in 1908 served as a passenger and freight boat from Forsyth to the Branson railroad. It was also an excursion boat. Pictured on the* far right *against the rail are Pearl and Walter Moore of Taney County, Missouri.*

From the Carl Moore Collection.

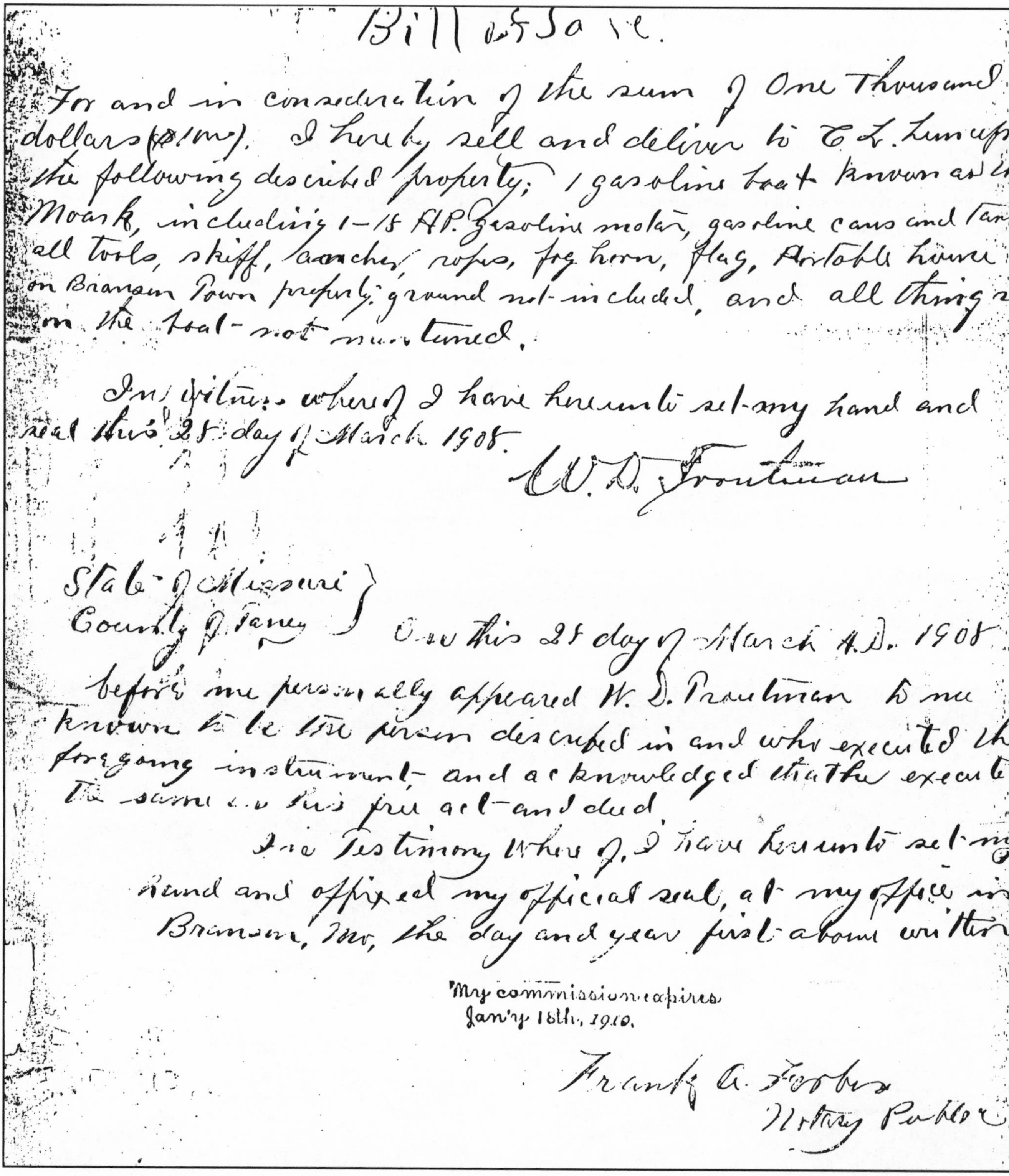
Bill of Sale.

For and in consideration of the sum of One Thousand dollars ($1000). I hereby sell and deliver to C. L. [illegible] the following described property; 1 gasoline boat known as the Moark, including 1-18 H.P. gasoline motor, gasoline cans and tank, all tools, skiff, anchor, ropes, fog horn, flag, portable house on Branson Town property, ground not included, and all things on the boat not mentioned.

In witness whereof I have hereunto set my hand and seal this 28 day of March 1908.

W. D. Troutman

State of Missouri }
County of Taney } On this 28 day of March A.D. 1908

before me personally appeared W. D. Troutman to me known to be the person described in and who executed the foregoing instrument and acknowledged that he executed the same as his free act and deed.

In Testimony Whereof, I have hereunto set my hand and affixed my official seal, at my office in Branson, Mo, the day and year first above written.

My commission expires
Jan'y 18th, 1910.

Frank A. Forbes
Notary Public

Bill of Sale for Moark.

From the Carl Moore Collection.

his mule was a regular part of the daily schedule for Ted Magness, owner of the general store. When the mailboat appeared, Ted loaded the mail sack onto the back of his mule, and they headed to his store. His wait at the lake was usually a short one. As one old timer said, "You could set your clock by the *Sammy Lane* 'cause she brung the mail the same time every day."[18]

The first *Sammy Lane* was built up Turkey Creek and made its maiden voyage in June 1913. The *Sadie H.* was licensed in 1916. By the late 1920s, Hobart McQuarter had ten boats running, including the *Joseph H.*, the *Mohawk,* the *Dan Mathews,* the *Patty-Jo,* the *Issac Walton,* the *Samoline,* the *Jim Lane,* and the *Shepherd of the Hills.* One of the most popular was the *Virginia Mae,* a double-

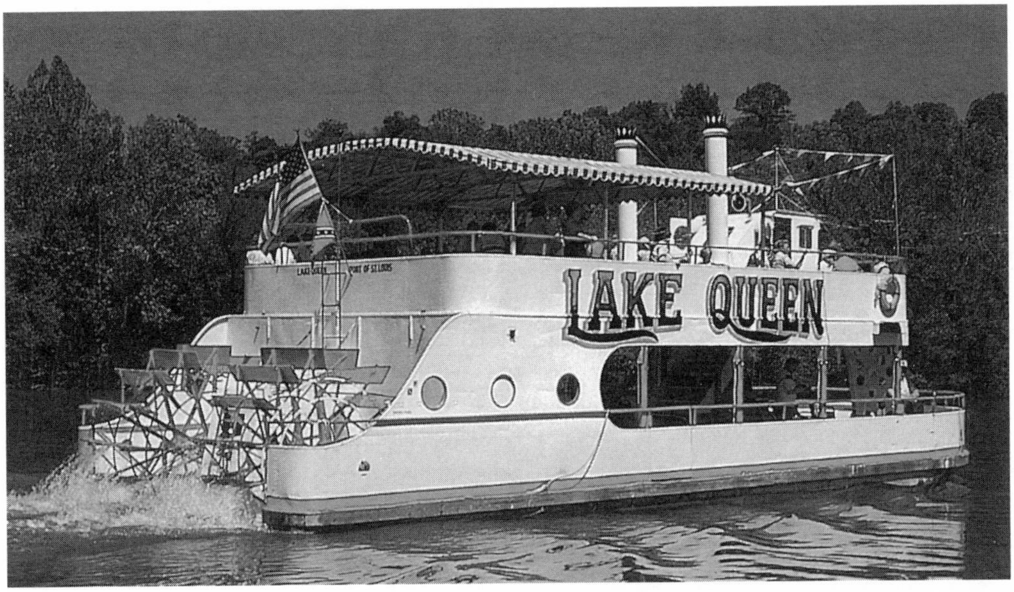

The Lake Queen *tours Lake Taneycomo at Branson, Missouri, under the direction of Capts. Bob and Margi Colerick.*

Photo courtesy of Bob and Margi Colerick.

The showboat Branson Belle *operates from White River Landing on Table Rock Lake. Making its maiden voyage in April 1995, the* Branson Belle *is believed to be the largest excursion vessel built for a land-locked waterway.*

Courtesy of White River Landing.

decker named after McQuarter's daughter. During the '20s and '30s, a popular excursion included dancing to melodies played by a live band all the way from Branson downriver to Rockaway Beach and back.

The Sammie Lane Boat Line was taken over by Vi and Lyn Asselin in 1964. As an enhancement to their river trips, the Asselins introduced the Sammy Lane Pirate Cruise, an excursion along Lake Taneycomo that is filled not only with beautiful scenery but also with history and tales of White River. The Colericks, the current owners of Sammy Lane Boat Dock are proudly carrying on the tradition passed to them. The Colericks also own the *Lake Queen,* a paddle-wheel riverboat that has served on Lake Taneycomo for many years and was purchased from Capt. Lane Sagers. The *Lake Queen* offers daytime and evening excursions, some of which include a meal. For a brief time in 1995 and '96, Lake Taneycomo was also served by the *Princess* riverboat, owned by Howard Grenier and his sons. The *Princess* offered scenic excursion trips, some with meals.

The newest riverboat on White River in the Branson area is the *Branson Belle.* The *Branson Belle* is a palatial showboat that made its maiden voyage in April 1995. Operating out of White River Landing on Table Rock Lake, the spectacular riverboat offers both meals and live entertainment. A joint venture of Kenny Rogers and Silver Dollar City, the *Branson Belle* is believed to be the largest excursion vessel built for a landlocked waterway. The sternwheeler measures 256 feet by 74 feet by 65 feet and can comfortably seat 650 to 700 passengers in its atrium where they are dined and entertained in a turn-of-the-century setting.

Though their numbers steadily decreased, steamboats plied White River until the late 1930s. In 1930, the Choctaw

Transportation Company was busy in the Lower White, carrying a variety of freight. In August of that year, the steamboat *Robert H. Romunder* towed supplies for the Union Bridge Company of Kansas City; that company held the contract for the pier work at the site of construction of the new Clarendon bridge over the White River. Another steamboat, the *Robert Sanford,* brought supplies for the bridge contractors, the Austin Bridge Company of Dallas, Texas. The *Robert H. Romunder* also stayed busy transporting logs for the F. T. Dooley Lumber Company. The logs were placed on the riverbank about forty miles below Clarendon, where they were picked up and delivered by boat to the Choctaw Transportation river terminal at the Missouri Pacific tracks. The steamboat worked in both the White and the Arkansas Rivers. The *Sears,* another logging boat, was also busy during that period.

In 1933, the *Mary Woods No. 2* was officially placed into service hauling lumber for the Woods Lumber Company. The 132-foot boat was designed by Eugene Woods, president of the company. The vessel had an all-steel hull with a beam of 26 feet and draft of 4 feet. Its steam-driven engines were 350 horsepower. As has been mentioned, the *Mary Woods No. 2* is now permanently docked at the Jacksonport State Park on White River.

The number of steamboats running in the White River dropped substantially each year, until they eventually disappeared, the victims of a more modern transportation system. The superb passenger packets, with their steam calliopes, elaborately fitted staterooms, elegantly furnished cabins, and talented musical ensembles have faded, unceremoniously, into the past. No longer do their twin ribbons of smoke ride the breeze. No longer does the scent of their burning pine knots fill the air. And no longer do the tones of their melodious whistles float along the river; but perhaps, by perusing this book, the reader can "float lightly, speed swiftly and safely" on a steamboat ride along the White River.

Log boat Sears. *Photo was taken at a logging landing at Jacksonport. The steamer was used to push log barges up White River.*

Photo courtesy of Jacksonport Courthouse Museum.

The Mary Woods II *is docked at Jacksonport State Park. Built in 1931 to haul log rafts on the White River, the stern-wheeler was donated to the park by the Potlatch Corporation in 1967.*

Photo by Sammie Rose.

PART III

FERRIES

"I remember we lived on the farm where I was born there by *Nave's Ferry.* Daddy came in—I was about five years old—and said the steamboat is coming up the river, and I went to the door and I saw it go up the river. My granddad Adams used to freight to Springfield for the merchants in Protem. He had an old Springfield wagon, and he hauled eggs and produce to Springfield and brought back things for the store. I was born about a quarter of a mile from that ferry on this side."[1] So spoke Willa Nave Brown (most people call her Bill) as she and her sister, Fern Nave Boone, described their lives near the banks of the White River. Mrs. Brown's ancestors were quite active in ferries along the White, as was she in later years.

Willa and Fern's father, Tobe, bore the name of his grandfather, Jacob Wilson Nave, who built the original *Nave's Ferry.* Willa's husband, Joe, assisted his father, Baxter Brown, in running the *Brown's Ferry,* located downriver from the *Nave's Ferry.* In 1923, the young couple bought *Brown's Ferry* from the elder Brown. Baxter Brown built the ferry, initially, because of a need to reach portions of his farm which lay on the other side of the river, land that was inaccessible in times of heavy rains. Many of the White River ferries came into existence out of that same necessity and, once in place, were utilized not only by family and neighbors but also by strangers as well when the population of the region increased.

The sight of the White River during times of high water could be a terrifying one for early settlers, particularly if no ferry existed along their chosen route. In Doug Mahnkey's book *Hill and Hollow Stories* (School of the Ozarks Press, 1975), he tells about the first time the White was seen by a family moving to the area from Kentucky. They had camped for several days at Springfield, Missouri, before proceeding to a spot near Forsyth on the banks of the river. When the grandmother stuck her head out of the wagon and saw the expanse of water, she yelled at her son, "My God, son! Ain't they some way around this?"

In addition to providing transportation for natives and newcomers, the presence of the ferries contributed to the expansion of commerce along the river. These landings often served as ports where transfer of cargo was made to smaller water craft that transported the merchandise to destinations located on the tributaries of the White, or to wagons that carried the goods to inland settlements.

Most of the families who operated these early ferries lived near the river, and the method of running the business was simple. At many of them, the traveler need only "holler" when he arrived at the river's edge. The ferryman or a member of his family would appear from their nearby home or a field in which they were working and would "carry" the customer across. At other ferry sites, a large iron bell was utilized to summon the operator.

Prior to the advent of water-powered sawmills, the early ferries were simply large rafts. Ferryboats constructed of sawed lumber made their appearance in the late 1840s or early 1850s. Most of the early ferries were poled, or "lugged," across the water by the ferrymen, who learned from experience how to utilize the river's current to assist in the crossing. In later years, cables were also used to expedite the trip. The cable, usually fastened to a large tree, was strung from bank to bank across the river. Mounted on the cable was a large pulley to which a heavy rope was connected. The other end of the rope was hooked to a windlass on the ferry so that the ferryman, by turning the windlass, could change the position of the ferry. If the craft was pointed upstream, the pressure of the current would turn the windlass until the front end of

Nave's Ferry, *located at Lead Hill, formerly Dubuque, where West Sugar Loaf Creek empties into White River. Jake Nave built this ferry. Later it was owned by William Thomas Raley. The* Lady Boone *steamboat was built at the town of Dubuque also.*

Photo courtesy of Wanda Hutchenson.

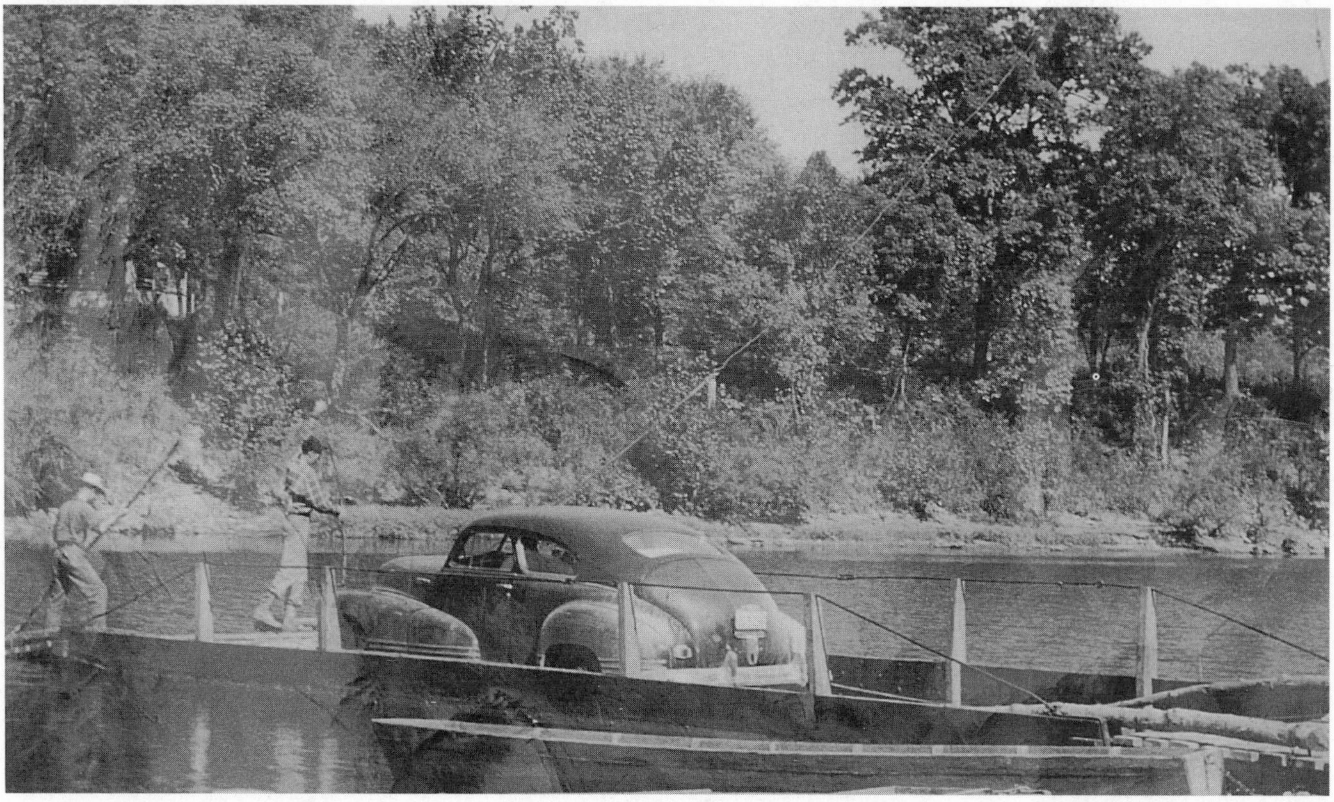

Moore's Ferry, *about 1947. Carl Moore and Ed Falk pole or "lug" the ferry across White River.*

Photo courtesy of Carl Moore.

the vessel was at the correct angle, and the ferry would be pushed slowly across the river by the water's flow. When the steamers began plying the White, the vessels sounded their bell to warn the ferryman to lower the ferry cable so that they might approach and/or pass the landing without danger to their smokestacks. On more than one occasion, a steamer lost its stacks to a ferry cable.

As the White River basin developed and river traffic increased, ferry operators, unless the ferry was a private one, were required by law to be licensed and bonded by the county courts. For a number of years, the state license fee in Missouri was two dollars, while the county fee usually varied from ten to thirteen dollars per year. Bond was usually set at five hundred dollars. Service charges collected by the ferry operators were set by the individual county courts, and in 1889 the following rates were typical:[2]

Wagon and 2 yoke of oxen or 4 horses	\$.75
Wagon and 1 yoke of oxen or 2 horses	\$.50
One-horse carriage and 1 horse	\$.35
Man and horse	\$.25
Cattle by the head	\$.10
Sheep and hogs by the head	\$.05
Footman	\$.10

Most people, grateful for the transportation, were quite willing to pay the ferry fees. There were occasional travelers, however, who attempted to take advantage of the ferryman by giving a variety of excuses for not paying today, accompanied by a solemn promise to pay tomorrow. Dom Ingenthron of Taney County, Missouri, once told Doug Mahnkey about a ferry operator who hoped to avoid such problems by posting the following verse at his ferry:

As man to man is so unjust
And I know not in whom to trust
As I have trusted to my sorrow
You pay today, I'll trust tomorrow.

At some ferry crossings, the service rates during periods of high water were different from those charged at times of low water. Rates for Independence County, Arkansas, in February 1911 show that difference (see illustration).

Ferriage Rates

STATE OF ARKANSAS,
County of Independence.

I, T. M. WALDRIP, Clerk of the County Court for said County, do hereby certify that the following ferry rates for High and Low Water have been fixed by the County Court of said County, and Ferry Keepers are prohibited from collecting a greater amount than herein fixed.

Low Water Rates		High Water Rates	
For man and horse	10c.	For man and horse	20c.
For 1-horse wagon or buggy	15c.	For 1-horse wagon or buggy	25c.
For 2-horse wagon or buggy	20c.	For 2-horse wagon or buggy	35c.
For 4-horse wagon	40c.	For 4-horse wagon	60c.
For 6-horse wagon	60c.	For 6-horse wagon	75c.
For footman	5c.	Fcr footman	10c.
For loose stock	5c.	For loose stock	10c.
For automobile	25c.	For automobile	50c.

Given under my hand this 18th day of February, 1911.

T. M. WALDRIP, Clerk.

Ferriage rates, Independence County, Arkansas.

Courtesy of Wilson Powell.

Ferry operators were sometimes fiercely competitive. In the early days of the region's development, *Talbert's Ferry,* in Marion County near Yellville, Arkansas, was a primary landing for the area. It was later owned by Lee Denton and was known as *Denton's Ferry.* Denton apparently became upset when, less than a mile down the White from him, W. C. McBee placed a ferry into operation. McBee's river land included the mouth of Fallen Ash Creek; and he not only built a ferry there, but a grist mill, a cotton gin, and a warehouse. Like good businessmen everywhere, ferry operators along the White took their occupation seriously. The emergence of *McBee's Landing* created a formidable threat to business at *Denton's Ferry,* and a battle was in the making. Whether the following story is indeed true or not, it certainly conveys the sense of intense competition that existed between these two ferry owners. A sentence from the *Mt. Echo* newspaper of Marion County, Arkansas, reads: "We understand that Mr. Lee Denton, 'Buck-eyed' up on mean whiskey went down river and painted McBee's Landing and his 4X ferry red last week."[3]

The busiest ferries became part of the overland routes between major towns. Others primarily served local communities. Many were located near the spot where a tributary emptied into the White. Several of them, because of changes in operators, were called different names at various times during the course of their existence. As road and bridge construction improved, the need for the ferries lessened, and by 1993 only one was still in operation across the White River.

In discussing some specific White River ferries, it seems appropriate to start near the White's origin and travel downriver. The upper reaches of White River were surrounded by dense wilderness and tough prairie when Peter Van Winkle, owner of the *Van Winkle Ferry,* settled there about 1853. A native of the state of New York, Van Winkle migrated to Illinois early in life, where he remained until adulthood. He first visited the White River area, around Fayetteville, between 1837 and 1840. About 1850, however, Van Winkle briefly returned to Illinois from Arkansas, then spent some time in Texas. In 1853, he came back to White River country to stay and settled in eastern Benton County.

Van Winkle had little formal education but became a skilled

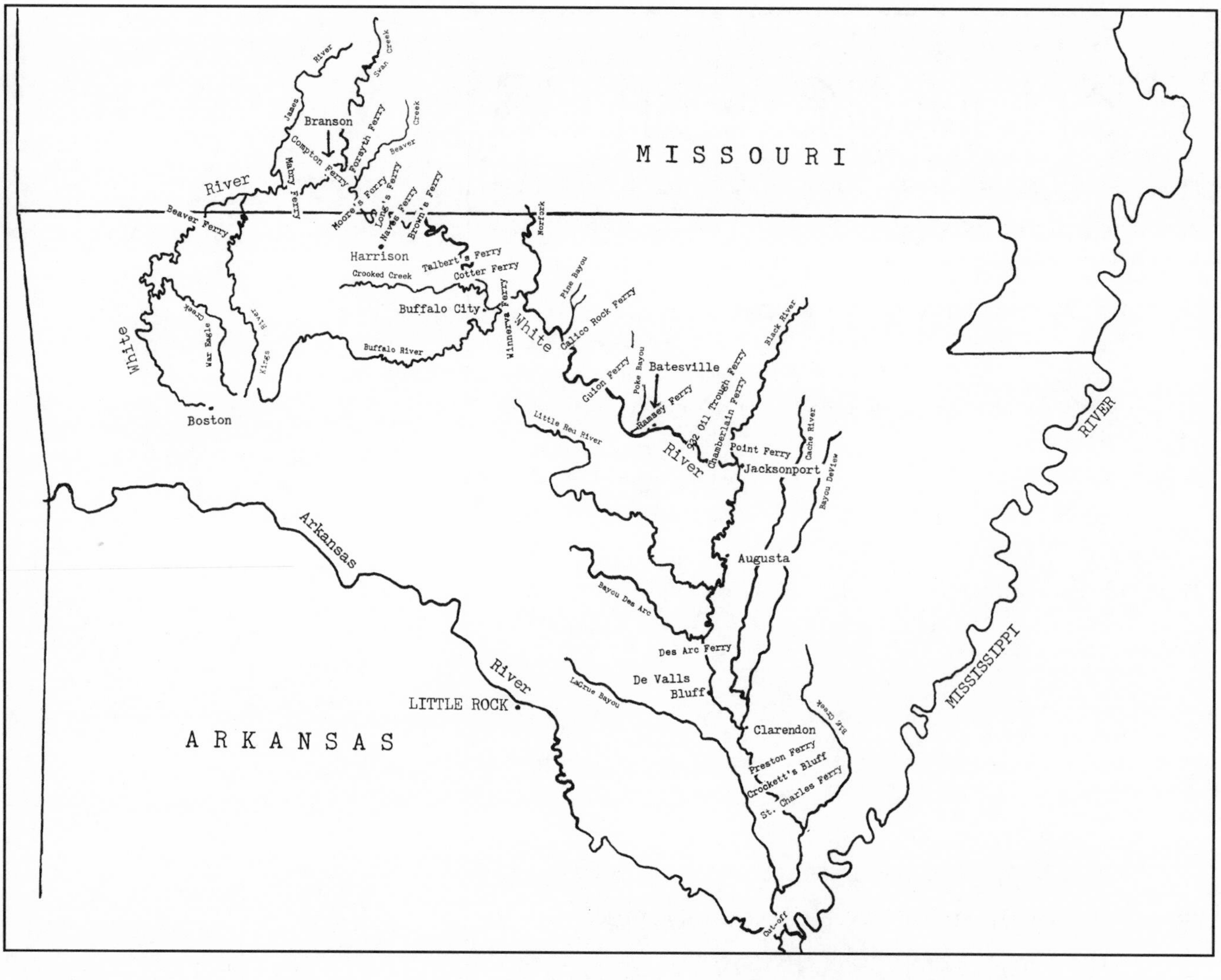

White River ferries. Due to space, all ferries are not shown on this map; a complete listing of ferries and their location is in the back of the book.
Sketch by Sammie Rose.

farmer, blacksmith, and mechanic. During his early years in northwestern Arkansas, he held several contracts with settlers who were attempting to break up the heavy prairie sod that stretched west and north of Fayetteville to the Missouri border. To handle the job, he designed a special plow, pulled by several yoke of oxen. The implement was a boon for the pioneers. Around 1858, Van Winkle built a steam sawmill on Little Clifty Branch, a spring-fed brook that empties into War Eagle, a White River tributary. Van Winkle was active in the lumbering business for a number of years; his first milling efforts had been with an oxen-powered portable sawmill.

In January 1882, Van Winkle purchased twelve acres of land lying on both the east and the west banks of the White River, near the War Eagle mouth, and established *Van Winkle Ferry*. His customers could use the ferry free of charge, but other ferry patrons paid fifty cents. Throughout his life, Van Winkle acquired a great deal of land in the area and was a very successful lumberman. At the time of his death, in February 1882, he was acknowledged to be one of the wealthiest businessmen in the region. The approximate location of the *Van Winkle Ferry* was slightly downriver from the present Horseshoe Bend Recreational Area on Beaver Lake.

One of the earliest ferries to operate on the White was located at Beaver, Arkansas, near the present town of Eureka Springs. Wilson A. Beaver moved to the area from Tennessee in 1835. In 1857, Beaver bought the land where the ferry was already operating from John and Sarah Williams. Williams had held title to the

Beaver Ferry *across White River was replaced by a one-lane "swinging" or suspension bridge, which is still in use, on Arkansas Highway 187.*

Photo courtesy of Eureka Springs Museum.

Beaver Ferry *was named for Wilson A. Beaver, a prominent early Arkansan. This current-powered ferry was used to haul material to build the railroad bridge, shown in the background, across White River at the Narrows in 1883.*

From the Sam Leath Collection, Eureka Springs Museum.

land as far back as 1852, when it was referred to as the "Recter place on White River."[4] Whether Recter operated a ferry at the spot is unknown. Squire Beaver, who had a large farm and a number of slaves, eventually owned much of the valley where the ferry was located. He ran the ferry for a while with George F. Wilson, then Wilson operated the ferry by himself.

During the Civil War, *Beaver Ferry* was used to transport Union troops across the river on their way to the battle at Pea Ridge. The store that existed at Beaver at the time was converted into an infirmary for wounded soldiers. Because of its location on a primary road along Butler Creek, *Beaver Ferry* was always a busy one. Following the war, the little village of Beaver grew, and on September 22, 1879, a post office was established there. Squire Beaver became the first postmaster, serving during 1879 and 1880. The name was later changed from Beaver Ferry Post Office to simply Beaver Post Office. There was a large rock quarry operating near the village at that time, and the town had several small houses in which the quarry laborers lived. It was a busy crossroads and also had a hotel.

Patrons of *Beaver Ferry* were varied, ranging from local to commercial. Lumber from a mill at the mouth of Leatherwood Creek was regularly brought to the ferry to be transported across White River to markets in Missouri. *Beaver Ferry* ceased operation when a toll bridge was built at the turn of the century. The water-powered craft was called back into service, however, when a flood washed out the bridge about the time of construction of the railroad. The ferry continued to run until 1926 when the bridge which stands today was built. A small bridge, reminiscent of the famed Golden Gate Bridge, the span is a picturesque reminder of earlier days in Northwest Arkansas.

Beaver Ferry *in the 1920s at Beaver, Arkansas. Note two Model A cars on the ferry and a covered wagon on the approach.*

From the Sam Leath Collection, Eureka Springs Museum.

Ferries powered by the river current were used to take travelers across the White River. One ferry operator, W. W. Kimberling, had two bridges and later a town named after him.

Credit unknown.

Near where the James River empties into the White in Missouri was the site of the *Maberry Ferry* (also known as *Mabry Ferry* and later as *Kimberling Ferry*). Another of the earliest to operate on the river, it dates back to pre–Civil War days. The White was about three hundred feet wide at the point where the ferry crossed. Run by Reuben Maberry, the ferry was a busy one because it was part of the Old Wilderness Road that extended from Springfield, Missouri, south into Arkansas. The operation was renamed the *Kimberling Ferry* in 1870 when William Wesley Kimberling Sr. assumed its handling. In 1867, after serving in the Union army, Kimberling married and bought a farm on the north side of the White River, where he established a store. He bought the *Maberry Ferry* in 1870 with Henry Thomas. The ferryboat was quite old and worn. After assuming ownership, the two men built a new craft that was about forty-two feet long and twelve feet wide with banisters on both sides and gates at each end. At all times, two canoes were kept tied to the vessel in case of accident, though no serious mishaps occurred with the ferry.

The *Kimberling Ferry* carried a variety of passengers through the years, including large numbers of hogs, cattle, and sheep. Herdsmen from Arkansas would head for market in Springfield, Missouri, driving not only their own stock but animals they had purchased along the way. Some stock owners were known to move their animals into the area for other reasons as well. Occasionally, at tax assessment time, a stockman from Arkansas would drive his stock to the land near the ferry and let it range there. When it was time for the assessors to appear in Missouri, and the tax officials in the herdsman's part of Arkansas had moved on, the animals were returned to their home.

Money and records for the *Kimberling Ferry* were kept in a "stand-table" built by Wesley Kimberling's brother. Since there was no bank located in the vicinity, the amount kept at the ferry could be substantial at times, so concern for theft was always there. The business was robbed at least once. The ferry ran from the south side of the river, and remained in operation until a bridge was built across the White in the 1920s as part of the construction of Highway 13 through the area. On December 10, 1922, the *Kimberling Ferry* made its final run after having been operated by the Kimberling family for fifty-two years.

The point where Turkey Creek empties into the White was the location of the *Turkey Creek Ferry*. During the late 1880s, it was operated by Henry C. and J. T. Berry. In the years 1893 to 1899, it became known as the *Hawkins Ferry* after William M. and A. J. Hawkins assumed its operation. During a portion of the 1890s, the ferry was licensed without fees by the county court because of the small number of customers. Since there was no town of Branson at the time, the operation was considered mostly an accommodation ferry for those few who needed it. The busiest years at the *Hawkins Ferry* were in 1903 at the beginning of railroad construction in the area and in 1913 during completion of the White River bridge by the dam company. In 1901 and 1909, J. A. Vanzandt was the licensed operator. During 1904 and 1905, the ferry license was issued to Charles M. Thompson and William E. Cox.

Compton Ferry, *1907. The ferry was located at the mouth of Roark Creek. Henry Compton was licensed as operator. Joe Snapp was one of his assistants.*

Photo courtesy of Don Garner.

At the mouth of Roark Creek was the *Roark Ferry,* commonly known as the *Compton Ferry* because Henry Compton was the licensed operator. Joe Snapp served as one of his assistants. The ferry was busiest after rail service was completed through Branson in 1906. The new road from Forsyth to Branson provided the ferry with considerable traffic. The creation of Lake Taneycomo on the White in 1911, and the construction of the river bridge at Branson, ended the need for the *Compton Ferry.*

During the late 1870s, the *Boston Ferry* was in operation about three and one-half miles below the *Compton Ferry.* It was operated by William S. Boston and gave competition to an older ferry, the *Hensley Ferry,* located a short distance below it. In 1870, William S. Boston purchased some river bottomland on the south side of White River just upriver from the *Hensley Ferry.* When he saw how busy *Hensley Ferry* was because of its location on the Harrison-Springfield Road, Boston opened an alternate route along the main divide west of the Bull Creek watershed and established the *Boston Ferry* as part of that route. The alternate became known as the Boston Road and was opened sometime between 1875 and 1879. Boston sold both the ferry and his farm in 1884.

Another of the oldest White River ferries, dating to Civil War days, the *Hensley Ferry* was located a short distance below Oak Grove Point, near the mouth of Bull Creek in Missouri. Built by William Hensley, the ferry was later run by his sons, George and Jim Hensley. When the railroad came to Springfield in 1870, a great deal of commercial traffic from markets downriver utilized the ferry since it was part of the Harrison-Springfield Road. It was not uncommon for fifty to one hundred freight wagons to pass over the road daily. The *Hensley Ferry* was also one of the steamboat landings. For a while there was a large rooming house at the crossing. Claribel Rose Hensley, wife of Elmo Hensley, held fond memories of evenings spent at the boarding house while visiting there, evenings filled with the strains of fiddle music, laughter, and stories. The ferry became one of the most profitable in the area. It was that business which prompted Boston to start the competitive ferry mentioned earlier. The *Hensley Ferry* lost its usefulness with changes in routes and the creation of Lake Taneycomo when Powersite Dam was built in 1911.

A ferry called *Chapman Ferry* ran briefly near Chapman Hollow in Missouri. Though it's existence was short, it was quite busy for a while, handling about the same number of travelers as the *Compton Ferry.* W. W. Jones was one of the licensed operators for the ferry, while Sam Brown was its last operator, just prior to the creation of Lake Taneycomo.

The White River crossing near Forsyth, Missouri, was a major one and had a number of ferries operating there at different times. According to county records, the earliest ferry operator actually licensed at this site was Bennett P. Parrish in 1886. Parrish ran the ferry, known as the *Parrish Ferry,* from 1886 to 1897. Around 1897, a rival operation was created by Dr. F. V. Baldwin near the Parrish site. The *Baldwin Ferry* was licensed from 1897 to 1911. From 1897 to 1905, a ferry license at Forsyth was also issued to the Jesse A. Tolerton Ferry Company. The *Parrish Ferry* at Forsyth was replaced in 1919 by a two-span steel bridge.

During the Civil War, a ferry at Forsyth figured substantially in battle strategy. On January 19, 1863, Federal troops under the command of General Herron arrived at the White River on the opposite shore from Forsyth. Realizing the importance of maintaining an outpost in that section of the state bordering Arkansas, General Herron considered it vital that he occupy Forsyth. The river, because of high water, could not be forded. There was, however, a ferry operating at the site, and the ferryboat ran continuously for more than eight days and nights, moving all the troops and vehicles across the river.

Forsyth bridge and ferry. The oldest county record lists Bennett P. Parrish as being licensed in 1886, with Robert Parrish licensed from 1891 to 1896 to operate a ferry at Forsyth. A competition developed from 1897 to 1905 between Dr. F.V. Baldwin and Jesse A. Tolerton, both licensed and operating ferries at the same time. It is believed that Tolerton took over the Parrish Ferry, *also called the* Forsyth Ferry.

Photo courtesy of Carl Moore.

The Parrish Ferry *at Forsyth, Missouri. Ira Parrish, Forsyth druggist, and his dog pose for a picture on a ferry at the Forsyth landing.*
Photo courtesy of Irene Reynolds.

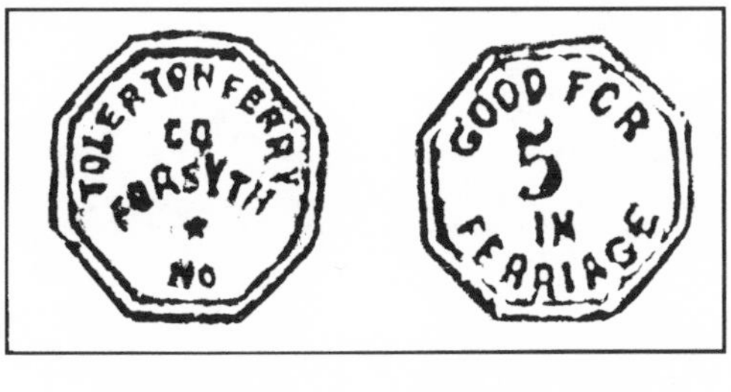

Token issued by Tolerton Ferry Company of Forsyth, Missouri. From 1897 to 1905 Dr. F.V. Baldwin and Jesse A. Tolerton were both licensed and operated ferries at Forsyth.
From the Elmo Ingenthron Collection.

Quite near the Forsyth location was the *Swan Creek Ferry,* located at the mouth of the Swan. The operation was brief, appearing just prior to the construction of a bridge at the site, which ended the need for the ferry.

A ferry known as the *Beaver Creek Ferry* ran near the mouth of Beaver Creek from about 1894 to the early 1900s. In 1903 the operation was known as the *Kissee Mill Ferry.*

Another ferry operating in the early 1900s was the *Cedar Creek Ferry* near Cedar Creek's entrance into White River. In 1902, a Mr. Beeler was its operator. The name changed to the *Blackwell Ferry* in 1910 when a Mr. Blackwell owned it.

Near the mouth of Trigger Creek, still in Missouri, was the *Trigger Creek Ferry,* better known as *Moore's Ferry* because Isaac Moore built it originally. Like the *Blackwell Ferry* above it, *Moore's Ferry* offered a more direct route to the important trading centers of Kirbyville, Hollister, and Branson for the people living in the Cedar Creek–Protem area. The exact date of its first operation is not known. During the years 1906 through 1910, a license for operation of the ferry was issued to Isaac Moore, though he may have operated it for several years prior to that date. Following the years of operation by the Moore family, one of the last ferrymen at *Moore's Ferry* was Olen Austin. Austin would sometimes have to use his team of horses, Rex and Prince, to pull cars ashore when they became stuck on the sand bar while departing the ferry, so the animals were usually close by.

The last operator of *Moore's Ferry* was Wylse Yandell. Thelma Johnson, his daughter and a resident of Kirbyville, Missouri, had fond memories of the ferry and her father's dedication to its operation. One of those memories was of a trip taken with her father when she was just a small girl. He took Thelma and other family members on a trip down the White to visit some ferry landings downstream. Thelma remembered seeing at least three between *Moore's Ferry* and Elbow Shoals: the *Ellison's,* the *Cornell,* and the *Nave's Ferry.* Wylse Yandell (his full name was James Wilson Yandell)

Moore's Ferry, *with Isaac Moore, his wife, Elizabeth, and granddaughter, Ethel. Located at the mouth of Trigger Creek, the ferry was built by Moore, who operated it for many years.*

Photo courtesy of Carl Moore.

Moore's Ferry. *Leaning against the rail is Olen Austin, operator. His wife is the lady in the* center *of the ferry with the hat on.* The Trigger Creek Ferry, *better known as* Moore's Ferry, *was built by Isaac Moore, who ran it for many years near the mouth of Trigger Creek. In later years it was operated by Olen Austin and Wylse Yandell and on a help-yourself basis.*

Photo courtesy of Maxine McGlauchlen.

Olen Austin is shown with his team, Rex and Prince. The horses were frequently used to pull cars out if they became stuck while disembarking from Moore's Ferry *when Austin operated it.*

Photo courtesy of Maxine McGlauchlen.

was a true riverman who loved the White and who, though he respected the river, had no fear of it. He once told Thelma that there was no reason for anyone to drown if one would just keep one's senses and not "try to swallow the whole river."[5] Anyone could float and travel with the water long enough to reach safety, he said.

The Yandells owned a farm near the ferry, and Wylse Yandell became the ferry's primary operator during its final years of operation. Since it was considered a community ferry at that time, no fee was charged for its use. More than once, the craft was loosened from its moorings by a storm, and Yandell would have to retrieve it. At least once, it had to be rebuilt by Yandell, but the community always contributed funds for any repairs which had to be done to the ferry. After a particularly damaging flood took its toll on their farm, Yandell and his wife moved into Branson, but he continued to go to *Moore's Ferry* for some time. In fact, he often made the trip by foot, despite the miles it was from his home in town. When Yandell was not available to operate the ferry, it was run on a "help-yourself" basis. Often, the craft would be left on the opposite shore and Yandell would have to retrieve it when he arrived at the ferry site. Wylse Yandell, in his black hat, overalls, and chambray shirt, was a familiar and welcome sight at *Moore's Ferry;* he was part of a tradition that was missed when it disappeared. The ferry continued in operation until the building of Bull Shoals Dam across the White River in 1953 created Bull Shoals Lake.

Just below the mouth of Elbow Creek, 464.5 miles from the mouth of the White River, was *Long's Ferry.* It was in operation for a number of years during the 1880s and 1890s. The ferry was owned by Judge John Long, whose family had come from Mason City, Iowa, shortly before the Civil War. The Longs owned land on both sides of the river, as well as a cotton gin and a large warehouse where merchandise brought by the steamboats was stored. According to Doug Mahnkey, in his book *Hill and Hollow Stories,* Judge Long's grandson, Elza Long, remembered hearing steamboats that were en route to Forsyth give two blasts on their whistles as a signal for the ferry cable to be lowered so the boat might pass over it. Because it was on one of the primary routes to Springfield, Missouri, long lines of freight wagons from the south would frequently form while waiting to board *Long's Ferry.* The lines became particularly long during cotton season.

The *Nave's Ferry,* as previously mentioned, was built by Jake Nave and was another of the early ferries operating on the river. It was later known as the *Raley Ferry* when William Thomas Raley assumed its ownership. The ferry was located at the foot of a small shoal where West Sugar Loaf Creek emptied into White River—today this site is a part of Bull Shoals Lake.

Brown's Ferry, originally built by Baxter Brown to reach his land on the opposite shore, as mentioned earlier, was another busy one because of its location on Yellville Road, which ran from Arkansas to Protem, Missouri. In the late 1800s, Brown's ferriage fee was fifty cents per wagon. The wear and tear of the crossings and the elements took its toll on the ferryboats, and Brown had to build several replacement crafts during the years he ran the ferry. Usually Brown's vessels were built of pine shipped in from southern Arkansas. In 1923, Baxter Brown's son, Joe, who was married to Willa Nave, bought the ferry. During their tenure as owners, Joe and Willa Brown built two replacement ferryboats. The last one constructed by Joe Brown was made from lumber cut in a mill owned by Joe Burleson at Pyatt, Arkansas. Two wagons or two cars could be ferried per trip on that ferry. Under the management of both Baxter and Joe Brown, *Brown's Ferry* ran from the late 1800s until 1952 when Bull Shoals Dam was built. The resultant Bull Shoals Lake covered some of the Brown's land, and the ferry ceased operation due to the lake waters. After selling seven acres of their land to the government for the Highway 125

The William Thomas Raley Ferry *at Lead Hill, Arkansas, was owned by Raley and operated by Larkin Shaffer. Raley is pictured here headed for his horse, with the ferry in the background. In earlier years the ferry was owned by Jake Nave. It was located at the mouth of West Sugar Loaf.*
Photo courtesy of Kathryn Adams.

Brown's Ferry, *across White River from Arkansas to Protem, Missouri, was built in the late 1800s by Baxter Brown. His son, Joe, and Joe's wife, Willa, known as "Bill," later built and ran two ferries at site.* Pictured left to right, *an unidentified man, Jacob Wilson (Tobe) and Jane Nave, Patsy Fern Taneyhill (little girl), and ferry owner Baxter Brown.*

Photo courtesy of Mrs. Joe Brown.

The Peel Ferry *is on Arkansas Highway 125. It was put into operation after Bull Shoals Dam was built.* Peel *replaced* Brown's Ferry *to Protem, Missouri. A 471-cubic-inch diesel marine engine powers the tug* Spring Bank *that tows this ferry across the lake in seven minutes.*

Photo by Sammie Rose.

boatdock on the south side of the lake, Joe and Willa Brown moved to Protem, where they also moved their general store.

Quite near the location of the old *Brown's Ferry* is the only White River ferry still in operation in 1998. Part of Arkansas Highway 125, the *Peel Ferry* crosses Bull Shoals Lake from Peel, Arkansas, to Protem, Missouri. The ferry came into existence thanks to a community effort following the formation of the lake. In 1967, fifty members of the Peel community formed Marion County Ferry, Inc., and raised about thirty-three thousand dollars, enabling them to equip Bull Shoals Lake with a ferry. Operation of the ferry was turned over to Marion County in September of the following year. It was run as a toll facility until December of 1969 when the Arkansas Highway Department leased the ferry. On August 15, 1970, the highway department purchased the ferry for twenty-three thousand dollars, and it continues to operate the facility today. The ferry runs during daylight hours and averages about one hundred vehicles per day. It is operated by two crews with three men per crew: the pilot and two deckhands.

Equipment for the *Peel Ferry* consists of two sixty-by-twenty-foot barges, one for regular traffic and one for fuel traffic, and two tugs. Currently, the tug *Spring Bank* operates with the barge *Lady Marion* for regular daily travel. Until recently, a tug named *Little Joe* was used with the barge *Toad Suck* to ferry fuel trucks that have to be transported by themselves, and to carry overflow vehicles during peak traffic times; however, the *Little Joe* is no longer being utilized. The *Toad Suck* was previously run as the *Toad Suck Ferry* across the Arkansas River near Conway, Arkansas. A twin-paddle-wheel ferry during its Toad Suck days, the barge was hauled by the

Arkansas Highway Department on a lowboy trailer to the Peel location. It was a two-day trip that drew many a puzzled look along the way. The barge *Lady Marion* was built by Don Baker, the Norris brothers, and Paul Yarber of Newark, Arkansas. Their welding expertise will be discussed when we review the *Guion Ferry,* another of the six steel ferries constructed by these men.

The *Pace Ferry* was located seven miles above the present site of Bull Shoals Dam near the mouth of Sister Creek. It was part of the old Flippin-Oakland Road in Arkansas. The road was the route taken by most of the freight consigned to Oakland merchants from the railroad at Flippin. That, plus local travelers, kept *Pace Ferry* quite busy from the late 1800s through the 1930s. Prior to 1918, the ferry was operated by Joe Pace and his son, Gus. In 1934, its operator was Warren Pace.

About 407 miles from the mouth of the White River, just above Water Hill, was *Mooney's Ferry.* The site of a well-known woodyard for the steamboats, the landing was a popular one in the late 1800s. In April 1888, W. C. Jones of the *Mountain Echo* reported that four or five hundred bales of cotton remained at *Mooney's Ferry* awaiting transport because the White was too low for the steamboats to pass Buffalo Shoals. Johnny Cake, chief of the Delaware, lived at a large spring in what became known as Tucker Bottoms, a fairly short distance from the later site of *Mooney's Ferry.*

A primary landing for all types of river traffic through the years was *Talbert's Ferry,* 405.4 miles from the mouth of White River, near the old Yellville Road. Established in the 1830s by three Talbert brothers, Fed, Walt, and Sam, the crossing was one of the oldest above the mouth of Buffalo River. The Talberts came to the

The Pace Ferry *was owned by Joe Pace and was on the Flippin-Oakland Road in Arkansas on White River. Frost operated the ferry in 1915. Here a mule was used for pulling the ferry into the bank.*

Photo courtesy of Jim Gaston.

Formerly Talbert's Ferry, *later owned by Lee Denton and called* Denton Ferry. *This ferry crossing was located 405.4 miles from the mouth of White River. Here, the poled or "lugged" ferry has a surrey carrying five passengers pulled by four horses. Note steamboat in the background.*

Photo courtesy of Jim Gaston.

area about 1824 or earlier and had a good relationship with their Indian neighbors.

As mentioned previously, Peter Cornstalk, a Shawnee chief in the 1830s, performed many kind acts for the white pioneers, as did Johnny Cake, the Delaware chief. Johnny Cake's band was living near Tucker Bottoms when Fed Talbert had to make a trip to the land office in St. Louis to lay claim to his land. Before departing, Talbert asked the Delaware chief to send some of his men each day to check on Mrs. Talbert and their children. Johnny Cake was more than happy to oblige. The morning following Talbert's departure, some Indian braves went down to the river on the west side and saw Mrs. Talbert on the other bank wave, the agreed upon signal that all was well. About an hour after signaling to the Indians, Mrs. Talbert happened to glance across the White and saw a huge black bear sauntering down to the water. She assumed it was just going for a drink of water, but as she watched, the bear jumped into the river and began swimming across. Just prior to his departure, Fed Talbert had killed a deer, and his wife figured the bear had caught scent of the fresh venison. Frightened, Mrs. Talbert quickly gathered her children inside the log cabin and boarded the only door with a heavy bar. They were hardly barricaded when the bear started shaking the door. Mrs. Talbert seized a sharp broad axe, the only weapon available to her for their defense. The cabin was not well chinked, and after having no success with the door, the animal peered into the cabin through the chinks. It finally decided to climb up to the loose board roof, using the chinks to scale the wall. When the bear reared up on its hind legs and thrust its paws into a chink, one paw went clear through. Swinging the axe with all her might, Mrs. Talbert severed about six inches of the paw from the rest of the leg. A great roar of pain was heard, and the injured animal gave up its quest and limped up a hollow, leaving a trail of blood.

When Johnny Cake's men came to the opposite shore the next morning, Mrs. Talbert signaled for them to cross. She showed them the bear's paw as she related details of the encounter. The Indians followed the animal's trail to a sort of cave, where it was resting. After killing and skinning the creature, the braves returned to the cabin and left a hindquarter for Mrs. Talbert and her children. The remainder of Fed Talbert's absence was uneventful at the cabin, but the Indians were very faithful in checking on Mrs. Talbert each morning.

In 1837, Walter Talbert sold the ferry site to Jesse Goodman, the keelboatman who ran a trading post there. Among Goodman's employees at the trading post was his nephew, W. B. Flippin. Flippin was clerking in the trading post when John Benge and his band of Cherokees reached *Talbert's Ferry* on their trek to their assigned lands in Oklahoma. Flippin later described the event in an article in the *Mountain Echo* of June 30, 1899:

> Many of the Cherokees were well dressed and riding good horses; fine looking men . . . the majority of them were poorly clad—some of the women only having blankets wrapped around them, several carrying papooses wrapped in a blanket or some kind of cloth and fastened to the backs of their mothers. Seeing so many, I wondered that I did not hear a scream from a single papoose. . . .
>
> It was winter when they came to White River; ice was frozen over along the banks of the river. I was to assist the ferryman in setting the host across the river in a very ordinary ferryboat with two oars to row with. Instead of their stopping to make terms to cross the river in the ferryboat, they pretended to halt, but waded across the river, men and women, all except a few who had horses or carriages. . . . It reminded me of a drove of cattle crossing a stream. The river was unusually low at this time, but it was over two hundred yards wide . . . They camped shortly after crossing the river and built up fires and remained all night. . . .
>
> There came that evening to the camp a large fine looking man . . . who had recently come to the county. . . . Micajah Hogan . . . had come for the purpose of gambling with the Indians, which he did that night, and won a considerable amount of money.
>
> Next day early the host moved on, but two Indians crossed back over the river. Hogan returned and put up at the house of the ferryman. I learned that the name of one of the Indians was Benge, a sub-chief, the other a tall active looking Indian, who's name was Young. He immediately told Hogan his business was to play a game of cards with him. Hogan readily consented. They sat on a large log and commenced playing what is known as seven up. Hogan kept talking. Presently a crowd gathered to see the game. Young hardly ever spoke. . . . I noticed Hogan was losing about every game.
>
> They were betting freely, playing out a hand. Hogan came in one of being out, as they called the end of the game. Hogan threw down the cards and cried out in a loud voice, "Out?"
>
> "Yes," said the Indian. "out of Hell, and a pity for that!" Young got up and said, "I am satisfied. I have won back all the money you won from me last night."
>
> Benge, during the game, kept speaking in Indian to Young. Hogan told him to speak in English and cursed Benge, whose eyes fairly shown with fire, returning the compliment and drew out a fine silver handled pistol. Hogan told him that he had no arms.
>
> Benge said, "You shall not have that for an excuse," and pulled out a mate to the pistol he had and offered it to Hogan, but he refused to take it.
>
> I expected to see Benge shoot him, but he let fly a volley of oaths, cursing Hogan and the whites saying they had taken their homes from them, and compelled them to go from the homes of their fathers to a land they knew nothing of in the far west. . . .
>
> Benge was a large square built man and appeared as vicious as an enraged lion. Benge and Young mounted their horses and rode off. . . .[6]

At some ferry crossings during their trek to Oklahoma, the Indians were charged larger fees than normal or were refused passage and forced to ford the water. That may have been one reason for the band's decision to ford the White at *Talbert's Ferry* rather than waiting to be carried across.

Talbert's Ferry figured prominently during the Civil War, not only because of its strategic location but also because of the

Confederate saltpeter mines in the area. Several skirmishes occurred at the ferry. As previously mentioned, *Talbert's Ferry* was later called *Denton Ferry* when purchased by Lee Denton, who ran it for many years. *Denton Ferry* continued in operation until the early 1930s. Baxter Hurst and E. B. Wood were the last owners of *Denton Ferry.*

Near the mouth of Fallen Ash Creek, 404.1 miles from the White River's mouth, W. C. McBee built a store and grist mill and established *McBee's Ferry* about 1886 or 1887. *McBee's Ferry* was on a direct line from Yellville to Mountain Home, and his 4X ferry-boat was a very strong craft that could carry substantial freight. The site was also an important steamboat landing. Samuel Bayless, grandfather of Rex Bayless from Cotter, ran the woodyard there that supplied fuel for the steamers. According to Bayless, it would usually take the steamers twenty-four hours to travel upriver from Batesville to the landing, but only twelve hours for the return trip downriver. In addition to the store, mill, and woodyard, McBee constructed a beautiful sixteen-room residence at the landing. The ferry was active for many years.

There were two ferries mentioned at Buffalo City, near where the Buffalo River empties into White River, one on either side of the river. When W. E. Winner founded the town of Winnerva in Baxter County in 1892, across the river from Buffalo City, his plans included the *Winnerva Ferry.* The ferry was run by Mathew Barton, known to many as "Uncle Mat." The town and the ferry's future was connected to construction of a railroad line to Missouri, and the project proved a failure, though the ferry continued for a while. On the Marion County side of the White near Buffalo City was *Walton's Ferry.* In June of 1893, the steamboat *Randall* laid a cable for *Walton's Ferry.* No mention was made of the duration of the ferry's operation, but it was particularly busy while the mines on Buffalo River were producing.

Shipp's Ferry, 384.1 miles from the mouth of White River, was located upstream from Calico Rock, Arkansas, about six miles from the North Fork. Shipp's Landing was mentioned as early as the 1850s, and the ferry was in service for many years. During a number of those years, *Shipp's Ferry* was run by the father of Junior Cobb. Junior Cobb is an excellent woodcarver who lives at Three Brothers; he first began selling his carvings to the ferry's patrons. The Cobb children grew up on the river, and for a while the family lived in a cave near *Shipp's Ferry.* Prior to the building of Bull Shoals Dam, the entire family would sometimes put in a johnboat quite a distance upriver and float all the way down to the Batesville lock, harvesting mussel shells for the button industry and camping on the riverbank along the way. The first ferries at Shipp's Landing were wooden, including the craft run by Cobb

Shipp's Ferry, *located upstream from Calico Rock, 384.1 miles from the mouth of White River, was between the* Nelson *and* Hindman Ferries. *It was in service for many years. Paul Yarber, a welder from Newark, Arkansas, worked on the building of the ferry shown here.*

Photo courtesy of Johnnie M. Gray.

that was just large enough to carry two cars. In its later years of operation, when it became part of the state highway system, the ferry was constructed of steel and was another one of those built by the Norris brothers, Paul Yarber, and Don Baker.

The *Norfork Ferry* was located near the mouth of the North Fork of White River, southeast of Buffalo City. When the North Fork of White River was dammed in the late 1940s, the *Henderson Ferries* crossed the newly formed Norfork Lake. Departing from approximately the same spot on U.S. Highway 62, one ferry carried passengers across Norfolk Lake to Henderson, Arkansas, while the second ferry crossed the lake to a point which connected with a northern route to Missouri. These boats were flat barges with tugboats attached to the sides for power, and they could carry fifteen to eighteen cars. Though some people thought of the *Henderson Ferries* as White River ferries, they were actually Norfork Lake ferries.

Rex Bayless of Cotter, Arkansas, remembered early days at *Norfork Ferry* when there were several whiskey stills in the area, and moonshiners were pretty protective of their business. The ferry was sometimes involved in that protection. The Baxter County sheriff at the time had a twin brother whose hunting plans were once delayed at the ferry because of the stills. The brother and another fellow went to *Norfork Ferry* to cross over to go deer hunting. The ferryman at the ferry, however, kept postponing the crossing because he thought the brother was the sheriff and that the guy with him was a "revenuer." It took a while, but the hunters finally convinced the riverman that they were not the law, and they were taken across. The warning system that involved the

This ferry is possibly Calico Rock Ferry. *Note the load of cattle penned in the middle of ferry by placing a board across each end to balance the cattle's weight. Propulsion was by "lugging," also called poling.*

Photo courtesy of Wilson Powell.

Calico Rock Ferry *and bridge in 1966. This ferry was a current-powered "floating bridge." It was located on Arkansas Route 5 between Mountain Home and Sylamore.*

Photo courtesy of Johnnie M. Gray.

ferryman was simple but effective. When questionable passengers approached, they were delayed at the crossing until a fellow who stayed in a nearby cabin could build a fire so the smoke would alert those in the hills. Upon seeing the smoke signal, a mounted man on the mountain would carry the message from still to still, enabling the moonshiners to have everything hidden by the time the law arrived.

Another of the poled wooden ferries, the *Calico Rock Ferry* was located near the town of that name and was 360.5 miles from the mouth of White River. The ferry was part of State Highway 5 from Mountain Home to Sylamore. Its operation ceased about 1966 when a new bridge was built on the highway.

The *Sylamore Ferry,* near Mountain View, Arkansas, was located 343.3 miles from the mouth of the White. It was an important community ferry for several years. The ferry was retired by the Arkansas Highway Department in the mid-1970s.

One of the last ferries to cease operation on the White River was the *Guion Ferry,* which connected Stone and Izard Counties in Arkansas on State Highway 58. In the 1800s, the location was called *Wild Haw Landing* and was an important steamboat landing. It is a beautiful spot, situated in a deep valley surrounded by towering bluffs, and is another place on the White where the river is a dividing line. The wooden ferryboat at *Guion Ferry* was destroyed by a tornado in 1929 but was replaced. Wooden crafts were used there until the 1940s, when operation was suspended for a time. In 1962, a steel ferry was placed in operation and was run by the local communities it served until 1970, when the state took over its operation.

The Sylamore Ferry*'s last day of operation was May 20, 1976. Located near Mountain View, Arkansas, it was 343.3 miles from the mouth of the White River.*

Postcard photo courtesy of Maxine Curtis.

The Guion Ferry *was one of the last "floating bridges" to be replaced by a stationary bridge. The ferry carried Arkansas Highway 58 across White River 331.1 miles from the river's mouth.*

Photo courtesy of Phyllis Rossiter.

The steel ferry at Guion was one of the six ferries built by Cecil, Dickson, and Fred Norris; Paul Yarber; and Don Baker. Cecil Norris contracted most of the jobs, and Yarber and Baker were the principal welders. Welding is a hot job, and the smoke and heat within the compartments of the ferries could become intense while the welders were joining some fifteen hundred pounds of welding rods used in a steel ferry the size of the *Guion Ferry.* Using a forge blower, fresh air was forced into the work area through hoses, but the amount of air that could be blown in to the welders was limited, so there was a great deal of danger associated with the job. Fortunately, these men were good friends and looked out for one another. Dickson Norris usually placed the sheets of steel on the outside and held the primary responsibility of checking on the welders within the ferry. Fred Norris did a lot of cutting of the steel for specific areas. All of the workers took great pride in their work. Experienced welders, such as these, were like artists and could recognize the work done by another welder as though it was signed by the "artist" himself. By 1988, *Guion Ferry* had outlived its usefulness and was closed when a new bridge was constructed at the site.

Farther down the White, 320.8 miles from its mouth, near Penter's Bluff, was *Wall's Ferry.* Built by Grandison M. Wall about 1860, it was run by the Wall family until 1908. Wall's license to operate the ferry in 1860 cost five dollars for one year. The ferry landed at the foot of Penter's Bluff on the opposite side of White River from the Wall farm, which was on the south bank of the river. During the Civil War, Grandison Wall served as a private for the Confederacy, enlisting at *Hess Ferry,* about four miles downriver. He was described as an honest, gentle man who lost his farm partially because he was always having to "bail out" some of his "wild bunch" of boys. One tale told about one or two of them hiding their whiskey under the pilings of the ferry. Another story mentioned their hand-walking across the White River on the ferry cables. No matter the era, it seems youngsters can always provide excitement.

Penter's Bluff has held a special fascination for youngsters throughout the ages. The account of one youthful escapade was repeated year after year by some Penter's Bluff families. A group of young men were hunting near the bluff when a challenge was issued to see who could venture nearest the edge of the precipice. One lad, a little too daring, fell over the bluff into a large cedar tree below. Once his companions were assured he was not seriously injured, they decided to have some fun at their friend's expense and told him they were going home. Actually, two of them went for a rope while the others hid nearby. The unlucky lad thought he had been deserted. At first, he looked down, and he prayed. Then he looked up and, in questionable language, implored his friends to lift him up. The stranded youth's actions alternated between prayer and colorful pleas to be lifted until his pals returned with a rope and hoisted him to safety. Understandably, he resented the laughter from his friends, and the subject was a rather touchy one for a while.[7]

In the December 25, 1913, issue of the *Batesville Guard,* the *Wall's Ferry* "Country Correspondent" mentioned that George Tosh was "talking of putting in a ferry and blacksmith shop" there, but there is no record of his having done so.

Thought to be Point *or* Jacksonport Ferry. *Note the elephant and horse side by side on the ferry, as well as two very old cars.*

Photo courtesy of Wilson Powell.

The *Hess Ferry,* in existence prior to *Wall's Ferry,* was one of the earliest on the White and was located about 317 miles from its mouth. The ferry dated back to pre–Civil War days and was well known by steamboat pilots and other rivermen.

Just a short distance downstream from the *Hess Ferry,* at 315.9 miles from the mouth of the White, was another 1800s operation. The *Grigsby's Ferry* became known as the *O'Neal Ferry* in the 1900s when it served the O'Neal community. Pearl fever struck the village when a Mr. Hall from Bellmore found a gem while using mussels for fish bait about two miles below the ferry. He sold the pearl for eighty dollars, a significant amount for the early 1900s. Through his love of fishing, Hall had stumbled upon one of the richest mussel beds ever found in White River. The discovery caused a great deal of excitement, and many residents combed the river for more of the treasures. As mentioned in the steamboat chapter, shelling on White River was quite popular at the turn of the century and remained so into the 1930s. The harvesters would steam the shells open, pitch out the flesh, and check for pearls. Shell buyers would purchase the cleaned mussel shells by the pound. Pearl buyers were interested only in the jewels. The meat was not only used for fish bait but also, according to Rex Bayless, fed to pigs. As you can imagine, some of the piles of mussels could become rather rank during the summer.

One of the first ferries on White River was *Shield's Ferry,* located by the farm of Nathaniel and James Shield, upriver from Batesville near Chataunga Mountain. There is no mention of how long the ferry was operated by the Shields, but on January 27, 1816, their farm was sold to Joab Hardin, and on November 4, 1817, Hardin was granted a license to operate the ferry. *Shield's Ferry* ran until at least 1828.

On November 4, 1817, John Wyatt was granted a license to run a ferry across White River at the mouth of Bayou Saladore, between *Shield's Ferry* and Batesville. A road had been laid out, in 1816, from the village of Lawrence, Missouri, to Bayou Saladore, so it was hoped the crossing would be a busy one. Wyatt was allowed to charge the same rates as the *Morris Ferry* and the *Graham Ferry* below him, plus he could levy a fee of three cents per head for hogs and sheep. *Wyatt's Ferry* ran for about twelve months, after which Wyatt simply quit or was forced out of business. On November 3, 1818, John L. Lafferty was awarded Wyatt's ferry license. The ferry continued for quite some time.

Since there was a good potential for growth in the region, competition for the ferries around Batesville became keen just prior to 1820. On November 3, 1818, the same day that Lafferty was given a permit to run the *Wyatt's Ferry,* his friend Joab Hardin acquired a license to operate a ferry on the opposite side of the

This cable ferry across White River near Newark, Arkansas, was known as the Chamberlain Ferry. *It utilized the current for power, plus was poled or "lugged." J. W. Frieze later owned this ferry that was operated by Paul Yarber's father and older brother. In 1889, fare for some ferries was ten cents for a footman, fifty cents for a wagon and yoke of oxen or two horses, and twenty-five cents for a man and horse.*

Photo courtesy of Paul Yarber.

river from Lafferty. Since Hardin still had his upriver ferry, this was probably an attempt to control competition at the Saladore crossing. Joab Hardin lived in a log hut near the river where he ran *Hardin's Ferry.* His ferryboat was a crude one described as two small canoes lashed together, with some split clapboards laid across them. Schoolcraft, the Englishman who traveled down White River in 1819, mentioned *Hardin's Ferry.* Whether he was referring to *Hardin's Ferry,* at this site, or *Shield's Ferry,* the one Hardin ran upriver, is not clear.

In December 1816, Henry Morris was given a permit to operate the *Morris Ferry* at the "ford above Poke Bayou." About the same time, a license was granted to Moses Graham for a ferry approximately one mile below the mouth of Poke Bayou, so competition for the ferry business was intense. It is unknown just how long Morris operated his ferry, but the ferry owned by Moses Graham, which was located near Batesville and was 300.8 miles from the mouth of the White, lasted a long time and later became known as *Ramsey's Ferry.*

Graham was an important early settler who lived on a farm at the Poke Bayou ferry site and, until 1817, had also owned a farm at the mouth of Poke Bayou. After paying a five dollar fee, Graham received his license for the ferry below Poke Bayou on December 23, 1816. Ferriage rates were set as follows: man and horse, 25 cents; four-wheeled carriage and team, one dollar; two-wheeled carriage and two horses, 50 cents; loaded horses, 25 cents; loose horses and cattle, 12 1/2 cents per head; footmen, 12 1/2 cents; two wheeled-carriages and one horse, 37 1/2 cents. Graham was always aware of the business potential of the area and owned various properties at different times.

In December 1819, in need of additional money to complete a negotiation for land at Bell Point, Arkansas, Graham sold his farm and ferry near Poke Bayou to Charles Kelly and William Ramsey. Following the purchase, Kelly lived at the farm and ran the ferry for a few months but then sold it to his brother-in-law, Ramsey, and the conveyance became known as *Ramsey's Ferry.* Heavy rains in 1890 caused White River to rise substantially, and a ferryman at *Ramsey's Ferry* was swept away in an accident caused by the high water. The *Ozark Queen,* the last steamboat to be built for the passenger and freight trade above Batesville, was launched at the dock below *Ramsey's Ferry* in September of 1896. The ferry ran until 1928, when a one-mile bridge was completed. Until construction of the bridge, *Ramsey's Ferry* provided the only means of crossing White River at Batesville.

The ferries in the Batesville area, like many on White River, were frequently of importance during the Civil War, carrying troops across the waterway. A tragedy occurred at Batesville in May of 1862 when eleven Union soldiers drowned while crossing White River on a ferryboat. A report of General Curtis on May 12, 1862, stated: "By accident Captain Thomas G. McClelland and 10 men of the Third Illinois Cavalry were drowned yesterday in crossing White River. . . . My means for crossing the river are very trifling."[8] The exact location of the ferry accident was not given.

The family of Paul Yarber, the welder from Newark mentioned earlier, was involved with the operation of several ferries below Batesville. Paul's father, Will, and his oldest brother, George, worked on the *Russell Ferry* near Magness; it was one of the earliest ferries in that section of the White River. During the Civil War, some Confederate forces were headquartered briefly at *Russell Ferry.* Ferry sites were important all along the river during the course of the conflict. Yarber's family also worked on the *Chamberlain Ferry* near Newark. Owned by J. W. Frieze, the *Chamberlain Ferry* was another of the wooden cable ferries that was poled, or "lugged," across the river.

For about ten years during the late 1930s and early 1940s, Paul

Left to right, W. T. Yarber and his sons, George and Paul, who operated the Oil Trough Ferry *in the 1930s and 1940s. The ferry was located on White River near Newark, Arkansas.*

Photo courtesy of Paul Yarber.

Yarber ran the *Oil Trough Ferry,* another wooden ferry. There were seldom mishaps on the vessel, but there was one Yarber remembers vividly. It was during a period of high water and ice in February of 1940. Yarber, along with Edgar Magness, the ferry's owner, were maneuvering the ferryboat across White River when the accident occurred. The craft was carrying a Missouri-Pacific bus loaded with passengers. Floating in the river were chunks of ice that constantly bashed against the ferry, and, worse, sometimes stacked up against it. He and Magness would continually angle the boat so that the ice might go around the craft. Occasionally, it would even go under the boat. The rope cables of the vessel became covered with ice from freezing rain and the splash-up from the ferry, making them too large to go through the pulleys. Yarber would take an iron bar and break the ice from the ropes, but that action also caused the cables to fray. The weight of the bus, plus the chunks of ice, caused the "bull rope" fastened to the whiplash to break and fling through the air. Because the rope was a vital part of steering the ferryboat, the craft and its passengers were, momentarily, at the mercy of the river. Screams of terror were heard from those within the bus, but with the calmness of experience, Yarber and Magness soon had the situation under control and safely delivered their charges to the opposite shore. Such excitement was somewhat routine for rivermen, but the trip was probably one remembered for a lifetime by those aboard the bus.

Along with his experiences dealing with ferries on the White River, Paul Yarber also harvested mussel shells. Like all rivermen who grew up on the White, Yarber spent a great deal of time on and in White River and has a deep affection for and appreciation of the waterway.

In 1941, the *Oil Trough Ferry* was sometimes called the "Oil Trough Barge" because it was then a flat-bottomed, engine-propelled scow that was guided on a steel cable. Fare at the time was twenty-five cents for passenger cars and fifty cents for trucks. The ferry was located on Arkansas Highway 14.

Perhaps one of Arkansas's best-known ferries across White River was the *St. Charles Ferry.* Located 59.5 miles from the mouth of the White, on the lower reaches of the river between Marvell and DeWitt, it was the only ferry on the Arkansas section of the Great River Road. The *St. Charles Ferry* operated toll free as part of State Highway 1 and ran twenty-four hours a day. It was adjacent to the White River National Wildlife Refuge, a tremendous wilderness area that is bustling with wildlife, particularly birds, since it is on a natural flyway. In 1981, the ferry was replaced by a bridge.

While we have discussed only some of the White River ferries

The Des Arc Ferry *was a current-powered ferry, later replaced by a bridge on Arkansas Highway 38. Des Arc also had a steamboat landing, and a large sidewheeler was named for the town.*

Photo courtesy of Wilson Powell.

within our text, we have included on the list of ferries all the operations we found in our research. Because there were also several private ferries run only for personal or limited, local use, we have probably missed some. Some may have been called other names at different times, dependent upon their operator. We do feel, however, that this is the most complete list of White River ferries to date. Perhaps it will serve as a starting point from which other "history detectives" can continue. Like the steamboats, ferries served a vital role in the settlement and development of the White River basin. No longer a part of the White River scene, their importance lies in the past, but hopefully, through this book, their contribution will be remembered.

Crockett's Bluff Ferry *on White River.*

Photo courtesy of Johnnie M. Gray.

STEAMBOATS

Chronological Order

1831 ....*Waverly*
1831 ....*Laurel*
1831 ....*Bob Handy*
1832–33...........*Reindeer*
1832–33...........*Volant*
1833 ....*William Parsons*
1834 ....*La Fourche*
1834 ....*Ottawa*
1836 ....*Tecumseh*
1836–40...........*Mt. Pleasant*
1837–38...........*Mt.Vernon*
1838.................*William Hurlbert*
1838–39...........*Steubenville*
1839 ....*Daisy*
1840 ....*Batesville* (first one)
1841 ....*De Kalb*
1841 ....*Franklin*
1841 ....*Governor Yell*
1841–43...........*Victoria*
1842 ....*Pawnee*
1842 ....*Rialto*
1842–43...........*Bunker Hill*
1843 ....*Dove*
1844 ....*Little Ben Franklin*
1844 ....*Marietta*
1844 ....*Nick of the Woods*
1844 ....*Rolla*
1844 ....*Sarah*
1844 ....*Yucatan*
1844–45 ....*Carrier*
1844–48 ....*Batesville* (second one)
1845 ....*Chicago*
1845 ....*Glazer*
1845 ....*Wasp*
1845–46 ....*Wabash Valley*
1845–51...........*Clermont*
1845–58 ....*General Morgan*
1846 ....*Georgia*
1846 ....*Pink*
1846–47...........*Cote Joyeuse*
1848 ....*Kate Kirkwood*
1848–49 ....*Governor Bent*
1848–49 ....*Storm*
1848–50 ....*Julia*
1848–51...........*Lt. Maury*
1848–51...........*Major Barbour*
1849 ....*J. L. Webb*
1849 ....*North Alabam*
1849–50 ....*Conductor*
1850 ....*Dispatch*
1850 ....*Pearl*
1850 ....*Santa Fe*
1850–51 .... *Eureka*
1851.................*Clermont No. 2*
1851.................*F. H. White*
1851.................*J. B. Gordon*
1851–56...........*Julia Dean*
1851, 1858–59 ....*St. Francis*
1852.................*Amazon*
1852.................*C. Hayes*
1852.................*Emily*
1852.................*Financier*
1852.................*Ironton*
1852.................*Jefferson*
1852–54...........*Naomi*
1852–54...........*Yohogany*
1853–55...........*Ben Lee*
1853–55...........*Mary L. Daugherty*
1853–56...........*James Laughlin*
1854 ....*Caroline*
1854 ....*Falcon*
1854 ....*Fawn*
1854 ....*Obion*
1854–55...........*Illinois Belle*
1854–55...........*Luella*
1854–55...........*Sangamon*
1854–56...........*Exchange*
1854–56...........*National*
1854–58...........*Thomas P. Ray*
1855 ....*Ingomar*
1855 ....*Justice*
1855–57...........*Jesse Lazear*
1855–58...........*Evansville*
1856 ....*Col. Drennen*
1856 ....*Joan of Arc*
1856 ....*Young America*
1856–57...........*North Star*
1856–61...........*Sam Hale*
1857.................*Comet*
1857.................*Editor*
1857.................*J. Morrisett*
1857.................*Louisa*
1857–59...........*Return*
1858 ....*Eve*
1858 ....*Persia*
1858 ....*Titanis*
1858 ....*W. M. Lawrence*
1858–59...........*Fortune*
1858–59...........*Oakland*
1858–59...........*William Campbell*
1858–60...........*Audubon*
1858–60...........*Badger State*
1858–60...........*City of Knoxville*
1858–60...........*Europa*
1858–60...........*Grand Glaize*
1858–60...........*Interchange*
1858–60...........*John Briggs*
1858–60...........*Medora*
1858–60...........*Monongahela Belle*
1858–60...........*Nebraska*
1858–60...........*W. H. Langley*
1858–61...........*Admiral*
1858–61...........*Mary Patterson*
1858–63...........*Pocahontas*
1859 ....*Arkansas Traveler*
1859 ....*A. W. Quarrier*
1859 ....*Charm*
1859 ....*Crescent*
1859 ....*Editor*
1859 ....*E. M. Ryland*
1859 ....*Evansville*
1859 ....*Interchange*
1859 ....*Louisiana Belle*
1859 ....*Rose Douglas*
1859 ....*Tennessee Belle*
1859–60...........*Belvidere*
1859–60...........*Frontier City*
1859–60...........*Hazel Dell*
1859–60...........*St. Francis No. 2*
1859–60...........*Tennessee Belle*
1859–60...........*William H. Langley*
1859–61...........*Iatan*

1859–62 .... *Novelty*
1859–63 .... *General Pike*
1860 .... *Acacia Cottage*
1860 .... *Carrier*
1860 .... *Daniel B. Miller*
1860 .... *Favorite*
1860 .... *Izetta*
1860–61 .... *Golden State*
1860–61 .... *Masonic Gem*
1860–61 .... *New Moon*
1860–61 .... *Tahlequah*
1860–63 .... *Kanawha Valley*
1860–66 .... *Des Arc*
1860, 1872–73 .... *Maysville*
1861 .... *Cadet*
1861 .... *J. J. Cadot*
1861 .... *Ohio Belle*
1861 .... *S. H. Tucker*
1861 .... *Sovereign*
1861–62 .... *Cambridge*
1862 .... *Empire City*
1862 .... U.S. gunboat *Benton*
1862 .... *General Bragg*
1862 .... *Golden Era*
1862 .... *Maurepas*
1862 .... *Tyler*
1862 .... *White Cloud*
1863 .... *Altoment*
1863 .... *America*
1863 .... *Arago*
1863 .... *Bertha*
1863 .... *Conestoga*
1863 .... *Cricket*
1863 .... Gunboat *No. 25, Covington*
1863 .... *Creole Belle*
1863 .... *Crescent City*
1863 .... Gunboat *No. 12, Curlew*
1863 .... *Dacotah*
1863 .... *Des Moines City*
1863 .... *Diurnal*
1863 .... Gunboat *No. 38, Exchange*
1863 .... Gunboat *No. 30, Fawn*
1863 .... *Florence*
1863 .... *Gilliam*
1863 .... *H. A. Homemyer*
1863 .... Gunboat *No. 15, Hastings*
1863 .... *H. R. W. Hill*
1863 .... *J. S. Pringle*
1863 .... *Kaskaskia* (one of two last Confederate boats)
1863 .... *Lebanon*
1863 .... *Marmora*
1863 .... *Mill Boy*
1863 .... Gunboat *No. 37, Naumekeg*
1863 .... *Progress*
1863 .... *Q. Lloyd*
1863 .... *Robert Hamilton*
1863 .... *Rose Hambleton*
1863 .... *Sallie List*
1863 .... *Silver Cloud*
1863 .... *St. Louis*
1863 .... *Thomas T. Patton*
1863 .... *Tom Suggs (Tenas)* (one of two last Confederate boats)
1863 .... Gunboat *No. 8, Tyler*
1863 .... Gunboat *No. 55, Undine*
1863 .... USS *Lexington*
1863 .... *William R. Glasgow*
1863 .... *William Wallace*
1863–64 .... *Eclipse*
1863–64 .... *Ella*
1863–64 .... *Emma No. 2*
1863–64 .... *Dove*
1864 .... *Argonaut*
1864 .... *B. M. Runyan*
1864 .... *Canton*
1864 .... *Dickey*
1864 .... Gunboat *No. 51, Fairy*
1864 .... *Kate Hart*
1864 .... *Kenton*
1864 .... *Lilly Martin*
1864 .... *M. S. Mepham*
1864 .... *Omaha*
1864 .... *Prairie State*
1864 .... *Queen City*
1864 .... *Sir William Wallace*
1864 .... *Sunny South*
1864 .... *St. Cloud*
1864 .... *Venus*
1864–65 .... *Commercial*
1864–65 .... *Fanny Ogden*
1864–67 .... *Rowena*
1864, 1870s .... *Celeste*
1865, 1896–97 .... *Tycoon*
1866 .... *Agnes*
1866 .... *Centralia*
1866 .... *Goldfinch*
1866 .... *Harry Dean*
1866 .... *John D. Perry*
1866 .... *J. R. Hoyle*
1866 .... *Justice*
1866 .... *Kate Bruner*
1866 .... *Lady Franklin*
1866 .... *Lena*
1866 .... *Loma*
1866 .... *Petrolia*
1866 .... *Zouave*
1866–67 .... *J. S. McCune*
1866–67 .... *Cherokee* (first)
1866–67 .... *Clermont*
1866–71 .... *Emma C. Elliot*
1867–68 .... *F. W. Brooks*
1868 .... *Laura*
1868 .... *Liberty*
1868 .... *Lily*
1868 .... *Norman*
1868 .... *Tempest*
1868–69 .... *Converse*
1869 .... *Malta*
1869 .... *Natoma*
1869–70 .... *Liberty No. 2*
1869–71 .... *Argos*
1869–76 .... *Batesville* (third one)
1869–76 .... *Legal Tender*
1870 .... *Mayflower*
1870–72 .... *R. P. Walt*
1870–73 .... *Pat Cleburne*
1870–78 .... *City of Augusta*
1870–80 .... *John Howard*
1870s .... *Columbia*
1870s .... *Mary Boyd*
1870s .... *Sioux City*
1871 .... *Sally V*
1870s .... *T. H. Allen*
1871 .... *Hartford*
1871 .... *Osage*
1871 .... *Seminole*
1871–72 .... *Jennie Howell*
1871–73 .... *Emma C. Elliott*
1872 .... *Glasgow*
1872–73 .... *Jessie*
1872–80 .... *Arch P. Green*
1873 .... *Clarai*
1873 .... *Ranger*
1873–74 .... *Cora Belle*
1873–74 .... *Mary Miller*
1874 .... *George W. Cheek*
1875 .... *Quickstep*
1875–77 .... *Duck*
1876 .... *St. Francis Belle*
1876 .... *Fannie Tatum*
1876–77 .... *Trader*
1877 .... *Music*
1877 .... *Ruth*
1877–79 .... *Alberta*
1877–79 .... *C. B. Warner*
1877–79 .... *Winnie*
1877–80 .... *John Howard*
1877–81 .... *McArthur*
1877–83 .... *Hard Cash*
1877–85 .... *Milt Harry*
1878 .... *Red Wing*
1878–79 .... *Hope*
1879 .... *Marlin Speed*
1879 .... *Maumelle*
1879 .... *Ouachita Belle*
1879–80 .... *Florence Meyer*
1879–81 .... *Jennie Stinson*
1879–81 .... *Josie Harry*
1880–83 .... *Alberta No. 2*
1880–83 .... *Whitewater*

1880–85 .... *Lady Boone*
1881 .... *Bedford*
1881 .... *Red Cloud*
1881–83 .... *Cherokee* (second)
1882 .... *Belle of Ottawa*
1883 .... *Dean Adams*
1884 .... U.S. snagboat *Picayune*
1884–85 .... *Joe Peters*
1884–86 .... *Alberta No. 3*
1884–87 .... *John F. Allen*
1884–91 .... *Chickasaw*
1885 .... U.S. snagboat *Henry Sheldon* (last boat to Forsyth)
1885–86 .... *De Smet*
1886 .... *Wild Boy*
1886–87 .... *New Home*
1887 .... *Decker*
1887–88 .... *Governor James P. Eagle*
1887–88 .... *Ralph*
1887–91 .... *General Charles H. Tompkins*
1888–89 .... *Tom Hess*
1888–90 .... *Katie Maxfield*
1889 .... *Bright Star*
1890–92 .... *The White Eagle*
1891 .... *Golden Gate*
1891–92 .... *Rowena Lee*
1891–92 .... *Des Arc* (second)
1892–93 .... *Randall*
1892–93 .... *Ralph E. Warner*
1892–96 .... *J. A. Woodson*
1893–95 .... *Myrtle*
1893 .... Barge named *Sandy* (to work with *Myrtle*)
1893 .... U.S snagboat *Chauncey B. Reese*
1893 .... *Oakland*
1893–1905 .... *A. R. Bragg*
1893–97 .... *Rex*
1894 .... *Dauntless*
1895–96 .... *T. E. Morrison*
1895–96 .... *G. M. Sivley*
1896 .... *Black Diamond*
1896–97 .... *Josie Sivley*
1896–1903 .... *City of Idaho*
1896–1903 .... *Ozark Queen*
1897 .... *Portia*
1897–1900 .... *New Mattie*
1897–98 .... *Mary F. Carter*
1899–1900 .... *Choctaw* (built for White, never ran on it)
1900–01 .... *Dea*
1900–01 .... *G. W. Lyons*
1900–01 .... *Harry Waltz*
1900–01 .... *Grace Smith*
1900–01 .... *Iverness*
1900–01 .... *Jessie Blair* (gasoline-powered)
1900–01 .... *Orlando* (old *Ora Lee*)
1900–01 .... *Troubador*
1900–01 .... *C. E. Taylor*
1900–03 .... *City of Peoria*
1901 .... *Buck Elk*
1901 .... *Eagle*
1901 .... *Evening Star*
1901 .... *Kennedy*
1901 .... *Welcome*
1901–02 .... *Lotus*
1901–02 .... *Quickstep*
1901–04 .... *J. D. Galloway*
1901–06 .... *Joe Wheeler*
1902 .... *Eureka* (gasoline-powered)
1902 .... *Kate Adams*
1902–03 .... *Cleveland*
1902–04 .... *Krata*
1902–06 .... *F. W. Tucker*
1902–06 .... *Susan*
1903 .... *Current View*
1903 .... *Hosmer*
1903 .... *Jack Rabbit*
1903 .... *Josie*
1903 .... *Mary Carter*
1903 .... *Monarch*
1903 .... *Ondine*
1903 .... *Russell Lord*
1903 .... Arrival of steam locomotive from Batesville to Cotter
1903–05 .... *George Pope*
1904–05 .... *A. D. Allen*
1904–05 .... *Bob West* (gasoline-powered)
1904–05 .... *Cora Lee* (gasoline-powered)
1904–05 .... *J. Taylor* (gasoline-powered)
1904–05 .... *Little Abby* (gasoline-powered)
1904–05 .... *Peerless* (gasoline-powered)
1904–05 .... *Twins*
1904–10 .... *Alda*
1905 .... *Dolly B*
1906 .... *Minnehaha*
1906 .... *Myrtle Corey*
1906 .... Snagboat *Quapaw*
1907 .... *Liberty*
1907 .... *John P. Usher* (Forsyth to Branson)
1907–08 .... *Miriam*
1907–09 .... *Choctaw*
1907–1920s .... *Pocahontas*
1908 .... *Jim Duffy*
1908 .... *Leader*
1908 .... *Moark* (gasoline-powered)
1908 .... *Cleveland*
1908 .... *Grand*
1908–10 .... *G. W. Huff*
1908–10 .... *Rock City*
1910 .... *Columbia*
1910 .... *Star* (second)
1910–11 .... *Lillian H.*
1910–15 .... *Mary S. Lucas*
1911 .... *Niggerhead*
1912–21 .... *F. W. Tucker No. 2*
1913–25 .... *Missouri*
1915 .... *Rustler* (gasoline-powered)
1915–17 .... *City of Muskogee*
1922 .... *Ursie Boyce*
1924–25 .... *Lightwood*
1930 .... *Robert H. Romunder*
1930 .... *Robert Sanford*
1930 .... *Huston*
1930 .... *L. G. Neal*
1930 .... *C. W. Huffs*
1930 .... *Sears*
1933 .... *Mary Woods II*

While every attempt has been made to include all steamboats that traveled White River, some made only a single trip or two, and many were switched from one river to another, so we may have missed some. We apologize for any omissions.

Ferries

From Upper White to Lower White River

Van Winkle ....Near mouth of War Eagle, Arkansas
Beaver................Near Eureka Springs, Arkansas
Kimberling ....(*Maberry* or *Mabry*) Below James River, Missouri, 1870 to 1922
Turkey Creek ....(*Hawkins*) Near mouth of Turkey Creek, Missouri, 1880s by Berry, 1893–99 by Hawkins
Compton.............(*Roark*) Mouth of Roark Creek, Missouri
Boston ....Below Hollister, Missouri, late 1870s, sold in 1884
Hensley ....Near mouth of Bull Creek, Missouri; one of oldest (near Civil War time) and most profitable, used until Powersite Dam was built
Chapman ....Chapman Hollow, Missouri; Sam Brown, last operator
Parrish...............At Forsyth, Missouri; 505 miles from mouth of White River; 1886–87, Parrish; 1897–1911, Tolerton Ferry Co.; closed in 1919 when steel bridge was built
Baldwin ....Second ferry at Forsyth, Missouri; 1897–1911, started by Dr. Baldwin; 505 miles from mouth
Swan Creek..........At mouth of Swan, Missouri, briefly, prior to building bridge
Beaver Creek.........Missouri, 1894 (in 1903, *Kissee Mill*)
Blackwell ....(*Cedar Creek*) Missouri; 1902, Beeler, operator; 1910, Blackwell, operator
Moore's ....(*Trigger Creek*) Missouri, continued until Bull Shoals dam was built
Ellison's ....Exact location unknown, between *Moore's* and *Long's*
Cornett ....Exact location unknown, above *Long's*
Long's................Just below Elbow Shoal; 464.5 miles from mouth
Nave's................(*Raley*) Near West Sugar Loaf; built by Jake Nave; William Thomas Raley was a later operator
Holt ....Exact location unknown
Stoke's .... Exact location unknown
Bradley ....Near mouth of Big Creek, east from Protem
Brown's ....Yellville Road to Protem; late 1800s until 1952; built by Baxter Brown; son Joe, later owner
Peel ....Peel, Arkansas, to Protem, Missouri; still operating on State Highway 125; in 1968 began going across Bull Shoals Lake
Pace..................Seven miles above Bull Shoals Dam near Sister Creek; part of old road to Flippin, Arkansas
Howe ....458.5 miles from mouth
Collis ....Exact location unknown
Noe's.................Above Jimmy Creek
Blair's................Between Noe's and Howard's Creek
White's ....412.2 miles from mouth
Mooney's............407.1 miles from mouth
Talbert's ....(*Denton's* later) Near old Yellville Road, Sumner Shoal; 405.4 miles from mouth; one of the oldest
Denton ....Late 1800s through 1915 or so; 405.4 miles from mouth; run by Lee Denton (same as *Talbert's*)
McBee's ....Mouth of Fallen Ash Creek; 404.1 miles from mouth of White River
Cotter ....(*Lake*) Near Cotter
Red Fox ....Below Cotter
Walton..............At Buffalo City, on Marion County side
Winnerva Landing ..Across from Buffalo City, in Baxter County, operated by Mathew Barton
Hayes ....At Howell's Landing, 390.1 miles from mouth
Nelson's.............386.9 miles from mouth
Shipp's ....Upstream from Calico Rock; 384.1 miles from mouth
Hindman ....383.2 miles from mouth
Wingmar ....Between *Shipp's* and Big Creek
Norfork ....Old ferry was southeast of Buffalo City; 377.9 miles from mouth
Calico Rock.........Near town of Calico Rock; 360.5 miles from mouth
Sylamore............Near Mountain View, Arkansas; 343.3 miles from mouth
Guion................Crossed at Guion on State Highway 58; 331.1 miles from mouth; Wild Haws Shoal
Wall's ....Penter's Bluff; near old Lock No. 3 above Batesville; 320.8 miles from mouth
McClelland's ....320.1 miles from mouth
Hess................. About 317 miles from mouth
Grigsby's............315.9 miles from mouth; later *O'Neal's*, for the community
Shield's ....1816–28; west of Batesville near Chataunga Mountain (known in 1976 as Dean Mountain); 1817, Joab Hardin, operator
Wyatt's..............At mouth of Bayou Saladore; licensed in 1817 to J. Wyatt, who ran it about 12 months; November 1818, license to John L. Lafferty; part of road connection from Lawrence, Missouri, to White River

Hardin's	1818–19; opposite *Shield's;* mentioned by Schoolcraft, 1819
Morris	Downriver from *Shield's,* at "ford above Poke Bayou"
Gainor's	Exact location unknown
Gaymore	303.7 miles from mouth
Harris	1899, near Batesville
Ramsey's	(*Graham* when run by M. Graham) 300.8 miles from mouth; main ferry for Batesville
Greenbriar	Below Batesville, just above *Raynor*
Raynor	Below Batesville
Russey	291.9 miles from mouth
Russell	Near Magness, between Batesville and Jacksonport
Arnold	278.0 miles from mouth
Oil Trough	Near Jacksonport; Arkansas Highway 14; 277.3 miles from mouth
Chamberlain	Between *Oil Trough* and Jacksonport
Point	Where Black River enters; 264.8 miles from mouth, near Jacksonport; across Black River
Robertson	244.3 miles from mouth, below Newport
Grand Glaize	241.7 miles from mouth
Hatch	West side; 4 miles above Augusta; during Civil War
Des Arc	Near Des Arc; 147.7 miles from mouth
Clarendon	Near town of Clarendon; 100.5 miles from mouth
Preston	Near Preston Bluff, below Clarendon; 84.2 miles from mouth
Crockett's Bluff	1880s; Maddox Bay; 67.6 miles from mouth
Simpson	61.6 miles from mouth
St. Charles	Free ferry near White River National Wildlife Refuge; replaced in 1981 by bridge; 59.5 miles from mouth

Note: Schoolcraft mentions a *Morrison's Ferry* between Batesville and Penter's Bluff in 1819.

NOTES

PART I

Keelboats and Flatboats

1. *Independence County Chronicle* 13, no. 1 (October 1971): 14.
2. Ibid.
3. *Independence County Chronicle* 13, no. 2 (January 1972): 4.
4. *Batesville North Arkansas Times,* March 28, 1868.
5. Hugh Parks, *Schoolcraft in the Ozarks* (Van Buren, Ark.: Press-Argus Printers, 1955), 140.
6. *Izard County Historian* 10, no. 2: 38–39.
7. W. E. Bevins, *Makers of Jackson County* (n.p., n.d.), 11–12.

PART II

Steamboats: 1831–1860

1. Duane Huddleston, "Of Racehorses and Steamboats," *Independence County Chronicle* 14, no. 2 (January 1973): 40-43.
2. *Batesville (Arkansas) News,* May 9, 1839.
3. Ibid., October 8, 1840.
4. *Arkansas State Gazette and Democrat,* February 14, 1851.
5. *Memphis Weekly Appeal,* January 7, 1852.
6. Ibid.
7. Capt. Charles Warner, "Independence Co. Packet Boating from Fulton to Finish," *Independence County Chronicle* 3, no. 4 (July 1962): 3–25.
8. *Batesville (Arkansas) Guard,* June 23, 1941.
9. *Arkansas Gazette,* June 9, 1845.
10. S. C. Turnbo, "Fireside Stories of the Early Days," *Taney County Republican,* April 26, 1956.
11. *Des Arc (Arkansas) Citizen,* April 22, 1859.
12. Ibid., September 28, 1859.
13. *Batesville (Arkansas) Daily Guard,* January 18, 1941.
14. John Q. Wolf, "Early Days on White River," *Arkansas Gazette,* September 22, 1940, Sunday magazine section.
15. *Batesville Guard,* February 28, 1935.
16. Ibid.
17. Ibid., March 8, 1941.
18. *Arkansas State Gazette and Democrat,* June 4, 1852.
19. *Memphis Daily Appeal,* December 10, 1854.
20. Ibid., February 17, 1854.
21. Story from Hope Lynch, Clarendon, Arkansas.
22. *Memphis Daily Appeal,* September 17, 1854.
23. Ibid., February 5, 1857.
24. Arkansas Reports, vol. 19, Arkansas Supreme Court, January 1858.
25. *Batesville (Arkansas) Independent Balance,* February 27, 1857.
26. *Des Arc (Arkansas) Citizen,* December 11, 1858.
27. Ibid., May 18, 1859.
28. Ibid., May 25, 1859.
29. Ibid., January 8, 1859.
30. Ibid.
31. Ibid., September 14, 1859.
32. Ibid., February 11, 1859.

Steamboats: 1861–1865

1. *Des Arc (Arkansas) Constitutional Union,* January 18, 1861.
2. Ibid., February 1, 1861.
3. Ibid.
4. Ibid., February 8, 1861.
5. Lady Elizabeth Watson, *Fight and Survive!* (Conway, Ark.: River Road Press, 1974), 6.
6. Ibid., 8.
7. Ibid., 10.
8. *Des Arc (Arkansas) Semi-Weekly Citizen,* March 14, 1861.
9. *Little Rock Daily State Journal,* January 10, 1862.
10. Ibid., January 11, 1862.
11. Watson, *Fight and Survive!,* 27.
12. Fletcher Pratt, *Civil War on Western Waters* (New York: Henry Holt and Co., 1956), 126.
13. Watson, *Fight and Survive!,* 79.
14. *Arkansas Gazette,* May 8, 1938.
15. *Memphis Daily Bulletin,* April 22, 1864.
16. Watson, *Fight And Survive!,* 96–98.
17. Ibid., 105–6.
18. *Memphis Daily Bulletin,* October 27, 1864.
19. Ibid., January 19, 1865.
20. Ibid., February 11, 1865.

Steamboats: 1866–1900

1. *Jacksonport (Arkansas) Herald,* March 31, 1866.
2. *Des Arc (Arkansas) Weekly Citizen,* July 28, 1866.
3. *Memphis Daily Bulletin,* May 20, 1867.
4. Ibid., August 18, 1867.
5. *Batesville North Arkansas Times,* August 17, 1867.

6. *Searcy (Arkansas) White County Weekly Record,* February 29, 1868.
7. *Memphis Avalanche,* April 15, 1868.
8. Ibid., May 20, 1868.
9. *Memphis Daily Appeal,* January 30, 1869.
10. *Arkansas Gazette,* October 4, 1870.
11. *Memphis Daily Appeal,* October 2, 1869.
12. Ibid., November 25, 1869.
13. *Arkansas Gazette,* July 27, 1869.
14. *Memphis Daily Appeal,* January 21, 1870.
15. Donald T. Wright, "Best Steamboat Picture Find of 1959 to This Date," *Waterways Journal* 73 (August 29, 1959): 11–12.
16. *Memphis Daily Appeal,* February 3, 1870.
17. *Arkansas Gazette,* July 22, 1870.
18. Ibid., November 30, 1870.
19. *Memphis Avalanche,* July 3, 1871.
20. *Batesville (Arkansas) Republican,* February 26, 1873.
21. *Arkansas Gazette,* March 8, 1873.
22. *Pocahontas (Arkansas) Weekly Observer,* December 16, 1873.
23. Ibid., April 14, 1874.
24. *Batesville (Arkansas) Guard,* June 24, 1941.
25. *Memphis Public Ledger,* November 30, 1875.
26. *Batesville North Arkansas Times,* April 20, 1876.
27. *Memphis Public Ledger,* October 3, 1876.
28. Ibid., August 5, 1876.
29. *Batesville (Arkansas) Guard,* January 25, 1877.
30. Ibid., February 28, 1877.
31. Ibid.
32. Duane Huddleston, "The Batesville Mardi Gras," *Independence County Chronicle* 10, no. 1 (October 1968): 40–41.
33. *Searcy (Arkansas) White County Record,* April 28, 1877.
34. *Batesville (Arkansas) Guard,* September 13, 1877.
35. Ibid.
36. Ibid., August 29, 1878.
37. Ibid., September 19, 1878.
38. *Memphis Public Ledger,* March 29, 1879.
39. *Arkansas Gazette,* May 8, 1879.
40. *Memphis Public Ledger,* November 20, 1879.
41. P. Guntharp, undated newspaper clipping, Jacksonport Courthouse Museum, Jacksonport, Arkansas.
42. *Batesville Guard,* February 9, 1881.
43. P. Guntharp, undated newspaper clipping, Jacksonport Courthouse Museum, Jacksonport, Arkansas.
44. *Batesville Guard,* November 23, 1881.
45. Ibid., August 2, 1882.
46. *Arkansas Gazette,* November 13, 1938.
47. Ibid.
48. *Memphis Commercial Appeal,* April 7, 1937.
49. *(Pocahontas, Arkansas) Randolph Herald,* January 1, 1885.
50. *Batesville Guard,* March 8, 1941.
51. *(Yellville, Arkansas) Mountain Echo,* April 16, 1886.
52. *Batesville Guard,* June 5, 1941.
53. Ibid., May 7, 1886.
54. Capt. Charles Warner, "The Warners of Batesville," *Independence County Chronicle* 10, no. 1 (October 1967): 23–24.
55. "The Hess's Record," *Batesville (Arkansas) Progress,* December 28, 1889.
56. *Batesville (Arkansas) Weekly Record,* February 6, 1941.
57. *Mountain Echo,* April 24, 1891, quoted from the *Springfield Democrat.*
58. Ibid., January 12, 1894.
59. Ibid., October 6, 1893.
60. *Arkansas Gazette,* May 18, 1894.
61. Duane Huddleston, "Navigation of the Buffalo River . . . ," *Independence County Chronicle* 10, no. 1 (October 1968): 12.
62. *Mountain Echo,* May 1, 1896.
63. Walter L. Isom, personal interview, August 2, 1968, Rea Valley, Arkansas.
64. *Memphis Commercial Appeal,* date uncertain.

Steamboats: 1900–1917

1. *Newport (Arkansas) Daily Independent,* May 1, 1901.
2. *Memphis Commercial Appeal,* August 31, 1950.
3. Ibid.
4. *Newport Daily Independent,* July 8, 1901.
5. Steamboat Bill column, "Melody in the Ozarks," *Waterways Journal* 59 (March 9, 1946): 19.
6. *Newport Daily Independent,* November 16, 1901.
7. *Independence County Chronicle* 25, no. 4 (1984).
8. *Mountain Echo,* June 6, 1902.
9. Walter L. Isom, personal interview, August 2, 1968, Rea Valley, Arkansas.
10. Elmo Ingethron, personal interview, August 20, 1987, Kirbyville, Missouri.
11. *Newport (Arkansas) Weekly Independent,* March 10, 1905.
12. *Newport (Arkansas) Daily Independent,* May 10, 1905.
13. *Batesville (Arkansas) Daily Guard,* June 24, 1941.
14. *Newport Daily Independent,* May 17, 1907.
15. Ibid., May 18, 1907.
16. *Newport Weekly Independent,* May 24, 1907.
17. *Branson (Missouri) Beacon,* Sesquicentennial Celebration, July 4, 1987.

PART III

Ferries

1. Willa Brown, personal interview, 1989, Protem, Missouri.
2. Elmo Ingenthron, personal notes and interview, 1988, Kirbyville, Missouri.
3. *(Yellville, Arkansas) Mountain Echo,* November 19, 1886.
4. Beaver history, Beaver Post Office, Beaver, Arkansas.
5. Thelma Johnson, personal interview, 1991, Kirbyville, Missouri.
6. Duane Huddleston, "Cherokee Incident at Talbert's Ferry," *Independence County Chronicle* 11, no. 1 (October 1973): 59–63.
7. M. Farnham and W. Clark, "Penter's Bluff," *Independence County Chronicle* 20, no. 3 (April 1979): 5.
8. A. C. McGinnis, "Eleven Union Soldiers Drown . . . ," *Independence County Chronicle* 17, no. 2 (January 1976): 16–17.

GLOSSARY

aft .... Toward the stern or tail of a boat.

beam .... The breadth of a boat at its widest point.

bill of lading .... A written receipt given by a carrier for goods accepted for transportation.

boom .... A horizontal beam used for raising and lowering gangplanks and cargo.

bow .... The front of the boat.

bulkhead .... Any wall or partition on a boat.

calliope .... A musical instrument equipped with steam whistles and played from a keyboard.

capstan .... Spool on boat deck placed upright, which is turned either manually or mechanically and used for winding a cable or raising a weight.

channel .... The bed of a stream or waterway.

cordelle .... A long rope attached to a riverboat that is used to pull the vessel over difficult spots.

dikes and wing dams .... Structures, usually of rock or wood, built from the bank into the river that funnel the water and foster self-scouring to provide an adequate amount of water in the channel.

doctor engine .... The engine that pumps water to the boiler on a steamboat.

dory .... A boat with a narrow, flat bottom, high bow, and flaring sides.

draft .... The depth of a boat from the waterline to its keel.

eddy .... A current at variance with the main current in the river, especially one having a swirling motion.

fore .... Toward the bow or front of a boat.

foredeck .... The forward end of the main deck.

freeboard .... The portion of the side of a hull that is above the water, between the main deck and gunwale. The upper edge of a boat's sides.

hold .... The entire cargo space in a vessel.

hull .... The hollow, lowermost portion of a vessel, partially immersed in the water, that supports the remainder of the boat.

howitzer .... A cannon having a comparatively short barrel.

jackstaff .... Flagpole.

keel .... A structural beam running from bow to stern, to which the boat's frame is attached.

lap-welded .... Over-lapped.

levee .... A landing place for vessels; also a sloping embankment constructed to prevent overflow during high water.

lighter .... A long, narrow boat used to lighten the load of a larger boat when it is having navigational difficulties.

lock .... Chamber built at one side of a river dam for the purpose of raising and lowering vessels in transit.

master .... On a steamboat, the officer in charge. Short for "master mariner."

mouth .... The end of a river where it empties into another body of water.

mud clerk .... Second clerk, whose duties included going out in all weather on unpaved levees to receive or deliver freight.

packet .... A boat that carries mail, passengers, and goods regularly on a fixed route.

pilot .... The officer who steers the boat.

port .... Looking forward, port is the left-hand side of a boat.

rivulet .... A very small stream of water.

roustabout .... Deckhand, man employed in the deck department who works for the mate, generally handling freight, cleaning up, etc.

sawyer .... A snag that has an up and down motion in the water. Frequently hidden under the water.

side-wheeler .... A steamboat with a paddle wheel on each side.

slaked lime .... Lime combined with water to form calcium hydroxide.

snag .... Any driftwood, including whole trees, in the river.

snag boat .... A steamboat equipped with machinery capable of raising snags from the river.

snake-barge .... Two or more barges connected by rope and utilized to float cargo and/or timber downriver.

sounding .... Process of determining the water's depth.

stacks .... Smokestacks on a vessel.

stage .... Sometimes called gangplank, it is a forty-to-sixty-foot-long boardwalk that swings out ahead of steamboats and is lowered at landings with its heel on the forecastle and the other end on the bank. Used to get on and off the boat.

starboard .... Looking forward, starboard is the right-hand side of the boat.

steamboat .... A vessel that is propelled by an engine driven by steam under pressure. Also called a steamer.

steer .... To steer, the pilot keeps the boat coming ahead, traveling faster than the current, and negotiates the point, bend, bridge, et cetera. To flank, he puts the boat in reverse, gets lined up, then allows the current to help him through the spot. Since the boat is going slower than the current, the pressure of the current against the hull holds the desired position in the channel.

stern .... The back of the boat.

stern-wheeler .... A boat propelled by a paddle wheel located at the stern.

tinclad .... A wooden boat with its hull covered with sheet iron for protection during wartime. Also called an ironclad.

towboat .... River vessel designed to push barges.

tributary .... A stream of water that flows into a larger body of water.

wharf .... A structure built at the shore, maintained for boats to tie up.

yawl .... A rowboat or skiff that belongs to a large boat.

INDEX

C

D

T

Y

Z